CRITICAL REFLECTIONS ON THE EU'S DATA PROTECTION REGIME

This book brings together leading academics working on data protection law in the EU to analyse the most notable developments, and the most significant changes, which have occurred during the first five years of the GDPR.

The book includes contributions analysing the efficacy of the Regulation's consent-based model, the struggle to regulate AdTech using the provisions of the GDPR, the controversy surrounding US-EU data sharing and the interaction of the Regulation with EU Fundamental Rights and other secondary laws regulating data.

The book is unique in setting out to record a period of rapid development – and significant challenge – for EU law through its examination of these episodes in the life of the Regulation in a single text. Each chapter examines the changes introduced by the GDPR, analyses the effect of the Regulation in practice, and maps what the next five years holds for one of the world's most influential data privacy laws. The lineup of the editorial and author team reflects the pioneering role of female academics in data protection and GDPR discourse.

In highlighting the controversies and conflicts which the Regulation has faced in its first five years, the book illuminates the significance of the GDPR's introduction in advancing our thinking about the function, form, and future of data protection law, and outlines those matters that remain to be resolved as the GDPR moves towards its first decade in force.

Hart Studies in Information Law and Regulation: Volume 3

Hart Studies in Information Law and Regulation

Series Editors
Tanya Aplin (General Editor)
Perry Keller (Advisory Editor)

This series concerns the transformative effects of the digital technology revolution on information law and regulation. Information law embraces multiple areas of law that affect the control and reuse of information, data and digital tools – intellectual property, data protection, privacy, freedom of information, state security, tort, contract and competition law. 'Regulation' is a similarly extensive concept in that it encompasses legal and non-legal modes of control, including technological design and codes of practice.

The series provides cross-cutting analysis and exploration of the complex and pressing issues that arise in a society where digital infrastructures are now pervasive and when massive volumes of digital information are shared globally. These issues include access to data; sharing, reuse, and governance of data; open source and public sector data; the legitimacy and transparency of training data; propertisation of data and digital tools; freedom of expression and information access rights; privacy rights and data protection regimes; and the role of the state and private entities in safeguarding the public interest in the uses of data.

In the spirit of representing the diverse nature of its topics, the series embraces various methodologies: doctrinal, comparative, empirical, theoretical, historical and socio-legal, and particularly welcomes monograph proposals.

The series is especially open to perspectives from jurisdictions or regions which have traditionally been underrepresented in the scholarly literature.

Recent titles in this series:

Constitutionalising Social Media
Edited by Edoardo Celeste, Amélie Heldt and Clara Iglesias Keller

Cybersecurity, Privacy and Data Protection in EU Law: A Law, Policy and Technology Analysis
Maria Grazia Porcedda

Critical Reflections on the EU's Data Protection Regime: GDPR in the Machine
Edited by Róisín Á Costello and Mark Leiser

Critical Reflections on the EU's Data Protection Regime

GDPR in the Machine

Edited by
Róisín Á Costello
and
Mark Leiser

•HART•
OXFORD • LONDON • NEW YORK • NEW DELHI • SYDNEY

HART PUBLISHING

Bloomsbury Publishing Plc

Kemp House, Chawley Park, Cumnor Hill, Oxford, OX2 9PH, UK

1385 Broadway, New York, NY 10018, USA

29 Earlsfort Terrace, Dublin 2, Ireland

HART PUBLISHING, the Hart/Stag logo, BLOOMSBURY and the Diana logo are trademarks of Bloomsbury Publishing Plc

First published in Great Britain 2024

A catalogue record for this book is available from the British Library.

A catalogue record for this book is available from the Library of Congress.

Library of Congress Control Number: 2024944262

ISBN: HB: 978-1-50997-784-0
ePDF: 978-1-50997-786-4
ePub: 978-1-50997-785-7

Typeset by Compuscript Ltd, Shannon

Dr Róisín Á Costello BL

For Davy

Dr Mark Leiser

A special thank you to all the academics, students, privacy professionals, and regulatory theorists with whom I have shared and discussed ideas. A particular expression of gratitude is reserved for Professor Andrew Murray of the London School of Economics who instilled in me the obligation to remain objective as an academic and demanded that I always think critically.

Any professional or scholarly work I undertake is only possible because of the incredible support I have at home. I love you, Lorna & Zuri, Jack & Emily, for making my life remarkable. It's most certainly never a dull moment.

ACKNOWLEDGEMENTS

The idea for the volume was born at the TILTing Perspectives conference held at the University of Tilburg in 2018. We had long wanted to work on a project together, and we settled upon the idea of bringing together a group of academics and practitioners to critically reflect on the capacities and shortcomings of the GDPR, which, at the time, was newly entered into force. Our plans were disrupted and delayed by COVID-19 and, in 2021, we realised that the first five years of the Regulation on which we spent so much of our time reflecting were fast coming to a close.

There has been much to consider in those first five years. Indeed, few laws can claim to have generated so rapidly a volume of judicial decisions, policies, guidelines, and commentary equal to the GDPR. Fewer still could claim to have had such an impact not only on how we define legal concepts but also on how the full range of society, from a single citizen to a multinational corporation, goes about its business.

At the time of TILTing Perspectives, some among the academic community harboured reservations about the GDPR, particularly concerning the complexity of the GDPR, the broad range of powers it bestowed upon regulators, and an ever-expanding scope of authority. There was also some scepticism towards the perception of the GDPR as a panacea for the excesses of big tech. Gradually, a body of colleagues began to grow who shared a desire to engage critically with data protection law and to query its limits and potentials. It is on this body of work which we seek to draw in this volume, which we hope will offer an account of the challenges which the Regulation has faced in its first half-decade, and how well (or badly) it has risen to its task during that period.

We are very grateful to the contributors to this volume for generously giving their time and expertise in commenting on a range of these developments. As with any edited collection, the following book is a testament to the collegiality and cooperative spirit of our academic community. We are particularly aware of how fortunate we are to work in an area that is characterised by such rich exchanges of ideas and such genuine openness to collaboration. Dr Leiser would also like to thank Saba Üzeltürk for her assistance with graphics, proofing and for providing general feedback on the text of the introduction.

We are equally grateful to the team at Hart and the series editors who welcomed our proposal for this volume, offered constructive advice as we prepared it, and worked so diligently on bringing it to you, the reader.

As always, we are grateful to our loved ones, family members, friends, and colleagues in our home institutions whose support is fundamental to all our endeavours. We are particularly grateful to all the students, colleagues, and professionals who have entertained our ideas, offered insights and analysis, as well as feedback on this project.

Róisín Á Costello, Mark Leiser
Dublin – Amsterdam
July 2024

CONTENTS

CONTRIBUTORS

Róisín Á Costello is an Assistant Professor of EU Law in the School of Law at Trinity College Dublin and a practising barrister.

James Kneale is a practising barrister and has formerly worked for the Irish Data Protection Commission and for the Legal Service for the Council of the European Union.

Mark Leiser is an Assistant Professor at the Vrieje University of Amsterdam.

Gianclaudio Malgieri is an Associate Professor of Law and Technology at Leiden University and the co-Director of the Brussels Privacy Hub.

Anna Nelson is Research Assistant for the Leverhulme Trust funded project 'FemTech surveillance: Gendered digital harms and regulatory approaches' at the University of Sheffield.

Katherine Nolan is a Lecturer in Law at Ulster University.

Bart W Schermer is a Professor of privacy and cybercrime at eLaw, the Centre for Law and Digital Technologies at Leiden University.

Anastasia Siapka is a PhD Candidate at the KU Leuven Centre for IT & IP Law.

Maria Tzanou is a Senior Lecturer in law at the University of Sheffield.

Michaël Van den Poel is a Research Engineer at the EDHEC Augmented Law Institute on the Interdisciplinary Project on Privacy (IPoP) and PhD Student at the Law, Science, Technology and Society (LSTS) Research Group at the Vrije Universiteit Brussel).

Tijmen HA Wisman is an Assistant Professor at the Vrije Universiteit Amsterdam.

Lex Zard is a researcher and lecturer as well as a PhD candidate at eLaw, the Centre for Law and Digital Technologies at Leiden University.

TABLE OF CASES

Decisions of the Court of Justice

Decisions of the General Court

European Court of Human Rights

Decisions of the Dutch Courts

Decisions of the Courts of England and Wales

Decisions of the Irish Courts

TABLE OF LEGISLATION

Regulations

Directives

Draft Legislation

Decisions

Introduction

RÓISÍN Á COSTELLO AND MARK LEISER

I. Text and Context

The enactment of the General Data Protection Regulation (GDPR)[1] in 2016 and its entry into force in May 2018[2] marked a significant milestone in the evolution of data protection laws, reflecting an ambitious endeavour to protect personal data in an era increasingly defined by and through digital transactions. Designed to offer a more integrated and harmonised framework across the European Union, the GDPR sought to empower individuals to exercise control over their personal information, thereby setting a new global standard for data protection.

Rarely has so much been expected of a legal measure. From the outset, however, there were reasons to wonder whether the move from the old to the new regulatory regime would present as smooth and progressive a transition as possible. The Regulation was complex, bestowing a broad range of regulatory powers on national supervisory authorities, delegating a significant enforcement burden to the lead supervisory authority within the Union, and continuing to operate based on a notice and consent architecture which had already proven to be only partially effective under the Regulation's predecessor directive.

The Regulation has subsequently been criticised for furthering the conflation of privacy and data protection rights as well as leading a movement in which EU values have been imposed on jurisdictions whose legal systems are not compatible with such a direct adoption of European data protection laws. The Regulation is subject to ongoing criticisms about its enforcement (or lack thereof). The appeal in *Schrems II* and ongoing concerns about the capacity of lead supervisory authorities to act as global regulators illustrate that much remains to be resolved in maximising the effective operation of the Regulation in practice.

In the first five years of its operation, several of these areas of scepticism have borne academic fruit. As the contributions to this volume detail, both scholars

[1] Regulation (EU) 2016/679 of the European Parliament and of the Council of 27 April 2016 on the protection of natural persons with regard to the processing of personal data and on the free movement of such data, and repealing Directive 95/46/EC (General Data Protection Regulation).

[2] See GDPR, art 99. The GDPR entered into force in 2016, but only became applicable on 25 May 2018.

and practitioners have generated thought-provoking work on the prioritisation of consent as the primary, default basis for the processing of personal data – and have given others pause to question to what extent informational requirements as part of notice and consent architectures can compensate for the information asymmetries, decisional fatigue, and regulatory burdens that accompany modern online business practices. Controversies over the ad-tech eco-system, dark patterns, and scraping of personal data to supply large-scale language-learning modules, all addressed in this volume, stem partly from these basic consent-based concerns.

This volume comes nearly three-quarters of a decade after the entry into force of the GDPR, and its contributions were penned as the Regulation's first half-decade faded in the rearview mirror. Our hope is, that by gathering contributions from leading voices in modern European and data protection law to offer critical reflections on the controversies and challenges that have marked these early years of the Regulation's existence, we might assist in identifying what challenges will arrive in the law's second half-decade – and how we might best respond to them as a European community.

As academics interested and indeed invested in the interpretation and enforcement of data protection law, we hope that this volume can offer a guide to a selection of the central questions and controversies that have defined data protection law since 2018. This volume is not exhaustive thus while Chapter 6 of this collection will address the *Schrems I* and *Schrems II* litigation, both decisions and the debate which surrounds them about the feasibility and desirability of data localisation[3] are part of a broader trend of turning outwards in the early years of the GDPR (admittedly carried over from the Data Protection Directive), and intersection of adequacy of the Union's external projection of constitutional values[4] which cannot be exhaustively contained within the scope of this volume.[5]

II. The Contributions to this Volume

Chapter 1 of this volume, authored by Tijmen HA Wisman, is aptly titled 'The Problem of Invisible Power in Data Protection Law'. This chapter delves into the

[3] Theodore Christakis, 'European Digital Sovereignty, Data Protection and the Push toward Data Localisation' in Anupam Chander and Haochen Sun (eds) *Data Sovereignty: From Digital Silk Road to the Return of the State* (Oxford University Press, 2023) 371.

[4] See, Federico Fabbrini and Edoardo Celeste, 'The Right to be Forgotten in the Digital Age: The Challenges of Data Protection Beyond Borders' (2020) 21 *German Law Journal* 55. On considering the impact of the Regulation on the global south see Cara Mannion, 'Data Imperialism: The GDPR's Disastrous Impact on Africa's E-Commerce Markets' (2020) 52(3) *Vanderbilt Journal of Transnational Law* 685. On imperial and colonial narratives in data scholarship more broadly see Nick Couldry and Ulises A Mejias, 'Data Colonialism: Rethinking Big Data's Relation to the Contemporary Subject' (2019) 20(4) *Television and New Media* 336; Róisín Á Costello, 'The Brussels Effect: Regulatory Standard-Setting and Constitutional Conflicts in Post-Brexit Privacy Law' in Edoardo Celeste et al (eds) *Data Protection and Digital Sovereignty Post-Brexit* (Hart, 2023) 165.

[5] See generally, Federico Fabbrini et al (eds) *Data Protection Beyond Borders: Transatlantic Perspectives on Extraterritoriality and Sovereignty* (Hart, 2021).

intricate challenges posed by the enforcement and application of the General Data Protection Regulation (GDPR) in protecting individual rights against the backdrop of increasing digital surveillance and data processing by public authorities. Wisman provides a compelling historical context, tracing the evolution of data protection from early computerisation to the current GDPR framework.

The chapter critiques the practical shortcomings of GDPR, particularly its failure to counteract the asymmetrical power dynamics between citizens and state apparatus that often remain hidden behind bureaucratic processes. Through rigorous analysis and case studies, such as predictive analytics practices by UK local councils and administrative data processing in the Netherlands, Wisman exposes how data protection laws, while extensive, often fall short in practice, leaving individuals vulnerable to unaccountable governmental decisions. This critical examination sets the stage for a broader discussion on the need for robust legal frameworks that ensure transparency and fairness in the digital age.

Chapter 2, 'Assessing the Impact of Impact Assessments: Practical Questions Related to Article 35 GDPR', by Bart W Schermer offers an insightful exploration of the implementation and effectiveness of Data Protection Impact Assessments (DPIAs) under Article 35 of the GDPR. Schermer argues that there is a 'procedural vagueness' inherent to the DPIA requirement and, in particular, the role of the prior consultation of Article 36 of the GDPR which compromises the, ostensibly, 'risk-based' approach championed by the GDPR in its impact assessment process. Schermer notes that the increasing use of DPIAs, and thus the greater awareness of privacy and data protection issues, has resulted in a 'net positive' for those rights. But he also contends that the codification of DPIAs under the GDPR has led to an inherent vagueness that is not conducive to a coherent use of impact assessments in the way the GDPR envisages.

By integrating theoretical perspectives and empirical data gathered through surveys among Dutch privacy professionals, the chapter sheds light on the practical challenges and inconsistencies faced by those tasked with conducting DPIAs. The discussion extends into the procedural integration and overlaps with other risk assessment tools, such as those for AI systems, illustrating the complex compliance landscape and the ongoing struggle to balance risk management with regulatory requirements.

In Chapter 3, 'The Question of Consent in European Data Protection', Róisín Á Costello and Mark Leiser examine the intricate dynamics of consent within the framework of European data protection legislation. They critically assess how consent is operationalised as a mechanism for user empowerment and the protection of individual autonomy while also exploring its practical and theoretical challenges. The authors argue that, while the GDPR has positioned consent at the core of the data protection regime, the reality of obtaining genuine, informed consent in the digital age is fraught with complexities.

This includes issues around the autonomy of data subjects and the effectiveness of consent as a tool in the face of evolving technologies such as artificial intelligence and large language models that push the boundaries of traditional data processing practices. Through this exploration, the chapter highlights the gaps between regulatory ideals and market practices, suggesting that a re-evaluation of consent mechanisms is necessary to better align with the principles of fairness, transparency, and accountability envisioned by the GDPR.

In Chapter 4, 'Five Years of the Illegitimacy of Surveillance Advertising', Lex Zard moves to consider one the great controversies of the GDPR in its first five years, namely how the GDPR can, and should, contend with the challenges to consent – and indeed the Regulation more generally – posed by the ad-tech eco-system and what has been termed 'surveillance capitalism'.[6] Zard argues that surveillance-based economies of the type described, which operate on a 'Consent-or-Pay' model, can be valid but that this requires the existence of genuine choice between services, and accessibility in terms of price point among other conditions. At a basic level, Zard notes that the risks to consumers' physical or mental integrity or dignity in such a consent or pay scheme requires a higher standard of consent in certain situations, such as when advertising employment or housing opportunities.

In Chapter 5, 'Re-imagining Data Protection: Femtech and Gendered Risks in the GDPR' Anastasia Siapka, Maria Tzanou and Anna Nelson examine the GDPR from the perspective of gender. While the Regulation adopts a gender-neutral approach, they observe that gender is largely absent from the text of the Regulation more broadly and, indeed, from academic debate and consideration.[7] The authors argue that gender matters under the GDPR and that the Regulation's current gender-blind approach fails to recognise that personal data (and data gaps), as well as data subjects and risks of processing can be *gendered*. On this basis, they contend that the GDPR should be gender responsive and should explicitly acknowledge and engage with gendered risks for both symbolic and normative reasons. They propose a series of *de lege lata* routes to foreground gendered risks in data protection law, including using feminist DPIAs.

The authors also propose that the GDPR should evolve to acknowledge and mitigate these risks by integrating a gender perspective into its framework, thus enhancing the regulation's ability to safeguard against discrimination and uphold the rights of all individuals, particularly in sexual and reproductive health. The chapter reimagines the legal frameworks and emphasises the need for broader societal engagement in shaping laws that recognise and address the nuances of gender and technology.

In Chapter 6, 'Data Transfers, Schrems and the Future of Data Transfers under the GDPR', James Kneale delves into the complex landscape of international data transfers under the GDPR. It focuses on the landmark Schrems cases and their profound impact on the legal frameworks governing data privacy between the EU and the US. This chapter navigates the turbulent legal journey sparked by privacy

[6] See Shoshana Zuboff, *The Age of Surveillance Capitalism: The Fight For A Human Future at The New Frontier of Power* (1st edn, Public Affairs 2019).

[7] Though see Gianclaudio Malgieri and Gloria González Fuster, 'The Vulnerable Data Subject: A Gendered Data Subject?' (2022) 13 *European Journal of Law and Technology* 1.

activist Max Schrems, whose activism led to significant judicial rulings, including the invalidation of both the Safe Harbour and Privacy Shield agreements. In particular, Kneale argues that there is potential for a 'Schrems III' in light of the CJEU's findings that Safe Harbour and Privacy Shield did not ensure an equivalent level of protection of data subjects' rights to that guaranteed in the EU legal order.

In Chapter 7, 'Silent Reforms of the GDPR in the EU Digital Market Legal Revolution' Van den Poel and Malgieri argue that, despite the seeming retrenchment of the GDPR as a static text which this view endorses, the Regulation has been in almost constant evolution in its first half-decade – through its interpretation by the Court of Justice, national courts and DPAs albeit absent changes to the text itself – but also through a series of 'silent reforms' accomplished through several adjacent regulations. The authors have identified five such reforms located in three pieces of secondary law, namely the AI Act, the Digital Services Act and the Data Act.

What emerges, they argue, is a '*fil rouge*' of progression and cautious optimism as profound and important reforms are silently woven into the 'intricate tapestry of legislative measures that have collectively redefined the landscape of data protection'.

In Chapter 8, 'Data Protection's Intersections: Reconciling Data Protection Requirements with Regulated Data Use Beyond the GDPR', Katherine Nolan, examines how the GDPR intersects with, and is influenced by, other legislative instruments. This chapter interrogates the complexities of lawful data processing, emphasising that compliance extends beyond the GDPR into a web of overlapping regulations that govern data usage across various sectors.

Nolan methodically explores the nuances of how the GDPR interacts with other laws, such as the ePrivacy Directive, the Digital Markets Act, the Data Governance Act and the Data Act, which all impose additional data processing obligations. She articulates how these legislative frameworks impact and complicate the enforcement and application of data protection laws.

By focusing on how these laws integrate with or diverge from the GDPR, Nolan provides insights into the evolving landscape of EU digital governance, underscoring the challenges and opportunities presented by this intricate legal matrix. Her analysis contributes significantly to understanding the broader implications of data protection regulations, highlighting potential regulatory overlaps, gaps, and the ongoing need for harmonisation in digital governance. What emerges is a complex picture in which the apparently solid foundations and scope of the GDPR are rendered more subject to flux than initially appears.

Finally, in Chapter 9, 'Article 82 GDPR and Non-Material Damages: Torn Between Social and Economic Function?' Róisín Á Costello examines one of the most recent controversies which has come before the courts in respect of the interpretation of the GDPR, namely how and whether non-material damages can be awarded for harm suffered under the Regulation. The chapter outlines the rapidly expanding pool of decisions from the European Court that consider this issue and argues that they represent a concrete example of the attempts by the European Union to embed its commitments to fundamental rights within the architecture of market-based secondary laws.

Using a political-economy analysis which draws on the work of Karl Polanyi,[8] Costello argues that the CJEU's decisions in respect of Article 82 expose just how far data protection law has travelled from its own expressed roots of being a market-enabling branch of EU law – intended to facilitate a more competitive European market and how much data protection law has come to be regarded as an integrated and active part of the Union's fundamental rights architecture exposing the CJEU's (and the Union's) evolving relationship to ordoliberal regulatory approaches – and the integration (or perhaps reintegration) of the social and market aspects of the Union's constitutional identity.

[8] Karl Polanyi, *The Great Transformation: The Political and Economic Origins of Our Time* (2nd edn, Beacon Press, 2001) , 171 *et seq.*

1

The Problem of Invisible Power in Data Protection Law

TIJMEN HA WISMAN

I. Introduction

The advent of computers has enabled public authorities to collect personal data, disseminate it to other authorities and maintain comprehensive dossiers on individuals. These dossiers can fuel the subsequent decisions of public authorities in relation to individuals. In the European Union (EU), when such personal data is processed by administrative authorities, the General Data Protection Regulation (GDPR) applies to ensure a measure of legal protection for the individual.[1] In practice, this protection often falls short.

In 2019, a group of UK researchers, identified 53 local councils using predictive analytics in order to 'score' individuals without any 'means for people who had been scored to know their score, how it was generated and how to interrogate it'.[2] As a result, a person can be labelled (it does not necessarily have to be a score) without being informed of the label or given an opportunity to contest it even though it may impact how the individual is treated. The report's authors observe that 'data scores come to order the *contours of citizenship*, shaping the deserving and undeserving, risky and the vulnerable, and, ultimately, the terms upon which access to and participation in society might occur'.[3] This reveals how the invisible web of personal data compounded and cemented by administrative authorities is fundamental to the relationship between citizens and the state.

By the early 1970s, governments in the US and Europe had already recognised that the individual ought to be protected against the increasingly computerised

[1] Regulation (EU) 2016/679 of the European Parliament and of the Council of 27 April 2016 on the protection of natural persons with regard to the processing of personal data and on the free movement of such data, and repealing Directive 95/46/EC [2016] OJ L119.

[2] Lina Dencik et al, 'The Golden View: Data-driven Governance in the Scoring Society' (2019) 8 *Internet Policy Review* 6 and 14. Available at: https://policyreview.info/pdf/policyreview-2019-2-1413.pdf accessed 8 December 2023. The GDPR was in force in the UK at the time.

[3] ibid 19.

machinery of the state. In the US, a report was issued by the Ministry of Health, Education & Welfare which argued that the power asymmetry created by the introduction of computerised record-keeping raised concerns in relationships between individuals and authorities active outside of law enforcement (hereafter referred to as 'administrative authorities'), since data processing activities in law enforcement were subjected to constitutional and statutory limitations.[4] Many of the concerns in the report revolved around due process, a complex concept which captures the thought that individuals need protection against arbitrary or unjustified government action, which could already be found in the Magna Charta Liberatum.[5] Due process received special attention, because computerised record-keeping facilitated the exercise of invisible informational power leaving citizens unaware of, and unable to defend themselves against, the decisions of administrative authorities. The effect of computers on the exercise of invisible power by administrative agencies requires enhanced protections for people confronted by them.[6] Instead of drawing inspiration from existing due process protections to find an answer to the problem of invisible power, the report's authors exclusively addressed it through a particular concept of privacy, defying dictionary definitions, as 'mutuality' in record keeping.[7]

The counterparts of due process in the European context can be found in the Council of Europe's (hereinafter CoE) European Convention on Human Rights (ECHR), namely in the right to a fair trial, the right to an effective remedy, and on the national and EU level, the right to good administration.[8] Data protection law from its early inception in the European context proclaimed the ambition to protect all rights and fundamental freedoms. Given this broad ambition, a response including innovative approaches to rights important for the legal protection against the computerised state machinery, such as the right to a fair trial and an effective remedy, would have been in line with the concerns sparked by computers.[9] Instead, European data protection laws followed the US focus on a

[4] Secretary's Advisory Committee on Automated Personal Data System, *Records, Computers and the Rights of Citizens* (U.S. Department of Health, Education & Welfare 1973).

[5] Ola J. Settem, *Applications of the 'Fair Hearing' Norm in ECHR Article 6(1) to Civil Proceedings*, Springer 2016, 8.

[6] Ricardo Lilo Lobos, *Understanding Due Process in Non-Criminal Matters* (Ius Gentium: Comparative Perspectives on Law and Justice 97, Springer 2022) 246–247.

[7] *Records, Computers and the Rights of Citizens* (n 4), 40.

[8] D.J. Galligan, *Due Process and Fair Procedures* (Oxford University Press 1996) 212–225. It can also be found on the national level in principles of good administration. At EU level there is Article 41 of the Charter of Fundamental Rights which provides a right to good administration and includes a right to be heard before any individual measure which would affect her or him adversely is taken, a right to have access to his or her file and the obligation of the administration to give reasons for its decision. The Charter, however, is not applicable to national administrative agencies which are not implementing EU law in their operations. See Migle Laukyte, 'Averting Enfeeblement and Fostering Empowerment: Algorithmic Rights and the Right to Good Administration' (2022) 46 *Computer Law & Security Review* 1–14. Available at: www.sciencedirect.com/science/article/pii/S0267364922000607?via%3Dihub, accessed 15 February 2024.

[9] See Preamble and Article 1 Convention 108, Recital 2 and Article 1(1) Directive 95/46/EC of the European Parliament and of the Council of 24 October 1995 on the protection of individuals with

peculiar conception of privacy. The relativity of the right to privacy, particularly in the EU, has contaminated aspects of data protection seeking to address the problem of invisible power, despite the fact that this problem is fundamental to political systems where openness and transparency should be the norm.

Against this background of fundamental transformation in public administration caused by information technologies, this chapter aims to explore the extent to which data protection law effectively addresses the threats to the legal protection of individuals posed by the problem of invisible power. This problem is defined within the context of the original concerns that gave rise to data protection law in the US and the European context, including the Council of Europe and the EU. Section 3 analyses the relevant legal protection regime in the current EU data protection law. The final substantive section focuses on two notorious examples from the practice of Dutch state institutions to reveal the shortcomings of the existing legal regime.

II. The Introduction of Computing and the Invisible Power Problem

Early data protection laws emerged amidst concerns over the amplification of state apparatus' informational power by computers and its potential impact on individual legal protection. These concerns were present both in the US and in Europe, considered in turn below.

Fair Information Practice in the US

In 1973, a stern alarm was sounded in a US report named 'Records, Computers and the Rights of Citizens'. The report, authored by a diverse group including social service professionals, legislators, government and private industry managers, researchers, lawyers, private citizens, and field experts, anticipated contemporary concerns surrounding information and communication technologies (ICT). It illuminated the risks associated with widespread computerisation. A central theme was the concern over government's invisible exercise of power through data processing, especially outside the context of law enforcement where protections for due process were in place.[10] In its foreword, the authors of the report noted that a more centralised record keeping on individuals 'demands a hard look at the adequacy of our mechanisms for guaranteeing citizens all the protections of due process in relation to the records we maintain about them'. This quote shows

regard to the processing of personal data and on the free movement of such data *OJ L 281 (DPD)*, Recital 2 and Article 1(2) GDPR.

[10] The focus of this chapter is also data processing outside the context of law enforcement.

two important and inextricably linked phenomena: the advent of computers enabling novel state power dynamics over citizens, and the imperative to redefine citizen rights and safeguards to mitigate potential abuses, ensure fairness, and balance the executive branch's heightened power resulting from computerisation.[11]

Within this context, the report refers to the concept of due process on a number of occasions. The authors delve into the emergence of interconnected information access, raising concerns about potential denial of citizens' rights, benefits, and public goods without their knowledge or ability to challenge such actions.[12] Decision-making based on undisclosed information or information without its source revealed was deemed contrary to fundamental principles of due process.[13] They foresaw bureaucracies prioritising efficiency through computerised record-keeping, potentially compromising due process for citizens. These concerns reveal the contours of an invisible and intangible informational power, which can be wielded against an oblivious person.

Due process further reappears in the report in a discussion about intelligence data, originally collected by law enforcement agencies, further processed by other organisations for a range of purposes, including eligibility for employment, including in civil service, access to public benefits, permits and licences.[14] Assessments of eligibility are commonly conducted by administrative authorities, whose data-processing activities are often minimally, if at all, constrained by legal safeguards and constitutional limitations. This example demonstrates how the extensive powers of one agency, justified by critical objectives like national security, might encroach upon the operations of other agencies handling less significant matters.[15]

Within this context, the report signals a deficiency in mechanisms enabling citizens to assert their legal position, encompassing not only rights but also softer entitlements such as status and benefits, in dealings with public authorities. To address the increasing state-citizen power asymmetry driven by computerisation, the authors identify the need to grant citizens the right to know *what* is on records, *how* these records are used and the right to participate in the formation of information on record.[16] The authors mention that the concerns about computer-based record keeping can be linked to a redefinition of personal privacy related to personal data record keeping understood in terms of *mutuality*: The procedures affording an individual the right to participate in his own records were coined 'fair information practices', which came to feature in substance in the US Privacy Act of 1974.[17]

[11] *Records, Computers and the Rights of Citizens* (n 4), 75.

[12] ibid 120. Due process considerations such as the right to be heard are not only important for rights, but also benefits, see Giacinto della Cananea, *Due Process of Law Beyond the State: Requirements of Administrative Procedure*, Oxford Academic 2016, 43.

[13] *Records, Computers and the Rights of Citizens* (n 4), 61.

[14] ibid 75.

[15] ibid 20.

[16] ibid 60–62.

[17] Gloria González Fuster, *The Emergence of Personal Data Protection as a Fundamental Right of the EU*, (Springer 2014) 35–36.

This focus on privacy can only be warranted following a redefinition, which the authors implicitly acknowledge deviates from the standard dictionary definition and distracts from the fact that computerised record-keeping actually affects the legal position of the individual vis-à-vis the state.[18] It is therefore questionable whether the report's authors contributed to the protection of this legal position by referring to the relevant problem as one of privacy which the authors themselves describe as a value which is neither absolute nor constant.

It is this non-absolute nature of privacy that supported the proposal that procedures for *fair information practice* would not have to be followed if specifically authorised by law.[19] This raises the question in the US context whether elementary considerations of due process should be so easily circumvented by the legislator. Given the constitutional nature of some protections of due process, the legislator's mandate to sideline them implies that an individual's legal position can be changed without her or his involvement. This is a significant step back compared to the protections of due process in criminal law evident, for instance, in the Fifth Amendment. This notion appears to contradict elementary considerations of due process, as alluded to by the authors themselves in a quote from Justice Felix Frankfurters:

'The heart of the matter is that democracy implies respect for the elementary rights of men, however suspect or unworthy; a democratic government must therefore practice fairness; and fairness can rarely be obtained by secret one-sided determination of facts decisive of rights … No better instrument has been devised for arriving at truth than to give a person in jeopardy of serious loss notice of the case against him and opportunity to meet it.'[20]

Early Discourse on Data Protection in Europe

In the then European Community, early discussions revolved around data processing, with a document from the European Commission primarily focusing on the competitiveness of the European data processing industry against the US.[21] Data processing was identified as a force 'penetrating virtually every walk of life, transforming management and administration, education and science' and identifying its potential to determine the structure of society.[22] The Commission stated that the creation of databanks made the rules of access to them vital and described them to be of 'basic constitutional importance' pointing to the need to establish 'common ground rules'.[23] The European Parliament followed suit by adopting a

[18] ibid 38.
[19] ibid 41.
[20] ibid 242.
[21] Commission, 'Community Policy on Data Processing' (Communication) 1973 SEC(73) 4300 final.
[22] ibid 1.
[23] European Parliament, 'Resolution of the European Parliament on the protection of the rights of the individual in the face of developing technical progress in the field of automatic data processing' [1975] OJ C60/48.

resolution stating that 'a directive on "individual freedom and data processing" is an urgent necessity', not only from the perspective of citizens, but also because of the need to harmonise legislation.[24] The European Parliament called for the establishment of a special committee to examine proposals relating to 'the right of the individual to see and dispute the stored information'.[25] This resolution was based on an interim report of the Legal Affairs Committee, originally introducing the value of 'personal freedom and data processing'. To address this, the primary objective of the report is to examine 'the more restricted field of intrusion on privacy by misuse of automatic data processing techniques, of identifying the dangers and studying the ways in which they may be minimised'.[26] In short, the anticipated major change in legal protection due to the rise of data processing technologies, which would revolutionise state administrative processes and expand the informational power of public authorities, was pinpointed as a particular aspect of the right to privacy.

Beyond the European Community, in 1981, the Council of Europe (CoE) adopted Convention 108 in which privacy was positioned as the most prominent value.[27] The Explanatory Report does reveal a recognition of concerns beyond the right to privacy already in the first sentence: '[t] he object of this convention is to strengthen data protection, i.e. the legal protection of individuals with regard to automatic processing of personal information relating to them'.[28]

Data protection is positioned as the legal protection of individual presumably affected by the processing of personal data. This is explicitly linked to 'decisions affecting individuals [...] based on information stored in computerised data files' and the duty for those responsible for the files to guarantee that 'the undeniable advantages they can obtain from automatic data processing do not at the same time lead to a weakening of the position of the persons on whom data are stored'.[29] These quotes show an understanding that the introduction of computerised data files creates a new type of concern which should be addressed by new rules.

From the very beginning data protection claimed to be protecting all rights and fundamental freedoms; given this broad ambition, an approach including these rights would have been in line with the concerns data protection law seeks to address.[30] The singular focus of the drafters of the CoE Convention 108 on a very

[24] ibid.

[25] ibid.

[26] Legal Affairs Committee of the European Parliament (Rapporteur: Lord Mansfield), 'Interim Report on the protection of the rights of the individual in the face of developing technical progress in the field of automatic data processing' 1975, Document 487/74, 7.

[27] Article 1 Convention for the Protection of Individuals with regard to Automatic Processing of Personal Data (Convention 108). Fuster (n 17) 78–84.

[28] Council of Europe, *Explanatory Report to the Convention for the Protection of Individuals with regard to Automatic Processing of Personal Data* (Strasbourg, 28.1.1981), 1.

[29] ibid.

[30] See Preamble and Article 1 Convention 108, Recital 2 and Article 1(1) DPD, Recital 2 and Article 1(2) GDPR.

particular conception of the right to privacy therefore does not seem to be motivated by sound legal reasoning, but by docility to the fresh US doctrine instead.

One can question whether putting the onus of data protection on the right to privacy may result in the relativity of the latter being applied to the former. Although relativity is appropriate with respect to some aspects of data protection law, the same cannot be claimed when data protection and due process aspects coincide. The right to a fair trial and an effective remedy are *unqualified rights* within the framework of the European Convention on Human Rights (ECHR) as opposed to the right to private life which is a *qualified right*.[31] A qualified right in the ECHR contains a qualification clause establishing the requirements under which a right can be interfered with, e.g. under Article 8(2) of the ECHR. The right to a fair trial and the right to an effective remedy do not contain such a clause, which is not to say they are absolute, but it does demonstrate that these rights are not as relative as the qualified rights.[32] The right to a fair trial is one of the cornerstones of constitutional democracy and the rule of law. Since the ECHR was drafted against the backdrop of fear for the rise of totalitarian societies, characterised by the opaque exercise of state power, it is surprising that these considerations of legal protection seem to hinge on formal decisions of the state such as sanctions, measures, fines or criminal prosecution. This protection starts from the rather naïve assumption that state sanctions are deployed only in the public eye. It denies the possibility of an invisible (and in some cases malevolent) exercise of power. The emerging threats of computerised data processing were a great moment to revisit these naïve assumptions present in the ECHR and to bolster and redefine existing rights to a fair trial, effective remedy, and good administration, rather than simply replicating a US-style privacy law.

The Convention 108 offered measures which could, to some extent, contribute to addressing these concerns: the data protection principles, the data subjects' rights and the duty for Member States of the CoE to give effect to them. In theory this would effectively offer the data subject the right to be aware of the processing of personal data and the right to challenge the contents of a file. In the explanatory report, data protection principles are condensed into two fundamental legal standards: ensuring that collected data is accurate, relevant, and not excessive for its purpose, and ensuring that its use is appropriate.[33] This reveals a very narrow conception of legal protection where data subjects' rights serve as instruments for the efficiency of data processing entities, with correctness seen merely as a requirement for efficiency.

[31] Bernadette Rainey, Elizabeth Wicks and Clare Ovey, *Jacobs, White & Ovey: The European Convention on Human Rights* (Oxford University Press 2010) 9.

[32] How relative Article 6 ECHR is in practice is another matter. See Ryan Goss, The Disappearing 'Minimum Rights' of Article 6 ECHR: the Unfortunate Legacy of *Ibrahim* and *Beuze* (2023) 23(4) *Human Rights Law Review* 23.

[33] Explanatory Report (n 28) 9.

The Convention 108 protections are subject to a regime of exceptions and restrictions in Article 9. The explanatory report illustrates the aspired relativity of the data protection law in the clarification that the Convention's text 'has been modelled after that of the second paragraphs of Article 6, 8, 10 and 11 of the [ECHR]'.[34] The mention of Article 6 of the ECHR (the right to a fair trial) here is a striking mistake, since this is not a qualified right. On the contrary, Article 6(2) of the ECHR contains the presumption of innocence which is an absolute principle; coincidentally this can also be harmed by practices enabled by the exceptions to data protection law where public authorities share shadow administrations containing secret judgments on a person's character.

These early foundations for data protection laws in Europe reveal common concerns with the US, discussed next.

The Common Concern of Invisible Power

Two important problems created by the introduction of computers which challenge individuals' legal protection emerge from the discussions in the US and Europe. The first is the *lack of transparency* (hereinafter '*the opacity problem*') surrounding the processing of personal data. Personal data can be collected, shared, enriched, and increasingly mined to derive new information from it, all without citizens being aware of either the process or the outcomes. This processing can result in an invisible web of data, which public authorities may then utilise to make decisions regarding rights, privileges, benefits, taxes, arrangements, or access to other public goods. The personal data processed can effectively constitute a body of presumed information used to evaluate whether a citizen meets the conditions to be entitled to (or have a right to) a certain public good, service, status or other entitlement.

The second problem is *the inability of the citizen to challenge the body (or elements thereof) of presumed information* established by a public authority or network of public authorities used to base their decisions on. Another variation of this issue arises when individuals are confronted with informal decisions, such as receiving a label, score, or judgment of character, based on presumed information, without the ability to challenge it. This problem, and the variant thereof, amounts to the *indefensibility problem.*

While this chapter does not intend to address exhaustively all the problems which might arise in this context, it is sufficient to establish that there is a *problem of invisible power* consisting of the opacity and the indefensibility problems facilitated by the processing of personal data. In this context, the following section examines how EU data protection law addresses this issue, focusing on the GDPR and its predecessor, the Data Protection Directive.

[34] ibid 10.

III. Legal Protection against Invisible Power in EU Data Protection Law

Although the GDPR has replaced the 1995 Data Protection Directive (hereinafter DPD), the latter merits attention in this section as it helps to shed light on the development of legal protections offered in EU data protection law against administrative authorities. Both the DPD and the GDPR were more extensive and included more elements addressing legal protection against actions of the executive empowered by personal data processing compared to Convention 108. These elements can be divided into two categories, addressed in the first two subsections. First, there are *transparency obligations* consisting of a duty for the data controller to provide information to the data subject (hereafter 'information duty') and a data access right for the data subject. Second, there is a right to protection against automated decision-making. The third subsection discusses the regime of legal restrictions to elaborate on the extent to which the DPD and the GDPR address the problem of the invisible power of administrative authorities.

Information Duty and Access Right

The DPD established an information duty for data collected from the data subject directly (Article 10) or through a third party (Article 11). Transparency obligations are linked to fairness in recital 38 which states that for processing to be fair the data subject must be in a position to learn of the existence of the processing operation. The scope of this information duty was not well specified. Besides the identity of the controller and the purposes of the processing, it provided for a residual category under 'any further information' with some examples. One example category included the existence of the right to access and rectification but did not mention automated decision-making.

Article 11(2) of the DPD provided two types of exceptions to the information duty. It provided the possibility for a data controller to not provide information to a data subject, particularly where that data is processed for statistical, historical or scientific research purposes, when this would be impossible or require disproportionate effort or if the recording or disclosure is expressly laid down by law and Member States provide 'appropriate safeguards'.[35] The first exception is a discretionary exception which provides a margin of discretion to the data controller to assert that informing the data subject would require a disproportionate effort. The second exception is a legal exception allowing discretion for national legislators to derogate from the information duty, provided they do so 'expressly' and adopt appropriate safeguards, although without specifying these safeguards.

[35] DPD, art 11(2).

Article 12 of the DPD did contain an access right which involved a category on 'knowledge of the logic involved in any automated processing of data [...] at least in the case of automated decisions referred to in Article 15(1)', the latter addressing basically the same scope of decisions addressed in Article 15(1)(h) of the GDPR. Article 12(b) of the DPD contained the right to rectification, erasure and blocking in case the processing does not comply with the DPD 'in particular because of the incomplete or inaccurate nature of the data'. Although Article 12 of the DPD did not contain a subparagraph allowing for exceptions, Article 13(1) provided the possibility for Member States to adopt legislative measures to restrict the scope of obligations and rights provided for in Articles 10, 11(1) and 12. It is notable that the DPD did not permit legislative restrictions of Article 11(2), which mandated the requirement for 'appropriate safeguards'.

Even though the GDPR offered no significant expansion concerning the information duty and the access right, it did improve some of the relevant aspects of the provisions. The information duty has become more precise and includes the necessary information for a data subject to exercise her or his rights of access, rectification, erasure and restriction, also with respect to further processing. These rights for the data subject were outlined in separate articles, but fundamentally, they have not changed in a manner that would afford the data subject significantly more legal protection compared to the DPD. Both the DPD and the GDPR provide a range of recitals and provisions which constitute a duty for the data controller to give data subjects enough information to effectively exercise their rights. The GDPR, however, does anchor this duty more firmly in certain provisions such as Article 12(2). Nevertheless, both the DPD and GDPR also allow the legislator to limit this duty.

What could be viewed as an improvement of the information duty is the explicit adoption of the information category: 'the existence of automated decision-making, including profiling, referred to in Article 22(1)' and 'meaningful information about the logic involved, as well as the significance and the envisaged consequences of such processing for the data subject'.[36] Whether this improves the information duty itself compared to the DPD can be contested. The scope of the information duty is equal to and thus as limited as the scope of Article 22(1) of the GDPR. Even though the specification of the information categories contributes to the clarity, these are formulated in a closed manner in the GDPR as opposed to the open formulation in the DPD. The open formulation in the DPD of 'any further information' would reasonably include any type of decision-making, without being limited to automated decisions with legal or similar effects. In this sense, the DPD offered more protection since the closed information duty in the GDPR implies that the data controller does not violate his information duty if he does not provide information that falls outside the scope

[36] GDPR, arts 13(2)(f) and 14(2)(g). Recital 71 is also relevant in this respect and will be discussed in the next subsection.

of Article 22. Overall, this would imply that the general information duty in the GDPR has become more restricted.

Some authors have argued that there exists a right to an ex post explanation regarding automated decision-making, ensured by the combination of information duties and access rights and link this to the initial expectations that computer processes would be transparent in their operations, which they deem more relevant now than ever.[37] The CJEU seems to have confirmed this in a recent judgment, in which it identified that the controller is subject to additional information obligations under Article 13(2)(f) and Article 14(2)(g) of the GDPR.[38]

The scope of exceptions for data which is collected directly from the data subject stayed approximately the same under the GDPR. An extra exception was added in Article 14 regulating the situation in which data is not directly collected from the data subject. Article 14(5)(b) of the GDPR provides that the information duty does not apply when it 'is likely to render impossible or seriously impair the achievement of the objectives of the processing'. The GDPR recitals do not provide clarity on this exception. Article 29 of the WP claimed that this exception can only be relied on if data controllers can demonstrate that providing the information alone would 'nullify the objectives of the processing'.[39] Such a strict interpretation cannot be defended based on the text of Article 14(5)(b) of the GDPR which explicitly states that it is sufficient for a data controller to demonstrate that providing information is likely to seriously impair the achievement of objectives.

This provides a data controller with a margin of discretion with respect to the decision of whether information should be provided. The example given by Article 29 of the WP is the signalling of suspicious activity by a bank and sending this data to the financial law enforcement authority. Thus, the disclosure to the authority is laid down by law, so the exception in this example seems to be based rather on Article 14(5)(c) in conjunction with Article 23(1)(e) of the GDPR.

This exception appears more applicable to processing in a horizontal relationship, where no public third party is involved and the processing is conducted to gather evidence of fraud, such as covertly recording employee theft in a workplace. Here, a margin of discretion for the data controller is necessary. It is highly questionable whether the same margin of discretion should be accorded to public authorities which engage in processing while performing their administrative

[37] Gabriela Zanfir-Fortuna, 'Article 13. Information to be Provided Where Personal Data are Collected from the Data Subject' in Steve Peers and others (eds), *The EU Charter of Fundamental Rights: A Commentary* (Hart 2014) 416. Andrew D. Selbst and Julia Powles, 'Meaningful Information and the Right to Explanation' (2017) 7 *International Data Privacy Law* 233, 235. Gianclaudio Malgieri and Giovanni Comandé, 'Why a Right to Legibility of Automated Decision-Making Exists in the General Data Protection Regulation' (2017) 7 *International Data Privacy Law* 247. For an opposing view see Sandra Wachter, Brent Mittelstadt and Luciano Floridi, 'Why a Right to Explanation of Automated Decision-Making Does Not Exist in the General Data Protection Regulation' (2017) 7 *International Data Privacy Law* 80.

[38] Case C-634/21 *SCHUFA* [2023] EU:C:2023:957, [56].

[39] Article 29 Working Party, 'Guidelines on transparency under Regulation 2016/679' (2017) WP260 rev.01, 31.

duties. This grants them the authority to decide on exceptions to transparency, which should ideally be specified in a law directly addressing this issue, rather than automatically left to the discretion of any public authority under the GDPR.

Protection against Automated Decision-making

Both the DPD and the GDPR provide protection against automated decision-making. After the adoption of the GDPR a discussion started over the precise content of this protection, in particular whether it is 'a right to be exercised by a data subject' or whether it is 'a qualified prohibition on a particular type of decisional process'.[40] Article 15 of the DPD imposed a duty on Member States 'to grant the right to every person not to be subject to a decision which produces legal effects' or 'significantly affects' the person when it is 'solely based on automated processing of data intended to evaluate certain personal aspects relating to him'.[41] The inclusion of decisions that produce legal effects or similarly significantly affect a person in this provision can be seen as an attempt by the legislator to encompass decisions that operate outside formal procedures, potentially enhancing the legal protection of individuals. In the second paragraph, it introduced exceptions on the prohibition quite similar to the alternative criteria for making processing legitimate in Article 7 of the DPD. This could be done on the basis of entering into or the performance of a contract, although only 'suitable measures to safeguard his legitimate interests' are mentioned in the Directive referring only to an example 'such as arrangements allowing him to put his point of view', with no further details.[42] The other exception is when it is authorised by law 'which also lays down measures to safeguard the data subject's legitimate interests', but no concrete requirements are established with respect to the form and substance of these measures.[43]

Article 22 of the GDPR, the counterpart of Article 15 of the DPD, has a similar structure in its first two paragraphs while also adding the criterion 'consent' as an exception. When the processing is authorised by law this should 'lay down suitable measures to safeguard the data subject's rights and freedoms and legitimate interests'.[44] This raises the question how the scope of Article 22(1) of the GDPR – decisions which produce legal effects or similarly significantly affect a person – relates to the seemingly broader scope of safeguards in Article 22(2)(b) which applies to rights, freedoms and legitimate interests. The enumeration of these broad categories implies a recognition that automated decisions can affect the contours

[40] Lee A Bygrave, 'Article 22. Automated Individual Decision-Making, Including Profiling' in Steve Peers et al (eds), *The EU Charter of Fundamental Rights: A Commentary* (Hart 2014) 530.

[41] DPD, art 15(1). The scope is a bit different than GDPR, art 22(1) which focuses on automated decisions 'including profiling'.

[42] ibid art 15(2)(a).

[43] ibid art 15(2)(b).

[44] GDPR, art 22(2)(b).

of citizenship, but it is not certain when these meet the threshold established in Article 22(1). The uncertain meaning of 'legal or similarly significant effects', as well as the 'decision based solely on automated processing' essentially grants a level of discretion to public authorities to organise administrative processes to fall outside of the scope of Article 22 of the GDPR. This is at odds with the rationale behind data protection law to protect the individual, creating a serious risk of circumvention.[45] The recent *SCHUFA* case is important in this context as the CJEU, relying on recital 71, defends a broad scope of the term 'decision', including decisions evaluating personal aspects relating to a person.[46] This broad interpretation of 'decision' is justified by a teleological interpretation of Article 22(1) of the GDPR which 'reinforces the effective protection intended by that provision'.[47]

In Article 22(3) of the GDPR, the suitable measures to safeguard data subject's rights and freedoms are explicitly provided when the processing is for entering into, or performance of a contract, or is based on consent 'at least the right to obtain human intervention on the part of the controller, to express his or her point of view and to contest the decision'.[48] The specific measures for automated decision-making in the GDPR are an improvement as compared to the DPD, but it is telling that this improvement does not cover decisions authorised by law. Recital 71, however, has caused some confusion as it enumerates various grounds for automated decision-making and concludes with a statement on the appropriate measures such processing should entail, including specific information provision to the data subject and the right to human intervention, expression of their viewpoint, explanation of the decision reached after assessment, and the ability to challenge the decision. The wording of Article 22 of the GDPR appears to leave room for the legislator to adopt other suitable measures.[49] According to the interpretation of Article 29 of the WP, all safeguards mentioned in recital 71, as well as Article 22(3), apply to all automated decisions.[50] The legislator explicitly omitted these safeguards from decisions authorised by law in the text of Article 22(2)(b) and relegated them to a non-binding recital. This divided academics about the margin of discretion delegated to the legislator. In *SCHUFA*, the CJEU made a preliminary point on this matter whereby the interpretation of EU law depends not only on words, but also on context, objective and purposes pursued by the act.[51] The Court leaves no room for doubt regarding the interpretation of recital 71 and Article 22(2)(b),

[45] A similar warning was issued in recital 27 DPD.

[46] Case C-634/21 *SCHUFA* (n 40), [45].

[47] ibid para 60.

[48] GDPR, art 22(3).

[49] Margot Kominski, 'The Right to Explanation, Explained', *Berkeley Technology Law Journal* 34: 189, 198.

[50] Article 29 Working Party, 'Guidelines on Automated individual decision-making and Profiling for the purposes of Regulation 2016/679', (2017) WP251rev.01, 27.

[51] Case C-634/21 *SCHUFA* (n 40), [41]. This references Case C-579/21 *Pankki S* EU:C:2023:501, [38] and the case law cited.

affirming that automated decisions authorised by law must include, among the suitable measures, the right for individuals to obtain human intervention from the controller, express their viewpoint, and challenge the decision.[52] This ruling, if respected by Member States, will greatly benefit the legal protection of the people.

Legal Restrictions

The DPD and GDPR both contain a separate article allowing for legal restrictions. It allows for limitations on some of the provisions of data protection law, while imposing requirements similar to Article 8(2) of the ECHR in the DPD or Article 52 of the CFEU in the GDPR. This means there needs to be a law providing for the limitation which respects the essence of all fundamental rights and freedoms and is a necessary and proportionate measure in a democratic society in order to safeguard a broad set of objectives ranging from national security to important economic of financial interests.[53] These restrictions are not categorised into specific areas such as monitoring and investigation, nor do they mention safeguards, suggesting that a broad margin of discretion is delegated to the legislator.

Article 13 of the DPD did not allow restrictions on the protection against automated decision-making of Article 15, but the GDPR does. The GDPR allows for restrictions on Articles 12–22, which includes the transparency obligations and the protection against decisions based on automated processing. Recital 73 elaborates that restrictions concerning decisions based on profiling can be imposed by Union or Member State law. The extent to which these restrictions may be applied is subject to new case law, but the precedent set in *SCHUFA* provides ground for cautious optimism.

Restrictions need to respect the essence of rights, therefore cannot entail the general suspension of a right or void it of its basic content.[54] The structure of Article 23 also implies that it imposes exceptions to a rule and, following the logic of human rights, should be applied restrictively. Recital 41 provides that a legal basis can also be substantive law and establishes the requirement that a legislative measure must be clear and precise and its application foreseeable to the person subject to it. This can be read in conjunction with Article 23(2) of the GDPR which requires that legislative measures must contain specific provisions for a set of eight categories when relevant. Two of the categories especially applicable to the problem of invisible power are the scope of the restrictions introduced, and the risks to the rights and freedoms of data subjects.[55] Restrictions which enable the invisible exercise of power increase the risks to the rights and freedoms of data subjects.

[52] ibid [65]–[66].

[53] These objectives have been expanded with three categories in the GDPR.

[54] European Data Protection Board, 'Guidelines 10/2020 on restrictions under Article 23 GDPR' (2021) Version 2.1, 7.

[55] GDPR, arts 23(2)(c) and 23(2)(g).

If restrictions enable administrative authorities to exercise invisible power, this would undercut the ability of data subjects to defend themselves against decisions affecting their rights, freedoms and legitimate interests. Recital 4 provides that the GDPR respects all fundamental rights and explicitly mentions the right to an effective remedy and to a fair trial. It follows from Article 23(1) that restrictions should respect the essence of the right to a fair trial and an effective remedy. The CJEU has ruled that legislation failing to allow individuals to pursue legal remedies to access their data, or to obtain rectification or erasure of their data, does not respect the essence of the fundamental right to effective judicial protection.[56] Therefore, there is again reason for optimism regarding the leeway afforded to legislatures to circumvent the legal protection offered in the GDPR.

Restrictions on transparency and measures against automated decision making may transform processing activities of an administrative authority into a form of secret surveillance. In line with ECtHR case law which imposes a higher standard of foreseeability on legislation providing such competences, the law imposing the restriction should be formulated with sufficient precision to enable the individuals to understand when it would apply to them.[57] Furthermore, there should be a clear indication of the conditions under which an administrative authority is permitted to employ secretive measures, along with justification for their necessity in relation to a specified purpose.[58]

The following section examines to what extent these provisions offer protection in practice.

IV. The Protection against Invisible Power in Practice

The system of rights and safeguards set in EU data protection law accompanied by a broad range of exceptions (with an even broader range of exceptions in the GDPR) has its implications for the exercise of invisible power. This section analyses certain practices of Dutch state agencies suggesting that EU data protection law offers little to no substantive protection against the invisible power of administrative authorities in practice.

Data Protection and the System Risk Indication

An early example of proactive personal data utilisation by administrative authorities involves linking their files to determine a citizen's eligibility for social benefits. For instance, if the file of the social benefits authority is linked to the file of the

[56] Case C-362/14 *Schrems* [2015] EU:C:2015:650, [95].

[57] Recital 8 GDPR; EPDB, p. 13.

[58] *Copland v The United Kingdom* App no 62617/00 (ECtHR, 3 April 2007), [46].

authority maintaining records of incarcerated individuals, and incarceration is a criterion for benefit exclusion, it can automatically be inferred that the citizen is ineligible for those benefits.[59] This practice followed a reactive logic, linking data to specific conditions determining an individual's entitlement to benefits.

A pilot called 'Black Box' implemented from 2008 to 2010, signalled a departure from this reactive logic. Black Box was described by the Ministry of Social Affairs and Employment as a 'professional and secured organisational provision in which data could be linked anonymised through special software. Only the risk population is made retrievable and delivered back to the client'.[60] The Ministry of Social Affairs investigative unit SIOD – the 'Social Intelligence and Investigative Service' – was responsible for developing risk profiles in order to select high-risk persons. The Dutch Data Protection Authority (hereinafter DPA) investigated the SIOD and Black Box concluding that the duty to provide information to the data subject was violated. It sanctioned the Ministry which defended itself by arguing that Article 43 Wbp (the Dutch law which implemented Article 13 DPD) allowed for exceptions to the information duty. The DPA disagreed and emphasised that exceptions should be made restrictively and that the SIOD should balance their own interests against that of the individual on a case-by-case basis.[61]

After 2010, Black Box resurfaced with a new name 'System Risk Indication' (hereafter SyRI) in a Dutch law.[62] The purpose of SyRI was to identify individuals (and companies) whose data suggested non-compliance or fraud related to labour, social security, or tax laws.[63] The legislation specified seven executive bodies permitted to collaborate, the data categories authorised for risk profiling, and the generation of 'risk reports.' These reports essentially merged citizens' personal data from various public authorities into interinstitutional files through file linking, employing a secret risk model, and shared among project partners. The risk model comprised 'risk indicators' indicating an elevated likelihood of fraud or unlawful behaviour.[64] A risk report meant that a person was considered worthy of investigation for fraud or non-compliance with legislation.[65]

Despite previous sanctions by the DPA regarding general exceptions to the information duty, the legislator introduced, in the explanatory memorandum of the SyRI legislation, another information duty exception that was general in

[59] Kamerstukken II 1997–1998, 25 892, nr 3, 94.

[60] Zenc commissioned by the Ministry of Social Affairs and Employment, 'Onderzoeksrapportage Wbp/Black Box' (2011) 4.

[61] Letter from DPA to the Minister of Social Affairs and Employment, 'Besluit tot oplegging last onder dwangsom' 8 februari 2011, 9.

[62] A 'Besluit' is lower legislation adopted by the Minister without the direct involvement of Parliament.

[63] Article 65 of the Law SUWI, which has been annulled due to the judgment of the Court. An increased risk of the text of Article 65(2) Wet SUWI states the 'misuse of public funds and public facilities in the area of social security and income-related schemes, tax and contribution fraud or non-compliance with labour laws'.

[64] Tweede Kamer, 2012–2013, 33 579, nr 3, 38.

[65] ibid 3.

nature.[66] The legislator claimed the 'data subject' was informed about the SyRI instrument and the potential for file linking when applying for benefits. However, because data processing was mandated by law, the controller would provide further information to the data subject upon request regarding the specific legal requirements governing the recording or disclosure of relevant data.[67] In the 'Data subjects' rights' section, it was stated that citizens processed in SyRI would not be informed due to the disproportionate effort required and the risk of individuals adapting their behaviour.[68] The data subject can submit a request, but whether it will be accommodated 'depends on the question whether monitoring compliance with the legal requirements will prevent this. In that context, a concrete balancing of interests will take place'.[69] According to the legislator, issuing a risk report does not carry legal consequences. If a risk report prompts further action, the interest in monitoring legal compliance prevents disclosing information to the data subject until a formal investigation commences.[70] If no investigation is commenced, the fact that the risk report concerns 'information of strategic significance (modus operandi)' could 'outweigh the need for disclosure'.[71]

The legislator used the explanatory memorandum to introduce a general restriction on the DPD transparency obligations. Moreover, he used the general discretionary exception in data protection law, giving administrative authorities complete discretion in deciding whether citizens will be informed, thereby unilaterally setting crucial conditions for their legal protection. All of this occurred without explicitly stating it in the law. However, even if it were explicitly stated, it would not change the fact that citizens' legal protection is contingent upon administrative authorities interested in depriving them of such protection. The DPA issued an opinion on the proposed SyRI law, not critiquing any transparency aspects but objecting to the proposal on other grounds.[72]

The SyRI law passed in both chambers of the Dutch Parliament in 2014 without a single vote against it. After few years in operation, SyRI was challenged in court by a group of Dutch NGOs claiming a breach of Article 8 ECHR and various GDPR provisions including Articles 14 and 22. In its 2020 judgment, the court of first instance struck SyRI down. Regarding legal protection, the court strongly emphasised that the secrecy surrounding the risk model and risk indicators prevents citizens from verifying the generation process of the decision tree mentioned by the State. As a result, citizens cannot defend themselves against the submission of a risk report about them, nor can they assess whether their data

[66] ibid 23.
[67] ibid.
[68] ibid.
[69] ibid 24.
[70] ibid 23.
[71] ibid 23–24.
[72] Letter from DPA to the Minister of Social Affairs and Employment, 'Advies conceptbesluit SyRI' 18 februari 2014.

has been processed on correct grounds.[73] According to the court, '[t]he right to respect for private life also means that a data subject must reasonably be able to track their personal data'. Viewing this case from a positive perspective, one could interpret the court as affirming a non-negotiable precondition: citizens must have the right to information regarding risk profiling to effectively challenge the lawfulness of data processing. However, merely five paragraphs later, the court asserted that the SyRI legislation lacked adequate safeguards to render the interference caused by SyRI proportionate: '[w]ithout insight into the risk indicators and the risk model, or at least without further legal safeguards to compensate for this lack of insight. (…)'.[74] In the SyRI case, the court essentially returned the issue to the legislator, permitting the continuation of the exercise of invisible power. While celebrated as a triumph for privacy, this case can also be interpreted as a validation of data protection law's failure to impose constitutional constraints on the exercise of invisible power by administrative authorities.[75]

Data Protection and the Fraud Signal Facility

The second example of invisible power concerns a database by the Dutch Tax Service called the Fraud Signal Facility (*Fraude Signalering Voorziening* hereinafter FSV). The FSV was a secret database in which people (and companies) could be registered for a plethora of different reasons. The DPA divided them into three main categories: internal signals of fraud, external signals of fraud and information requests from external governmental organisations.[76] Special categories of data including ethnicity, medical data and judicial records were stored in FSV of 13 000 citizens, 11% of the total of registered citizens.[77] This system played an important part in operations of the Dutch Tax Service in which parents who made minor errors in their requests for benefits were forced to pay back tens of thousands of euros and has become known internationally as the childcare benefits scandal.[78] This scandal forced the government to resign. FSV played an important part in branding people as fraudsters after they were disproportionately punished for minor errors. People could receive the '1x1' registration (featuring as a checkbox) in FSV which indicated that a special team of the unit *Invordering* (Collection)

[73] *SyRI v NJCM* [2020] NL:RBDHA:2020:1878, [6.90].

[74] ibid para 6.95.

[75] Tijmen Wisman & Merel Hendricks, 'The SyRI Victory: Holding Profiling Practices to Account', (*Digital Freedom Fund Blog*, 23 April 2020). Available at: https://digitalfreedomfund.org/the-syri-victory-holding-government-profiling-to-account/ accessed 26 February 2024.

[76] DPA, Belastingdienst Verwerkingen van persoonsgegevens in de Fraude Signalering Voorziening, (Onderzoeksrapport) 2021, z2020-04615, 15–18.

[77] Pricewaterhouse Coopers commissioned by the Tax Service, 'Onderzoek effecten FSV Particulieren' 2021, 12.

[78] Anna Holligan,'Dutch Rutte government resigns over child welfare fraud scandal', (*BBC.com*, 15 January 2021). Available at: www.bbc.com/news/world-europe-55674146 accessed 26 February 2024.

had to settle the claim, which otherwise would happen automatically.[79] At the level of the directorate *Toeslagen*[80] (Benefits) this was seen as an indication of possible fraud whilst the team responsible for claiming the money back interpreted it as proven fraud.[81] As a result, these individuals were frequently denied personal payment arrangements or amicable debt settlements, compelling them to repay significant debts over a span of 24 months.[82] A total of 40% of the citizens registered in the FSV ticked the box '1x1'.[83]

Another label people would get is 'O/GS', which is an acronym for the Dutch words 'Opzet/Grove Schuld' ('Intent/Gross Negligence'). In a memo on measures to expedite the process of handling requests for personal payment arrangements, after the Tax Service's disproportionate reclaiming of childcare benefits, discussions centred on the inability to swiftly process 7,000 outstanding requests using the current methods and procedures.[84] To expedite the process, it was decided that all childcare benefit debts exceeding €3,000 would automatically be labelled as O/GS. Debtors would also automatically receive the label O/GS if their total debts, including housing and healthcare benefits, exceeded €5,000.[85] Even a mere suspicion of fraud could lead to individuals being added to a 'monitoring list' or an 'exclusion list', hindering the resolution of benefit requests.[86] The FSV data were shared with multiple state institutions, municipalities, law-enforcement institutions such as the police and public prosecutor's office, private parties, societal organisations and even the Ministry of Justice.[87]

During a debate on the report, Dutch politician Pieter Omtzigt remarked that the presence of over 100,000 individuals and companies on blacklists, unaware of their status and facing significant legal repercussions, signalled a severe failure of the Dutch constitutional state. The automatic assignment of a fraud label frequently led to denial of favourable payment arrangements for the substantial debts arising from childcare benefit reclaiming. This situation often resulted in entire families facing bankruptcy, with dire consequences, particularly for families with young children. The ensuing poverty and stress led to circumstances increasing the risk of children being removed from their parents by child protection services.[88]

[79] Onderzoek effecten FSV Particulieren (n 77) at 30.

[80] ibid 11. One thing that does not become clear in the report is how the directorate of Toeslagen relates to the unit of Invordering.

[81] ibid 11.

[82] ibid.

[83] ibid.

[84] Belastingdienst, Memo Versnellingsmaatregelen TG-304, 9 February 2016.

[85] Auditdienst Rijk *Ministerie van Financiën*, 'Grensbedragen O/GS en MSNP' (Onderzoeksrapport), 6 July 2021.

[86] ibid 31.

[87] Pricewaterhouse Coopers commissioned by the Tax Service, 'Onderzoek Gegevensdeling met Derden', 2022, 12.

[88] NOS, 'Kabinet: meer hulp toeslagenouders, uit huis geplaatst kind niet zomaar terug' (*nos.nl*, 12 May 2022). <https://nos.nl/artikel/2428594-kabinet-meer-hulp-toeslagenouders-uit-huis-geplaatst-kind-niet-zomaar-terug> accessed 8 February 2024.

Many reports were dedicated to identifying the violated rights. Given that the data processing schemes within FSV resemble a complex puzzle of registrations, with personal data leaking from one leaky basket to another, facilitated by computing devices, one might expect the GDPR to play a significant role in the legal analysis provided in the reports written by consultancy firms commissioned by the Tax Service, the DPA and parliamentary commissions.

One of the reports on FSV issued by Pricewaterhouse Coopers specifically focused on the effects of FSV on benefits and addressed the question of the lawfulness of the decision-making and subsequent actions on the basis of the FSV.[89] The GDPR led the authors to observe only violations of privacy principles due to misinterpretation of data, over-accessibility of data and storing data longer than necessary.[90] The fact that the FSV and the fraud labels functioned as a blacklist did not result in any findings with respect to the GDPR, but were found to have violated numerous principles of good administration.[91] Since giving these labels formally did not constitute decisions it is doubtful whether the Dutch principles of good administration actually applied.

The report of the DPA set the tone with respect to the terms in which this gross injustice was denoted: lawfulness, purpose specification, accuracy and storage limitation were violated and the Tax Service had not made an effort to rectify or erase the 'non-updated personal data'.[92] Certainly, they could have been more critical regarding the fraud labels assigned to individuals, effectively constituting automated decisions with significant impacts on people's lives. Despite the sentimental speeches by the chairman of the DPA on the plight of the victims,[93] the main focus was placed on the lack of a legal basis which seemingly would have also compensated for the lack of transparency.[94] The label of fraud was reduced to a matter of accuracy: citizens did not get the correct label or the label was not updated.[95] Overall, one might be led to the conclusion that secret fraud labels could be legitimised by embedding them into law. While this may seem like an excessively positivist approach to the issue, it is apparently what the GDPR facilitates and enables in practice.

A parliamentary commission issued the report 'Blind to man and justice' in which the authors observe that a false dichotomy was created between 'fighting fraud and the protection of personal data'.[96]

While such an observation is appreciated for recognising that data protection revolves around fundamental principles of procedural justice, the remainder of

[89] See (n 77) at 9.
[90] ibid 12.
[91] ibid 46–47.
[92] DPA, 61.
[93] DPA, Speech Aleid Wolfsen over onderzoek FSV, 29 October 2021, 1 and 2.
[94] ibid 3.
[95] ibid 4.
[96] Parlementaire Enquéte Fraudebeleid en Dienstverlening, 'Blind voor Mens en Recht', Kamerstukken II 2023–2024, 35 867, nr 6, 37.

the report illustrates how the data protection perspective often limits the ability to address issues beyond mere legality.

The authors of the report concluded that the right to respect for private life was frequently violated, echoing the DPA's assertion that the processing of personal data lacked a lawful basis. This reduction of flagrant injustice to a mere matter of legality, akin to the DPA's stance, suggests the ability the state to legalise injustice.[97]

It was noted that the FSV had effectively functioned as a blacklist, stigmatising individuals as fraudsters. However, this observation serves to underscore that recognising this injustice does not necessarily lead to more fundamental conclusions about rights violations. The most basic observation can be found in the foreword, where the authors emphasise that without appropriate measures, changes, and safeguards, the tax benefits scandal could recur tomorrow.[98] The conclusion that additional safeguards are needed to prevent another fundamental rights scandal appears more fitting than simply noting that individuals received incorrect labels. The lens of data protection law distorts the perception of reality and trivialises the conclusions drawn. These conclusions highlight the inadequacy of GDPR provisions in addressing the issue of invisible power. The notion of shadow administrations enabling the invisible punishment of individuals is reminiscent of themes found in a Kafkaesque novel and is wholly misplaced in a constitutional democracy.

V. Conclusion

While the precise reason why privacy became the focal point in legal responses to concerns stemming from the advent of computing may remain elusive, it is evident that this approach did not yield rules adequately addressing the problem of invisible power.

The latest legal response, the GDPR, does not alter this reality. Compared to the DPD, the GDPR offers greater clarity on transparency obligations, but also expands discretionary exceptions for the data controller. Legal protection against automated decision-making has been enhanced through the introduction of specific measures for individuals, although the efficacy of these improvements concerning decisions authorised by law arguably relies on the CJEU judgment in the *SCHUFA* case. The ambiguous scope of Article 22(1) of the GDPR gives public authorities the discretion to establish decision-making systems that may not fall within its purview. Furthermore, the GDPR brought protection against automated decision-making under the regime of restrictions. Therefore, uncertainty persists

[97] ibid 38.

[98] ibid 10. NOS 'Levens van mensen door overheidsfalen vermorzeld, kan morgen weer gebeuren' (*nos.nl*, 26 February 2023). Available at: https://nos.nl/collectie/13957/artikel/2510458-levens-van-mensen-door-overheidsfalen-vermorzeld-kan-morgen-weer-gebeuren accessed 17 April 2024.

regarding the extent to which the legislator can depart from the obligation to implement specific suitable measures to safeguard the rights, freedoms, and interests of data subjects.

While legal ambiguities may stimulate doctrinal discussions, they undermine legal protection and legal certainty. In practice, these ambiguities allow executive bodies to opportunistically interpret the law, often opting for the path of least resistance, which may circumvent transparency and legal protections for individuals. Evidence of this phenomenon is apparent in the Netherlands, where both the legislator and executive adopt a pragmatic approach to the GDPR, frequently invoking its numerous exceptions. While this approach may stimulate academic discourse, it leaves vulnerable individuals and their families without the protection they seek against administrative authorities.

The GDPR enables a flawed interpretation of the protection afforded by fundamental rights within this framework, allowing the safeguards against invisible power to be undermined by both the legislator and executive. Consequently, it contradicts the often-stated ambition of data protection laws to safeguard all fundamental rights when data is processed, even implying that the protection of fundamental rights can be nullified by legislative action. The examples from Dutch administrative practice vividly illustrate the repercussions of the lack of comprehensive legal protection in data protection law.

The unimaginable injustice endured by families in the Netherlands, inflicted upon them invisibly by Tax Service administrations and evaluated by different state institutions based on the GDPR, paints a grim picture of the protection it offers in practice. While we should avoid uncritically generalising the lessons from this, it's safe to say that the GDPR lacks structural protections that establish clear limits and safeguards against secret administrations. While court victories could bolster these limits, the events in the Netherlands highlight that legal protection against invisible power is too crucial to rely solely on NGOs, media and the judiciary.

2

Assessing the Impact of Impact Assessments: Practical Questions Related to Article 35 of the GDPR

BART W SCHERMER

I. Introduction

In this chapter I explore how the requirement of Article 35 of the GDPR to conduct a data protection impact assessment (DPIA) has been implemented in practice. In particular, I will look at those elements of the DPIA requirement that may hinder its effectiveness in practice. Getting an insight into the practical application of Article 35 of the GDPR will help us to determine whether the goals of reducing the risks of a processing activity to the rights and freedoms of natural persons is achieved in practice.[1]

In this chapter I will discuss several questions and issues that may emerge while conducting DPIAs in practice. In particular, I will focus on the 'procedural vagueness' of the DPIA requirement and the role of the prior consultation of Article 36 of the GDPR. By analysing these issues, I hope to propose improvements for the legal framework provided under the GDPR and its application in practice.

Methodology

The main method for the collection and analysis of information was desk research. The desk research involved an examination of primary and secondary legal sources, including legislation, case law, guidance from supervisory authorities and academic literature.

To get further insight into the performance of DPIAs in practice, a short survey was held under privacy professionals. The survey consisted of 18 multiple

[1] See GDPR, Recitals 75 and 84.

choice, Likert, and open-ended questions. The survey was seeded under 435 Dutch respondents, more or less evenly split between the public and private sector.[2] 61 respondents filled out the survey.[3] The respondents were mainly DPOs, privacy officers or (in house) privacy lawyers (82 per cent).[4] Given the homogeneity of the sample I am fairly confident that the responses adequately reflect how the performance of DPIAs is perceived by privacy professionals in practice. Given the small sample size however, and the fact that only Dutch privacy professionals were interviewed, I cannot make any statements based of this survey with a very high degree of confidence. Nevertheless, I feel that the survey gives some interesting practical insights that are useful for our analysis.

Finally, this chapter was informed by the personal experiences of the author, having performed numerous DPIAs as a privacy and data protection consultant over the past 15 years.

Reading Guide

The chapter is structured as follows. In section II, I will briefly explore the origins of the DPIA and explain the DPIA requirement as set forth in Article 35 of the GDPR. In section III, I discuss how vagueness in Article 35 of the GDPR and limited guidance from the data protection authorities have led to questions on how to perform effective DPIAs in practice. In section IV, I discuss the prior consultation of Article 36 of the GDPR. Section V will take the findings from sections III and IV and explore whether there is room for improvement. I conclude with a short summary and conclusion in section VI.

II. The DPIA Requirement of Article 35 of the GDPR

The GDPR takes a risk-based approach to data protection.[5] It is up to the data controller to assess the risks of a particular processing activity to the rights and freedoms of natural persons and determine which measures are necessary to remove those risks or reduce them to an acceptable level. These measures, often called 'controls' in the literature on risk management, can include, but are not limited to

[2] There are an estimated 10,000 DPOs in the Netherlands (see www.autoriteitpersoonsgegevens.nl/fg-informatie), but the total population of privacy professionals in the Netherlands is unknown. We estimate the total population of privacy professionals to be around 30,000 to 40,000.

[3] The response rate (14%) is relatively low because the survey was seeded under a broader professional population to help increase the size of the sample. These professionals were asked to forward the survey to relevant privacy professionals in their organisation.

[4] The remainder of the group mostly had related functions such as (chief) security officer.

[5] See Recital 74. See also: https://ec.europa.eu/justice/Article-29/documentation/opinion-recommendation/files/2014/wp218_en.pdf.

processes, policies, devices, and practices.[6] One control that is often used in the context of risk management is that of impact assessments. Impact assessments are risk management tools that are used in a variety of settings. An impact assessment can be described as 'the process of identifying the future consequences of a current or proposed action'.[7]

As early as the 1960s technology assessments were performed to better help understand the impact of technological developments on society.[8] Impact assessments were also extensively used in the environmental context. There, Environmental Impact Assessments (EIAs) were used to assess the impact of policy- and decision-making on the biophysical world.[9] For instance, the *Convention on the Conservation of Migratory Species of Wild Animals* required countries, amongst others, to take action to avoid any migratory species to become endangered in the future.[10] This implies that countries must anticipate and predict the effects of their actions on wild animals.[11] While the treaty itself does not prescribe the use of an impact assessment, impact assessment have proven to be effective tools in complying with treaty responsibilities.[12]

The same logic can be applied to data protection and data protection legislation. It is the responsibility of the data controller to ensure that there are minimal risks to the rights and freedoms of data subjects that result from personal data processing. DPIAs function as a tool to identify and appraise risks, creating a basis for removal or mitigation of the identified risks. Indeed, prior to the GDPR Privacy Impact Assessments (PIAs) were already a fairly common practice in data protection.[13]

With the introduction of Article 35 of the GDPR the use of an impact assessment as a tool to assess risks in the context of data protection became a legal obligation. So, prior to the GDPR, DPIAs were effective controls to enable compliance with data protection legislation, whereas now the use of the control itself has become a legal requirement. Introducing specific data protection controls in the legislation to improve compliance in practice was a deliberate choice of the legislator.[14] Unlike its predecessor the personal data protection directive, which

[6] See for instance: ISO 31000:2018 Risk Management – Guidelines.

[7] See www.iaia.org/uploads/pdf/What_is_IA_web.pdf.

[8] Elin Palm, Sven Ove Hansson, 'The Case for Ethical Technology Assessment (ETA)' (2006) 73 *Technological Forecasting & Social Change* 73, 543.

[9] Mark Everard, 'Environmental Impact Assessments', in Max Finlayson et al. (eds) *The Wetland Book I: Structure and Function, Management, and Methods* (Springer, 2018), 851.

[10] Convention on the Conservation of Migratory Species of Wild Animals, Bonn, 23 June 1979.

[11] Convention on the Conservation of Migratory Species of Wild Animals, Seventh meeting of the conference of the parties, Bonn, 18–24 September 2002, Impact Assessment and Migratory Species, UNEP/CMS/Conf.7.16 23 August 2002 Agenda item 11(b).

[12] ibid.

[13] See, e.g., Roger Clarke, 'Privacy Impact Assessment: Its Origins and Development' (2009) 25(2) *Computer Law Security Review* 123.

[14] Katerina Demetzou 'Data Protection Impact Assessment: A Tool for Accountability and the Unclarified Concept of 'High Risk' in the General Data Protection Regulation' (2019) 35(6) *Computer Law & Security Review*, 3.

had very few specific requirements on governance and compliance, the GDPR has several mandatory data protection controls alongside the DPIA requirement. These include the appointment of a Data Protection Officer (GDPR, Art 37), keeping a register of processing activities (GDPR, Art 30), maintaining appropriate data protection policies (GDPR, Art 24(2)) and implementing privacy by design and by default (GDPR, Art 25).

A DPIA serves a twofold purpose. First of all, it is a mechanism to identify the risks to the rights and freedoms of the data subject, assess the severity of these risks, and determine measures that will remove these risks altogether, or reduce them to an acceptable level.[15] Second, the DPIA is an accountability measure to display compliance with the GDPR.[16]

A DPIA must, at a minimum, cover the following aspects according to Article 35(7) of the GDPR:

(a) a systematic description of the envisaged processing operations and the purposes of the processing, including, where applicable, the legitimate interest pursued by the controller;
(b) an assessment of the necessity and proportionality of the processing operations in relation to the purposes;
(c) an assessment of the risks to the rights and freedoms of data subjects; and
(d) the measures envisaged to address the risks, including safeguards, security measures and mechanisms to ensure the protection of personal data and to demonstrate compliance with the GDPR, taking into account the rights and legitimate interests of data subjects and other persons concerned.

Not performing a DPIA might result in important risks being overlooked, leading to non-compliance with the GDPR. But not performing a DPIA that includes all the elements above may also result in a non-compliance, regardless of the fact that the actual processing activity itself may be legitimate. In December 2023, the Dutch data protection authority (*Autoriteit Persoonsgegevens*, or *AP*) issued International Card Services BV (ICS) with a fine of €150,000 for not performing a DPIA.[17] While ICS had a DPIA triage process in place, it failed to identify the processing activity under discussion as 'high risk', therefore a specific DPIA was not performed. ICS argued that the normal risk assessment procedure that was followed should be equated to performing a DPIA. However, the AP argued that this was not the case as the risk-assessment was too generic and did not explicitly cover all the elements set forth by Article 35(7) of the GDPR.[18]

[15] Eleni Kosta, 'Article 35 Data Protection Impact Assessment' in Christopher Kuner and others (eds), *The EU General Data Protection Regulation (GDPR): A Commentary* (Oxford University Press 2020), 668.

[16] Demetzou (n 14).

[17] Autoriteit Persoonsgegevens, Boetebesluit ICS, 18 December 2023.

[18] ibid, paras 29, 30.

III. Procedural Vagueness

In the years after the entry into force of the GDPR, guidance was given by data protection authorities and different methodologies, templates and software applications were developed to facilitate compliance with Article 35.[19] While these initiatives have done a lot to improve compliance, questions still remain in the practical application. Most of these questions can be attributed to the abstract wording of the DPIA requirement and its vagueness on the proper procedure for conducting a DPIA.[20] While the necessary contents of a DPIA are specified in Article 35(7) of the GDPR, Article 35 does not prescribe the actual process of doing a DPIA. This leads to questions in practice on when and how to perform a DPIA.

The 'procedural vagueness' enshrined in Article 35 is deliberate.[21] Dalla Corte and Van Brakel observe that the GDPR has a 'meta-regulatory' nature.[22] Rather than setting strict guidelines for conducting DPIAs, the GDPR sets out the principles and high-level requirements and leaves it up to organisations how to best implement these requirements in their operations.

Researchers have also recommended that the legislator not to be too prescriptive when it comes to DPIA methodologies.[23] While this makes sense, the procedural vagueness may also lead to misconceptions on how to conduct a DPIA, leading to sub-optimal results. The procedural vagueness in the GDPR is thus both a bug and a feature. On the one hand, not prescribing a clear methodology for doing a DPIA leaves flexibility for data controllers to conduct them in a way that is most appropriate to their circumstances. On the other hand, not being clear (enough) may lead to incomplete and ineffective DPIAs in practice.

The Article 29 Working Party on Data Protection (WP29), currently the European Data Protection Board (EDPB), has shed some light on this issue by providing some further guidance in their Guidelines on Data Protection Impact Assessment.[24] The EDPB suggests a five-step approach for conducting a DPIA that can be visualised as follows:

[19] For an overview see: Georgios Georgiadis, Geert Poels, 'Towards a Privacy Impact Assessment Methodology to Support the Requirements of the General Data Protection Regulation in a Big Data Analytics Context: A Systematic Literature Review', (2002) 44 *Computer Law & Security Review* 1–15.

[20] See, e.g., Georgios (n 19); Amir Shayan Ahmadian, Daniel Strüber, Volker Riediger, Jan Jürjens, 'Supporting Privacy Impact Assessment by Model-based Privacy Analysis' (2022) Proceedings of the 33rd Annual ACM Symposium on Applied Computing – SAC' 18, 1467–74; Lorenzo Dalla Corte, Rosamunde van Brakel, '*Data Protection Impact Assessment Methods for the Urban Environment: A Report for the Commissie Persoonsgegevens Amsterdam*' (Tilburg Institute for Law and Technology 2022), 25.

[21] Georgiadis (n 19).

[22] Dalla Corte (n 20).

[23] Dariusz Kloza, Niels van Dijk, Raphaël Gellert, István Böröcz, Alessia Tanas, Eugenio Mantovani, Paul Quinn 'Data Protection Impact Assessments in the European Union: Complementing the New Legal Framework Towards a More Robust Protection of Individuals' (2017) d.pia.lab *Policy Brief No 1*/2017, 4.

[24] Article 29 Data Protection Working Party, 'Guidelines on Data Protection Impact Assessment (DPIA) and determining whether processing is "likely to result in a high risk" for the purposes of

Figure 2.1 The DPIA process according to the EDPB[25]

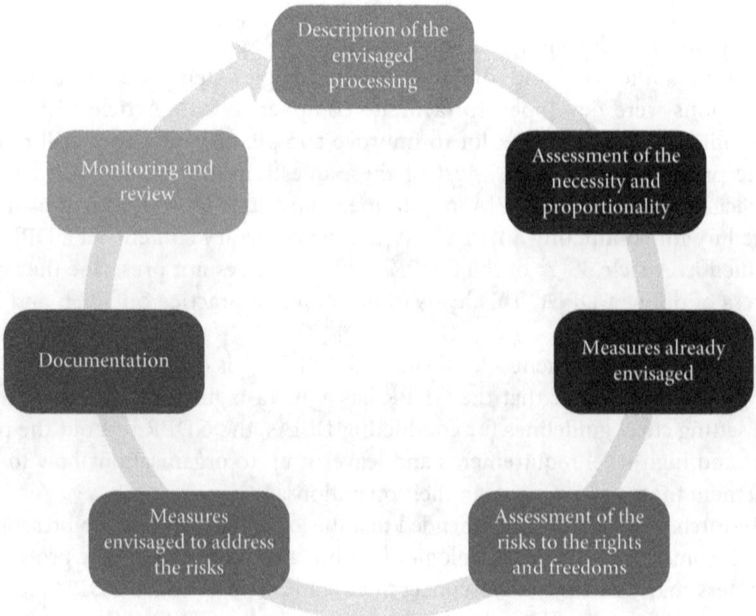

Furthermore, Annex 2 of the Guidelines specify the criteria for an acceptable DPIA. They are primarily an ordered list of the requirements set forth in Article 35(7) of the GDPR and the associated recitals.

While the Guidelines give a high-level overview of the process, they lack detailed information and best practice on how to conduct a DPIA. In particular, the guidance lacks clarity on how different stakeholders within the organisation must be engaged and how risk-reducing measures can be incorporated into the design process. Furthermore, the guidance is somewhat confusing. The second step in the process according to the EDPB, is an assessment of the proportionality and the subsidiarity of the envisaged processing. Only after that does the actual risk assessment follow. This is strange, as it is only after having identified all possible alternatives and risk-reducing measures, that you can say something sensible about the necessity of the processing (subsidiarity and proportionality) and thus the legitimacy of the processing. While the EDPB states that the risk assessment is an iterative process and the discussion on proportionality and subsidiarity may need to be revisited, its place in the overall process flow is strange nonetheless.[26]

Regulation 2016/679', Adopted on 4 April 2016, as last Revised and Adopted on 4 October 2017. 17/EN 248 rev.01.

[25] See https://ec.europa.eu/newsroom/article29/items/611236/en.

[26] ibid, 16.

Apart from the (limited) guidance by the WP29/EDPB, different national data protection authorities have provided DPIA methodologies.[27] However, these have been criticised for being too theoretical.[28] They lack practical advice on how to assess risks, including an objective way to assess and present privacy impacts and the efficiency of countermeasures.[29] Furthermore, the methodologies and associated templates focus, for the most part, on the process of documenting the results of a DPIA and less on the actual process of risk assessment (i.e. how do you effectively assess the risk of a processing activity).

The vagueness of Article 35 of the GDPR and the limited guidance provided by the supervisory authorities have raised several questions in practice, most notably:

- What is the proper scope of a DPIA?
- When should a DPIA conducted and what should the focus be?
- What is the role of the DPO in the DPIA process?

These questions are discussed below.

Scope

The first question raised in practice is what the scope of a DPIA should be. Should a DPIA, for instance, be limited to a particular part of a processing activity (such as a new IT system) or should the entire process be assessed?

Another question related to scope is whether only data protection risks should be assessed, or whether all risks to the rights and freedoms of data subjects should be addressed in a DPIA. The GDPR specifically refers to the 'rights and freedoms of natural persons' in Recital 75. These include privacy and data protection risks, but they may also cover other risks such as discrimination. It thus makes sense to interpret the DPIA requirement to cover all potential risks for the data subject, in so far as they can be attributed to the processing of personal data.

In our survey I found that DPIAs mostly focus on privacy and data protection risks. The impact of data processing on other civil and political rights was considered by 69 per cent of the respondents whereas social, cultural and economic rights were only considered by 39 per cent. When asked for the reasons why they had not included these rights, the most common answer was that it was not relevant in the context of the processing. However, a number of respondents also replied that it was not included in the DPIA template nor was it mandatory under the GDPR.

[27] See www.cnil.fr/en/PIA-privacy-impact-assessment-en and https://ico.org.uk/for-organisations/uk-gdpr-guidance-and-resources/accountability-and-governance/guide-to-accountability-and-governance/accountability-and-governance/data-protection-impact-assessments/.

[28] Georgiadis (n 19); Ahmadian (n 20).

[29] Georgiadis (n 19) at 11.

To what extent future risks should be addressed in a DPIA is also unclear. Technology assessment and value-sensitive design specifically take into account future risks.[30] How a technology might impact society in the medium-to-long term is one of the key reasons for carrying out technology assessment.

A specific issue when it comes to scope is the interaction with other risk assessment instruments now and in the future. Within the GDPR, for instance, there might already be overlap between the DPIA and Transfer Impact Assessment (TIAs).[31]

Of particular relevance for the near future is the potential overlap between AI Impact Assessments (AIIAs) and DPIAs. Training and using AI systems oftentimes involves the processing of personal data, so a DPIA is necessary when there is a high risk for data subjects. At the same time, deploying an AI system that makes decisions regarding natural persons will likely also warrant performing an AIIA. Indeed, under the AI Act, when an AI system is considered high risk, a fundamental rights impact assessment must be conducted.[32]

While DPIAs and AIIAs differ in scope and application, they do share many similarities. In the Netherlands, central government entities must perform DPIAs and record the results in a uniform format (*Model DPIA Rijksdienst*). When using AI they are also required to perform a Human Rights Impact Assessment for Algorithms (*Impact Assessment Mensenrechten en Algoritmen*). An assessment of both templates found a great deal of overlap between the two instruments.[33] Therefore, the Dutch Ministry of the Interior and Kingdom Relations issued guidance on how to deal with this overlap.[34]

To avoid additional burden for data controllers, providers and users of AI systems, further guidance from the EDPB and/or the newly formed Artificial Intelligence Board on how to perform both types of assessments simultaneously is very welcome.

Apart from the interplay between AIIAs and DPIAs there are also other potential areas where DPIAs may intersect with other impact assessments in the future. One such area is that of children's rights. Given the potential impact of digital services on the rights of children, there is in an increasing call to make a Child Rights Impact Assessment (CRIA) mandatory.[35]

[30] See, e.g., Batya Friedman and David Hendry, *Value Sensitive Design, Shaping Technology with Moral Imagination* (MIT Press, 2019).

[31] See: https://edpb.europa.eu/sme-data-protection-guide/international-data-transfers_en.

[32] See Article 27 AI Act (European Parliament legislative resolution of 13 March 2024 on the proposal for a regulation of the European Parliament and of the Council on laying down harmonised rules on Artificial Intelligence (Artificial Intelligence Act) and amending certain Union Legislative Acts (COM(2021)0206 – C9-0146/2021–2021/0106(COD)), P9_TA(2024)0138).

[33] Ministerie van Binnenlandse Zaken en Koninksrijksrelaties, 'Handreiking gezamenlijk gebruik IAMA en Model DPIA Rijksdienst', 19 januari 2023.

[34] ibid.

[35] See, e.g., Sudeshna Mukherjee, Kruakae Pothong and Sonia Livingstone, 'Child Rights Impact Assessment: A Tool to Realise Child Rights in the Digital Environment' (5Rights Foundation 2021). In the Netherlands Parliament requested the Dutch government to explore the possibility of a mandatory

A CRIA will no doubt overlap with a DPIA, as digital services generally process personal data of children. Furthermore, when AI is used, there might also be a need to do an AIIA. When formal templates or methodologies are prescribed for individual impact assessments, this might lead to additional administrative burdens for organisations.

Finally, Article 34 of the Digital Services Act requires platforms to conduct a risk assessment.[36] While this risk assessment differs significantly in terms of scope and application from the DPIA requirement and is only applicable to 'very large online platforms' it is another example of mandatory risk assessment in EU legislation.[37]

To summarise, uncertainty with regard to the scope of a DPIA has resulted in assessments that are often arbitrary and whose content and quality vary widely on a case-by-case basis.[38] This issue is further compounded by the abundance of DPIA methodologies and templates available for controllers to choose from.[39] Issues will likely persist given the fact that the data protection authorities give very little concrete guidance on DPIAs and do not provide public feedback on DPIAs they have assessed. This is to be expected given the oftentimes confidential or sensitive nature of DPIAs, but guidance by the authorities on what constitutes a proper DPIA and how it should interact with other risk assessment instruments, might help improve the overall quality of DPIAs.

Timing and Focus

A second question that arises as the result of procedural vagueness is *when* to conduct a DPIA. It is clear from the GDPR that a DPIA needs to be conducted prior to the processing. However, the GDPR does not state in which stage of the design process a DPIA should take place. Indeed, the Spanish Data Protection Authority (the *Agencia Española Proteccion* Datos, or *AEPD*) argues that the GDPR only has authority over the actual data processing.[40] The rights and freedoms of data subjects are comprised when the data are processed. Therefore, a DPIA should be carried out before these rights are compromised. As such, the GDPR does not require organisations to conduct a DPIA already in the design or implementation phase, it just requires the DPIA to be completed *prior* to the

child rights impact assessment. See www.tweedekamer.nl/kamerstukken/moties/detail?id=2022Z13691&did=2022D28223.

[36] Regulation (EU) 2022/2065 of the European Parliament and of the Council of 19 October 2022 on a Single Market for Digital Services and amending Directive 2000/31/EC (Digital Services Act), OJ L 277.

[37] Besides these legally required impact assessments organisations may also have internal impact assessments such as business impact assessments leading to a further stacking of impact assessments.

[38] Dalla Corte (n 20).

[39] ibid.

[40] Agencia Española Proteccion Datos, 'Risk management and impact assessment in the processing of personal data', June 2021, p 131.

processing. Having said that, the Spanish DPA does strongly advise data controllers to start the DPIA before the actual design and implementation.[41] In practice, a DPIA may be part of the earliest stages of a design process, but it is also possible that it is conducted nearer the end of the process. It is advisable, though, to do a DPIA early in the development cycle, as it is still relatively cheap and easy to make changes.[42] In this regard, the DPIA requirement of Article 35 has a clear, but seldom mentioned, synergy with Article 25 of the GDPR (privacy by design and by default). During the assessment risks that have been identified can be removed or mitigated through changes in the design, satisfying the requirements of Article 25.

While it is most beneficial to perform a DPIA early in the design of a product or service, it is not uncommon that DPIAs are carried out near the end of the design process. Our survey showed that 18 per cent of the respondents start with their DPIA near the end of the development cycle; 28 per cent start near the beginning of the development cycle; and 30 per cent conducted the DPIA throughout the development.[43]

The twofold function of a DPIA both as a risk assessment tool and an accountability instrument may contribute to the fact that not all organisations start early in the development cycle. Organisations likely focus their efforts on being compliant with the legislation, rather than seeing a DPIA as a valuable tool to improve their products and services. Indeed, our survey showed that the primary driver for doing DPIAs in many organisations is compliance, rather than the intrinsic motivation to improve the design: 41 per cent of the respondents answered that compliance is the main driver, while only 18 per cent answered that improving the design was the main goal. For the remainder of the respondents both goals were equally important. However, the data from our survey did not show that those organisations that are more focused on compliance than improvement are more likely to perform the DPIA near the end of the development cycle. While organisations that were more focused on improving the product or service were slightly more likely to do a DPIA early in the development cycle, they were almost equally likely to start near the end. Conversely, those organisations that were more focused on compliance were also somewhat more likely to start a DPIA at the beginning of the development cycle. This probably reflects that a DPIA is oftentimes part of a project initiation process within an organisation.

When it comes to executing a DPIA, it is advised to do this with an interdisciplinary team and mindset.[44] With an interdisciplinary team, the knowledge, skill and competencies of each team member can be leveraged to identify risks and propose effective mitigation.[45] However, given that a DPIA is a legal requirement,

[41] ibid 131.

[42] Kloza (n 23) at 5.

[43] The remaining respondents answered 'other', with responses stating that this depended on the type of processing, it was decided on a case-to-case basis, and even that DPIAs were conducted after the start of the processing.

[44] Luis Sánchez and Ross Mitchell, 'Conceptualizing Impact Assessment as a Learning Process' (2017) 62 *Environmental Impact Assessment Review*, 195.

[45] ibid.

DPIA methodologies seem to be geared more towards privacy and compliance professionals than engineers. Notario et al. note that few privacy practices or approaches are specifically addressed at dealing with privacy from a system engineering perspective, language and mindset.[46] While their work predates the implementation of the GDPR, there are no indications that their observation is no longer accurate. Indeed, our survey showed that oftentimes IT-related roles are not even part of the DPIA process. While most of the organisations (77%) involved IT-related roles in the DPIA process, 23 per cent of the respondents answered that only the business and the DPO/privacy office were involved in doing DPIAs.

The Role of the DPO

A third question that is raised by the procedural vagueness, is the role and position of the data protection officer (DPO).[47]

Article 39(1) of the GDPR tasks the data protection officer with: (1) providing advice where requested on the performance of a DPIA and (2) monitoring the performance of DPIAs. A survey published by the EDPB shows that 85.2 per cent of DPOs give advice on DPIAs. However, when asked about their involvement in monitoring the performance of DPIAs, only 69.2 per cent of DPOs (median) answered that they were involved in monitoring DPIAs.[48]

Most organisations by now know that the data controller (i.e. 'the business') is responsible for doing a DPIA, not the DPO. In our survey, 60 per cent of the respondents answered that the business is responsible for executing a DPIA within their organisation, while just 6 per cent answered that the DPO is responsible. Nevertheless, questions on the role of the DPO remain, in particular regarding the status of the advice of the DPO.

Article 35(2) of the GDPR states that the data controller shall seek the advice of the DPO when conducting a DPIA. In particular, the DPO must advice on the following key aspects:

- what safeguards to apply to mitigate any risks to the rights and interests of the data subjects;
- whether the data protection impact assessment has been correctly carried out; and
- whether its conclusions (to go ahead with the processing and what safeguards to apply) comply with data protection requirements.[49]

[46] Nicolas Notario, Alberto Crespo, Samuel Martin, Jose del Alamo, Daniel Le Metayer, Thibaud Antignac, Antonio Kung, Inga Kroener, David Wright, 'PRIPARE: Integrating Privacy Best Practices into a Privacy Engineering Methodology' (IEEE 2005).

[47] Kloza (n 23) at 4.

[48] EDPB (2024), Coordinated Enforcement Action Designation and Position of Data Protection Officers Adopted on 16 January 2024.

[49] Data Protection Working Party, Guidelines on Data Protection Officers, adopted on 13 December 2016, as last Revised and Adopted on 5 April 2017, 16/EN WP 243 rev.01, art 29.

The EDPB has clarified what should be done if the advice of the DPO is not followed. In its Guidelines on the role of the DPO, the EDPB states the following: 'if the controller disagrees with the advice provided by the DPO, the DPIA documentation should specifically justify in writing why the advice has not been taken into account'.[50] The EDPB argues in its Guidelines on Administrative fines that not following the advice of the DPO can be indicative of an intentional breach:

> Circumstances indicative of intentional breaches might be unlawful processing authorised explicitly by the top management hierarchy of the controller, or in spite of advice from the data protection officer or in disregard for existing policies (…).[51]

For situations where the (correct) advice of the DPO is knowingly and willingly disregarded or misinterpreted, this is a straightforward conclusion. Disregarding the advice of the DPO indicates intentionality which, in turn, may contribute to e.g. a higher fine. Furthermore, in civil procedures, disregarding the advice of the DPO may be indicative of tortious behaviour by the data controller, making the data controller liable for damages suffered by data subjects.

However, what might also happen in practice is that the data controller and the DPO will make a different assessment of, for instance, the proportionality of a processing activity. It is likely, given the role and the position of the DPO, that they will 'take the side' of the data subject, focusing more on their interests, than on the general interest or on the interest of the data controller. The data controller on the other hand will focus on the goals of the processing and attach more weight to that side of the equation. As such, an assessment of the proportionality (and even the subsidiarity) may yield different outcomes for both actors. It is questionable whether in situations where there is such a difference of opinion, not following the advice of the DPO must be considered 'indicative of an intentional breach'. Doing so might give the DPO an outsized role in the decision-making process, because the advice of the DPO will be followed to the letter out of fear of sanctions from the supervisory authority. Conversely, we must also not downplay the consequences of disregarding the advice of the DPO as this will undermine the authority and position of the DPO.

Finally, the level of knowledge of the DPO is also relevant when discussing the position of the DPO and the value of their advice in the context of DPIAs. In their survey, the EDPB expresses concern when it comes to the level of knowledge required for the performance of the task of a DPO.[52] The GDPR requires the DPO to have 'expert knowledge' on data protection. When this knowledge is not present, it might affect the ability of the DPO to advice on DPIAs, which in turn negatively affects the performance of the DPIA.

[50] ibid 17.

[51] EDPB, 'Guidelines 04/2022 on the calculation of administrative fines under the GDPR', version 2.1, adopted on 24 May 2023.

[52] EDPB, 'Coordinated Enforcement Action Designation and Position of Data Protection Officers', adopted on 16 January 2024, 18.

IV. Article 36 of the GDPR

One of the most enigmatic articles in the GDPR is Article 36. It reads as follows:

> The controller shall consult the supervisory authority prior to processing where a data protection impact assessment under Article 35 indicates that the processing would result in a high risk in the absence of measures taken by the controller to mitigate the risk.

The idea is that when there is a high risk to the rights and freedoms of the data subject, the processing may not commence without prior consultation of the data protection authority. However, the exact conditions for doing a prior consultation and the role of the data protection authority are somewhat unclear.

The first question that is raised by the wording of Article 36 of the GDPR is whether the assessment of the risk must be done after risk-reducing measures have been introduced, or prior to them being introduced. The wording of the article seems to suggest the latter ('in the absence of measures taken by the controller'), but this seems to defeat the purpose of having to do a DPIA in the first place. The whole idea of doing a DPIA is that the controller assesses the risks and comes up with risk-reducing measures. It is not the task of the data protection authority to conduct a DPIA and come up with risk-reducing measures that should then be taken onboard by the controller to reduce the risk. As such, the most logical interpretation of Article 36 is that a prior consultation is only necessary when the residual risk of the data-processing activity remains high (i.e., the remaining risks after measures that the data controller is willing and able to take).[53] Recital 84 supports this idea:

> (…) Where a data-protection impact assessment indicates that processing operations involve a high risk which the controller cannot mitigate by appropriate measures in terms of available technology and costs of implementation, a consultation of the supervisory authority should take place prior to the processing.

We may deduce from this wording that when the residual risk is high (i.e. high risk after all risk-reducing measures have been taken), the data controller should consult the data protection authority. The EDPB Guidelines on DPIAs also take the position that the requirement is triggered by a situation where there is high residual risk.[54]

The data protection authority gives written advice to the controller regarding the risks of the processing activity. It could, for instance, suggest alternative risk-reducing measures to those considered by the data controller, or maybe reiterate

[53] See, Cecilia Alvarez Rigaudias and Alessandro Spina, 'Article 36 Prior Consultation', in Cristopher Kuner et al. (eds), *The EU General Data Protection Regulation (GDPR): A Commentary*, (Oxford University Press 2020), 684.

[54] EDPB, 'Guidelines on Data Protection Impact Assessment (DPIA) and determining whether processing is "likely to result in a high risk" for the purposes of Regulation 2016/679', 4 October 2017, 19.

that the measures dismissed by the data controller need to be implemented to reduce the risk to an acceptable level. It might even be that the data protection authority evaluates the risk differently than the data controller (arguing that it is lower). The UK's Information Commissioner's Office (ICO), for instance, notes on its website that it may conclude that the risks have been sufficiently mitigated and the controller may carry on with the processing.[55]

The data controller is, of course, free to ignore the advice of the data protection authority and carry on with the processing regardless. However, both during and after the consultation, the data protection authority is free to leverage its entire enforcement arsenal at the controller.[56] Knowing and willingly contravening the advice of the data protection authority therefore seems ill-advised.

The advice of the data protection authority does not seem to cover advice on the legal basis for processing nor should it be interpreted as a mechanism for prior authorisation. While this is not entirely clear from the wording of Article 36, it can be inferred *a contrario* from Article 36(5) of the GDPR. This paragraph allows for national legislation that makes consultation on processing activities conducted in the public interest mandatory and subject to prior authorisation. Given that it is allowed at the national level to diverge from the standard rules of the GDPR in this particular instance, I may deduce that authorisation is normally not covered by Article 36. We can find further support for this argument on for instance the website of the Dutch data protection authority. The AP explicitly states in their Article 36 intake form that they will not give any advice on the legal basis for processing, and that this assessment is the responsibility of the data controller.[57]

Given that the AP does not assess the legal basis, it also does not assess the necessity of the processing activity (proportionality and subsidiarity). As such, an authorisation does not make a lot of sense as this would need to entail a balancing test between the risks for the rights and freedoms of data subjects and the interests of the data controller. This interpretation also seems to match with the title of Article 36 of the GDPR: it is a prior consultation, not a prior authorisation. Finally, it aligns with the natural role of a data protection authority: it supervises compliance with the requirements of the GDPR, but it is not the ultimate arbiter on what is considered legitimate when it comes to data processing. This position is reserved for the legislator and the judiciary. When the data protection authority makes decisions on what is considered necessary in a democratic society when it comes to data protection, they may overstep their authority.

From a practical perspective though, this interpretation raises the question as to how useful a prior consultation is for the data controller. If I follow the above reasoning, the main benefit of a prior consultation would be to achieve greater clarity on the position of the data protection authority vis-à-vis a particular processing

[55] See https://ico.org.uk/for-organisations/uk-gdpr-guidance-and-resources/accountability-and-governance/data-protection-impact-assessments-dpias/do-I-need-to-consult-the-ico/#do7.

[56] See GDPR, art 36.

[57] See www.autoriteitpersoonsgegevens.nl/themas/basis-avg/praktisch-avg/voorafgaande-raadpleging.

activity and perhaps get some 'free advice' on risk-reducing measures. However, while it is not entirely outside the realms of possibility, it does seem rather unlikely that a data protection authority would make a more favourable assessment of the residual risk than the data controller. In general, data protection authorities are stricter and more cautious when it comes to data protection risks than the average controller. So, the likely outcome is that the data protection authority will take more and/or stricter risk-reducing measures. In those situations, the data controller is probably better off not starting the project altogether. This raises questions about the practical use of Article 36 of the GDPR. Surprisingly, though, our survey found that 23 per cent of respondents had applied for a prior consultation in the past.[58] In that light, calling Article 36 a 'dead letter' is too much of a stretch.

V. Room for Improvement?

While the DPIA requirement is not without its flaws, I argue that making DPIAs mandatory has had an overall positive effect on privacy and data protection. As a result of their legal obligations, data controllers now actively consider the risk of their data protection activities and take measures to address these risks, increasing the level of data protection within organisations. This conclusion is supported by our survey. 50 per cent of the respondents agreed with the statement that DPIAs have contributed to a higher level of privacy and data protection within their organisation, while 29 per cent strongly agreed with this statement.[59]

While DPIAs contribute to a higher level of data protection (at least in the perception of the privacy professional) the business is less enthusiastic. When given the statement 'the business is positive about conducting DPIAs' only 31 percent of the respondents agreed. 32 per cent disagreed and 37 per cent answered 'neutral' (neither positive nor negative). When asked what the reasons were for the negative perception cost, complexity, time investment and not understanding the benefits were those most cited. Given that the business is ultimately responsible for conducting DPIAs, this poses a risk to the effectiveness of the DPIA requirement.

The negative perception can, in part, be attributed to the vagueness of the article and the limited guidance by the supervisory authorities. When asked what they would like to improve, respondents amongst other things mentioned more clear procedures and templates, integration with other types of assessments, shorter turnover times and a decoupling of the privacy by design process and the reporting requirements.

[58] Note that I did not limit the answer to a certain time period, so this answer could encompass the entire career of the respondent.

[59] It must be noted that there could be some bias in these results as I have surveyed privacy professionals who are probably more inclined to think that privacy measures have a positive effect.

Many of the questions surrounding DPIAs flow forth from the 'meta-regulatory' nature of the GDPR.[60] The GDPR does not prescribe measures or technologies to be used, but rather it hopes to leverage existing risk-management procedures within organisations.[61] This, however, inevitably leaves a measure of vagueness in the law, as it must cater to many different scenarios and organisations. It is difficult to create legislation that is both broadly applicable and concrete at the same time. While it could be made more prescriptive and it describe the 'ideal' process for conducting a DPIA, this will inevitably come at the cost of the flexibility of the requirement, resulting in data controllers being shoehorned into a methodology that does not match with their organisation. Furthermore, it is highly questionable whether there actually is something like an 'ideal' methodology when doing DPIAs.

Given the above, I propose the following measures to improve the effectiveness of DPIAs in practice. These measures are mainly aimed at the legislator and the data protection authorities.

- *Support and share best practice.* A survey on DPIAs conducted under European Institutions by the EDPS found that data controllers would like to see best practice, for instance in the form of example DPIAs.[62] By showing data controllers what the effective procedures for carrying out DPIAs are, and showing what a good DPIA report looks like, data controllers can better focus their efforts. While it could be argued that this is a task for the market, more clarity on what a data protection authorities expect from data controllers is of added value.
- Provide guidance on how DPIAs and privacy by design can complement one another. Current guidance seems to be focused too much on the final DPIA report and less on the process of improving products and services. More emphasis could be placed on the role of a DPIA as a tool for improving products and services, rather than on it being a legal requirement. To this end it is especially important to emphasise the need for including designers and developers in the DPIA process.
- Consider how different risk assessments tools can be integrated into a single process. With the proliferation of risk assessment requirements in, amongst others, the GDPR, DSA and AI Act, the compliance burden on organisations may grow significantly. This may further antagonise businesses, leading to a 'tick the box' culture. By integrating different assessments into a manageable and comprehensive whole, the process of risk assessment can be streamlined, keeping business impact at an acceptable level.

When it comes to Article 36 of the GDPR, improvements to the actual text are possible. In any case, Article 36 should more accurately reflect the logic of

[60] Dalla Corte (n 20) at 11.
[61] ibid, 10.
[62] EDPS, 'Survey on Data Protection Impact Assessments under Article 39 of the Regulation' (2020) case 2020-0066.

Recital 84, i.e. it should make clear that a prior consultation is only possible when the outcome of a DPIA is that the residual risk of a data-processing activity remains high, despite the measures taken by the data controller.

Also, possibilities to include some form of prior authorisation could be explored. There are situations where controllers may feel the need to forge ahead with a processing activity, given its (societal) importance.[63] In these situations, a system of prior authorisation could be beneficial. In such a system there would not just be an assessment of the risk-reducing measures, but also an assessment of the necessity of a processing activity. While this might give data protection authorities too much 'residual law making power', it would solve situations in which there is a pressing need to process data, but a lack of clarity about the legal basis for processing.[64] Finally, the mechanism of prior consultation could also play a role in those situations where there is a difference of opinion between the data controller and the DPO.

VI. Conclusion

A DPIA can be a valuable tool to mitigate privacy and data protection risks. By mandating the use of this tool through Article 35 of the GDPR it has gained more wide-scale adoption. As such, it can be argued that Article 35 has been a net positive for privacy and data protection. But while DPIAs have proven to be useful tools to mitigate risks, their application is not without its flaws. In part, these flaws can be traced back to the codification of the DPIA requirement in the GDPR. The inherent vagueness of Article 35 of the GDPR has led to a multitude of different procedures, templates and methodologies that are not necessarily focused on improving products or services through privacy by design, but rather on accountability.

To improve the effectiveness of DPIAs in practice, guidance could be given on the proper scope and timing as well as its interaction with other risk-management instruments and impact assessments. To this end it would also be beneficial to share best practices and feedback on DPIAs. When it comes to Article 36 of the GDPR, the wording could be improved. Furthermore, ideas on prior authorisation could be further explored.

[63] As mentioned, art 36(5) to some extent already allows for a mechanism of prior authorisation.

[64] Rebecca Ong, '*Mobile Communication and the Protection of Children*' (Leiden University Press, 2010).

3

The Question of Consent in European Data Protection Law

RÓISÍN Á COSTELLO AND MARK LEISER

I. Introduction

The European Union's data protection landscape has long emphasised the importance of consent as a tool for user empowerment and safeguarding individual autonomy. The importance of consent is not an innovation of the General Data Protection Regulation (GDPR). Directive 95/46/EC (DPD) provided the basis for establishing consent as a central component of the Union's data protection regime over two decades before. The DPD provided that consent was the primary basis for processing under Articles 7(a) and 8(2), with Article 2(h) requiring that such consent be freely given, specific, and informed. These were framing values and priorities that were, in large part, carried over to the GDPR, and their echoes are evident, inter alia, in the wording and framing of Articles 4(11), 6(1)(a), 7 and 9(2)(a) as well as in Recitals 32, 42 and 43. Yet it is evident that the Regulation, far from simply affirming the role of consent within data protection law, reaffirmed consent as the fulcrum of the EU data protection framework more broadly. Thus, Article 7, in conjunction with Article 4(11) and Recital 32, presents a clear set of criteria for consent integrated within a market-oriented framework which seeks to embed respect for Fundamental Rights within the digital market.

In this chapter, we explore the consent infrastructure within the GDPR and its integration within the constitutional framework of EU law. Despite its normative importance, consent has proven to be challenging to define in a manner that fully reflects the choices consumers face in online markets and successfully upholds the autonomy interests it seeks to protect. This complexity not only underscores the intricacies of consent as a normative anchor and a practical threshold for action but (for those of us engaged in a critical appraisal of the GDPR) provides an impactful example of the interaction of law and theory in modern privacy and data protection law and theory.

Part II of this chapter examines the role and definition of consent within the GDPR. Part III examines the relationship between autonomy and consent within data protection law and, indeed, as part of broader privacy theory leading to Part IV, in which we examine the normative concerns raised by others about the centring of consent within data protection law. Parts V to VII examine two of the practical, technology-led challenges to deferring to consent-led models of the GDPR.

In particular, we examine how the role of consent in artificial intelligence (AI) engages in data scraping for use in training Large Language Models (LLMs). This examination will focus on how consent is obtained, whether current consent-based practices and protections are adequate, and how they can be improved to respect individual autonomy and comply with the requirements of the GDPR. Second, and leading to the examination undertaken by our colleague Lexo Zard in Chapter 4 of this volume, we explore the deceptive techniques or 'dark patterns' employed by the AdTech industry to obtain consent for collecting and using personal data in the behavioural advertising ecosystem.

By dissecting these two practices and their attendance mechanisms and strategies, as well as how they push the boundaries of lawful consent, this chapter seeks to highlight areas for regulatory improvement and suggest ways to ensure that consent mechanisms are normatively coherent as well as practically transparent, fair and effective in safeguarding user privacy in the digital age.

II. Consent and the GDPR

Consent is a primary and, in some views, the default mechanism which facilitates the operation of the GDPR and achieves the vindication of data subjects' rights to data protection and privacy. Consent is defined under Article 4(11) of the GDPR as a 'freely given, specific, informed and unambiguous indication of the data subject's wishes by which he or she, by a statement or by a clear affirmative action, signifies agreement to the processing of personal data relating to him or her'. This definition offers the presumptive basis for processing under Articles 6 and 9, which provide that personal and sensitive personal data may be processed based on consent or explicit consent.

Pursuant to Article 6 of the GDPR, the processing of personal data is lawful only if and to the extent that at least one of the listed conditions is present, of which the data subject's consent is listed first. By Article 9(2)(a), GDPR is the first basis on which the presumptive ban on the processing of special categories of personal data may be set aside if a data subject has given explicit consent to the processing of their data. While both Articles 6 and 9 of the GDPR note the further basis for processing, consent offers the first, most basic, and presumptively preferable basis for processing both data categories in most cases.

This position is reinforced by Recitals 42 and 43 of the GDPR,[1] which reaffirms the data controller's duty to ensure consent is present. Article 7 further

[1] Recital 42 requires that processing based on the data subject's consent should be demonstrable by the data processor and in the context of a written consent, safeguards should be put in place to ensure

supplements the definition of consent provided in Article 4(11) with specific practical conditions which must be met to establish that the consent obtained is valid. These supplemental requirements are, of course, only relevant where consent forms the basis for processing under Article 6(1)(a) or concerning specific processing operations involving sensitive data under Article 9(2)(a) or fully automated decision-making by Article 22(2)(c) of the GDPR. What is particularly interesting regarding the position of consent under Article 7 is that the obligation is placed on controllers to innovate to find means of supporting and enabling consent.[2]

Consent is not only a primary concern within the regulatory architecture established by the GDPR but also a matter of constitutional importance within the scheme of EU law. As the Article 29 Working Party emphasised in its Opinion 15/2011 on the definition of consent, inviting data subjects to accept a data processing operation should be subject to rigorous requirements 'since it concerns the fundamental rights of data subjects and the controller wishes to engage in a processing operation that would be unlawful without the data subject's consent'.[3] The EDPB, citing this emphasis on consent, has noted that the 'crucial role of consent' is underlined by Articles 7 and 8 of the Charter of Fundamental Rights of the European Union (CFREU).[4]

Though the EDPB does not expand on the precise relationship between the CFREU and consent, it is implicit from the Guidelines' text and contextual reading of the GDPR that autonomy plays a central role in data privacy within the regulatory scheme which the Regulation underpins.[5]

III. Consent and Autonomy

The EDPB has noted that consent can only be an appropriate lawful basis if a data subject is offered control and is given a genuine choice about accepting or declining the terms offered and, importantly, declining them 'without detriment'.[6] In addition, the Guidelines provide that where consent is 'obtained in full compliance with the GDPR, consent is a tool that gives data subjects control over whether or not personal data concerning them will be processed. If not, the data subject's control becomes illusory, and consent will be an invalid basis for processing, rendering the processing activity unlawful'.[7] These comments link consent to the data subject's autonomy – in the form of control and free choice.

that the data subject is aware that they are giving consent and the extent to which it is being given. Recital 43 provides that in assessing whether consent has been freely given, consent should not be considered to have been given where there is a clear imbalance between the subject and controller.

[2] A position emphasised by the Article 29 Working Party Opinion 15/2011 on consent and reaffirmed by the EDPB, 'Guidelines 05/2020 on Consent under Regulation 2016/679' (4 May 2020).

[3] Opinion 15/2011 on the definition of consent (WP 187), 8.

[4] EDPB, Guidelines (n 2) at 5.

[5] Drawing in particular on the orienting role of control as outlined in GDPR, Recitals 7 and 75.

[6] EDPB (n 2) at 5.

[7] ibid.

The idea of linking control and privacy rights, an umbrella under which we might generally group data protection, is not new. In this respect, the normative link that the Regulation clearly envisages between personal control, autonomy and privacy protection is well established. The 'control-based' approach to privacy is perhaps most associated with the work of Westin,[8] though it has equally been advanced and interrogated by Fried,[9] Scanlon[10] and Bok[11] and Boyd[12] (among others) and emphasises the link between control over personal information and the details of an individual's private life on the one hand, and autonomy or freedom on the other.[13]

The work of Westin, who is perhaps the most prominent of those who had advanced this control-based approach to privacy, was used by Fried who has defined privacy as fundamentally linked to the capacity to choose for ourselves what information we disclose and how and with whom we form relationships[14] – an articulation that evidently maps to the data protection view articulated in the GDPR.[15]

In this linking of autonomy, control and privacy, autonomy can be understood as mirroring Raz's concept of 'people controlling, to some degree, their destiny, fashioning it through successive decisions throughout their lives'.[16] As the EDPB Guidelines echo, autonomy requires an adequate range of morally acceptable options and meaningful choices free from manipulation, coercion, or excessive undue influence.[17] Autonomy should thus be understood as the capacity for individuals to make choices that result from deliberative action. In keeping with this Razian idea of autonomy, choosing between bad options may not constitute autonomy.

This normative relationship between consent, control and individual autonomy has emerged as a central debate among scholars in the first five years of the GDPR.[18] A particular focus of concern has been on whether, in a digital market offering limited services, many or all of which have similar terms of service, data subjects can be said to have meaningful choices such that a notice and consent

[8] Alan Westin, *Privacy and Freedom* (Atheneum, 1967), 7.

[9] Charles Fried, 'Privacy' (1968) 77(3) *Yale Law Journal* 475.

[10] Thomas Scanlon, 'Thomson on Privacy' (1975) 4(4) *Philosophy and Public Affairs* 315.

[11] Sissela Bok, *Secrets: On Ethics of Concealment and Revelation* (Pantheon Books, 1982).

[12] Danah Boyd, 'Social Network Sites as Networked Publics: Affordances, Dynamics, and Implications', in Zizi Papacharissi (ed), *Networked Self: Identity, Community, and Culture on Social Network Sites*, (Routledge, 2010) 38.

[13] Allen 1988; Jean L Cohen, *Regulating Intimacy: A New Legal Paradigm* (Princeton University Press, 2002).

[14] Fried (n 10) at 482.

[15] ibid 485. Fried considers that the central normative value of this vision is that it allows us the space to develop meaningful relationships with others – a view of privacy and the right to private life, which is evident in the jurisprudence of the ECtHR.

[16] Joesph Raz, 'Autonomy, Toleration and the Harm Principle' in Susan Mendus (ed), *Justifying Toleration: Conceptual and Historical Perspectives* (Cambridge University Press 1988), 369.

[17] Paul Bernal, *Internet Privacy Rights*, (Oxford University Press, 2014), 24–5.

[18] ibid 372.

model like that operated by the GDPR can offer a normatively coherent, and practically feasible regulatory architecture.

When thinking about consent, distinguishing between 'thick' and 'thin' consent models is helpful. 'Thick' models of consent shape, and allow the individual consenting to shape, their interaction with those forces and actors around them, thus constituting an expression of individual autonomy.[19] Thick consent models are, in essence, those envisaged by the GDPR in its most idealised context. They are premised on a choice landscape characterised by absolute voluntariness, free from asymmetries of bargaining power, and replete with numerous competing participants between whom an individual may choose without suffering a detriment.

In contrast, 'thin' consent models are those in which, as the EDPB fears, consent is illusory – a functional but ultimately superficial exercise of choice. Thin consent models have little or no regard for the practical impacts of structural power, individual capacity or market dominance and emphasise the existence of choice rather than engaging with the substance of the options available to data subjects and the reduction to their deliberative capacity, which results when there is only a choice between bad choices.

One source of criticism levelled at the GDPR's notice and consent architecture has been that, while it espouses commitment to a thick model of consent, it does not function effectively in the digital market due to restricted choice and regulatory burdens and thus, in practice, is a thin consent model given its operation in a digital market that is characterised by a few private actors who, due to their dominance, effectively operate as standard setters for the contractual terms used by new entrants and those employed among the existing market players. This feature of the digital market means that individuals enjoy little functional choice as to the terms on which they consent to contracts for particular services or goods and undermines a crucial presupposition of a 'thick' consent model – by narrowing the capacity for choice at the source.

In such a setting, the argument that a user may seek equivalent services or goods elsewhere is impractical, while the argument that a user can 'opt-out' and choose none of the offerings is, at best, disingenuous, failing to acknowledge the social and cultural damage occasioned by failing, or being unable to engage with, the digital market.[20] Compounding this is the presence within the digital market of 'lock-ins', which restrict consumer choice by obstructing interoperability, restricting consumers from using content provided by one seller on devices provided by another, and obstructing the operation of effective competition in which consumers can participate.[21] The second difference between digital and traditional

[19] Tom L Beauchamp, 'Autonomy and Consent', in Franklin Miller, and Alan Wertheimer (eds), *The Ethics of Consent: Theory and Practice* (Oxford University Press, 2009).

[20] *Smith v Maryland* 422 US 735 (1979), Marshall and Brennan JJ dissenting articulated this necessity particularly well.

[21] Kyle Wiens, 'Apple Shouldn't Get to Brick Your iPhone Because you Fixed it Yourself' *Wired*. Available at: www.wired.com/2016/02/apple-shouldnt-get-to-brick-your-iphone-because-you-fixed-it-yourself/,

markets relates to the volume and density of the terms individuals are asked to consent to.[22] The evidence is that the volume of terms to which data subjects are asked to agree when seeking to participate in the digital market and the low levels of choice between providers of goods and services mean that individuals often need to be made aware of the content and implications of their consent.[23]

All of this matters because consent, as an expression of individual autonomy,[24] functions to alter the morality of another actor's conduct, which means otherwise impermissible actions are rendered legally, socially, and permissible.[25] When consent becomes superficial or 'thin', this transformative power and the normative resonance of the autonomy claims that consent possesses fall away.[26] Thus, it is unsurprising that consent use as a normatively transformative practice has emerged as a site of controversy in the context of the GDPR.

IV. The Problem with Consent

This conflict over the validity of the GDPR's recourse to consent has been particularly contextualised by the practical reality that in the digital market, the preconditions necessary for valid consent – capacity, voluntariness and meaningful choice – cannot, as noted above, always be clearly and neatly satisfied in the

accessed 8 August 2023; Luis E Hestres, 'App Neutrality: Apple's App Store and Freedom of Expression Online' (2013) 7 *International Journal of Communication* 1265; Chaim Gartenberg, 'Amazon strikes deal with Apple to sell new iPhones and iPads' *The Verge* Available at: www.theverge.com/2018/11/9/18079340/amazon-apple-iphone-ipad-watch-beats-deal-selling-products-online.

[22] Jonathan A Obar and Anne Oeldorf-Hirsch, *Clickwrap Impact: Quick-Join Options and Ignoring Privacy and Terms of Service Policies of Social Networking Services* (York Univeristy; Quello Centre, Michigan State University and University of Connecticut 2017); Jonathan A Obar and Anne Oeldorf-Hirsch, 'The Biggest Lie on the Internet: Ignoring the Privacy Policies and Terms of Service Policies of Social Networking Services' (2018) 1 *Information, Communication & Society* 1.

[23] This has been repeatedly demonstrated in the context of privacy choices, Rainer Bohme and Stefan Kopsell, 'Trained to Accept? A Field Experiment on Consent Dialogs' (Proceedings of the SIGCHI Conference on Human Factors in Computing Systems); Simone van der Hof Bart Custers, Bart Schermer, Sandra Appleby-Arnold and Noeline Brockdorff, 'Informed Consent in Social Media Use – The Gap between User Expectations and EU Personal Data Protection Law' (2013) 10 *SCRIPTed* 435; Neil Richards and Woodrow Hartzog, 'The Pathologies of Digital Consent' (2019) 96(6) *Washington University Law Review* 1461; Elettra Bietti, 'Consent as a Free Pass: Platform Power and the Limits of the Informational Turn' (2020) 40 *Pace Law Review* 307; Elizabeth Edenberg and Meg Leta Jones, 'Analysing the Legal Roots and Moral Core of Digital Consent' (2019) 21(8) *New Media and Society* 509.

[24] Ruth Faden and Tom L Beauchamp, *A History and Theory of Informed Consent* (Oxford University Press 1986), 277.

[25] Heidi M Hurd, 'The Moral Magic of Consent' (1996) 2 *Legal Theory* 121, 123; Elizabeth Edenberg and Meg Leta Jones, 'Analysing the Legal Roots and Moral Core of Digital Consent' (2019) 21 *New Media & Society* 1804; Meg Leta Jones, 'The Development of Consent to Computing' 41(1) (2019) *IEEE Annals of the History of Computing Governance and Computing* 34.

[26] Franklin G Miller and Alan Wertheimer, 'Preface to a Theory of Consent: Beyond Valid Consent' in Franklin G Miller and Alan Wertheimer (ed), *The Ethics of Consent: Theory and Practice* (Oxford University Press 2010), 203; John Simmons, *Moral Principles and Political Obligations* (Princeton University Press 1979), 76.

way the Regulation envisages.[27] Thus, for example, a choice may be freely given, specific, informed, and unambiguous in the manner envisaged by Article 4(11) of the GDPR and may still lack the morally transformative power it is intended to attribute to the action consented to because the data subject making that choice has no functional, alternative option within the market or the offerings available to them. In such circumstances, consent cannot fulfil its purpose of assessing whether and under what conditions fundamental rights may be limited or abolished as quickly and cleanly as the GDPR envisages.

The consent that operates in the digital market is, thus, not continuously contiguous with the 'thick' version of autonomy identified in the text of the Regulation, which is characterised by capacity, voluntariness, and meaningful choice. Instead, consent may be an unpredictable moderator of autonomy – operating at times as a thin, formalist expression of choice that has little regard for the practical impacts of structural power, individual capacity or market dominance and, at others, as a real signifier that substantive 'thick' conceptions of autonomy are at work.

Thus, consent is only sometimes as helpful a proxy for ensuring autonomy as it initially suggests. Bietti, describing this phenomenon, has therefore described the notice and consent model adopted in the GDPR as 'not only normatively futile but also positively harmful'[28] and argues that

> The discourse of autonomous consent and the assumptions that underlie it positively harm consumers in two ways: by imputing responsibility on users for outcomes that no one could have reasonably chosen and by focusing attention on the wrong kinds of values and creating collective resistance around alternatives that should be promoted. It seems that notice and consent, in fact, act as technologies of power: a default practice that has become hard to contest and is part of the background of assumed facts about our digital environment. When faced with the effects of such a default practice, entrepreneurs and regulators too often recite arguments about the absolute importance of individual autonomy. They say that individuals need greater control over their digital lives, and consent is our best if not the only, option. These responses are symptomatic of a dismaying lack of imagination around existing and future alternatives.'[29]

Not all authors have gone this far. Zarksyand Lemley have argued that notice and consent models like those employed under the GDPR produce greater awareness of terms, make for more informed consumers and generate greater power for individuals to make meaningful choices.[30] However, as many scholars have argued, this view may be somewhat more idealistic than reality can admit. Consent is often

[27] And as part of what Margot Kaminski refers to as an instrument of 'binary governance' Margot E Kaminski, 'Binary Governance: Lessons from the GDPR's Approach to Algorithmic Accountability', (2019) 92(6) *Southern California Law Review* 1529.

[28] Elettra Bietti, 'Consent as a Free Pass: Platform Power and the Limits of the Informational Turn' (2020) 40(1) *Pace Law Review* 307.

[29] ibid 313.

[30] Tal Z Zarsky, 'E-Contract Doctrine 2.0: Standard Form Contracting in an Age of Online User Participation' (2008) 14 *Michigan Telecoms and Technology Law Review* 303; Mark A Lemley, 'Terms of Use' (2006) 91 *Minnesota Law Review* 459.

given without severe consideration or conscious deliberation and, in some models of online interaction, may not even meet the threshold for voluntariness that the GDPR establishes.[31] This is not to exclude a notice and consent model altogether. Richards and Hartzog have argued that reliance on consent can be beneficial. Still, they note that it will be most valid when it is infrequent, when the potential harms resulting from the choice are clear and easily understood, and when individuals have the correct incentives to choose consciously and thoughtfully.[32]

As we transition from a broad examination of consent within the GDPR framework to the nuanced challenges posed by the age of AI, several pivotal questions arise. First, we must consider whether the traditional notion of consent applies to publicly available data and how this intersects with data protection principles. Second, the legal requisites for consent have become increasingly complex with the advent of technologies like generative AI, which rely on extensive scraping of data (much of which will contain personal identifiers) from the internet. This practice raises critical questions about the legitimacy of using vast amounts of scraped data to train AI models, especially in light of the GDPR's consent requirements. Third, the role of supervisory authorities in regulating and holding accountable entities like OpenAI and other language model providers is paramount. The interventions of such authorities could be instrumental in shaping the landscape of lawful data use in AI development.

Finally, this discussion will inevitably lead us to scrutinise whether the current issues surrounding consent in AI and data scraping serve as further evidence of the fundamental flaws within the consent paradigm, especially when considering AI's rapid advancement and integration into everyday life. This exploration will delve into the complexities of consent in an era where technological advancements continuously expand and redefine the boundaries of data protection.

V. Challenges to the GDPR's General Consent Framework from AI

As discussed in the previous section, consent must be freely given, specific, informed and unambiguous, setting a high standard for data protection. However,

[31] Bart W Schermer et al, 'The Crisis of Consent: How Stronger Legal Protection May Lead to Weaker Consent in Data Protection' (2014) 16 *Ethics of Information Technology*, 171–82; Lisa M Austin, 'Enough About Me: Why Privacy is about Power, Not Consent (or Harm)' in Austin Sarat (eds) *A World Without Privacy: What Law Can and Should Do?* (Cambridge University Press, 2014), 131; Gabriela Zanfir, 'Forgetting About Consent: Why the Focus Should Be on "Suitable Safeguards"' in Serge Gutwirth, Ronald Leenes and Paul De Hert (eds), *Reloading Data Protection* (Springer, 2014), 237; Bert-Jaap Koops, 'The Trouble with European Data Protection Law' (2014) 4 *International Data Privacy Law* 250.

[32] Neil Richards and Woodrow Hartzog, 'The Pathologies of Digital Consent' (2018) 96 *Washington University Law Review* 1461.

the advent of AI, particularly in advanced algorithms and machine learning, presents challenges that extend beyond the conventional boundaries envisaged by the GDPR.[33] AI's capability to process and analyse vast amounts of data on an unprecedented scale raises significant questions about the applicability of traditional consent mechanisms.

For instance, the use of AI in predictive analytics, behavioural advertising and personalised services relies on aggregating and processing personal data in ways that individuals may not fully anticipate or understand when giving consent.[34] Furthermore, AI's reliance on large datasets for training complicates the notion of specific and informed consent, as AI's eventual applications can be diverse and not fully known during data collection.[35] This scenario necessitates re-evaluating consent frameworks to ensure they remain practical and relevant in AI, where data use and processing dynamics have evolved significantly.

LLMs, such as GPT (Generative Pre-trained Transformer), underpin some of the most advanced AI applications today, from natural language processing to content creation. These models are trained on extensive corpora of text data, often sourced through web scraping – the automated collection of publicly available online information.[36] Data scraping, the automated process of collecting information from public domains, is critical for amassing the large-scale datasets required for training these AI models. While instrumental in advancing AI capabilities, this practice navigates a complex landscape of data availability and ethical use, especially when personal data is involved. This method allows LLMs to assimilate various language patterns, idioms, and knowledge, generating responses that mimic human-like understanding.

These technologies can also produce deepfakes and manipulate information, thereby challenging data integrity and potentially contravening the GDPR.[37] The array of risks includes creating biased data sets, which can perpetuate and amplify societal biases in harmful ways.[38] Moreover, the 'black-box' nature of AI systems complicates efforts to achieve transparency and accountability, particularly under

[33] Aleksander Kesa and Tanel Kerikmäe, 'Artificial Intelligence and the GDPR: Inevitable Nemeses?' (2020) 10(3) *TalTech Journal of European Studies* 68.

[34] János Mészáros and Chih-Hsing Ho, 'Big Data and Scientific Research' (2018) 59 *Hungarian Journal of Legal Studies* 403; Helena Ursic Vrabec and Bart Custers, 'Legal Barriers and Enablers to Big Data Reuse' (2016) 2 *European Data Protection Law Review* 209.

[35] Philipp Hacker, 'A Legal Framework for AI Training Data – From First Principles to the Artificial Intelligence Act' (2021) 13(2) *Law, Innovation and Technology* 257.

[36] IBM, 'What Are Large Language Models (LLMs)?' (IBM Topics, 26 April 2024). Available at: www.ibm.com/topics/large-language-models#:~:text=LLMs%20are%20a%20class%20of%20foundation%20models%2C%20which,as%20well%20as%20resolve%20a%20multitude%20of%20tasks.

[37] Bart van der Sloot, 'Regulating Non-Personal Data in the Age of Big Data' in Maria Tzanou (eds) *Health Data Privacy under the GDPR* (Routledge, 2020) 85.

[38] Emily M Bender et al, 'On the Dangers of Stochastic Parrots: Can Language Models Be Too Big?' (2021) ACM Conference on Fairness, Accountability, and Transparency, 610.

GDPR requirements, which emphasise informed consent and the traceability of data processing activities.[39]

The expansive reservoirs of publicly accessible data embody a profound conundrum for the consent paradigm delineated by the GDPR. For example, data disseminated across social media platforms, discussion forums, and open databases frequently encompasses personal characteristics that, under GDPR stipulations, could be considered special category data and thus require unambiguous consent for their processing.[40] Yet one exception to this explicit consent requirement under Article 9 of the GDPR is where the data subject manifestly makes the data public.[41] Thus, a quintessential quandary emerges in the attempt to harmonise the inherently public domain of this data with the stipulation for individualised consent.

Given the data's open access, one might conjecture an implicit consent for its utilisation. Nonetheless, Article 9 unequivocally necessitates that consent be explicit, informed, and voluntarily proffered, thereby engendering debates regarding the legality of employing this data absent direct authorisation from the implicated individuals. This predicament demands a sophisticated comprehension of consent, particularly when addressing data that, despite being publicly accessible, was not ostensibly designated for extensive processing or analytical endeavours.

Advocate General Rantos clarified in *Schrems v Meta*[42] that manifestly making sensitive data public does not automatically remove the protections granted by Article 9 of the GDPR. However, the data still falls under the purview of Articles 5 and 6 and, where applicable, Article 7 of the GDPR. Thus, while Article 9(2)(e) allows for the processing of special categories of personal data that have been manifestly made public, this does not authorise the aggregation and analysis of such data for personalised advertising purposes 'in itself'.[43] The phrase 'in itself' is significant. While Article 9(2)(e) of the GDPR does not provide a standalone basis for processing sensitive data in this context, such processing might still be permissible under the conditions set out in Articles 5 and 6 of the GDPR.

Article 9(2)(e) of the GDPR effectively removes the 'special protection' granted to special category data. When a data subject voluntarily makes such data public, what was once 'protected' personal data becomes 'ordinary' data. However, the processing of this now non-sensitive data remains subject to the strictures set forth primarily in Articles 6 and 7 of the GDPR. Moreover, adherence to the principles detailed in Article 5 of the GDPR, such as the principle of purpose limitation

[39] Ognyan Seizov and Alexander J Wulf, 'Artificial Intelligence and Transparency: A Blueprint for Improving the Regulation of AI Applications in the EU' (2020) 31(4) *European Business Law Review* 611.

[40] GDPR, art 6(1)(a).

[41] ibid art 9(2)(e).

[42] Case C-446/21 *Maximilian Schrems v Meta Platforms Ireland Limited* EU:C:2024:366.

[43] ibid 45.

found in Article 5(1)(b), is obligatory. This principle insists that personal data be collected solely for specified, explicit, and legitimate purposes, and it is the responsibility of the data controller to demonstrate compliance with this criterion, as outlined in paragraph 2 of the related provision.

Thus, if a data subject makes personal data publicly available, this action could be interpreted under Article 9(2)(e) of the GDPR as having 'manifestly made public' the data. Nonetheless, this action alone does not justify the processing of personal data. In light of the Advocate General's interpretation in *Schrems*, even when a data subject makes personal data publicly available, it does not, by itself, authorise the processing of this or any other related data for purposes such as aggregating and analysing for AI, including LLMs or other processing activities not directly aligned with the initially declared purposes.

The insistence on explicit consent safeguards individual privacy and autonomy, ensuring that persons maintain sovereignty over their data. Obtaining consent for a specific purpose when using publicly available data presents significant complexities. These complexities underscore the need for more precise regulations and innovative frameworks that can effectively address the unique challenges of the digital environment. To comply with data protection principles, particularly the consent requirement, it is essential that consent is clearly tied to the specific purpose for which the data is used and that this purpose is explicitly communicated to individuals. How can scraping data from the Internet adhere to these principles? The challenge arises in ensuring that the use of scraped data for training LLMs adheres to data protection principles, especially considering the difficulty in obtaining individual consent for already public data.

VI. Reconciling Data Scraping Practices with GDPR Compliance: Challenges and Opportunities in the Digital Age

Data scraping, the automated aggregation of information from websites and publicly accessible databases serves diverse purposes, spanning academic inquiry to commercial exploitation. Yet, the legality and ethical dimensions of harvesting personal data sans the explicit consent of the implicated individuals engender intricate dilemmas. The situation mainly concerns data in the public domain, where the presumption of consent for collecting, processing and utilising personal information in manners unforeseen by data subjects is tenuous at best.

The GDPR, through its bedrock principles of 'lawfulness, fairness, and transparency',[44] mandates that personal data handling aligns with legal statutes, upholds equity towards the data subjects, and proceeds with manifest clarity. However, data

[44] GDPR, art 5(1)(a).

scraping activities frequently transgress these principles, especially regarding fairness and transparency, leaving individuals oblivious to the fate of their data once scraped. Furthermore, GDPR underscores purpose limitation and data minimisation principles,[45] prescribing that data collection targets specified, explicit, and legitimate ends and remains confined to what is indispensable for the intended processing activities. Mass-scale data scraping, in its propensity to repurpose or retain data beyond its initial scope, starkly contravenes these tenets, potentially culminating in uses of data that extend well beyond the stipulated initial objectives or necessitating data retention past its utility.

OpenAI claims that the purposes of collecting data that might be used to train or refine ChatGPT are clearly defined. For instance, the data could be explicitly collected to train language models to understand and generate human language responses.[46] Furthermore, they claim that data used to train ChatGPT is only processed in ways compatible with the model's initial purpose of improving language understanding and generation capabilities.[47] Restricting further processing is essential – any use of the data beyond these specified purposes, such as for unrelated commercial activities or data sharing with third parties without explicit consent, would be incompatible with the purpose limitation principle. To align further with GDPR principles, any personal data used in training the AI model is typically subjected to data minimisation and anonymisation techniques. These measures involve using only the data necessary for specific purposes and anonymising it to prevent the identification of individuals, thereby reducing privacy risks and ensuring compliance with GDPR.[48]

Thus, the apparent notion of implied consent derived from the public availability of data finds itself increasingly at odds with the GDPR's rigorous consent paradigms, prompting a recalibration towards a methodology that harmonises the legitimate utilities of data scraping with the imperatives of data subject rights. This recalibration could envisage the innovation of anonymisation techniques for scraped data, bolstered transparency regarding the objectives of data collection, and the institution of opt-out mechanisms for individuals, thereby navigating the fine line between the augmentation of digital-age utilities and the inviolable respect for individual data rights.

This situation underscores the need for clear guidelines and potentially new regulatory approaches to reconcile LLMs' operational requirements with the fundamental rights to privacy and data protection. A sophisticated regulatory approach, underpinned by a nuanced comprehension of consent's evolving dynamics in the digital era, is indispensable to navigating this complex landscape. Such an approach must transcend conventional boundaries, embracing a more granular understanding of consent that acknowledges the multifaceted nature of digital

[45] ibid art 5(1)(c).
[46] Available at: https://openai.com/policies/privacy-policy.
[47] ibid 2.
[48] ibid.

interactions and their varying expectations of privacy. Such an approach necessitates a recalibration of regulatory frameworks to accommodate the realities of digital data dissemination and a cultural shift towards a more discerning engagement with personal data found online. Forging a harmonious equilibrium between the essence of data protection and the vast potential of digital information necessitates an innovative rethinking of consent paradigms. This re-evaluation must encapsulate a broader recognition of the complexities inherent in digital consent, advocating for mechanisms that empower individuals with greater control and clarity over their data while fostering an environment where the collective benefits of digital data are not unduly curtailed.

Generative AI introduces complex challenges related to bias and data protection that have significant implications under the GDPR. These challenges include perpetuating biases through machine learning flaws, manifesting as discriminatory outputs in applications such as facial recognition or job screening processes, and favouring specific demographics. Additionally, the opaque nature of AI decision-making, often called the 'black-box' problem, complicates accountability and transparency, particularly in sectors where safety is critical. Another concern is the 'AI hallucinations' phenomenon, where Generative AI systems produce inaccurate or misleading information, which can be problematic under GDPR mandates. The use of extensive personal data by inherently non-transparent AI systems poses further challenges in maintaining GDPR compliance, especially concerning informed consent.

German data protection authorities, led by the Landesbeauftragte für den Datenschutz und die Informationsfreiheit (LfDI) in Baden-Württemberg, have exhibited proactive scrutiny in a detailed inquiry concerning ChatGPT's compliance.[49] The authorities' concerns about the potential for generative AI technologies to sidestep established data protection laws due to their disruptive nature emphasised the necessity of this thorough approach. The German inquiry is part of a broader European effort to regulate generative AI, as evidenced by the EDPB's establishment of a special task force.[50] While these questions reflect discussions at the national level, they align with broader European concerns about the adequacy of personal data processing by AI systems like ChatGPT. Moreover, this regulatory focus extends beyond Germany. For instance, Italy's Data Protection Authority has recently escalated scrutiny following alleged GDPR violations by OpenAI, leading to initial enforcement actions and ongoing evaluations in conjunction with the EDPB's task force.[51]

[49] Virtual Data Protection Office. 'Datenschutzrechtliche Prüfung von ChatGPT geht weiter: Landesdatenschutzbeauftragter stellt zusätzliche Fragen an OpenAI' [ungültige URL entfernt], 29 January 2024.

[50] European Data Protection Board (EDPB), 'EDPB resolves dispute on transfers by Meta and creates task force on Chat GPT', European Data Protection Board, 13 April 2023. Available at: www.edpb.europa.eu/news/news/2023/edpb-resolves-dispute-transfers-meta-and-creates-task-force-chat-gpt_en.

[51] S Dunn 'OpenAI's ChatGPT Facing Scrutiny in Italy for Data Protection Infringements [Online]. Crypto News Network' (30 January 2024). Available at: www.ccn.com/news/technology/openais-chatgpt-scrutiny-italy-data-protection-infringements/.

The intricate balance between harnessing the capabilities of data scraping and adhering to the GDPR emphasises the need for a nuanced approach to data consent. However, while the industry works to align these technical practices with legal standards, a parallel digital trend further complicates the landscape: using deceptive design strategies to circumvent user consent. This leads us from a discussion on the challenges of legitimate data use to the ethical and regulatory issues surrounding these manipulative design practices, setting the stage for a deeper exploration of how such tactics not only conflict with the principles of data protection but also fundamentally undermine user autonomy and informed decision-making.

VII. Circumventing the Consent Requirement Through Deceptive Design

The necessity for obtaining consent has led some companies to employ design strategies known as 'dark patterns', a term first coined by Brignull in 2010.[52] These are deceptive design techniques used to coerce, steer, or deceive users into making unintended decisions.[53] Recent scholarly work, including a taxonomy proposed by Gray et al., seeks a transdisciplinary approach to unify the study of dark patterns, aiming to avert fragmentation across research domains.[54] Despite increasing awareness of these deceptive designs, a gap often exists between privacy attitudes and behaviours.[55] Factors like information asymmetry and bounded rationality influence user decisions; users often lack the knowledge or psychological capacity to make fully informed choices.[56] Dark patterns exploit these psychological mechanisms, often leading to economic and non-economic harms, affecting privacy and autonomy and causing psychological distress.[57]

[52] Harry Brignull, 'Dark Patterns: Deception vs. Honesty in UI Design' (A List Apart, 1 November 2011). Available at: https://alistapart.com/article/dark-patterns-deception-vs.-honesty-in-ui-design/; See also Harry Brignull, 'Dark Patterns: User Interfaces Designed to Trick People'. UX Brighton Conference, Brighton, UK. Available at: www.slideshare.net/harrybr/ux-brighton-dark-patterns.

[53] European Data Protection Board, 'Guidelines 02/2022 on the Application of Article 60 GDPR' (EDPB, 14 March 2022). Available at: https://edpb.europa.eu/system/files/2022-03/guidelines_202202_on_the_application_of_article_60_gdpr_en.pdf.

[54] Colin M Gray et al, 'Mobilizing Research and Regulatory Action on Dark Patterns and Deceptive Design Practices' (2024) in *Extended Abstracts of the CHI Conference on Human Factors in Computing Systems* (CHI EA'24). Association for Computing Machinery.

[55] Idris Adjerid, Eyal Peer and Alessandro Acquisti, 'Beyond the Privacy Paradox' (2018) 42(2) *MIS Quarterly* 465.

[56] Mark Leiser, 'The Problem with "Dots": Questioning the Role of Rationality in the Online Environment' (2016) 30 *International Review of Law, Computers & Technology* 191.

[57] Christoph Bösch et al, 'Tales of Dark Patterns and Their Influence on Consumer Decisions' (2016) 14 *IEEE Security & Privacy* 45; Colin M Gray et al, (2018) 'The Dark (Patterns) Side of UX Design' in *Proceedings of the 2018 CHI Conference on Human Factors in Computing Systems*, 1.

Deceptive design refers to methods and strategies embedded within digital environments that manipulate user decision-making processes, leading to outcomes that users might not have chosen if fully informed or free from manipulation. These tactics exploit cognitive biases and can be intricately woven into surface-level user interfaces and the underlying system architectures.[58] They can range from overt nudges to subtler forms that are less detectable yet potentially more harmful, as they can influence behaviour without clear user awareness. These strategies are not confined to consumer law or data protection but span a range of disciplines, including digital rights, child protection, and algorithmic transparency. This interdisciplinary approach underscores the need for a definition that captures the broad impact of such designs beyond simple economic or privacy concerns.

Yet, targeted advertising has become crucial within the advertising industry, enhancing the likelihood of user engagement. Cookies were introduced in 1994 to facilitate stateful browsing amidst the inherently stateless HTTP protocol. Given the protocol's statelessness, each request to render a website is independent, devoid of any memory of previous interactions. Cookies allow storing small data fragments on web browsers, encapsulating data pertinent to authentication, user preferences, or session identifiers – such as maintaining items in a shopping basket while continuing to shop. A name, a value, an associated URL and an expiry date characterise each cookie; those related to that URL are transmitted upon a request from the browser to a server. However, this practice entails notable privacy risks, as tracking through cookies can reveal extensive and sensitive personal information. The European Union amended the e-Privacy Directive (PECD) in response to these concerns in 2009.[59] Article 5(3) of the PECD requires user consent to store or access information on a user's terminal equipment.

Cookies are categorised broadly into four types: strictly necessary cookies, which are indispensable for the website's essential functions; performance cookies, which collect anonymised data on visitor interactions to gauge popular pages; functional cookies, which enhance user experience by enabling personalised features like language settings; and targeting or advertising cookies, employed to monitor browsing behaviours for tailored advertising. Initially conceived to enhance user experience, a significant portion of today's cookies are now utilised for tracking, primarily to gather data for targeted advertising. Even essential cookies require clear disclosure of their purposes.

The most prevalent method of obtaining consent is through cookie banners, which vary widely in design due to the absence of standardised formats. Studies

[58] Mark Leiser AND Cristiana Santos, 'Dark Patterns, Enforcement, and the Emerging Digital Design Acquis: Manipulation Beneath the Interface' (Forthcoming, 2024) *European Journal of Law and Technology*. Vol. 15 No. 1 (2024): BILETA Special Issue, https://ejlt.org/index.php/ejlt/article/view/990.

[59] Directive 2002/58/EC of the European Parliament and of the Council of 12 July 2002 concerning the processing of personal data and the protection of privacy in the electronic communications sector (Directive on privacy and electronic communications) [2002] OJ L201/37.

identify three main types of banners: those that merely notify of cookie use, allow users to accept or decline cookies altogether and offer granular control over different cookie types.[60] One common manifestation is the strategic placement and design of "Accept All" buttons in cookie banners. These buttons are often prominently displayed and attractively coloured, making them more likely to be clicked.[61] Conversely, options that allow users to reject or customise their consent are typically less conspicuous, presented in smaller fonts, or tucked away behind multiple navigation steps. Such design not only skews user behaviour towards consent but also makes it challenging for users to understand the full scope of their consent and the data processing that will occur.[62]

These manipulative strategies exist along a visibility spectrum ranging from easily recognisable manipulations to those deeply embedded within the algorithms that govern digital interactions. This spectrum is crucial to understanding how they operate at different levels of user interaction and awareness. Enforcement actions and regulatory frameworks in the EU and elsewhere often focus on consumer and data protection aspects of these designs, highlighting their role in misleading users and violating privacy norms.[63] The growing use of complex algorithms and AI in crafting user experiences necessitates a definition that considers both the design elements visible to users and those that operate behind the scenes, influencing user behaviour in ways that are not immediately apparent.[64]

These designs pose significant challenges to acquiring user consent, particularly in digital environments. For example, pre-checked boxes for consent to data sharing or marketing communications are prevalent. These tactics exploit user inattention and inertia, leading users to grant permissions without explicit intention. They complicate the decision-making process by hiding essential information or making it difficult to access. Such manipulation includes confusing language, placing important details in fine print, or requiring users to navigate multiple menus to find privacy settings.

Pre-selected choices or default settings that inherently favour data collection without explicit user interaction pose significant challenges to informed consent. These default configurations may lead individuals to agree to more extensive data processing than they would if they were making an active, informed decision. Websites obscuring necessary information within complex navigational structures

[60] Arunesh Mathur, Mihir Kshirsagar and Jonathan Mayer, (2021) 'What Makes a Dark Pattern … Dark? Design Attributes, Normative Considerations, and Measurement Methods' in *Proceedings of the 2021 CHI Conference on Human Factors in Computing Systems*, 1.

[61] Than Htut Soe, Cristiana Teixeira Santos, Marija Slavkovik, (2022) 'Automated Detection of Dark Patterns on Cookie Banners: How to Do It Poorly and Why It Is Hard To Do It Any Other Way'. Available at: *arXiv preprint arXiv:2204.11836*, last accessed 30 March 2024.

[62] Cristiana Santos et al, (2021) 'Cookie Banners, What's the Purpose? Analyzing Cookie Banner Text Through a Legal Lens' *Proceedings of the 20th Workshop on Workshop on Privacy in the Electronic Society*, 187.

[63] ibid.

[64] Mark Leiser, 'Psychological Patterns and Article 5 of the AI Act' (2024) 1 *Journal of AI Law and Regulation* 4.

or using technical jargon impede users' decision-making. This practice contradicts the GDPR stipulations, which mandate that consent should be informed and rest upon a clear understanding of the data processing terms to which the user is consenting.

Such designs impair a user's ability to make informed choices, effectively burying the information needed to understand the requested consent. Users often find themselves in a position where they must agree to unrelated terms and conditions to access a service. This 'bundling' of consent forces users to accept all terms unrelated to the primary service under the guise of a single acceptance action. This practice undermines the principle of specific and informed consent, as it does not allow users to choose what they agree to independently. Specific design strategies complicate altering or withdrawing consent by embedding these options within cumbersome user interfaces or prolonging the opt-out process. This makes it challenging for users to withdraw consent and infringes on GDPR mandates, which uphold the user's right to revoke consent at any point quickly.

Some platforms implement deceptive design strategies that repeatedly prompt users to consent, a tactic known as 'nagging'. This can wear down user resistance and lead to consent being given to stop the interruptions. This type of consent is not genuine as it is given under duress and not out of an informed and free choice. Such strategies exploit users' cognitive biases, such as the default effect, where users are more likely to stick with pre-selected options, or decision fatigue, where users' ability to make optimal decisions deteriorates with the number of decisions they have made. These practices can significantly distort the consent process, leading to choices that do not reflect the user's preferences or interests. Children, in particular, are at a higher risk as they may lack the maturity to understand consent processes fully. Strategies targeting this demographic can lead to consent that is not genuinely informed, leveraging children's less developed cognitive skills to obtain agreement for data collection and processing that serve the platform's interests rather than the child's. They compromise the integrity of user decisions, violating principles of transparency, autonomy, and fairness that are foundational to user trust and legal compliance in digital interactions.

Obtaining user consent for data processing and tracking has become a critical requirement for website operators. With the increased scrutiny of data protection practices, particularly under the GDPR, businesses must ensure that their methods for securing consent are legally sound. To navigate this landscape, operators must avoid deceptive design practices and adopt transparent, user-friendly approaches that respect user autonomy. Recent legal judgments, such as the Rostock Regional Court's decision in September 2020, have reinforced the necessity for explicit and lawful consent mechanisms.[65] This case underscored several critical aspects of consent, which include the need for explicit consent where pre-ticked boxes or implied consent mechanisms, such as assuming consent from continued site

[65] Landgericht Rostock (Germany), 22 September 2020. Available at: www.vzbv.de/sites/default/files/downloads/2020/11/25/lg_rostock_15.09.2020.pdf.

usage, are deemed insufficient. The ruling emphasised the equivalence of options, ensuring that consenting and declining are presented as equally viable choices so that users do not feel coerced into giving consent. Moreover, transparency about data sharing is essential, particularly when data is shared with third parties, which must be disclosed and accessible.

The ruling advises website operators to adopt several compliance strategies to align with these legal requirements and best practices. They should use unambiguous language to explain the use of cookies and their impact on user experience and privacy, avoiding technical jargon or vague terms that could confuse users. Implementing mechanisms requiring users to actively select their preferences, such as toggling switches or checking boxes, is crucial to ensure that consent is explicit and informed. Consent banners or dialogues should present all choices – accept, reject, customise – equally, using the same font size, colour, and style. Designers should avoid making 'Accept' buttons more prominent or visually appealing than other options. Additionally, it is essential to allow users easy access to detailed settings to manage their cookie preferences or withdraw their consent at any time through a simple and intuitive interface. Website operators must be transparent and provide detailed information about the types of cookies used and the data each type collects, either directly on the consent banner or through easily accessible links.

Pre-selecting consent boxes, a practice now widely recognised as non-compliant with GDPR requirements for explicit consent, should be avoided. Operators should keep records of what each user has consented to, including what information was made available at the time of consent, ensuring that this documentation is easily accessible for both the user and the business. Regular reviews and audits of consent practices and privacy policies should be conducted to align with evolving legal standards and best practices, helping to identify and rectify issues before they become compliance risks.

Educating users about data privacy through clear and accessible informational resources is another crucial strategy. This approach helps build trust and ensures users make informed decisions. Finally, ensuring that consent mechanisms are effectively designed for all devices, especially mobile devices where a significant amount of web traffic occurs, is essential. Mobile interfaces should allow for easy navigation of consent choices without compromising usability. By implementing these strategies, website operators can ensure that their practices comply with legal requirements while respecting and protecting user rights. This approach mitigates legal risks, enhances the company's reputation, builds consumer trust, and supports a more ethical digital economy.

VIII. Conclusion

Consent has a crucial normative function and constitutional role within EU data protection law. However, as Edenberg and Leta-Jones have argued, the legitimacy of consent is not a binary question, and it must be evaluated contextually.[66] Consent should not, in other words, best 'the entire burden of protecting privacy'.[67] We must scrutinise both the normative role and the practical capacity of consent. Building on the foundation laid in the earlier sections of this chapter, it is clear that the GDPR's conceptualisation of consent has both fortified and complicated the legal architecture around data protection. The challenges become increasingly intricate as we have explored consent's complexities and evolving dynamics, especially in the digital age dominated by technologies like AI and extensive data analytics. The implications for policy, law, and individual rights are profound, necessitating a continuous re-evaluation of strategies to maintain the effectiveness and integrity of consent as a protective mechanism.

Looking forward, the discourse around consent must include the theoretical underpinnings and regulatory frameworks and the practical realities of implementing these concepts in a fast-paced digital environment. The burgeoning use of LLMs and the pervasive practices in AdTech to obtain consent for behavioural advertising presents quintessential examples where the existing frameworks often fall short. These areas, challenging the traditional boundaries of consent, underscore the urgent need for innovative regulatory approaches and more robust oversight mechanisms. The practice of scraping the internet for data, including personal data, to train LLMs like GPT highlights significant issues related to consent. The traditional model of obtaining explicit, informed consent becomes problematic when data is ubiquitous, and its use extends beyond the immediate context in which it was shared. This disconnect raises critical questions about the viability of consent frameworks designed for more straightforward data transactions. The shift toward using vast datasets for AI training necessitates reconsidering how consent is obtained, documented, and verified, ensuring it meets the stringent requirements set forth by the GDPR while also adapting to the scale and complexity of modern data use.

Similarly, the strategies employed in AdTech to secure consent for behavioural advertising often reveal a gap between regulatory expectations and market practices. The use of dark patterns and other manipulative tactics to obtain consent not only undermines user autonomy but also challenges the legal foundations upon which such consent is considered valid. Addressing these practices requires a concerted effort from regulators to tighten enforcement and redefine what constitutes genuine consent in contexts where sophisticated psychological triggers and opaque algorithmic processes drive user engagement.

To navigate these challenges, regulatory bodies and policymakers must engage in a dynamic process of adaptation and enforcement. This effort includes developing more precise guidelines on using personal data in AI, refining the legal interpretations of consent to address the nuances of digital interactions, enforcing

[66] Edenberg and Leta-Jones (n 23).

[67] Solon Barocas and Helen Nissenbaum, 'Computing Ethics: Big Data's End Run Around Procedural Privacy Protections', (2014) 57 *Communication of the ACM* 31, 33.

existing regulations with renewed vigour and focusing on real-world impacts rather than theoretical compliance. Moreover, data protection authorities play a crucial role in this landscape. DPAs need to be proactive, not only in enforcement but also in guiding organisations on best practices for obtaining and managing consent. Their role in educating users and data controllers on the evolving interpretations of consent and the ethical use of data is invaluable.

As we conclude this exploration of consent within the framework of European data protection law, it is evident that the journey towards a truly robust and effective consent mechanism is ongoing. The dual forces of technological advancement and evolving legal standards demand a dynamic approach to consent that respects individuals' rights while accommodating the practical realities of digital markets. The future of consent in data protection will likely see a greater emphasis on transparency, enhanced user controls, and a shift towards more granular choices for data subjects. These changes will require legislative and regulatory updates and a cultural shift in how organisations and individuals perceive and value privacy. By striving for a consent paradigm that is both meaningful and adaptable, we can navigate the complexities of modern data use without compromising the fundamental rights that lie at the heart of data protection law.

4

Five Years of the Illegitimacy of Surveillance Advertising

LEX ZARD

I. Setting the Stage

On 28 January 2010, on Data Protection Day, Commissioner Viviane Reding announced that digital transformation required personal data protection reform.[1] Commissioner Reding warned that surveillance advertising was a central challenge to Europeans' privacy.[2] Surveillance advertising is a business model that monetises websites and apps with advertiser money and without the consumer's monetary payment.[3] It has also been a central revenue stream for technology giants such as Alphabet (previously Google) and Meta (previously Facebook), which in 2023 were valued at $2.5 trillion.[4]

Surveillance advertising entails monitoring the behaviour of a consumer (or an internet user), algorithmically inferring their interests and traits (often referred to as 'profiling') and matching them with advertisements; therefore, it entails processing vast amounts of personal data.[5] Surveillance advertising is more often called online behavioural advertising (OBA) and is referred to interchangeably in the chapter.[6]

[1] See 'Europeans' Privacy Will Be Big Challenge in next Decade, Says EU Commissioner' (European Commission Press Release IP/10/63, 28 January 2010). Available at: https://ec.europa.eu/commission/presscorner/detail/en/IP_10_63, last accessed 16 November 2023.

[2] ibid. ('Our privacy faces new challenges: behavioural advertising can use your internet history to better market products.')

[3] See generally Shoshana Zuboff, *The Age of Surveillance Capitalism: The Fight For A Human Future at The New Frontier of Power* (First edition, PublicAffairs 2019).

[4] See 'Largest Companies by Market Cap' (*Companiesmarketcap*). Available at: https://companiesmarketcap.com/, last accessed 16 November 2023.

[5] See generally Frederik Zuiderveen Borgesius, *Improving Privacy Protection in the Area of Behavioral Targeting* (Wolters Kluwer, Information Law Series), vol 33 (2015).

[6] See Sophie C Boerman, Sanne Kruikemeier and Frederik J Zuiderveen Borgesius, 'Online Behavioral Advertising: A Literature Review and Research Agenda' (2017) 46 *Journal of Advertising* 363.

The Charter of Fundamental Rights of the European Union (CFREU) entered into force in 2009, shortly after Meta launched its advertising platform, including the controversial advertising *Beacon* that surveiled consumers over the Internet without their knowledge.[7] Article 8 of the CFREU established a regime in which personal data processing interferes with human rights unless there is a legal ground provided by law, for example, the *consent* of the person involved.[8] Indeed, under the Data Protection Directive 1995 (DPD), consumer consent was possibly the only legal ground that could legitimise surveillance advertising.[9] Nevertheless, incentivised by surveillance advertising profits, digital service providers have often collected consumer data in predatory ways. One prevalent way entailed showing consumers pre-ticked consent boxes which was later, in 2019, found illegal by the Court of Justice of the European Union (CJEU).[10]

Data protection reform was primarily intended to ensure consumers' authentic choices in an online environment by strengthening the rules for valid consent.[11] The surveillance advertising industry responded to the reform by avoiding asking consumers for consent altogether. On 25 May 2018, when the General Data Protection Regulation (GDPR)[12] entered force, Meta changed its legal basis for surveillance advertising practices from consumer consent to 'contractual necessity'.[13] Following initial litigation, Meta switched to 'legitimate interest', again resisting asking their consumers if they wanted to be tracked for surveillance advertising.[14] On 27 October 2023, the European Data Protection Board (EDPB) decided to ban Meta's surveillance advertising practices across the EU unless Meta asked

[7] See Betsy Schiffman, 'Facebook Is Always Watching You' *Wired* (4 December 2007). Available at: www.wired.com/2007/12/facebooks-is-al, last accessed 20 April 2023.

[8] Consolidated Version of the Charter of Fundamental Rights of The European Union [2012], OJ (C326) 391, art. 8 [hereafter CFREU]. See Jiahong Chen, *Regulating Online Behavioural Advertising Through Data Protection Law* (Edward Elgar Publishing, 2021) 92.

[9] See Frederik J Zuiderveen Borgesius, 'Personal Data Processing for Behavioural Targeting: Which Legal Basis?' (2015) 5 *International Data Privacy Law* [176]. Available at: https://academic.oup.com/idpl/article/5/3/163/730611, last accessed 1 May 2023. See Article 29 Data Protection Working Party, 'Opinion 06/2014 on the Notion of Legitimate Interests of the Data Controller under Article 7 of Directive 95/46/EC (WP217)' (2017) 17. ('[Contractual necessity] is not a suitable legal ground for building a profile of the user's tastes and lifestyle choices based on his clickstream on a website and the items purchased. This is because the data controller has not been contracted to carry out profiling, but rather to deliver particular goods and services, for example'.)

[10] Case C-673/17, *Planet49*, EU:C:2019:801.

[11] Bart W Schermer, Bart Custers and Simone van der Hof, 'The Crisis of Consent: How Stronger Legal Protection May Lead to Weaker Consent in Data Protection' (2014) 16 *Ethics and Information Technology* 171.

[12] Council Regulation (EU) 2016/679 of 27 April 2016 on the protection of natural persons with regard to the processing of personal data and on the free movement of such data, and repealing Directive 95/46/EC (General Data Protection Regulation) 2016 (OJ L 119)1 (hereinafter General Data Protection Regulation).

[13] 'Noyb.Eu Filed Complaints over "Forced Consent" against Google, Instagram, WhatsApp and Facebook' (*noyb*, 25 May 2018). Available at: https://noyb.eu/en/noybeu-filed-complaints-over-forced-consent-against-google-instagram-whatsapp-and-facebook, last accessed 2 May 2023.

[14] 'Meta (Facebook, Instagram) Switching to "Legitimate Interest" for Ads' (*noyb*, 30 March 2023). Available at: https://noyb.eu/en/meta-facebook-instagram-switching-legitimate-interest-ads, last accessed 7 April 2023.

its consumers for consent.[15] As a response, Meta now offers an 'Consent-or-Pay' model, in which consumers have to choose between consenting to give Meta their behavioural data for surveillance advertising or paying €9.99/month.[16]

Apart from Meta, the broader surveillance advertising industry, often called AdTech (referring to advertising technology facilitating the trade), has also been caught up in litigation that challenged the legitimacy of data processing practices within third-party surveillance advertising.[17] Since the entry into force of the GDPR, consumers visiting any given website online have been surveiled by hundreds of AdTech companies ('vendors'), what seems incompatible with the general principles of the EU data protection law.[18] Nevertheless, while there are serious concerns regarding the legitimacy of surveillance advertising, which is responsible for a large share of online advertising,[19] in 2018–2022, online advertising expenditure amounted to €330 billion in Europe.[20]

This chapter evaluates the legitimacy of surveillance advertising under Article 6 of the GDPR regarding the legal basis for processing personal data. For this purpose, it describes and analyses the enforcement and judicial processes since the GDPR entered into force until the end of 2023. This chapter gives particular attention to Meta's surveillance advertising practice, as Meta is both the primary beneficiary of and the standard setter in the surveillance advertising industry.

II. Regulating Surveillance Advertising

Surveillance advertising, or online behavioural advertising (OBA), shows consumers personalised advertisements based on behavioural data.[21] Surveillance advertising is one of several configurations of personalised online advertising. It entails 'profiling' or sorting consumers into segments based on interests

[15] European Data Protection Board, 'EDPB Urgent Binding Decision on Processing of Personal Data for Behavioural Advertising by Meta' (European Data Protection Board, 1 November 2023). Available at: https://edpb.europa.eu/news/news/2023/edpb-urgent-binding-decision-processing-personal-data-behavioural-advertising-meta_en, last accessed 16 November 2023.

[16] 'How We Show Ads in the European Region' (*Facebook Help Center*). Available at: www.facebook.com/help/631125599118423, last accessed 16 November 2023.

[17] Michael Veale and Frederik Zuiderveen Borgesius, 'Adtech and Real-Time Bidding under European Data Protection Law' (2022) 23 *German Law Journal* 226.

[18] 'RTB Online Ad Auctions' (*Irish Council for Civil Liberties*). Available at: www.iccl.ie/rtb/, last accessed 17 November 2023. See Scott Ikeda, 'Report on RTB: Adtech "Biggest Data Breach Ever Recorded", Online Behavior More Exposed in Countries Without Privacy Regulations' *CPO Magazine* (24 May 2022). Available at: www.cpomagazine.com/data-privacy/report-on-rtb-adtech-biggest-data-breach-ever-recorded-online-behavior-more-exposed-in-countries-without-privacy-regulations/, last accessed 13 October 2023.

[19] 'Digital Advertising Spending in Europe from 2006 to 2022' (*Statista*, May 2023). Available at: www.statista.com/statistics/307005/europe-online-ad-spend/, last accessed 16 November 2023.

[20] iab Europe has reported that surveillance advertising was responsible for 66% of all online advertising. 'Digital Advertising & Marketing: The Value of Digital Advertising' (*iabeurope*). Available at: https://iabeurope.eu/the-value-of-digital-advertising/, last accessed 13 January 2023.

[21] Boerman, Kruikemeier and Zuiderveen Borgesius (n 6) at 364.

('surf enthusiast') or traits ('household income top 10%') that artificial intelligence (AI) systems infer based on consumer's surveiled behaviour.[22] The consumer behavioural data that AI systems rely on for profiling include, among others, web browsing or social media behaviour, mouse cursor movements, geo-location, or keyboard stroke patterns.[23]

Digital platform providers, in particular Alphabet and Meta, are the most prominent *publishers* of surveillance advertising. They allow advertisers to advertise not only on their platforms (e.g., YouTube, Instagram) but also on websites and apps of the other digital service providers (e.g., online newspaper publishers) that join their networks (e.g., Google Display Network, Meta Audience Network).[24] These advertising networks are closed ecosystems where platform providers have end-to-end control of advertising sales and are called 'walled gardens'.[25] Alphabet dominates the search advertising market (Google Search, Google Display Network), and Meta dominates the social media advertising market (Facebook, Instagram, Meta Audience Network).[26] In addition, Alphabet dominates the open exchange market for surveillance advertising, also called AdTech, where all advertising networks, publishers, and advertisers bid for available ad spaces online.[27]

Surveillance advertising requires complex infrastructures and technological capabilities. It entails using AI systems to profile consumers, predicts advertising 'quality scores' and allocate advertising accordingly.[28] Advertising allocation in surveillance advertising is fully automated and occurs via real-time bidding (RTB) programmatic auctions.[29] Data optimise AI systems used in surveillance advertising.[30] For example, the party with the most data typically wins an RTB auction.[31] Therefore, surveillance advertising results in competition for consumer data collection and digital service providers to track consumers over the Internet,

[22] Lex Zard and Alan M Sears, 'Targeted Advertising and Consumer Protection Law in the European Union' (2023) 56 *Vanderbilt Journal of Transnational Law* 795, 800.

[23] Zuiderveen Borgesius (n 5) at 35–38.

[24] Competition and Markets Authority, 'Online Platforms and Digital Advertising: Market Study Appendix M: Intermediation in Open Display Advertising' (2020). Available at: www.gov.uk/cma-cases/online-platforms-and-digital-advertising-market-study.

[25] European Parliament, Policy Department for Citizens' Rights and Constitutional Affairs Directorate-General for Internal Policies, 'Regulating Targeted and Behavioural Advertising in Digital Services: How to Ensure Users' Informed Consent' (Study, PE 694.680, September 2021) 19. Available at: www.europarl.europa.eu/RegData/etudes/STUD/2021/694680/IPOL_STU(2021)694680_EN.pdf.

[26] Competition and Markets Authority (n 24).

[27] 'Antitrust: Commission Sends Statement of Objections to Google' (*European Commission*, 14 June 2023). Available at: https://ec.europa.eu/commission/presscorner/detail/en/ip_23_3207, last accessed 16 July 2023.

[28] European Parliament, Policy Department for Economic, Scientific and Quality of Life Policies, 'Online Advertising: The Impact of Targeted Advertising on Advertisers, Market Access and Consumer Choice' (Study, PE 662.913, June 2021) 25. Available at: www.europarl.europa.eu/thinktank/en/document/IPOL_STU(2021)662913.

[29] Veale and Zuiderveen Borgesius (n 17).

[30] European Parliament, Policy Department for Citizens' Rights and Constitutional Affairs Directorate-General for Internal Policies (n 25) 41–53.

[31] ibid.

typically by placing so-called 'cookies' on consumer devices.[32] As large platform providers such as Alphabet and Meta are 'gatekeepers' of the Internet and control access to consumer data, they dominate relative online advertising markets.[33]

Surveillance advertising can exploit consumers.[34] Consumer exploitation can lead to a direct economic detriment to the consumer (e.g., needless transactions) or structural harm through market failures, such as reduced innovation, reduced quality of content and services, increased prices, reduced welfare, and reduced trust in the market.[35] It can also contribute to *environmental harm* due to increased carbon emissions, battery overuse and electronic waste, as well as negatively affecting animal welfare.[36] It can lead to *affinity* harms such as discrimination and oppression of specific (often marginalised) groups.[37] Its *privacy* harms include emotional distress, disturbance, thwarted expectations, and anxiety.[38]

Consumer exploitation can lead to *authenticity* harms such as loss of (time for) consortium, leisure, and earnings.[39] It can also result in *integrity* harms that include adverse effects on mental and physical health and fitness of varying severity (e.g., self-harm, loss of life).[40] Lastly, consumer exploitation via surveillance advertising may lead to *dignity* harm or societal harm to future generations, democratic processes and consumer self-esteem by creating an online environment in which consumers cannot be vulnerable as they face the systemic risk of exploitation.[41]

[32] European Parliament, Policy Department for Economic, Scientific and Quality of Life Policies, 'Online Advertising: The Impact of Targeted Advertising on Advertisers, Market Access and Consumer Choice' (Study, PE 662.913, June 2021) 25. Available at: www.europarl.europa.eu/thinktank/en/document/IPOL_STU(2021)662913.

[33] European Commission, Directorate-General for Communications Network, Content and Technology and others, 'Study on the Impact of Recent Developments in Digital Advertising on Privacy, Publishers, and Advertisers' (2023) 37. Available at: https://data.europa.eu/doi/10.2759/294673.

[34] Joanna Strycharz and Bram Duivenvoorde, 'The Exploitation of Vulnerability Through Personalised Marketing Communication: Are Consumers Protected?' (2021) 10 *Internet Policy Review* 4. See, eg, Philipp Hacker, 'Manipulation by Algorithms. Exploring the Triangle of Unfair Commercial Practice, Data Protection, and Privacy Law' [2021] *European Law Journal* Available at: https://onlinelibrary.wiley.com/doi/full/10.1111/eulj.12389, last accessed 6 October 2023.

[35] *Tal Z Zarsky, 'Privacy and Manipulation in the Digital Age' (2019) 20 Theoretical Inquiries in Law* 172. Ryan Calo, 'Digital Market Manipulation' (2014) 82 *George Washington Law Review* 1025. See Competition and Markets Authority, 'Online Platforms and Digital Advertising: Market Study Final Report' (2020) 309–21. Available at: www.gov.uk/cma-cases/online-platforms-and-digital-advertising-market-study.

[36] Patrick Hartmann and others, 'Perspectives: Advertising and Climate Change – Part of the Problem or Part of the Solution?' (2023) 42 *International Journal of Advertising* 430. See Matti Pärssinen and others, 'Environmental Impact Assessment of Online Advertising' (2018) 73 *Environmental Impact Assessment Review* 177. See European Commission, Directorate-General for Communications Networks, Content and Technology and others (n 33) 89–96.

[37] Sandra Wachter, 'Affinity Profiling and Discrimination by Association in Online Behavioural Advertising' (2020) 35 *Berkley Technology Law Journal* 2.

[38] *Daniel Keats Citron and Daniel J Solove, 'Privacy Harms' (2022) 102 Boston University Law Review* 841.

[39] Cass R Sunstein, 'Manipulation as Theft' (2022) 29 *Journal of European Public Policy* 1959.

[40] Matija Franklin and others, 'The EU's AI Act Needs to Address Critical Manipulation Methods' (*OECD.AI*, 21 March 2023). Available at: https://oecd.ai/en/wonk/ai-act-manipulation-methods accessed 28 March 2023.

[41] European Commission, Directorate-General for Communications Networks, Content and Technology and others (n 33) 80–88. See 'Ledger of Harms' (*Center for Humane Technology*). Available at: https://ledger.humanetech.com/, last accessed 18 November 2023.

The legal framework of the European Union (EU) heavily regulates surveillance advertising. Firstly, as a business-to-consumer commercial practice, consumer protection law requires digital service providers to respect consumer autonomy.[42] The Unfair Commercial Practices Directive (UCPD), more specifically, establishes boundaries for consumer exploitation via surveillance advertising.[43] Secondly, the Directive on Privacy and Electronic Communications (ePrivacy Directive) regulates the tracking of consumers across the internet[44] while the General Data Protection Regulation (GDPR), the focus of this book, sets rules for processing personal data.[45] Thirdly, competition law grounded in Articles 101 and 102 of the Treaty of the Functioning of the EU (TFEU)[46] also protects consumers from exploitation.[47]

In 2022, the EU introduced the Digital Services Act (DSA) and the Digital Markets Act (DMA), which regulate platform providers and their advertising practices.[48] The DSA explicitly prohibits some forms of surveillance advertising aiming to safeguard against societal harms.[49] In contrast, the DMA aims to disperse the data power of the prominent platform service providers, such as Alphabet and Meta, to ensure contestability in digital markets, including in surveillance advertising, and safeguard the authentic choice of consumers.[50] Lastly, by 2024, the EU will likely finalise a proposal for the Artificial Intelligence Act (AIA) that sets further boundaries for consumer exploitation via artificial intelligence (AI), also when used for advertising.[51]

[42] Federico Galli, *Algorithmic Marketing and EU Law on Unfair Commercial Practices*, vol 50 (Springer International Publishing 2022). See also, Jan Trzaskowski, *Your Privacy Is Important to US!* (2021).

[43] Council Directive (EC) 2005/29 of 11 May 2005 concerning unfair business-to-consumer commercial practices in the internal market and amending Council Directive 84/450/EEC, Directives 97/7/EC, 98/27/EC and 2002/65/EC and Regulation (EC) No 2006/2004 O.J. 2005 (L 149)22 [hereinafter Unfair Commercial Practices Directive]. See Trzaskowski ibid. 29–31.

[44] Council Directive (EC) 2002/58 of 12 July 2002 concerning the processing of personal data and the protection of privacy in the electronic communications sector OJ 2002 (L 201)31 [hereinafter ePrivacy Directive].

[45] General Data Protection Regulation.

[46] Consolidated Version of the Treaty on the Functioning of the European Union [2016] OJ (C 202) 47 arts 101–02 [hereinafter TFEU].

[47] Inge Graef, 'Consumer Sovereignty and Competition Law: From Personalization to Diversity' (2021) 58 *Common Market Law Review* 471.

[48] Council Regulation (EU) 2022/2065 of 19 October 2022 on a Single Market For Digital Services and amending Directive 2000/31/EC (Digital Services Act) (Text with EEA relevance) OJ 2022 (L 277) 1. See Council Regulation (EU) 2022/1925 of 14 September 2022 on contestable and fair markets in the digital sector and amending Directives (EU) 2019/1937 and (EU) 2020/1828 (Digital Markets Act) OJ 2022 (L 265) 1.

[49] Digital Services Act, recital 69.

[50] Digital Markets Act. Note that, the DMA mentions 'choice' in the context of the consumer 23 times in the final text.

[51] Commission, 'Proposal for a Council Regulation Laying Down Harmonised Rules on Artificial Intelligence (Artificial Intelligence Act)', COD (2021) 0106 DRAFT (20 June, 2023) [hereinafter Proposal for Artificial Intelligence Act]. The cited version includes the European Commission proposal, as well as European Parliament (EP.AIA) and Council (C.AIA) mandates.

The EU legal framework safeguards against surveillance advertising harms in four significant ways: (i) by putting in place prohibitions for unacceptable surveillance advertising practices – for example, Article 26(3) of the DSA prohibits 'online platforms' from using special categories of data for OBA[52] and Article 28(2) of the DSA prohibits them from targeting minors with surveillance ads;[53] (ii) by ensuring consumer transparency through information disclosure rules – for example, Article 26 (1) of the DSA requires 'online platforms' to disclose information regarding OBA, such as the identity of an advertiser and ad-targeting criteria;[54] (iii) by putting in place risk assessment and mitigation rules, for example, Article 34 of the DSA requires very large online platforms (VLOPs) and search engines (VLOSEs) to conduct risk assessments of their surveillance advertising practices;[55] and (iv) by putting in place transparency and data access rules that enable enforcers to hold digital service providers accountable in their OBA practices, for example, Article 39 of the DSA requires VLOPs/VLOSEs to keep advertising repositories.[56]

One of the most potent legislative tools for safeguarding consumers against the harms of surveillance advertising is the GDPR. Surveillance advertising relies on data, such as consumers' browsing history (e.g., visited websites, used apps) or their on-service behaviour (e.g., clicks, likes), that in the EU qualifies as 'personal data' because it relates to an identified or identifiable individual.[57] This means that the GDPR prohibits all surveillance advertising unless the digital service provider actively legitimises it by meeting the requirements of Article 6(1) of the GDPR requirements.[58] In other words, all digital service providers that want to engage in surveillance advertising in the EU must comply with the GDPR, which regards the processing of personal data as prohibited *unless* service providers demonstrate they meet the legal grounds prescribed in Article 6(1).[59] The section below provides an analysis of how surveillance advertising can be legitimised.

[52] Digital Services Act, recital 69.

[53] ibid. art 28(3).

[54] ibid. art 26(1).

[55] ibid. art 34.

[56] ibid. art 39.

[57] Zuiderveen Borgesius (n 10). By the time the GDPR entered into force in 2018, there was consensus that OBA constitutes personal data processing because it enables singling out a particular individual, even without having data connected to a person's name. See, Frederik J Zuiderveen Borgesius, 'Singling out People without Knowing Their Names – Behavioural Targeting, Pseudonymous Data, and the New Data Protection Regulation' (2016) 32 *Computer Law & Security Review* 256. See GDPR, recital 30. ('Natural persons may be associated with online identifiers provided by their devices, applications, tools and protocols, such as internet protocol addresses, cookie identifiers or other identifiers such as radio frequency identification tags. This may leave traces which, in particular when combined with unique identifiers and other information received by the servers, may be used to create profiles of the natural persons and identify them.')

[58] *Urgent and Provisional Measures – Meta* [2023] *Datatilsynet* 21/03530-16 17.

[59] GDPR, art 6(1).

III. The GDPR and Legitimising Surveillance Advertising

Article 6(1) of the GDPR lists six legal grounds that can legitimise personal data processing activities.[60] Three of these six legal grounds are almost never thought to legitimise surveillance advertising: Article (1)(c) of the GDPR legitimises the processing of personal data that is directly required by law (legal obligation); Article (1)(d) of the GDPR legitimises processing that is in the vital interest of data subject (e.g., saving their life); and Article (1)(e) legitimises practices that are in the public interest (e.g., public health during a pandemic).[61]

In practice, digital service providers have relied on three other legal bases for surveillance. These three grounds are analysed in the next three sections in the following order: section III.A analyses the validity of processing surveillance advertising data because it 'is necessary for the performance of a contract' under Article 6(1)(b) of the GDPR; section III.B analyses the validity of processing surveillance advertising data due to 'legitimate interest' of publishers to engage in OBA under Article 6(1)(f); and section III.C analyses consumer's consent under Article 6(1)(a) as a legal basis for surveillance ads.

Contractual Necessity

Article 6(1)(b) of the GDPR allows the processing of personal data when this is 'necessary for the performance of a contract'.[62] This provision considers that sometimes contracts cannot be performed and services cannot be provided if the consumer does not provide personal data.[63] (e.g., a consumer pays with a credit card for a product available on an online marketplace and requests its delivery to their home address).[64] The digital service provider cannot process a purchase without bank details or deliver a product to the consumer's home address unless the consumer provides this data. In this case, Article (6)(1)(b) of the GDPR allows the online marketplace to process the consumer's card details and address based on contractual necessity.[65]

On 25 May 2018, when the GDPR came into force with strengthened requirements for consent, Meta updated its terms and conditions, stating that it processed

[60] ibid.

[61] GDPR, art 6(1)(e). Meta has previously argued that their surveillance advertising practices are in the public interest because they create infrastructure supporting the 'free' internet and fund the media. The CJEU regarded such an argument unsurprisingly invalid. Case C-252/21, *Meta v Bundeskartellamt*, EU:C:2023:537, [127]–[139].

[62] GDPR, art 6(1)(b).

[63] European Data Protection Board, 'Guidelines 2/2019 on the Processing of Personal Data under Article 6(1)(b) GDPR in the Context of the Provision of Online Services to Data Subjects' (2019) 2.

[64] ibid. 35.

[65] ibid.

the consumer personal data under Article 6(1)(b) of the GDPR because such data was necessary to perform a 'core service' of Meta's platforms (Facebook, Instagram), now framed as 'personalised experience', including personalised advertisement.[66] On the same day, *Noyb*, a digital rights organisation that can be said to act as the 'private prosecutor' for enforcing the GDPR,[67] filed a complaint with the Austrian Data Protection Authority (DPA).[68] Noyb argued that Meta had attempted to bypass the GDPR's strict consent requirements and engaged in illegitimate surveillance advertising.[69] As Meta's EU head office is located in Ireland, the Austrian DPA transferred the case to the Irish DPA.[70]

In 2014, the European Data Protection Board (EDPB) argued that contractual necessity was not a suitable legal ground for surveillance advertising within the context of the 1995 DPD which preceded the GDPR.[71] In 2019, the EDPB reiterated that digital service providers could not rely on Article 6(1)(b) of the GDPR as the legal basis for OBA.[72] However, in 2021, the Irish DPA published a *draft* decision suggesting that Meta's reliance on Article 6(1)(b) was valid.[73] The reasoning of the Irish DPA supported Meta's argument that *if* surveillance advertising was Meta's core service to consumers, then processing personal data for OBA was, indeed, necessary. The Irish DPA avoided evaluating the validity of the contractual clause that surveillance advertising was, in fact, Meta's core service to consumers, pointing to a lack of competence in evaluating the contract law.[74]

After several EU DPAs objected to the draft decision, the Irish DPA referred the case to the EDPB which, in July 2022, issued binding decisions that clarified that Meta could not rely on the Article 6 (1)(b) contractual necessity clause as the legal basis for processing personal data for surveillance advertising.[75] The EDPB argued that OBA involves processing an open-ended amount of consumer

[66] 'BREAKING: Meta Prohibited from Use of Personal Data for Advertising' (*noyb*, 4 January 2023). Available at: https://noyb.eu/en/breaking-meta-prohibited-use-personal-data-advertising.

[67] *The End of Online Behavioral Advertising* (CPDP Conferences, 2023). Available at: www.youtube.com/watch?v=FwMz7OLoOXI, last accessed 20 July 2023. *noyb* stands for 'none-of-your-business' and the full name of this organisation is the European Center for Digital Rights.

[68] 'Noyb.Eu Filed Complaints over "Forced Consent" against Google, Instagram, WhatsApp and Facebook' (n 13).

[69] ibid.

[70] Decision of the Data Protection Commission made pursuant to Section 113 of the Data Protection Act, 2018 and Articles 60 and 65 of the General Data Protection Regulation, (Dec. 31, 2022) (Ir.), 49.

[71] Article 29 Data Protection Working Party (n 9) 17. ('[Contractual necessity] is not a suitable legal ground for building a profile of the user's tastes and lifestyle choices based on his clickstream on a website and the items purchased. This is because the data controller has not been contracted to carry out profiling, but rather to deliver particular goods and services, for example.')

[72] EDPB, (n 63) 51–56.

[73] In the matter of LB (through NOYB) v Facebook Ireland Limited Draft Decision for the purposes of Article 60 GDPR of the Data Protection Commission made pursuant to Section 113(2)(a) of the Data Protection Act 2018.

[74] ibid 4.13.

[75] Binding Decision 2/2022 on the dispute arisen on the draft decision of the Irish Supervisory Authority regarding Meta Platforms Ireland Limited (Instagram) under Article 65(1)(a) GDPR, European Data Protection Board (28 Jul 2022).

personal data and cannot be 'strictly necessary' for the contract, even if the subject of the contract is personalisation, including advertising.[76] The EDPB explained that, while it may be less profitable, Meta could personalise advertisements based on limited consumer data, such as that consumers disclose when they sign up (e.g., age, gender and country of residence).[77] The EDPB further states that accepting contractual necessity as a valid legal basis for OBA would make 'theoretically any collection and reuse of personal data' lawful.[78]

Following the EDPB's binding decision, on 31 December 2022, the Irish DPA issued a €390 million fine to Meta, banned the company from engaging in surveillance advertising based on Article 6(1)(b) of the GDPR and gave the company three months to make their OBA practices GDPR compliant.[79] In response to this decision, Meta updated its terms and conditions; since 5 April 2023 it has continued to process personal data for surveillance advertising based on their claimed 'legitimate interest' under Article 6(1)(f).[80]

Legitimate Interest

In parallel to the *Noyb v Meta* litigation regarding Article 6(1)(b) of the GDPR, on 6 February 2019, *Bundeskartellamt* (The Federal Cartel Office), the German competition authority, prohibited Meta from combining personal data from different sources (mainly for surveillance advertising) without consumer consent.[81] Meta appealed the decision, and on 4 July 2023, the CJEU published its judgment in *Meta v Bundeskartellamt*.[82]

Among questions related to Meta's surveillance advertising practices, the CJEU considered whether Meta could rely on Article 6(1)(f) of the GDPR to process consumers' data for OBA. The court echoed the earlier guidance of the EDPB that the legitimate interest clause under Article 6(1)(f) requires that the processing of personal data meets three cumulative conditions:[83] (i) the publishers have a legitimate purpose; (ii) processing of personal data is necessary to meet this purpose ('necessity test'); and (iii) this purpose is balanced against the consumers' interests and fundamental rights ('balancing test').[84] The CJEU evaluated the case based on

[76] Data Protection Commission (n 70) at 49.
[77] EDPB (n 75) at 132.
[78] ibid.
[79] Data Protection Commission (n 70) at 113.
[80] See 'How Meta Uses Legal Bases for Processing Ads in the EU' (*Meta*, 4 January 2023)Available at: https://about.fb.com/news/2023/01/how-meta-uses-legal-bases-for-processing-ads-in-the-eu/, last accessed 7 April 2023.
[81] *Facebook, Exploitative business terms pursuant to Section 19(1) GWB for inadequate data processing* [2019] Bundeskartellamt B6-22/16.
[82] Case C-252/21, *Meta v Bundeskartellamt* (n 61).
[83] ibid [106].
[84] Article 29 Data Protection Working Party (n 9). See Zuiderveen Borgesius (n 9) at 167–70.

these criteria and established that Meta's reliance on Article 6(1)(f) for OBA was not GDPR compliant.[85]

Regardless of the CJEU judgment in *Meta v Bundeskartellamt*, Meta continued to process behavioural data on the ground of the 'legitimate interest'.[86] On 14 July 2023, the Norwegian DPA introduced urgent measures against Meta, banning the company's surveillance advertising practices for three months.[87] It also referred the issue to the EDPB which, on 27 October 2023, decided to extend the ban on Meta's OBA practices across the EU.[88] The Norwegian DPA conducted a thorough analysis of Article 6 (1)(f) of the GDPR based on the three conditions (legitimacy, necessity and balancing) which can be extrapolated to apply to digital service providers beyond Meta who are considering relying on Article 6(1)(f) for engaging in OBA.

Firstly, digital service providers must have a legitimate purpose – they cannot have a legitimate interest in engaging in explicitly prohibited practices. This means that digital service providers cannot claim the legitimacy of their purpose if they engage in forms of surveillance advertising that are explicitly prohibited. For example, Articles 26 and 28 of the DSA prohibit online platforms from engaging in surveillance advertising targeted at minors or using special categories of data. Assuming that some forms of OBA are not prohibited, engaging in such surveillance advertising could potentially provide a valid, legitimate purpose.[89] One argument is that legitimate interest in surveillance advertising is satisfying consumer preferences – as OBA entails showing consumers 'relevant ads' that are preferable to consumers.[90] Such an argument is illogical and indefensible as, in essence, it entails avoiding asking consumers to disclose their preferences (via consent) because it satisfies their preferences.[91] There are three other ways such legitimate purpose is typically framed: (1) surveillance advertising supports digital media (e.g., online newspapers) by funding digital services without consumers paying a monetary fee; (2) surveillance advertising is a form of marketing, which is a legitimate interest for *any* business; and (3) surveillance advertising serves a

[85] Case C-252/21, *Meta v Bundeskartellamt* (n 61)[117], [124]. ('in this regard, it is important to note that, despite the fact that the services of an online social network such as Facebook are free of charge, the user of that network cannot reasonably expect that the operator of the social network will process that user's personal data, without his or her consent, for the purposes of personalised advertising. In those circumstances, it must be held that the interests and fundamental rights of such a user override the interest of that operator in such personalised advertising by which it finances its activity, with the result that the processing by that operator for such purposes cannot fall within the scope of point (f) of the first subparagraph of Article 6(1) of the GDPR.')

[86] *Datatilsynet* (n 58).

[87] ibid.

[88] EDPB (n 15). Norway is not a Member State of the EU but is a member of the European Economic Area. The GDPR applies to Norway, and the Norwegian DPA is a member of the EDPB.

[89] See Chen (n 8) at ch 2.

[90] *Datatilsynet* (n 58) 16.

[91] ibid. ('Meta's allegation that Behavioral Advertising is in line with data subject's preferences, appears leveraged as an argument for why data subjects should not be able to freely exercise their preferences, which seems rather illogical.')

purpose of maximising the profit for publishers.[92] These aims can be considered legitimate given that they pass the necessity and balancing test of Article 6(1)(f) of the GDPR.

Secondly, the first two aims listed in the previous paragraph ('free internet' and 'legitimate marketing') cannot pass the necessity or proportionality test of Article 6(1)(f) of the GDPR. This test implies that processing data is 'strictly necessary' only for predetermined ends that cannot be attained by processing less data.[93] Surveillance advertising is not the only way digital service providers can engage in legitimate marketing or monetise consumer attention.[94] Segmented and contextual advertising provides alternative marketing strategies that can act as alternatives for funding the digital industry.[95] In contrast, the third aim ('profit maximisation') seems likely to pass the necessity test.[96] There is a perception in the industry that surveillance advertising generally optimises return on invested capital in advertising.[97] While there is contradictory evidence concerning the profitability of surveillance advertising for advertisers (compared to other advertising models), it certainly maximises the profit of gatekeepers such as Alphabet and Meta[98] because it involves processing almost unlimited amounts of data that gatekeepers can control and capitalise on.[99] Online advertising without surveillance data is likely to result in a significant reduction in profits for the gatekeepers. In 2019, the UK Competition and Markets Authority (CMA) found that profits of Alphabet and Meta far exceeded fair estimates.[100] The CMA attributed these excess profits to the gatekeepers' control of data, which gives them a competitive advantage in online advertising, implying the centrality of surveillance advertising in maximising their profits.[101]

[92] See Chen (n 8) at 55. See also *Datatilsynet* (n 58) 17.

[93] *Datatilsynet* ibid 17.

[94] See European Parliament, Policy Department for Economic, Scientific and Quality of Life Policies (n 28) at 16–20.

[95] Case C-252/21, *Meta v Bundeskartellamt* (n 61) at 150. See European Parliament, Policy Department for Economic, Scientific and Quality of Life Policies (n 28) at 16–21.

[96] *Datatilsynet* (n 58), 17.

[97] In 2016, 86% of digital advertising revenue in Europe was estimated to be derived from using behavioural data, with the predictions that such reliance would increase over time. See 'The Value of Digital Advertising' (*IAB Europe*). Available at: https://iabeurope.eu/the-value-of-digital-advertising/, last accessed 16 January 2023. See European Commission, Directorate-General for Communications Networks, Content and Technology and others (n 34) 115.

[98] *Datatilsynet* (n 58) at 17.

[99] See European Commission, Directorate-General for Communications Networks, Content and Technology and others (n 33) at 115, 120.

[100] CMA (n 32) at 67. ('We have found through our profitability analysis that the global return on capital employed for both Google and Facebook have been well above any reasonable benchmarks for many years. We estimated that the cost of capital for both Google and Facebook in 2018 was around 9%, whereas their actual returns have been substantially higher, at least 40% for Google's business and 50% for Facebook. This evidence is consistent with the exploitation of market power.')

[101] ibid 15. ('Advertisers and media agencies have told us that Google offers in-depth targeting options, driven by its unique and vast sources of data, while Facebook has the advantage of offering the ability to target specific audiences based on demographic characteristics, interests and location. This creates a substantial competitive advantage for Google and Facebook, both of which have access to more extensive datasets than their rivals.')

Thirdly, the aim of publishers to maximise profit via surveillance advertising can be regarded as a 'legitimate interest' under Article 6(1)(f) of the GDPR and can become the ground of processing if it satisfies the 'balancing test'.[102] Profit maximisation is part of entrepreneurial freedom that is protected as a human right in the EU as the 'freedom to conduct a business'.[103] Nevertheless, Article 6(1)(f) requires this interest to be balanced against the interests of other stakeholders, including consumers. Surveillance advertising can exploit consumers,[104] which can lead to economic and environmental detriment, discrimination, or injury to physical or mental integrity.[105] Surveillance advertising, as the infrastructure of the online environment, leads to the systematic threat of consumer exploitation.[106] This can be argued to violate *dignity*, which is the inviolable 'essence' of the rights in the EU.[107] Therefore, for surveillance advertising to pass the Article 6(1)(f) test, digital service providers must demonstrate they have weighed all interests and balanced them as per the general principles of the EU law.

In the case of Meta, the CJEU and Norwegian DPA decided that it had not adequately conduct such a balancing test, and, therefore, Article 6(1)(f) GDPR was not a valid legal basis for Meta to engage in surveillance advertising.[108] On 27 October 2023, the EDPB explicitly banned Meta from engaging in surveillance advertising on Article 6(1)(f) of the GDPR across the EU.[109] This litigation makes it apparent that for gatekeepers such as Meta, consumer consent is the only valid legal basis for engaging in surveillance advertising. The DMA further clarifies that designated gatekeepers must rely on consumer consent when processing data for surveillance advertising using data collected by third parties.[110]

This theoretically does not exclude the possibility of reliance on the legitimate interest of profit maximisation. Yet, such reliance would require rigorous risk assessment and mitigation exercises that demonstrate that a particular surveillance advertising practice is fair and does not infringe upon the dignity and integrity interests of consumers, which seems difficult.

The Belgian DPA evaluated the validity of relying on Article 6(1)(f) of the GDPR for companies engaging in surveillance advertising that are not gatekeepers

[102] Zuiderveen Borgesius (n 10) 167–70.

[103] Charter of Fundamental Rights of the European Union, art 16.

[104] See, e.g., European Parliament, Policy Department for Economic, Scientific and Quality of Life Policies (n 29) 35–38. See, e.g., Stigler Committee, 'Digital Platforms: Final Report' 336, 62–66.

[105] See European Commission, Directorate-General for Communications Networks, Content and Technology and others (n 33) at 66–103.

[106] See, e.g., Stigler Committee, (n 104) at 62–66.

[107] See Carsten Bäcker, 'Limited Balancing: The Principle of Human Dignity and Its Inviolability' in Jan-R Sieckmann (ed), *Proportionality, Balancing, and Rights: Robert Alexy's Theory of Constitutional Rights* (Springer International Publishing 2021). Available at: https://doi.org/10.1007/978-3-030-77321-2_4, last accessed 21 November 2023.

[108] Case C-252/21, *Meta v Bundeskartellamt* (n 61). See *Datatilsynet*, (n 58) at 18–22.

[109] European Data Protection Board (n 15).

[110] Digital Markets Act, art 5(2).

per se, such as smaller publishers, advertisers, and ad intermediaries.[111] This case was concerned with the Interactive Advertising Bureau (IAB) Europe Transparency and Consent Framework (TCF) that claimed to provide these companies (the industry refers to them as 'vendors') a valid legal basis for engaging in surveillance advertising.[112] The Belgian DPA's decision concerning the IAB Europe TCF asserts that these vendors could not rely on Article 6(1)(f) for surveillance advertising either.[113] While the Belgian DPA's decision awaits trial in the CJEU, IAB Europe has issued TCF 2.2, which relies on consumer consent instead of legitimate interest for surveillance advertising.[114]

Consent

As the analysis in the previous sections illustrates, surveillance advertising can be legitimised by Article 6(1)(a) of the GDPR or, if the consumer gives valid consent, to the digital service provider to process their data for surveillance advertising. Meeting the GDPR's consent is not a trivial task.[115] Section C is divided into five sub-sections: sub-section III.C.1. addresses the conditions for valid consent; sub-section III.C.2. analyses the validity of consent within the 'consent-or-pay' model; sub-section III.C.3. focuses on consumer consent in AdTech; sub-section III.C.4. explains consent requirements under the ePrivacy Directive and its relationship to Article 6(1) of the GDPR. Sub-section III.C.5 expands on the 'contractual' consequences of consumer consent to surveillance advertising; sub-section III.C.6. explores the surveillance advertising risks that consumer consent cannot legitimise; and sub-section III.C.7. describes cases in which higher level of (explicit) consent may be required for legitimising surveillance advertising.

Conditions

Acquiring legally valid consent is not a trivial task.[116] Consumer consent expresses their autonomy and their genuine preferences, which can waive a human rights

[111] *Decision on the merits 21/2022 of 2 February 2022, Gegevensbeschermingsautoriteit, DOS-2019-01377.*

[112] Michael Veale, Midas Nouwens and Cristiana Santos, 'Impossible Asks: Can the Transparency and Consent Framework Ever Authorise Real-Time Bidding After the Belgian DPA Decision?' (2022) *Technology and Regulation* 12.

[113] Veale and Zuiderveen Borgesius, (n 17) at 20. Victor Morel and others, 'Legitimate Interest Is the New Consent. Available at: Large-Scale Measurement and Legal Compliance of IAB Europe TCF Paywalls' (25 September 2023). Available at: http://arxiv.org/abs/2309.11625, last accessed 12 October 2023.

[114] Belgian Data Protection Authority, 'IAB Europe Case: The Market Court Refers Preliminary Questions to the Court of Justice of the EU' (9 July 2022). Available at: www.dataprotectionauthority.be/citizen/iab-europe-case-the-market-court-refers-preliminary-questions-to-the-court-of-justice-of-the-eu, last accessed 5 January 2023.

[115] See Zuiderveen Borgesius (n 9).

[116] See detailed overview on GDPR's consent requirements for OBA in Chen (n 8) at 113–20.

prohibition against the processing of their personal data.[117] Article 4(11) of the GDPR defines consent as a 'freely given, specific, informed, and unambiguous indication' of a consumer's wishes that is disclosed 'by a statement or an explicit affirmative action that signifies an agreement to the processing of personal data'.[118] In essence, the GDPR aims to ensure consumers give consent without manipulative and coercive influence.[119] Typically, determining the validity of consent requires evaluating whether consent is (i) informed, (ii) specific, (iii) unambiguous; and (iv) freely given.[120]

Firstly, *informed* consent means that digital service providers processing consumer personal data for surveillance advertising must disclose at least their identity and the purpose of processing (e.g., personalised advertising).[121] Such a disclosure must provide consumers with a substantial understanding of the agreement.[122] Article 7 of the GDPR clarifies that consent transparency entails more than mere information provision and that information should be provided in 'intelligible and easily accessible form, using plain language'.[123] For example, the French Data Protection Authority (DPA) has found that Alphabet violated requirements of 'informed' consent for surveillance advertising, as it provided information about purposes of processing in a 'generic and vague manner'.[124] This criterion can be considered violated if insufficient or inaccurate information is provided.[125] It can be argued that in the context of OBA, substantial understanding can only be ensured if digital service providers communicate the potential risks of agreeing to surveillance advertising (e.g., OBA may lead to integrity harms).[126]

[117] See European Parliament, Policy Department for Citizens' Rights and Constitutional Affairs Directorate-General for Internal Policies (n 25) at 58.

[118] General Data Protection Regulation, art 4 (11). ('"consent" of the data subject means any freely given, specific, informed and unambiguous indication of the data subject's wishes by which he or she, by a statement or by a clear affirmative action, signifies agreement to the processing of personal data relating to him or her;')

[119] See European Parliament, Policy Department for Citizens' Rights and Constitutional Affairs Directorate-General for Internal Policies (n 25) at 58–73.

[120] See Schermer, Custers and van der Hof (n 11). See also Veale and Zuiderveen Borgesius (n 17) at 236.

[121] General Data Protection Regulation, recitals 42, 32, 58.

[122] Schermer, Custers and van der Hof (n 11).

[123] General Data Protection Regulation, art 7, reci 58.

[124] 'The CNIL's Restricted Committee Imposes a Financial Penalty of 50 million Euros against GOOGLE LLC' (European Data Protection Board, 2019). Available at: https://edpb.europa.eu/news/national-news/2019/cnils-restricted-committee-imposes-financial-penalty-50-million-euros_en, last accessed 3 May 2023.

[125] Schermer, Custers and van der Hof (n 11).

[126] See European Parliament, Policy Department for Citizens' Rights and Constitutional Affairs Directorate-General for Internal Policies (n 25) 60. Disclosure of risk has been explicitly required in the now-stalled proposed ePrivacy Regulation. See Proposal for a Council Regulation concerning the respect for private life and the protection of personal data in electronic communications and repealing Directive 2002/58/EC (Regulation on Privacy and Electronic Communications) COM (2017) 10 [hereinafter Proposal for ePrivacy Regulation]. ('Information provided […] should include relevant information about the risks associated to allowing third party cookies to be stored in the computer, including the compilation of long-term records of individuals' browsing histories and the use of such

Secondly, consent must be *specific* or authorise a particular course of action.[127] This criterion requires digital service providers to ask consumers to consent to each processing activity if they undertake multiple processing operations (e.g., personalised feed and advertising).[128] For instance, the Norwegian DPA has found Grindr to violate the condition for 'specific' consent because the dating app asked for consent to OBA in a request bundled with the acceptance of the general privacy policy.[129] The specificity criterion is closely related to the criterion of informed consent, which aims to ensure that consumers are sure of what they are consenting to.[130] These criteria are particularly relevant in the context of surveillance advertising within gatekeeper ad networks (walled gardens) and in AdTech, where a multiplicity of third parties are involved.[131]

In the context of the designated gatekeepers, such as Alphabet and Meta, the DMA has clarified the requirement of specific consent in two provisions: Article 5(2)(a) of the DMA prohibits gatekeepers from processing consumer data for surveillance advertising that is collected by third parties (e.g., online newspapers, online games) that are part of their advertising networks (e.g., Google Display Network, Meta Audience Network) unless the consumer consents that the gatekeeper combines data from each third party.[132] Article 5(2)(b) of the DMA prohibits gatekeepers from combining consumer data between their different platform services (e.g., between Instagram and Facebook) unless the consumer consents to each processing activity separately.[133]

Thirdly, consent must be an *unambiguous* indication of the consumer's wishes.[134] This refers to the requirement that consent cannot be implied, for instance, because consumers access the website of the digital service provider.[135] In other words, there must be no doubt that the consumer consented to data processing.[136]

Fourthly, consent has to be *freely given* and, therefore, an expression of a consumer's genuine desire.[137] Digital service providers have to ensure that the

records to send targeted advertising. Web browsers are encouraged to provide easy ways for end-users to change the privacy settings at any time during use and to allow the user to make exceptions for or to whitelist certain websites or to specify for which websites(third) party cookies are always or never allowed.')

[127] Schermer, Custers and van der Hof (n 11).

[128] General Data Protection Regulation (n 31), recital 32.

[129] *Datatilsynet*, 'Administrative Fine – Grinder LLC' (2021) Offl. § 13 jf. fvl. § 13 (1) nr. 2.

[130] Schermer, Custers, and van der Hof (n 11) note 890 at 5.

[131] European Parliament, Policy Department for Citizens' Rights and Constitutional Affairs Directorate-General for Internal Policies (n 25) at 58.

[132] Digital Markets Act, art 5(2)(a).

[133] ibid.

[134] General Data Protection Regulation, art 4(11). ('"consent" of the data subject means any freely given, specific, informed and unambiguous indication of the data subject's wishes by which he or she, by a statement or by a clear affirmative action, signifies agreement to the processing of personal data relating to him or her;')

[135] Schermer, Custers and van der Hof (n 11) at 5.

[136] ibid. 7.

[137] General Data Protection Regulation, rec. 32.

consumer's decision-making is free of coercive and manipulative influences.[138] Article 7 of the GDPR lists two elements to consider when evaluating whether consent is freely given: (a) whether publishers provide alternative options;[139] and (b) whether there is an 'imbalance' between parties.[140] These two elements can help evaluate the legitimacy of the OBA industry's consent practices. Sub-section III.C.2. elaborates on the validity of consumer consent to surveillance advertising within the recently emerging 'Consent-or-Pay' model.

'Consent-or-Pay'

As the GDPR enforcement has demonstrated that consumer consent is the only legal basis for OBA, publishers are increasingly moving towards the 'Consent-or-Pay' ('OBA-or-Pay', 'Pay-or-OK', 'Surveillance-or-Pay') model in which they monetise their digital services either by surveillance advertising or by subscription fees paid for by consumers.[141] Significant legal uncertainty exists about whether consumer consent can be regarded as *freely given* within the Surveillance-or-Pay model.[142] In 2021, the German DPA of Lower Saxony (LfD) ruled that *Heise Online*, one of the largest online newspapers in Germany, used this model coercively and illegitimately.[143] However, the that Austrian and Spanish DPAs decided differently in similar cases.[144] The French DPA suggested that this model *can* be legitimised if a case-by-case assessment reveals that (i) the alternative is real and fair; and (ii) the price of a subscription is fair.[145]

The OBA-or-Pay model will reach the CJEU,[146] and it is most likely that case-by-case analyses and criteria similar to the one endorsed by the French DPA will be established. In essence, fairness in this context depends on the ability of the controller to ensure that consumers can *freely* choose which, of course, depends

[138] Veale and Zuiderveen Borgesius (n 17) 236. See Schermer, Custers and van der Hof (n 11).

[139] GDPR, art 7 (4). See European Data Protection Board, 'Guidelines 05/2020 on Consent under Regulation 2016/679' (2020) 8.

[140] European Parliament, Policy Department for Citizens' Rights and Constitutional Affairs Directorate-General for Internal Policies (n 25) at 63.

[141] Morel and others (n 113).

[142] ibid.

[143] The court recognised that such a model can be legal in principle but, in the case of *Heise Online* it was not. *Decision of the Data Protection of Lower Saxony regarding der Standard Tech rep* (Data Protection Lower Saxony). See noyb, '"Pay or Okay" on Tech News Site Heise.de Illegal, Decides German DPA' (*noyb*, 14 July 2023). Available at: https://noyb.eu/en/pay-or-okay-tech-news-site-heisede-illegal-decides-german-dpa, last accessed 23 July 2023.

[144] See generally, Morel and others (n 113). See 'Austria Challenges EU Newspapers' Pay-or-Cookie Walls' (www.euractiv.com, 12 April 2023). Available at: www.euractiv.com/section/media/news/austria-challenges-eu-newspapers-pay-or-cookie-walls/, last accessed 1 June 2023.

[145] 'Cookie walls: la CNIL publie des premiers critères d'évaluation' (*CNIL*, 16 May 2022). Available at: www.cnil.fr/fr/cookie-walls-la-cnil-publie-des-premiers-criteres-devaluation, last accessed 19 October 2023.

[146] '"Pay or Okay" – the Beginning of the End?' (*noyb*, 11 April 2023). Available at: https://noyb.eu/en/pay-or-okay-beginning-end, last accessed 22 November 2023.

on particular circumstances. The French DPA clarifies that consumer autonomy can particularly be limited in case there is an imbalance between consumers and digital service providers.[147] Such imbalance can, for example, exist when the user has few alternatives to the service. In *Meta v Bundeskartellamt*, the CJEU acknowledged that Meta's dominant position in the social network market was essential for determining the *freeness* of consumer consent.[148]

Therefore, the publisher's gatekeeping status is significant in evaluating whether consent is free from manipulative or coercive influence under the Surveillance-or-Pay model. In essence, one of the central aims of the DMA was to ensure consumers have free choice when facing gatekeeper services.[149] In actualising this aim, the DMA requires gatekeepers to ask consumers to consent to surveillance advertising and also to offer an 'equivalent' and possibly 'less personalised alternative' of their platforms that is not of 'degraded quality'.[150]

Since 30 October 2023, Meta has offered a 'Surveillance-or-Pay' model in the EU.[151] The company justifies this model by referring to the CJEU judgment in *Meta v Bundeskartellamt*, where the court mentioned the possibility that Meta could provide a subscription-based alternative to its services.[152] The CJEU didnot consider the validity of consent within the 'Surveillance-or-Pay' model, but rather, the 'necessity' of processing behavioural data for providing Meta's social network services.[153] The court reasoned that consumers must be able to reject the processing of such data that is not 'strictly necessary' for the contract and still receive the social network services, 'if necessary for an appropriate fee'.[154]

Nothing prohibits Meta from offering Facebook and Instagram solely via a subscription model. If Meta also offers a surveillance advertising-funded alternative, the validity of the consent to this alternative must be evaluated independently. This chapter argues that Meta misinterpreted the CJEU judgment and consumer consent (which waives their human rights protection) in their 'surveillance-or-pay' model is invalid.

Online newspaper publishing, where the 'surveillance-or-pay' model emerged, is a highly competitive market, and if a consumer is not happy with their options,

[147] 'Cookie walls: la CNIL publie des premiers critères d'évaluation (n 145).

[148] Case C-252/21, *Meta v Bundeskartellamt* (n 61) [150].

[149] Digital Markets Act. Consumer choice is mentioned 23 times in the DMA.

[150] Digital Markets Act, Recitals 36–37.

[151] 'Facebook and Instagram to Offer Subscription for No Ads in Europe' (*Meta*, 30 October 2023). Available at: https://about.fb.com/news/2023/10/facebook-and-instagram-to-offer-subscription-for-no-ads-in-europe/, last accessed 23 November 2023.

[152] Case C-252/21, *Meta v Bundeskartellamt* (n 61) [150]. ('Thus, those users must be free to refuse individually, in the context of the contractual process, to give their consent to particular data processing operations not necessary for the performance of the contract, without being obliged to refrain entirely from using the service offered by the online social network operator, which means that those users are to be offered, if necessary for an appropriate fee, an equivalent alternative not accompanied by such data processing operations.')

[153] Case C-252/21, *Meta v Bundeskartellamt* (n 61) [150].

[154] ibid.

they are likely to find a news source that either costs less or involves processing less data. In contrast, consumers accessing Facebook and Instagram cannot reasonably be considered to have an actual choice and express a genuine preference for surveillance advertising within the 'surveillance-or-pay' model. Facebook has more than 3 billion monthly active consumers (Instagram has 2 billion).[155] For many consumers, there are no reasonable alternatives they can use to connect with their families and friends.

As there are no reasonable alternatives to their services, consumer consent given to Meta for surveillance advertising since 30 October 2023, can be considered coercively influenced and, therefore, illegitimate under the GDPR. This suggests that, in general, if gatekeepers would like to monetise their services via surveillance advertising, they need to provide an alternative of their services that is 'equivalent', in a sense that the consumer does not pay for the service (as for surveillance advertising) and does not involve the processing of behavioural data (without degrading the quality of service). Such an alternative can, for example, be funded by random advertising or targeted advertising based on broad demographic or contextual information ('basic ads').

As for the subscription model, in the case of gatekeepers, it can be provided as the *third* alternative (Basic Advertising/Surveillance Advertising/Subscription) but not as the only alternative to the surveillance advertising-funded model. Recital 37 of the DMA also clarifies that gatekeepers must design their online interfaces in a way that does not coerce or manipulate consumers and ensure that giving consent (also for surveillance advertising) is as easy as withdrawing it.[156] This may suggest that gatekeepers must introduce a button or toggle that allows consumers to withdraw consent for surveillance advertising or alternate between 'Basic Advertising-Surveillance Advertising' options. In sum, the GDPR does not prohibit gatekeepers from providing their services *solely* via the subscription model but ensures that consent is *free* when gatekeepers choose to fund their services through surveillance advertising.

Lastly, another criterion for evaluating the *freeness* of cost within the 'surveillance-or-pay' model is the appropriateness of the fee charged to the consumer. So far, the German and Austrian DPAs have largely ignored disproportionate fees charged to the consumers. For example, *Heise Online* charged consumers 428 times more than they were earning per consumer via online advertising.[157] The exaggerated prices in the surveillance-or-pay model suggest that digital service providers provide an unreasonable or unfair alternative and coerce consumers towards choosing the surveillance advertising-funded versions.[158]

[155] 'Biggest Social Media Platforms 2023' (*Statista*, October 2023). Available at: www.statista.com/statistics/272014/global-social-networks-ranked-by-number-of-users/, last accessed 23 November 2023.

[156] Digital Markets Act, recital 37.

[157] See noyb (n 143).

[158] ibid.

Consent in AdTech

Acquiring informed, specific, unambiguous, and free consent is even more complicated in case surveillance advertising occurs in the open display advertising exchange often called 'AdTech'. As explained in section II, surveillance advertising occurring via AdTech includes hundreds of 'vendors', including publishers, advertisers, and ad intermediaries competing for advertising space in the real-time bidding (RTB) auction. Most of the open exchange is supported by the *OpenRTB* protocol provided by the Interactive Advertising Bureau (IAB) and the *Authorised Buyers* protocol provided by Alphabet. By December 2023, all vendors using both protocols are expected to implement 'Transparency & Consent Framework (TCF) 2.2.' provided by IAB Europe.[159]

TCF 2.2. emerged in response to the Belgian DPA's decision that, in February 2022, found the earlier versions of TCF to violate the GDPR.[160] On April 25, 2018, a month before the GDPR went into force, IAB Europe adopted an early version of TCF in order to help OpenRTB vendors engage in surveillance advertising.[161] Consent management platforms (CMPs) that emerged to facilitate earlier versions of TCF provided standardised cookie banners that collected consumers' cookie preferences in the 'Transparency and Consent String' and shared them with all TCF participants.[162] These versions of TCF entailed collecting consent to place third-party cookies to comply with Article 5(2) of the ePrivacy Directive.[163] As for processing data collected via these cookies for the purpose of OBA, early versions of TCF relied on legitimate interest prescribed in Article 6(1)(f) of the GDPR.[164] Therefore, when consumers accepted cookies on CMPs supporting early versions of TCF, they enabled hundreds and sometimes over 1,000 unknown vendors to track and target them for surveillance advertising.[165]

The Belgian DPA found that such reliance on Article 6(1)(f) of the GDPR by these third-party vendors violated the GDPR.[166] The Belgian DPA also found that acceptance of cookies could not be considered valid consent according to Article 7 of the GDPR for TCF participants to process consumer data for

[159] Kavya, 'Google and IAB TCF v2.2: How Publishers Can Stay Ahead with CookieYes' (*CookieYes*, 2 June 2023). Available at: www.cookieyes.com/blog/iab-tcf-cmp-for-publishers, last accessed 19 October 2023.

[160] 'TCF 2.2 Launches! All You Need To Know – IAB Europe' (*iab.Europe*, 16 May 2023). Available at: https://iabeurope.eu/all-news/tcf-2-2-launches-all-you-need-to-know/, last accessed 19 October 2023. Note that IAB and IAB Europe are not the same organisation.

[161] Veale and Zuiderveen Borgesius (n 17) at 230.

[162] Veale, Nouwens and Santos (n 112) at 13–14.

[163] ePrivacy Directive, art 5(3).

[164] Veale, Nouwens and Santos (n 112) at 13–14.

[165] Thea Felicity, 'Top 5 Best Consent Management Platforms in 2022 to Easily and Legally Manage User Data (*TechTimes*, 3 August 2022) 5. Available at: www.techtimes.com/articles/272671/20220308/top-5-best-consent-management-platforms-in-2022-to-easily-and-legally-manage-user-data.htm, last accessed 5 January 2023.

[166] *Gegevensbeschermingsautoriteit* (n 111).

surveillance advertising.[167] The Belgian DPA argued that too many actors are involved, and it would require disproportionate time for consumers to be meaningfully informed and understand to whom they are consenting and for what.[168]

In September 2022, upon appeal of the IAB Europe, the Belgian DPA referred the case to the CJEU, requesting a preliminary ruling on this matter.[169] While the CJEU judgment is not expected until 2024, the Belgian DPA requested IAB Europe to comply with the decision from 11 July 2023.[170] As a response, on 16 May 2023, IAB Europe introduced TCF 2.2., which includes new rules for TCF participants.[171] TCF 2.2. requires that the legal basis for OBA is consent from each of the 'vendors'. It seems that TCF 2.2. will decrease the number of vendors publishers can allow to track their consumers. It also requires publishers to show the *number* of vendors on the first layer of banners where consumers can accept placing third-party cookies for surveillance advertising.

Indeed, by 2024, TCF 2.2. will be implemented by almost all participants in AdTech and will provide improved protections for consumers relative to its earliest versions. However, there is much scepticism as to what extent it can ensure compliance with Articles 4, 6(1)(a), and 7 GDPR requirements for valid consent.[172] One hesitation is regarding the consent criteria to be informed and specific. It is doubtful that consent can be considered specific if, by one click, consumers consent to numerous ad vendors whose identities they do not see (even though they now see their number).[173]

Therefore, it is likely that to legitimise surveillance advertising, the industry needs to develop a stronger consent mechanism than TCF 2.2., suggesting the way ahead to be more centralised, where only a few ad intermediaries track consumers on most of the Web. This process parallels advancing 'local' or browser-based advertising tools, such as those developed under Alphabet's Privacy Sandbox.[174] Note that while safeguarding data breach or confidentiality harms (due to not sharing data with numerous third parties), such tools do not necessarily mitigate, and may indeed amplify, the exploitative nature of surveillance advertising.[175]

[167] ibid.

[168] ibid.

[169] ibid.

[170] 'IAB Europe Seeks Court Decision on Validation of The Action Plan as It Moves Forward with TCF Evolutions – IAB Europe' (https://iabeurope.eu/). Available at: https://iabeurope.eu/all-news/iab-europe-seeks-court-decision-on-validation-of-the-action-plan-as-it-moves-forward-with-tcf-evolutions, last accessed 4 May 2023.

[171] 'TCF 2.2 Launches! All You Need to Know – IAB Europe' (n 161).

[172] Veale, Nouwens and Santos (n 112). Morel and others (n 113).

[173] Veale, Nouwens and Santos (n 112). See also Tim Cross, 'IAB Removes Legitimate Interest from Reworked TCF' (*VideoWeek*, 16 May 2023). Available at: https://videoweek.com/2023/05/16/iab-removes-legitimate-interest-from-reworked-tcf/, last accessed 2 June 2023.

[174] Anthony Chavez, 'Expanding Testing for the Privacy Sandbox for the Web' (*Google: The Keyword*, 27 July 2022). Available at: https://blog.google/products/chrome/update-testing-privacy-sandbox-web/, last accessed 19 January 2023.

[175] See European Commission, Directorate-General for Communications Networks, Content and Technology and others (n 33) at 157–77.

Lastly, on 14 November 2023, the Irish Council of Civil Liberties published a report, 'Europe's Hidden Security Crisis', elaborating on how the AdTech ecosystem seriously threatens national security.[176] It has become increasingly difficult to find a way to deny or excuse the illegitimacy of AdTech (and RTB surveillance), making it clear that such a model is unsustainable.

Consent and ePrivacy

The surveillance advertising industry recognises that surveillance advertising in AdTech is unsustainable, not only because digital service providers do not have an appropriate legal basis for processing personal data, but also because these providers eavesdrop on the consumers by placing *cookies* on their devices, often violating ePrivacy Directive (ePD). Article 5(3) of the ePD requires digital service providers to have consumer consent to place trackers such as cookies on their devices that store information or gain access to information already stored in a consumer's devices.[177] It applies regardless of whether the consumer's information is classified as personal data under the GDPR.[178]

In Article 6(1)(a) of the GDPR, consent requirement as a legal ground for processing personal data is often conflated (and confused) with consent required under Article 5(3)of the ePD for placing trackers.[179] With the consumer's click on the 'accept all' button, digital service providers assume the consumer's GDPR consent, but hundreds of vendors also assume consent for placing tackers on consumer devices. Surveillance advertising-funded online environments have been filled with cookie banners requiring consumers to accept such cookies on many of the websites they visit, resulting in surveillance by hundreds of (often unknown) actors.[180]

In order to avoid the proliferation of cookie banners in the online environment, the EU proposed the ePrivacy Regulation in 2017.[181] The proposal included the requirement to centralise tracking decisions in browser settings that would

[176] Johny Ryan and Wolfie Christl, 'Europe's Hidden Security Crisis' (Irish Council for Civil Liberties (ICCL) 2023).

[177] ibid. 5(3).

[178] ibid 2(d). ('"Communication" means any information exchanged or conveyed between a finite number of parties by means of a publicly available electronic communications service.')

[179] Directive (EC) 2002/58 of the European Parliament and of the Council of 12 July 2002 concerning the processing of personal data and the protection of privacy in the electronic communications sector (Directive on privacy and electronic communications) OJ 2002 (L 201)31 [hereinafter ePrivacy Directive]. The consent for the placement of cookies is different from the legal grounds for processing personal data. For example, the ground for processing of personal data can be legitimate interest (e.g., marketing), but if such processing requires placement of tracking technologies, such placement still requires consent. The effect in this case is that publishers can provide their services only if consumers accept the cookies. Same is not true if the legal ground for processing is consent, in which case refusal to data processing cannot result in publisher suspending their services or content (otherwise it would not be freely given).

[180] ibid art 5(1).

[181] Proposal for ePrivacy Regulation (n 126).

allow consumers to choose how they wanted to be tracked over the Internet.[182] Such a rule allowed consumers to choose not to be tracked and threatened the surveillance advertising industry with heavy financial losses. This Regulation has been wholly stalled since the end of 2021.[183]

As the surveillance advertising industry is increasingly (en)forced to move away from tracking based on third-party cookies, it has started looking for other ways to connect consumers with browsing records and compile their behavioural profiles.[184] 'Device fingerprinting' is one method by which seemingly insignificant information about the device's features[185] This fingerprint can be used, for example, to combat fraud (e.g., identifying a person trying to log in to a site is likely an attacker who stole the credentials), but also to surveil a single consumer across different websites without their knowledge and without a way of opting out.[186] Device fingerprinting allows consumers to be tracked without cookies, but can also respawn deleted identifiers if the consumer deletes cookies.[187]

While device fingerprinting provides a privacy-invasive alternative tracking practice, some initiatives have successfully demonstrated the possibility of creating consumers' behavioural profiles while preserving the confidentiality of the data. *Adnostic* is a browser created in 2010 that allowed the creation of a behavioural profile of users and used them to target them with advertisements without sharing any data with other parties.[188] Similar privacy-preserving surveillance advertising alternatives such as Privad, AdVeil, and Brave are slowly entering the market.[189] On 16 November 2023, the EDPB published guidelines regarding the technical scope of Article 5(3) of the ePD which responds to various new tracking methods developed in the industry.[190] The EDPB clarifies that the consent requirement usually stays the same for these trackers.[191]

Alphabet has also started an initiative called Privacy Sandbox, in which the company considers various OBA alternatives that preserve the confidentiality of

[182] ibid.

[183] ibid.

[184] Zard and Sears (n 22) at 817.

[185] 'Cover Your Tracks' (*Electronic Frontier Foundation*). Available at: https://coveryourtracks.eff.org/learn, last accessed 19 January 2023.

[186] Nick Nikiforakis and others, 'Cookieless Monster: Exploring the Ecosystem of Web-Based Device Fingerprinting', *2013 IEEE Symposium on Security and Privacy* (IEEE Computer Society 2013). Available at: www.computer.org/csdl/proceedings-article/sp/2013/4977a541/12OmNCwlalM, last accessed 4 January 2023.

[187] Veale and Zuiderveen Borgesius (n 17) at 21.

[188] 'Vincent Toubiana et al., Adnostic: Privacy Preserving Targeted Advertising, Proceedings of the Network and Distributed System Symposium (March 2010). Available at: www.Crypto.Stanford.Edu/Adnostic/Adnostic-Ndss.Pdf.; 'Adnostic: Privacy Preserving Targeted Advertising' (*Adnostic*). Available at: https://crypto.stanford.edu/adnostic/ accessed 19 January 2023.

[189] Micah Altman and others, 'Practical Approaches to Big Data Privacy over Time' (2018) 8 International Data Privacy Law 29; European Commission, Directorate-General for Communications Networks, Content and Technology and others (n 34) 157.

[190] European Data Protection Board, 'Guidelines 2/2023 on Technical Scope of Art. 5(3) of ePrivacy Directive' (2023).

[191] ibid.

data – that is, do not share data with third-party providers. Alphabet is exploring various approaches such as Topics API[192] and FLEDGE.[193] These approaches aim to replace functionality served by cross-site tracking but maintain detailed lifestyle targeting of surveillance advertising.[194] Using Privacy Sandbox, alternatives for OBA can mitigate personal data breach and confidentiality concerns, but it is likely not to be able to address concerns about consumer exploitation in general. The move away of the industry from third-party tracking into browser-based or local surveillance advertising can further centralise power in advertising markets with large platform providers, making their surveillance advertising practices more exploitative.

Surveillance Contracts

Traditionally, legal scholars have avoided framing consent to surveillance advertising as entering into a contract with a publisher.[195] On the one hand, the protection of personal data is a fundamental right in the EU, therefore, it cannot be regarded as a commodity, such as money that can be traded in exchange for receiving digital services.[196] On the other hand, the increasing prevalence of adopting the 'Consent-or-Pay" model within publishers demonstrates that by choosing to access digital services funded by surveillance advertising, consumers enter into a ('data-for-access') bargain. Therefore, it would be counterintuitive to provide lesser protection for consumers when their economic bargain with the digital service provider also affects fundamental rights interests.[197]

The Digital Content Directive (DCD) acknowledges data-for-access bargains between consumers and digital service providers and ensures that consumers of these 'surveillance contracts' are protected with contractual remedies.[198]

[192] 'Topics API Overview' (*Chrome for Developers*, 25 January 2022). Available at: https://developer.chrome.com/docs/privacy-sandbox/topics/overview/, accessed 11 October 2023.

[193] Altman and others (n 190); European Commission, Directorate-General for Communications Networks, Content and Technology and others (n 34) 157.

[194] 'A Complete Guide to Google FLoC – What It Does and How It Works – How FloC Affects Privacy' (*Privacy Affairs*, 9 July 2022). Available at: www.privacyaffairs.com/google-floc/, last accessed 19 January 2023.

[195] Frederik Zuiderveen Borgesius, 'Consent to Behavioural Targeting in European Law – What Are Policy Implications of Insights from Behavioural Economics?' (Amsterdam Law School Legal Studies Research Paper No 2013-43, 2013) 4.

[196] Gianclaudio Malgieri and Bart Custers, 'Pricing Privacy – The Right to Know the Value of Your Personal Data' (2017) 34 *Computer Law & Security Review* 289.

[197] The German and Italian authorities have affirmed that data-for-access bargain is an economic transaction to which consumer protection rules apply. Kammergericht Berlin [KG][Higher Court of Berlin] Jan. 24, 2014, 5 U 42/12 at section B.2.bb (Ger.). See also, L'Autorita Graante Della Concorrenza e Del Mercato [AGCM] [Consumer Market Authority] 29 November 2018, Provvedimento n.27432 (It.).

[198] Digital Content Directive, art 3, recital 24 ('Digital content or digital services are often supplied also where the consumer does not pay a price but provides personal data to the trader. Such business models are used in different forms in a considerable part of the market. While fully recognising that the protection of personal data is a fundamental right and that therefore personal data cannot be

Article 3(1) of the DCD can be understood to apply only in situations when a consumer gives valid consent to the processing of personal data for surveillance advertising under Articles 6(1)(a) and 7 of the GDPR.[199] In other words, the bargain is not acknowledged when consumer personal data is processed because this is necessary to supply the digital content or comply with legal requirements (e.g., the obligation to identify users).[200] The DCD recognises that the GDPR has primacy in evaluating the validity of consent in surveillance contracts.[201] It affirms that although personal data is not a commodity if the consumer consents to an OBA contract, Article 3(1) of the DCD empowers them with contractual remedies.[202]

Therefore, Article 3(1) brings OBA contracts for digital services within the scope of the Consumer Rights Directive (CRD) and Unfair Contract Terms Directive (UCTD). This suggests that digital service providers must ensure the validity of consent under Article 7 of the GDPR and consumer protection rules regarding information disclosure, formation of contracts, withdrawal, non-conformity, remedies and provision of gratuitous content.[203] In other words, the validity of consent has to satisfy further contractual rules on incapacity, mistake, fraudulent behaviour, or exploiting vulnerability through coercion or manipulation.[204] Therefore, in case consent to surveillance advertising is found to be invalid, digital service providers would breach not only the GDPR but also national contract rules that entitle consumers to remedies such as damages.[205] Consumer protection law helps consumers demand the provision of services agreed upon via OBA contracts.[206]

Analyses of this chapter suggest that consent given within Meta's 'Consent-or-pay' model is invalid. Meta consumers can claim damages (possibly amounting to the required subscription fees).

Moreover, one of the central requirements of CRD is informing consumers about the total price of a contract.[207] However, digital service providers are

considered as a commodity, this Directive should ensure that consumers are, in the context of such business models, entitled to contractual remedies.')

199 Digital Content Directive, art 3, recital 24.

200 ibid, art 3(1), recital 25. See *also Commission Notice, Guidance on the Interpretation and Application of Directive 2011/83/EU of the European Parliament and of the Council on Consumer Rights*, O.J. 2021 (C 525) 1, 13.

201 See Digital Content Directive, recital 24.

202 ibid.

203 Marco Loos and others, 'The Regulation of Digital Content Contracts in the Optional Instrument of Contract Law' (2011) 6 *European Review of Private Law* 729, 733.

204 European Parliament, Policy Department for Citizens' Rights and Constitutional Affairs Directorate-General for Internal Policies (n 25) at 98.

205 See Natali Helberger, Frederik Zuiderveen Borgesius and Agustin Reyna, 'The Perfect Match? A Closer Look at the Relationship between EU Consumer Law and Data Protection Law' (2017) 54 Common Market Law Review 10.

206 ibid 2.

207 ibid 10.

exempt from the requirement to disclose the exact 'price' of surveillance contracts.[208] This exclusion is likely put in place to avoid putting a price tag on personal data that is protected as a fundamental right. Nevertheless, without disclosure of costs, surveillance contracts seem to have less protection than contracts with a monetary fee. To remedy this asymmetry, some have suggested that disclosing the monetary value digital service providers earn via surveillance contracts can provide 'material information' to consumers when agreeing to such an exchange.[209] Alternatively, digital service providers can disclose risks regarding entering surveillance contracts.

If personal data is regarded as a direct counter-performance to OBA contracts, an interesting implication would be that such counter-performance may be taxed.[210] It is improbable that any state will give such an interpretation, especially considering the re-assertion in the DCD that personal data is not a commodity.[211] Nevertheless, surveillance contracts must have similar protections as contracts with monetary payment, such as appropriate disclosure of surveillance risks upon agreement on a 'data-to-access' bargain. Section III.C.5. elaborates on the limitations of consumer consent for surveillance advertising as one of the risk mitigation instruments.

Managing Surveillance Risks

Article 34(1) of the Digital Services Act (DSA) requires the providers of Very Large Online Platforms (VLOPs) for example, Facebook, and Very Large Search Engines (VLOSEs), for example, Google Search, to 'diligently identify, analyse, and assess any systemic risks' that stem from the 'design or functioning of their service [...], including algorithmic systems'.[212] Article 34(1)(b) of the DSA clarifies that such risk assessment should take into consideration the severity and probability of actual or foreseeable harms to fundamental rights, such as human dignity (CFREU, art 1), privacy (CFREU, art 7), personal data protection (CFREU, art 8), freedom of expression (CFREU, art 11), non-discrimination (CFREU, art 21), children's rights, and consumer protection (CFREU, art 38).[213] Article 34(2) of the DSA clarifies that such risk assessment is particularly relevant in the context of recommender and advertising systems.[214] Recital 84 of the DSA clarifies that VLOPs/VLOSEs should focus on all relevant algorithmic systems, paying attention to data collection and use practices.[215]

[208] Digital Content Directive, art 2(7); See also Helberger, Borgesius, & Reyna (n 206) at 13.

[209] Malgieri and Custers (n 197). See also Sarah Spiekermann and Jana Korunovska, 'Towards a Value Theory for Personal Data' (2017) 32 *Journal of Information Technology* 62.

[210] See EU Report Targeted Advertising & Informed Consent at 77.

[211] See Digital Content Directive, art 24.

[212] Digital Services Act, art 34(1).

[213] ibid. art 34(1)(b).

[214] ibid. art 34(2).

[215] ibid. recital 84.

Surveillance advertising practices are likely to exploit consumer vulnerabilities, and this can lead to harms of varying severity, such as individual economic detriment or consumer humiliation by systemic threat of vulnerability exploitation. Understood this way, Article 34(1) of the DSA would require VLOPs/VLOSEs to include in their risk assessment evaluation how their surveillance advertising practices may result in consumer exploitation and consequent harm. Recital 81 is explicit with regard to manipulating minors, requiring VLOPs/VLOSEs to assess the risks of their practices 'concerning the design of online interfaces which intentionally or unintentionally exploit the weaknesses and inexperience of minors, or which may cause addictive behaviour'.[216]

Most importantly, Article 35 of the DSA requires VLOPs/VLOSEs to 'put in place reasonable and effective mitigation measures, tailored to specific systemic risks identified' in their risk assessments.[217] Such risk mitigation measures may include 'adapting their advertising systems and adopting targeted measures aimed at limiting or adjusting the presentation of advertisements in association with the service they provide'.[218] It is also important to highlight that the Digital Markets Act (DMA) can be understood to address the structural market risks of gatekeepers concerning consumer exploitation via surveillance advertising.[219]

Article 35(1)(i) of the DSA includes in its list of risk-mitigation measures 'taking awareness-raising measures and adapting their online interface in order to give recipients of the service more information'.[220] Therefore, acquiring consumer consent per Article 7 of the GDPR can mitigate *some*, but not all, risks of surveillance advertising.[221] The act of consent is a juridical act that waives the prohibition of processing personal data but also creates a contractual relationship.[222] In order for such a waiver to be considered valid, informational asymmetry regarding the risks must be corrected. In other words, it can be argued that consumers are able to consent to waive *only* the risks they were aware of (consent can mitigate surveillance risks *limited* to the extent of consumer awareness).

Moreover, even when consumers are aware of the risks, some can be regarded as unacceptable and, thus, impossible to waive. Firstly, unacceptable risks can be understood as significantly harmful outcomes for individuals, including physical or psychological detriment (integrity harms).[223] Secondly, such risks can be conceptualised as significantly harmful outcomes for society, including threats to future generations, democracy, and consumer humiliation (dignity harms).[224]

[216] ibid. recital 81.
[217] ibid. recital 35.
[218] ibid. art 35.
[219] Digital Markets Act, recital 14.
[220] ibid. art 35(1)(i).
[221] European Parliament, Policy Department for Citizens' Rights and Constitutional Affairs Directorate-General for Internal Policies (n 25) at 100.
[222] ibid. 98.
[223] ibid.
[224] ibid.

It is this logic that different versions of Article 5(1)(a)–(b) of the Artificial Intelligence Act (AIA) are attempting to codify. Some prohibitions (targeting minors, using sensitive data) establish the boundaries for unacceptable harms, including individual economic detriment to consumers (UCPD, art 5) or structural market harms (DMA, art 5, TFEU, art 102). Consumer consent cannot justify such risks.

With this in mind, the DSA rules on risk assessment and mitigation measures (DSA, arts 34 and 35) seem to provide a solid tool to hold VLOPs/VLOSEs accountable in that they do not engage in practices that lead to unacceptable risks and they take appropriate measures to manage other risks, such as data confidentiality risks. So far, the surveillance advertising industry has focused on innovating to mitigate data confidentiality harms (i.e., data breaches). For example, Alphabet Privacy Enhancing Technologies (PETs), likely to replace advertising which depends on third-party cookies, allowing the processing of large datasets necessary for behavioural personalisation without ever disclosing personal data to third parties.[225] While such measures mitigate the risks related to privacy harms, they do not tackle other harms such as consumer exploitation.

It is worth noting that while Article 34(1)(b) of the DSA does not mention evaluating risks to Article 37 regarding environmental protection, it requires such evaluation nevertheless.[226] Recital 81 of the DSA clarifies that the risk assessment is not limited to fundamental rights listed in Article 34(1)(b).[227] Therefore, it is appropriate for VLOPs/VLOSEs to conduct environmental protection risk evaluation regarding their OBA practices when there is a higher likelihood of consumer manipulation. The AIA explicitly intends to safeguard against the environmental risks of deploying and using AI systems.

Lastly, the DSA risk assessment and mitigation measures discussed in this section are addressed to the providers of VLOPs/VLOSEs (e.g., Facebook, Google Search). Indeed, the risk of surveillance advertising primarily stems from practices of these platform providers, particularly Alphabet and Meta, as they are the beneficiaries and standard setters in the industry. Nevertheless, this does not mean that smaller digital service providers, such as other 'online platforms' or publishers (e.g., online newspapers), are free from responsibility when they engage in surveillance advertising. OBA involves personal data processing, while Article 24 of the GDPR requires all digital service providers who use personal data for OBA to consider risks in their processing activities[228] and assigns the responsibility and burden of proof for compliance to digital service providers.[229] The principle of *fairness* requires digital service providers to balance their interests with consumer

[225] 'How We Achieve Privacy through Innovation' (*Google*, 1 February 2023). Available at: https://blog.google/technology/safety-security/how-we-achieve-privacy-through-innovation/, last accessed 6 June 2023.

[226] Digital Services Act, art 34 (1).

[227] ibid. recital 81.

[228] GDPR, recitals 42, 32, 58.

[229] ibid.

interests, to correct power asymmetries and to ensure that digital service providers do not infringe on inviolable consumer interests of integrity and dignity, regardless of whether the consumer has consented to process data for OBA.[230]

Moreover, under the GDPR, for surveillance advertising to be considered a legitimate practice, it not only has to be lawful (based on one of the legal grounds) but also *fair* and *transparent* (meet data protection principles of 'lawfulness, fairness, and transparency').[231] The principles of fairness and transparency are closely related to consumer autonomy, similar to consumer protection law unfairness and information principles. The GDPR enables autonomy by requiring digital service providers to *take proactive measures* to ensure that consumers understand how their data is used (the 'transparency paradigm') and that personal data is not used in a way that undermines consumer's interests, for example, by having a discriminatory effect, or by unfair balancing of interests (the 'fairness paradigm").[232] Central here is that the GDPR shifts the burden of proof towards the business to ensure that, in their attempt to ensure transparency, businesses do not merely disseminate information but ensure that consumers understand the information.[233]

Article 35 of the GDPR operationalises the fairness principle by requiring conducting a Data Protection Impact Assessment (DPIA) in high-risk situations.[234] A29WP guidelines regarding DPIA adopted in 2017 do not explicitly require digital service providers to conduct DPIA in all cases in which they conduct OBA.[235] Instead, as Article 35(3)(a) of the GDPR also clarifies in the example, OBA will require a DPIA in case it can be considered automated decision-making that has legal or similarly significant effects under Article 22 of the GDPR.

Indeed, if OBA is limited to smaller-scale digital service providers and does not combine data from other sources, it may be considered to have a low likelihood of algorithmic manipulation or cause severe consumer manipulation harms. Nevertheless, using AdTech can have risks similar to OBA practices of VLOPs/VLOSEs. With this in mind, it is recommended that all publishers engaging in OBA via AdTech also conduct DPIA to evaluate and mitigate risks of consumer manipulation. In essence, failing to conduct such a risk assessment can also be considered a breach of Article 5 of the UCPD requirement of professional diligence.[236]

[230] Damian Clifford and Jef Ausloos, 'Data Protection and the Role of Fairness' (2018) 37 *Yearbook of European Law* 130.

[231] GDPR, art 5 includes six data protection principles: (a) 'lawfulness, fairness and transparency', (b) 'purpose limitation', (c) 'data minimisation', (d)'accuracy', (e)'storage limitation', (f)'integrity and confidentiality'. ibid. art. 5.

[232] Gianclaudio Malgieri, 'The Concept of Fairness in the GDPR: A Linguistic and Contextual Interpretation', *Proceedings of the 2020 Conference on Fairness, Accountability, and Transparency* (Association for Computing Machinery 2020). Available at: https://dl.acm.org/doi/10.1145/3351095.3372868, last accessed 20 April 2023.

[233] Trzaskowski (n 42) 181–83.Thanks to Prof Mark Leiser for bringing this point to my attention.

[234] GDPR, art 5(1)(a), art 35.

[235] Article 29 Data Protection Working Party, 'Guidelines on Data Protection Impact Assessment (DPIA) and Determining Whether Processing is 'Likely to Result in a High Risk' for the Purposes of Regulation 2016/679, Wp248rev.01' (2017). Available at: https://ec.europa.eu/newsroom/article29/items/611236/en, last accessed 24 October 2023.

[236] Hacker, n.34.

Explicit Consent

In exceptional cases, the GDPR requires a higher standard of disclosing consumer preferences called 'explicit consent'.[237] Such explicit consent can be expressed, for example, by filling out a consent form or providing an electronic signature.[238] In the context of surveillance advertising, digital service providers must acquire such explicit consent from consumers if their practice falls under Article 22 of the GDPR.[239]

Article 22 of the GDPR requires explicit consent if personal data is used for 'automated decision-making, including profiling that has legal or otherwise significant effects' on the consumers.[240] This Article 22 prohibition reflects the data protection rules before the GDPR that were designed to restrict the use of computer systems for making decisions that could discriminate (e.g. in the employment context).[241] Recital 71 of the GDPR explicitly includes, as examples of such processing, the 'automatic refusal of an online credit application' and 'e-recruiting practices without human intervention' practices with *similar* significant effects.[242] Article 22 of the GDPR is particularly ambiguous, has limited case law and has been widely debated in academia.[243]

The extent to which Article 22 of the GDPR applies to surveillance advertising is also unclear. Firstly, it is unclear if algorithmic mediation of whether a consumer sees an advertisement can be considered an automated 'decision' within the meaning of Article 22. Secondly, whether such a decision produces legal or similarly significant effects is questionable.[244] In 2021, the so-called '*Schufa*' case was referred to the CJEU to decide whether using a particular credit scoring system constitutes an automated 'decision' under Article 22 of the GDPR.[245] The final judgment in *Schufa* is expected on December 7, 2023.[246] This judgment can clarify what constitutes an automated 'decision' and whether showing an advertisement falls within this criterion.

Nevertheless, the Article 29 Data Protection Working Party (A29WP) has previously acknowledged that surveillance advertising, in essence, constitutes such an automated 'decision' and instead makes falling of it under Article 22 GDPR dependent on whether its effects are significant.[247] In 2021, the Amsterdam

[237] General Data Protection Regulation, arts. 9(2)(a), 22(2)(c), recs 51, 71, 111.

[238] See Schermer, Custers, and van der Hof, at 5.

[239] General Data Protection Regulation, art. 22.

[240] ibid., Recital 71.

[241] Chen (n 8) at 122–23.

[242] General Data Protection Regulation, rec. 71.

[243] Andreas Hauselmann, 'The ECJ's First Landmark Case on Automated Decision-Making – a Report from the Oral Hearing before the First Chamber' (*European Law Blog*, 20 February 2023). Available at: https://europeanlawblog.eu/2023/02/20/the-ecjs-first-landmark-case-on-automated-decision-making-a-report-from-the-oral-hearing-before-the-first-chamber/ accessed 9 May 2023.

[244] Chen (n 8) at 122–23. Andreas Hauselmann (n 245).

[245] Case C-634/21, *OQ v Land Hesse (Schufa), Request for Preliminary Ruling, (2021)6 K 788/20WI.*

[246] Andreas Hauselmann, n.244.

[247] Article 29 Data Protection Working Party, 'Guidelines on Automated Individual Decesion-Making and Profiling for The Purposes of Regulation 2016/679' (2018).

District Court ruled in the so-called 'Uber ADM Case' that algorithmic matching of the drivers and consumers did not constitute automated decision-making because the interests of drivers and consumers were not 'significantly' affected.[248] Therefore, it is plausible that not all surveillance advertising will have effects *significant enough* to fall under Article 22 of the GDPR.

A29WP suggests several criteria for delineating between such surveillance advertising, for example, whether cross-site and third-party tracking takes place and whether the vulnerabilities of consumers are known to the businesses.[249] One example given by A29WP of surveillance advertising that falls under Article 22 targets a consumer with financial difficulties with gambling ads.[250] The A29WP also suggests that the significance of the impact can be established if decisions affect financial circumstances, access to health services, employment opportunities, and education.[251] Following this reasoning, this chapter argues that Article 22 of the GDPR applies to surveillance advertising when it involves advertising financial products, health services, gambling products, employment, housing opportunities, or presents algorithmically differentiated prices.[252]

Applying Article 22 to surveillance advertising suggests that the practice can only be legitimised by 'explicit' consent.[253] Such a higher standard of consent usually consists of a written statement or a signature of the consumer revealing the explicit desire of the consumer to be subjected to such processing, but it can also include signing a form, electronic signature, or two-step verification.[254] Consumers can also provide explicit consent by choosing (by ticking boxes) whether they want to receive surveillance advertising regarding areas that may have significant effects (e.g., employment). Explicit consent serves the purpose of clearing any doubt that the consumer wishes to accept such data processing.[255]

Lastly, this chapter argues that surveillance advertising must be regarded to fall under Article 22 of the GDPR in *all* cases in which it involves surveillance of consumers across websites. In cross-site surveillance advertising, consumers cannot reasonably expect how they can be targeted, and their vulnerabilities identified and exploited. Therefore, legitimising such practice likely requires a high standard of consent. Article 39(2) of the DSA, which ensures additional transparency measures for VLOPs/VLOSEs, may help further operationalise Article 22. In particular, Article 39(2)(e) of the DSA requires VLOPs/VLOSEs to make the main target parameters, including excluding consumers, publicly available.[256]

[248] C/13/687315 / HA RK 20-207, *Uber ADM, Rechtbank Amsterdam* (2023) ECLI:NL:GHAMS:2023:796.
[249] Article 29 Data Protection Working Party, (n 248).
[250] ibid.
[251] ibid.
[252] ibid.
[253] GDPR, art 22.
[254] ibid, art 9(2).
[255] Article 29 Data Protection Working Party, 'Guidelines on Consent Under Regulation 2016/679' (2018) 17/EN WP259 rev.01.
[256] Digital Services Act, art 39(2)(e).

Such transparency may shed light on ways in which surveillance advertising can lead to significant effects and, thus, cases in which digital service providers must ask for explicit consent.

IV. Conclusion

On 30 October 2023, the European Data Protection Board (EDPB) issued an urgent binding decision prohibiting Meta from engaging in surveillance advertising unless it found valid legal grounds under Article 6(1) of the GDPR.[257] This means that from 25 May 2018 to 30 October 2023, Meta has earned the most of its revenue in the EU through an illegitimate practice.[258] On the date of the EDPB decision, Meta switched to the 'Consent-or-Pay' model, charging its consumers €9.99 unless they consented to surveillance advertising.[259] This chapter argues that Meta's reliance on such a model is also illegitimate under Article 6 of the GDPR.

This chapter finds that as surveillance advertising can significantly negatively impact individuals and society, processing personal data for surveillance advertising can only be legitimised if digital service providers acquire consumer consent that reflects consumers' genuine preferences. In the 'Consent-or-Pay' model, consent can be valid given that the price is reasonable, and consumers have reasonable alternatives to the provided service. In the case of Meta, which is a gatekeeper, it provides services (Facebook, Instagram) to which only a few alternatives exist and consumers often depend upon them. Nothing stops Meta from charging a fee for these services. Nevertheless, consent to surveillance advertising cannot be regarded as legitimate if the only alternative to such consent is €9.99 for services for which no reasonable alternatives exist.

From 2018–2023, surveillance advertising was also mainly illegitimate in the open advertising exchange called AdTech. Irrespective of the GDPR and the ePrivacy Directive, the online environment has been plagued by exploitative practices designed to operationalise surveillance infrastructure.[260] As the industry recognises that such illegitimacy is not sustainable, it is moving towards local advertising methods (e.g., Alphabet's Privacy Sandbox) that do not share data with hundreds of vendors unknown to consumers. Nevertheless, while such local advertising techniques can minimise data breach harms, they also further centralise surveillance

[257] See European Data Protection Board, 'EDPB Urgent Binding Decision on Processing of Personal Data for Behavioural Advertising by Meta' (n 16).

[258] ibid.

[259] 'How Meta Uses Legal Bases for Processing Ads in the EU' (n 80).

[260] See European Commission, Directorate-General for Justice and Consumers, Behavioural Study on Unfair Commercial Practices in the Digital Environment: Dark Patterns and Manipulative Personalisation: Final Report(2022) (hereafter EC Study Dark Patterns and Manipulative Personalisation). See 'Manipulative Online Practices' (*European Commission*). Available at: https://ec.europa.eu/commission/presscorner/detail/en/ip_23_418 accessed 2 March 2023.

advertising in large platform providers, which can further translate into exploitation of the consumers and market exploitation.

This chapter also argues that consent to surveillance advertising takes the form of 'surveillance contracts', bringing the arrangement under the wing of consumer protection legislation. Not only do digital service providers have to ensure they meet requirements under Article 6(1) of the GDPR, but if they fail, they open themselves up to consumer claims for damages under the consumer protection rules. Moreover, while consumer consent can be seen as one of the risk-mitigation tools, there are some risks that such a consent cannot address. With such risks to consumers' physical or mental integrity or dignity, digital service providers must ensure such harm does not occur. Ensuring higher standard (explicit) consent in certain situations, such as when advertising employment or housing opportunities, and informing consumers of the surveillance risks can be appropriate measures to consider by digital service providers.

Lastly, in 2022, more than 50% of online advertising revenue went to Alphabet ($168.44 billion) and Meta ($112.68 billion).[261] These companies operate as a quasi-duopoly in surveillance advertising markets, mainly due to their 'data power' or competitive advantage in holding consumer data. These companies set the standards for the industry and it is essential that supervisory authorities make sure they cannot profit from illegitimate practices. With this in mind, this chapter calls for an urgent reaction of the national DPAs and the EDPB to the 'consent-or-pay' model adopted by Meta and ensuring that the company brings its practices into compliance with the GDPR.

Author's Note

This chapter was written in November 2023. Since then, there have been significant developments, in relation to the legitimacy of surveillance advertising, including THE CJEU's decision on 7 March 2024 in case C-604/22 regarding TCF and IAB Europe.[262] It is particularly worth noting that the EDPB responded to Meta's adoption of the 'consent-or-pay' model by publishing its opinion on 17 April 2024 regarding the use of such models by large online platforms.[263] It is unsurprising that the EDPB opinion largely echoes the reasoning found in this chapter, including a call for a third, free alternative as the means to ensure consumer consent is free in case they use services of gatekeepers, such as Meta.

[261] See Ronan Shields, 'Here Are the 2022 Global Media Rankings by Ad Spend: Google, Facebook Remain Dominant – Alibaba, ByteDance in the Mix' (*Digiday*, 13 December 2022). Available AT: https://digiday.com/media/the-rundown-here-are-the-2022-global-media-rankings-by-ad-spend-google-facebook-remain-dominate-alibaba-bytedance-in-the-mix/ accessed 12 January 2023.

[262] Case C-604/22, *IAB Europe*, 7 March 2024, ECLI:EU:C:2024:214.

[263] European Data Protection Board, 'Opinion 08/2024 on Valid Consent in the Context of Consent or Pay Models Implemented by Large Online Platforms' (2024).

5

Re-imagining Data Protection: Femtech and Gendered Risks in the GDPR

ANASTASIA SIAPKA, MARIA TZANOU AND ANNA NELSON

I. Introduction

The European Union's (EU's) General Data Protection Regulation (GDPR)[1] is considered 'the gold standard' for data protection laws worldwide.[2] Yet, it is a truism to state that it neglects gender. The Regulation itself adopts a gender-neutral approach: gender is notably missing from the specific provisions about the types of information revealing special category data as well as from the GDPR in general.[3] Academic debates on the GDPR (or data protection more broadly) and gender are also limited,[4] with the notable exception of Malgieri's and González Fuster's research into whether the 'gendered data subject' could be considered as 'vulnerable'.[5]

This chapter aims to address this regulatory and knowledge gap: it investigates the GDPR from a gender perspective to question whether the Regulation does/should explicitly recognise gender and, if so, how. In this regard, it makes three distinct contributions to the literature: First, it argues that gender *matters* within the GDPR. Using femtech as a case study at the intersection of data protection and reproductive and sexual rights, we show that technology-facilitated gendered

[1] Regulation (EU) 2016/679 of the European Parliament and of the Council of 27 April 2016 on the Protection of Natural Persons with regard to the Processing of Personal Data and on the Free Movement of Such Data, and Repealing Directive 95/46/EC (GDPR) [2016] OJ L119/1.

[2] See, inter alia, G Buttarelli, 'The EU GDPR as a Clarion Call for a New Global Digital Gold Standard' (2016) 6 *International Data Privacy Law* 77.

[3] Despite sex being a protected characteristic in EU anti-discrimination law, it is absent from GDPR, art 9 or any other GDPR provision. As explained in III.2, this omission is not merely formal or linguistic but rather reveals a substantive gap in the role that data protection rights (may) hold for the protection of sexual and reproductive rights.

[4] Jens T Theilen et al, 'Feminist Data Protection: An Introduction' (2021) 10 *Internet Policy Review* 1; Maria Tzanou, 'The Future of EU Data Privacy Law: Towards a More Egalitarian Data Privacy' (2020) 7 *Journal of International and Comparative Law* 449; Gloria González Fuster, 'Feedback to the Consultation on the White Paper on AI- Focusing on AI & Gender: An EU Law Perspective' (2020).

[5] Gianclaudio Malgieri and Gloria González Fuster, 'The Vulnerable Data Subject: A Gendered Data Subject?' (2022) 13 *European Journal of Law and Technology* 1, 1.

surveillance is inextricably linked with the sexual and reproductive rights of women and girls (or the lack thereof). The GDPR's gender blindness thus reveals a further omission: a lack of acknowledgment of the significance of data protection rights for the safeguarding of women's sexual and reproductive wellbeing and autonomy.[6] The GDPR's gender-blind approach fails to recognise that personal data (and data gaps),[7] as well as data subjects, and risks of processing can be *gendered*.

Second, the chapter argues that *gendered risks* should be encompassed by the GDPR's risk-based approach. In this regard, we first examine *in abstracto* the GDPR's risk-based approach, evaluating its conceptual limitations, interpretative gaps and practical implementation difficulties. We then articulate a conceptualisation of *gendered risks* for the first time in the data protection scholarship and identify types of gendered risks that are not currently captured by the GDPR's narrow focus on *individual* risks: these include *embodied*, *collective* and *societal* gendered risks.

Third, the chapter argues that the GDPR *should* be made gender responsive by explicitly acknowledging *gendered risks*. Such a recognition is significant for *symbolic* and *normative* reasons. We then re-imagine the GDPR and explore how this legislative framework could account for gendered risks *de lege ferenda*. Recognising that this re-imagination of the GDPR would require legislative intervention, we also offer a more moderate re-thinking of this instrument, placing gendered (especially collective) risks at the forefront of data protection. The proposed re-thinking of the GDPR both *de lege ferenda* and *de lege lata* provides several ways that legislators, courts, regulators and also data controllers could incorporate gendered risks in the interpretation, application and implementation of the GDPR.

The chapter is structured as follows: Part II examines the GDPR's risk-based approach, highlighting its conceptual ambiguities, the tension between risks and rights and the over-reliance on data controllers. Part III turns to the gendered risks that this approach has so far overlooked. It employs femtech as a case study of everyday techno-management of women's sexual and reproductive realities to explain why such experiences raise gendered concerns which are very relevant to data protection law. Part IV re-imagines the GDPR so that it becomes gender responsive. It introduces a definition of *gendered risks* and identifies different types thereof using examples from the femtech context. It then discusses the *symbolic* and *normative* significance of an explicit recognition of gendered risks within the GDPR. Finally, Part V concludes and reflects on future research.

[6] We recognise that not all those who menstruate, conceive and use 'femtech' are women, and that the impact of gendered risks may also be experienced by people who are not women. Further, we recognise that transgender men and non-binary individuals may face specific risks that are not captured by our analysis.

[7] Caroline Criado Perez, *Invisible Women: Exposing Data Bias in a World Designed for Men* (Vintage 2019).

II. Risk in the GDPR

The GDPR's Risk-based Approach

Within the GDPR, risk serves a dual role: as an object of regulation *and* a feature of the regulatory approach.[8] The former renders the GDPR a 'risk regulation', aiming to mitigate the risks of data-driven technologies and proactively safeguard individuals' rights.[9] The latter entails that the GDPR adopts a 'risk-based approach', implying the specific ways in which its provisions should be implemented to achieve these aims.[10]

Risk-based approaches facilitate and justify resource allocation based on the potential impact and likelihood of risks.[11] They allow regulators to 'channel their resources to those issues which pose the greatest risk to the achievement of their objectives', thereby enhancing efficiency.[12] Similarly, by dismissing unnecessarily burdensome obligations, the GDPR's risk-based approach seeks to ensure that data protection is effectively implemented.[13] Risk is integral to the accountability principle (GDPR, art 5(2)), which assigns data controllers the responsibility for ensuring and demonstrating that personal data processing complies with data protection principles.[14] The risk-based approach shapes this responsibility by both forming and triggering controllers' obligations.[15]

First, risk determines the technical and organisational measures controllers must implement for compliance. These measures should consider 'risks of varying likelihood and severity for the rights and freedoms of natural persons'.[16] Controllers need not implement all possible or the most demanding measures in

[8] Risk was not foreign to the GDPR's precursor, the Data Protection Directive (DPD), particularly concerning the security of processing (art 17) and checks by supervisory authorities (art 20). Risk has likewise implicitly justified the categorisation of certain personal data as special categories thereof (art 8): their sensitive nature increases the risk of adverse or discriminatory impacts, necessitating stricter conditions for their processing. However, it now permeates the GDPR throughout, holding a more prominent and functional role, as explained below.

[9] Claudia Quelle, 'The "Risk Revolution" in EU Data Protection Law: We Can't Have Our Cake and Eat It, Too' in Ronald Leenes et al (eds) *Data Protection and Privacy: The Age of Intelligent Machines* (Hart Publishing 2017) 33–62.

[10] ibid.

[11] Julia Black and Robert Baldwin, 'Really Responsive Risk-Based Regulation' (2010) 32 *Law & Policy* 181 cited in ME Gonçalves, 'The Risk-Based Approach under the New EU Data Protection Regulation: A Critical Perspective' (2020) 23 *Journal of Risk Research* 143.

[12] Julia Black, 'Risk-Based Regulation: Choices, Practices and Lessons Being Learnt' in OECD, *Risk and Regulatory Policy* (OECD Publishing 2010) 185–236, 186; cited in Gonçalves, ibid at 143.

[13] Article 29 Data Protection Working Party, 'Opinion 3/2010 on the Principle of Accountability' (WP 173, 13 July 2010); Article 29 Data Protection Working Party, 'Statement on the Role of a Risk-Based Approach in Data Protection Legal Frameworks' (WP 218, 30 May 2014).

[14] Article 29 Data Protection Working Party, WP 218, ibid.

[15] Katerina Demetzou, 'GDPR and the Concept of Risk: The Role of Risk, the Scope of Risk and the Technology Involved' in E Kosta et al (eds), *Privacy and Identity Management. Fairness, Accountability, and Transparency in the Age of Big Data*, vol 547 (Springer International Publishing 2019) 137–54.

[16] GDPR, art 24; Recital 74.

every case (e.g., even for small-scale, simple processing).[17] Rather, their accountability admits different levels, corresponding to 'the facts and circumstances of each particular case'.[18] Accountability obligations are then scalable, meaning that their scope is commensurate with the risk of the processing: higher or lower likelihood and severity of said risk warrant proportionately more or less demanding obligations.[19] Akin to 'calibrating' shooting equipment based on observed hits, controllers 'calibrate' their obligations based on the estimated risks of processing so that 'they hit the mark on the ground'.[20]

Second, other obligations are triggered only by risky or high-risk processing; when risk is absent, they remain inactive.[21] For instance, obligations to appoint an EU representative (Art 27(2)), maintain records of processing (Art 30(5)) and inform about data breaches (Arts 33–34) are waived when processing is unlikely to result in risk. Conversely, when processing might result in high risk, Article 35(1) mandates a data protection impact assessment (DPIA), evaluating risks to data subjects' rights and freedoms (Art 35(7)), while Article 36 (1) requires consulting supervisory authorities.

Overall, by forming and triggering controllers' obligations, the GDPR's risk-based approach additionally outlines the ways in which the materialisation of such undesirable outcomes should be prevented, e.g., through DPIAs.[22] A harm-based approach would instead favour an 'ex post, outcome-oriented review' over such 'design' obligations.[23] Harm-based approaches also concentrate on actual damage, whereas risk-based ones consider 'every potential as well as actual adverse effect'.[24]

Conceptual Ambiguities of Risk

This prominent role of risk in the GDPR contrasts sharply with the ambiguity surrounding its meaning. Recital 76 suggests assessing risk objectively 'by reference to the nature, scope, context and purposes of the processing'. Lacking a concrete framework, however, this requirement of objective assessment rings hollow. Recital 77 broadly recommends guidance through codes of conduct, certifications and guidelines – yet, the Article 29 Data Protection Working Party (WP29) avoids indicating relevant frameworks.[25] Slightly more concrete guidance

[17] Article 29 Data Protection Working Party, WP 173 (n 13); Quelle (n 9).

[18] Article 29 Data Protection Working Party, WP 218 (n 13).

[19] Demetzou (n 15); Milda Macenaite, 'The "Riskification" of European Data Protection Law through a Two-Fold Shift' (2017) 8 *European Journal of Risk Regulation* 506.

[20] Quelle (n 9); Arts 25(1) and 32(1) exemplify this calibration, positing that data protection by design and by default and security measures respectively should rely on the risks incurred by processing.

[21] Macenaite (n 19); Quelle (n 9).

[22] Quelle ibid.

[23] ibid.

[24] Article 29 Data Protection Working Party, WP 218 (n 13).

[25] Article 29 Data Protection Working Party, 'Guidelines on Data Protection Impact Assessment (DPIA) and Determining Whether Processing Is "Likely to Result in a High Risk" for the Purposes of Regulation 2016/679' (WP 248, 4 Apr 2017).

is available through examples. Recital 75 associates risk to rights and freedoms with the risk of 'physical, material or non-material damage', including cases where processing might:

- cause discrimination, identity theft, financial loss, reputational damage, loss of confidentiality, reidentification, or other significant economic or social disadvantage;
- obstruct data subjects' rights, freedoms and control over their data;
- concern special categories of personal data;
- lead to profiling that evaluates one's work, economic, health or other situation;
- concern vulnerable natural persons, particularly children; or
- involve numerous personal data and data subjects.

Recital 91 likewise considers risky the processing of special category data and processing that prevents data subjects from exercising rights or using services/contracts. This inductive approach, however, does not yield generalisable criteria for assessing types of risk beyond those mentioned in the examples.[26]

Even these examples, though, are inconclusive. Recital 75 conflates the outcomes of processing (e.g., discrimination) with processing itself (e.g., processing of special category data), obscuring which of the two should be assessed.[27] A way out of this confusion is plausible through the WP29's definition of risk as 'a scenario describing an *event* and its *consequences*, estimated in terms of severity and likelihood'.[28] Macenaite assigns risk to rights and freedoms to the category of *consequences* and protection of personal data to the category of the *event* leading to said consequences.[29] Processing that is risky, meaning non-compliant with data protection law, exposes natural persons to the risk of having their rights violated. Following this interpretation, 'a harm is the violation of a fundamental right stemming from the processing of data as well as the material and moral implication of the latter'.[30] Hence, risk assessment examines compliance of data processing and violations of rights/freedoms in tandem. Nonetheless, most GDPR provisions[31] suggest risk factors about processing itself; only Recital 75 provides risk factors about the violation of rights and freedoms and relevant negative consequences (eg, discrimination).

[26] Demetzou (n 15).

[27] This confusion is epitomised in art 35(1), which reads: 'Where a type of processing [...] is likely to result in a high risk to the rights and freedoms of natural persons, the controller shall, prior to the processing, carry out an assessment of the impact [...] on the protection of personal data.' It is, therefore, uncertain whether the object of assessment should be the risk to rights and/or to the protection of personal data. Raphaël Gellert, 'Understanding the Notion of Risk in the General Data Protection Regulation' (2018) 34 *Computer Law & Security Review* 279.

[28] Article 29 Data Protection Working Party, WP 248 (n 25). Emphasis added.

[29] Macenaite (n 19).

[30] Gellert (n 27) 282.

[31] For example, GDPR, art 35(3) and Recital 83.

Often intangible, these negative consequences resist the quantification typically required for risk assessments.[32] Such consequences are varied and subjectively perceived on the basis of individual and collective factors (e.g., experience, age, education, cultural norms and regulations).[33] In light of such variations, exposure to identical risks does not imply identical harm; certain individuals or groups might be more vulnerable to a risk or harm than others.[34] Although Recital 75 mentions vulnerable persons, it does not clarify who (besides children) is considered as such. More helpfully, the WP29 interprets vulnerability as a power imbalance between data subjects and controllers.[35] Hence, far from being objective or quantifiable, risk is individualised and relational, casting doubts on the GDPR's abstract risk-based approach and its suitability for addressing distinct vulnerabilities.[36]

In addition, although the GDPR is technologically neutral, its risk-based approach is not immune to contextual, including technological, change.[37] On a broader level, emerging technologies exhibit considerable complexity and autonomy, while processing and generating large volumes of data.[38] They introduce new or amplify existing risks. They likewise reveal new vulnerabilities as well as dimensions of rights and freedoms.[39] Key among the latter is the collective dimension of privacy, since data-driven technologies pose risks to not only individuals but also groups and society at large.[40] The GDPR's inclusion of such risks is not straightforward, leading to calls for the recognition of 'interdependent privacy' or 'group privacy rights'.[41] On a more specific level, risk changes within a single data processing activity, when its components (e.g., supporting factors) or context (e.g., purpose) evolve.[42] The latter also involves changes in the wider organisational or societal context of the processing activity – for instance, if 'new categories of natural persons become vulnerable to discrimination'.[43] To account for these

[32] Macenaite (n 19).
[33] ibid.
[34] Gianclaudio Malgieri, *Vulnerability and Data Protection Law* (Oxford University Press, 2023).
[35] The examples offered by the WP 29 are more diverse than the GDPR's, encompassing children, employees, those suffering from illnesses, asylum seekers, older people, and generally cases warranting special protection. Article 29 Data Protection Working Party, WP 248 (n 25).
[36] Macenaite (n 19).
[37] Demetzou (n 15).
[38] ibid.
[39] ibid; Article 29 Data Protection Working Party, WP 248 (n 25).
[40] Demetzou (n 15); Macenaite (n 19).
[41] Demetzou, ibid. A useful analysis of this dimension comes from Bieker, who refers to the 'duality of data protection law', including both an individual and a structural aspect, with the latter postulating requirements for the organisation of public and private entities when processing personal data, thereby encompassing holistic considerations of risk and power dynamics. He also argues for the *de lege ferenda* recognition of collective rights, especially of minorities or other vulnerable groups, through an extension of the term 'data subject' such that it would allow the enforcement of data subject rights by groups: Felix Bieker, *The Right to Data Protection: Individual and Structural Dimensions of Data Protection in EU Law* (TMC Asser Press, 2022).
[42] Article 29 Data Protection Working Party, WP 248 (n 25).
[43] ibid.

changes, risk needs a dynamic interpretation; this might, however, add to the obscurity of the risk-based approach.

This obscurity is exacerbated in terms of the subject(s) to whom risk refers. The WP29 excludes controllers' legitimate interests from the assessment: the risks of interest are those posed to individuals rather than the organisation performing the data processing (as happens with risk-based approaches in other fields).[44] Most risk-related provisions also mention natural persons instead of data subjects, encompassing individuals beyond those whose data are being processed.[45] This choice is welcome, given that data-driven technologies affect more individuals than the ones linked to the input data (e.g., through profiling).

Nevertheless, exactly whose risk is considered remains unclear. Individual subjects and processing activities are certainly included but the inclusion of collective subjects and processing is blurry. Although Recital 75 mentions 'significant social disadvantage' and 'processing that concerns numerous data subjects', these non-binding references appear to denote merely considerations of scale; their application to more structural risks or technological and business practices is questionable. At the other end, the WP29 holds that risk assessments should range 'from an impact on the person concerned by the processing in question to a general societal impact (e.g., loss of social trust)', which is too broad to reliably guide controllers.[46]

Tension between Risks and Rights

This risk-based approach co-exists with a conventional rights-based one, safeguarding data subject rights in Chapter III of the GDPR and the right to personal data protection throughout the text. This co-existence of risks and rights – especially as a 'risk to a right' – is challenging. In particular, the scalability of accountability obligations challenges the traditional rights-based approach. According to the latter, the right to data protection, as an EU fundamental right, should be upheld in a uniform manner, not based on risk.[47]

The same applies to data subject rights (eg, access, rectification, erasure, objection, transparency, right to be forgotten, right to data portability), which lack the scalability inherent in the risk-based approach. The right of access (Article 15), for instance, is absolute.[48] Controllers should take measures to fulfil this right when it is exercised – eg, through documentation.[49] However, it is unclear whether

[44] Article 29 Data Protection Working Party, WP 218 (n 13); Article 29 Data Protection Working Party, WP 248 (n 25).
[45] See, eg, arts 24(1), 25(1), 27(2), 32(1), 33(1), 34(1) and 35(1).
[46] Article 29 Data Protection Working Party, WP 218 (n 13).
[47] Quelle (n 9).
[48] ibid.
[49] ibid.

the right of access should be upheld regardless of the risk level (following the rights-based approach) or whether documentation obligations should be proportional to the risk level, allowing limited access rights in cases of low-risk processing (following the risk-based approach).

To address this ambiguity, the WP29 argued that 'the risk-based approach is being increasingly and wrongly presented as an alternative to well-established data protection rights and principles, rather than as a scalable and proportionate approach to compliance'.[50] It stressed that the risk-based approach should not compromise data subjects' rights; these should be respected to the same extent regardless of the risk of the processing examined.[51] The WP29 thus confined scalability to controllers' compliance in the context of the risk-based approach.[52] That the two approaches are distinct does not, however, mean that they are unrelated. As mentioned above, risk assessment examines compliant data processing *and* consequences on rights and freedoms, with higher/lower compliance leading to respectively higher/lower protection of rights. In that sense, the risk-based approach could foster rather than oppose the rights-based one.

The relation between the two approaches is further complicated by the rights pertinent to the risk-based approach. Although data subjects' rights and the right to data protection are expressly mentioned, the articulation of risk-related provisions suggests a broader scope. Recital 75 mentions 'risk to the rights and freedoms of natural persons' in general and offers varied examples of these, while Article 35(1) adopts the same phrasing. The WP29 elucidates that references to rights and freedoms imply 'the right to privacy but may also involve other fundamental rights such as freedom of speech, freedom of thought, freedom of movement, prohibition of discrimination, right to liberty, conscience and religion'.[53] Nevertheless, as with the risk factors and examples of Recital 75, this indicative enumeration of rights fails to consistently guide the implementation of the risk-based approach.

Even worse, there is no guidance about the possibility of negative consequences (ie, violation of rights) without an event (ie, non-compliant processing). A data processing activity might incur risks to natural persons' rights and freedoms despite appearing compliant, in the sense of following 'a reasonable and foreseeable interpretation of the rules and principles'.[54] Article 36(1) empowers supervisory authorities to take action against the intended data processing if they consider that 'the controller has insufficiently identified or mitigated the risk' but under the condition that the processing does not comply with the GDPR.

Similarly, the WP29 acknowledges authorities' role in 'carrying out enforcement procedures in case of non-compliance of controllers, which may imply

[50] Article 29 Data Protection Working Party, WP 218 (n 13).

[51] ibid.

[52] As the WP29 stated, 'a data controller whose processing is relatively low risk may not have to do as much to comply with its legal obligations as a data controller whose processing is high-risk' ibid.

[53] ibid.

[54] Quelle (n 9).

challenging risk analysis, impact assessments as well as any other measures carried out by data controllers'.[55] There is no acknowledgement, however, of the case in which data processing is superficially compliant – or at least cannot be promptly affirmed as non-compliant – yet still exposes natural persons to risk.[56] This omission is important, as the GDPR does not provide for an independent, general obligation to protect natural persons against risks to their rights and freedoms; such an obligation instead exists only in the context of implementing other GDPR provisions.

Over-reliance on Controllers

The ambiguity surrounding risk entails that its identification and management are left to the controllers' discretion. The role of interpreting the relevant provisions and implementing appropriate responses, a role hitherto confined to public entities, is now delegated to a private one.[57] Hence, this reliance on controllers departs from risk-based regulation as an approach commonly employed by governments and regulatory agencies.[58] This departure is not absolute, since supervisory authorities can challenge controllers' risk assessment and measures or adopt a risk-based approach to their own activities. Nonetheless, one might wonder whether the GDPR places 'unjustified faith in self-regulatory enforcement of data protection rules' and, relatedly, whether controllers are well placed to undertake these risk assessments.[59]

In particular, risk assessments should consider negative consequences that might be intangible (eg, significant social disadvantage), subjective (ie, dependent on one's risk perception) or related to values and norms (eg, discrimination). These aspects render risk contestable and difficult to anticipate or objectively measure. This difficulty is aggravated by controllers' flexibility in using risk assessment frameworks of their choice, raising further uncertainty about the level of data protection across the EU and controllers' liability for these methodological choices.[60]

Instead, the experience and views of those affected by data processing do not factor into the risk assessment. Pursuant to Article 35(9) on DPIAs, '[w]here appropriate, the controller shall seek the views of data subjects or their representatives on the intended processing, without prejudice to the protection of commercial or public interests or the security of processing operations'. With the appropriateness of such consultation being entrusted to the controllers' interpretation, this

[55] Article 29 Data Protection Working Party, WP 218 (n 13).
[56] Quelle (n 9).
[57] Gonçalves (n 11).
[58] Macenaite (n 19).
[59] ibid.
[60] ibid; Article 29 Data Protection Working Party, WP 248 (n 25).

obligation remains soft and far-fetched. Drawing on the exemption of commercial interests, private entities are likely to refrain from sharing details about their processing activities for the – actual or ostensible – purpose of safeguarding commercially sensitive information and retaining competitive advantages.[61]

Conversely, the articulation of risks by 'those who live with them and experience them' would benefit risk assessment and management.[62] Input by affected individuals would have two benefits; it would help controllers identify risks that might not be obvious as well as understand individuals' concerns and risk perceptions,[63] and it would help these individuals become aware of how their data are processed, thereby enhancing transparency and trust.[64] Even when data subjects are consulted, the provision does not require that their input is taken into account or that it feeds into measures to be adopted.[65] Equally, there are no provisions on whom such a consultation should involve and what procedures it should follow.[66] WP29's only guidance is that the controller's reasons for deviating from data subjects' input or avoiding to consult them in the first place should be documented.[67] Although the possibility of public engagement in principle exists under the GDPR, it regrettably remains 'of an informational nature and neither provides assurances of comprehensive risk identification nor guarantees a full-pledged protection from risks'.[68]

III. Gendered Risks and the GDPR

As section II illustrated, EU data protection law is undergoing a 'riskification'- understood as a 'move out from the limited boundaries of formal legality of processing of data and enforcement of individual rights against companies' and 'towards a model of "enforced self-regulation" for managing technological innovation in uncertain scenarios'.[69] This riskification occurs in overly broad and ambiguous ways and, more importantly, has not bothered to concern itself with the fundamental question: *whose* data protection risks matter within the GDPR?[70] Does the EU data protection law account for risks that are currently invisible in the GDPR? The following section takes a closer look at what we argue has been overlooked by the GDPR's risk-based approach, *gendered* risks, and discusses why they matter.

[61] Macenaite (n 19).

[62] Niels van Dijk, Raphaël Gellert and Kjetil Rommetveit, 'A Risk to a Right? Beyond Data Protection Risk Assessments' (2016) 32 *Computer Law & Security Review* 286.

[63] Macenaite (n 19).

[64] ibid.

[65] ibid.

[66] van Dijk, Gellert and Rommetveit (n 62).

[67] Article 29 Data Protection Working Party, WP 248 (n 25).

[68] Macenaite (n 19) at 531.

[69] Alessandro Spina, 'A Regulatory Mariage de Figaro: Risk Regulation, Data Protection, and Data Ethics' (2017) 8 *European Journal of Risk Regulation* 89.

[70] As Tzanou has put it, 'Data protection *for whom*?' See, Tzanou (n 4) at 454.

Surveillance of Women and Femtech

Women have, throughout history, experienced diminished levels of privacy as their bodies have been treated as 'property' of their fathers, husbands or men in general.[71] Privacy, as a right, has functioned as a double-edged sword for women, and popular conceptions of privacy have been criticised by prominent feminists as providing 'a shield for domestic violence'.[72]

Modern technologies have intensified the surveillance of women by providing 'almost limitless ways to harass and control' them.[73] As the UN Special Rapporteur on the Right to Privacy has observed, 'women can expect that nearly every detail of their intimate lives will be subject to multiple forms of surveillance by State as well as private actors, from domestic violence to sexual objectification and reproduction'.[74] Women must navigate 'hidden cameras, the possibility of recorded sexual assaults, threats of "revenge porn", … the proliferation of online mobs engaging in vicious campaigns of sustained sexualised abuse',[75] deepfakes,[76] cyberflashing,[77] and so on.[78] Technologically facilitated gender-based violence 'combines issues of gender inequality, sexualised violence, internet regulation, internet anonymity, and privacy'.[79]

A range of different actors are involved in the surveillance of women: from the market and private entities (such as employers, insurance companies, healthcare providers, advertisers) to intimate partners and ultimately governments.

Femtech has emerged as a new form of surveillance of women's bodies, health and reproductive choices and intimate relations. 'Femtech', a term coined by Ida Tin, the co-founder of menstrual tracking app Clue, refers to a multi-billion-dollar technology industry that offers a variety of technological tools to monitor and manage women's sexual and reproductive health and wellbeing.[80] It encompasses a broad range of software (apps) and hardware (wearables) aimed at supporting

[71] See Reva Siegel, '"The Rule of Love": Wife Beating as Prerogative and Privacy' (1996) 105 *Yale Law Journal* 2117; Michelle J Anderson, 'Marital Immunity, Intimate Relationships, and Improper Inferences: A New Law on Sexual Offences by Intimates' (2003) 54 *Hastings Law Journal* 1465.

[72] Catherine MacKinnon, *Toward a Feminist Theory of the State* (Harvard University Press 1991) 193; Elizabeth Schneider, 'The Violence of Privacy' (1991) 23 *Connecticut Law Review* 973.

[73] Human Rights Council, 'Report of the Special Rapporteur on the Right to Privacy' (A/HRC/40/63, 27 February 2019) para 72.

[74] ibid, para 81.

[75] Mary Anne Franks, 'Democratic Surveillance' (2017) 30 *Harvard Journal of Law & Technology* 425, 447.

[76] Mary Anne Franks and Ari Ezra Waldman, 'Sex, Lies and Videotape: Deep Fakes and Free Speech Delusions' (2019) 78 *Maryland Law Review* 892.

[77] Lewis Adams, 'Cyber-flashing convict is first to be jailed under new law' *BBC News* (London, 19 March 2024). Available at: www.bbc.co.uk/news/uk-england-essex-68543605.

[78] Ian Sample, 'Internet "Is Not Working for Women and Girls", says Berners-Lee' *The Guardian* (London, 12 March 2020). Available at: www.theguardian.com/global/2020/mar/12/internet-not-working-women-girls-tim-berners-lee; Human Rights Council 2019, A/HRC/40/63 (n 73), para 78.

[79] Human Rights Council 2019, A/HRC/40/63 (n 73), para 72.

[80] 'Femtech' also includes tools geared towards those working within the healthcare system (such as applications which improve screening for breast and ovarian cancer).

women and gender minorities to track, understand and manage their menstrual, reproductive and sexual health. Femtech apps track a range of different aspects of women's sexual and reproductive health, such as menstruation,[81] fertility[82] and menopause symptoms.[83] Data users input, for example, about flow rate is then used to make predictions about future experience (i.e., fertility windows and the start date of future menstrual cycles)[84] or to offer 'personalised' information about menstrual/reproductive health and symptom management.[85]

Femtech wearable devices are worn on the body and use sensors to gather information, such as breast milk production,[86] pelvic floor muscle movements,[87] changes to cervical fluid,[88] basal body temperature[89] and sleep patterns.[90] Using a connected app, wearables provide information or direct 'bio-feedback'; for example, smart pelvic floor trainers often use vibration to guide the user's exercises.[91] Finally, femtech also encompasses smart sex toys designed for use by women, such as smart vibrators[92] and smart dildos.[93] Many smart sextech are able to be remotely controlled, while some collect biometric data from the user.[94]

To understand the use and popularity of femtech apps and devices, it is necessary to situate these within the broader social and medical context within which they exist (and were developed). There is a recognised tendency to question whether women are trustworthy narrators of their own health and pain,[95] particularly regarding conditions related to the (dis)functioning of the womb.[96]

[81] Flo Health Ltd UK, 'Flo Period & Cycle Tracker, Apple App Store' (Version 9.41). Available at: apps.apple.com/gb/app/flo-period-cycles-tracker/id1038369065.

[82] FEMOMETER Ltd, 'Femometer – Fertility Tracker, Apple App Store' (Version 5.33.1). Available at: apps.apple.com/gb/app/femometer-fertility-tracker/id1529565125.

[83] Vira Health Ltd, 'Stella | Menopause Relief, Apple App Store' (Version 2.2.2). Available at: apps.apple.com/gb/app/stella-menopause-relief/id1577904186.

[84] Sarah Johnson, Lorrae Marriott and Michael Zinaman, 'Can Apps and Calendar Methods Predict Ovulation with Accuracy?' (2018) 34 *Current Medical Research and Opinion* 1587, 1587.

[85] See, eg, Kristin Mallon, 'Menopause Made Easier: How Femtech Can Transform Symptom Management' (*FemTech World*, 9 June 2023). Available at: www.femtechworld.co.uk/menopause/menopause-made-easier-how-femtech-can-transform-symptom-management/.

[86] Elvie, 'Elvie Trainer'. Available at: www.elvie.com/en-gb/shop/elvie-trainer.

[87] Elvie, 'Elvie Pump'. Available at: www.elvie.com/en-gb/shop/elvie-pump.

[88] kegg, 'The Science Behind kegg. Available at: kegg.tech/pages/science-behind-kegg.

[89] Tempdrop, 'Tempdrop: Monitor Your Fertility' Available at: www.tempdrop.com/en-gb.

[90] Oura, 'Oura Ring'. Available at: www.ouraring.com.

[91] See, eg, Intima, 'KegelSmart™'. Available at: www.intimina.com/kegel-smart; Elvie (n 85).

[92] Lioness, 'Products: Lioness Smart Vibrator'. Available at: www.lioness.io/products/the-lioness-vibrator.

[93] Lovense, 'Products: Gravity'. Available at: www.lovense.com/thrusting-vibrating-dildo.

[94] The Lioness Smart Vibrator, for example, collects information about the rhythm of pelvic floor movements during use to provide information about arousal and orgasm. Lioness, 'How it Works'. Available at: www.lioness.io/pages/how-it-works.

[95] Anna Nelson, 'Medical Records and Epistemic Injustice: A Women's Health Issue Worthy of Greater Attention' (*APA Blog*, 11 Sept 2023). Available at: www.blog.apaonline.org/2023/09/11/medical-records-and-epistemic-injustice-a-womens-health-issue-worthy-of-greater-attention/.

[96] See, eg, Stella Villarmea, 'When a Uterus Enters the Room, Reason Goes out the Window' in Camilla Pickles and Jonathon Herring (eds), *Women's Birthing Bodies and the Law: Unauthorised Intimate Examinations, Power and Vulnerability* (Hart 2020), 70–73; Elinor Cleghorn, *Unwell Women: A Journey Through Medicine And Myth in a Man-Made World* (Weidenfield and Nicolson 2021).

Those experiencing gynaecological symptoms are often 'not listened to'[97] and can face a 'battle' for diagnosis and treatment.[98] There are also substantial knowledge gaps regarding the ways that different gynaecological conditions manifest, as women's health remains under-researched.[99] Sexual, obstetric, post-partum and gynaecological health services are often under-resourced and subject to austerity measures,[100] struggling to meet patients' needs within an appropriate time frame or with satisfactory quality.[101]

Against this backdrop, women often feel that they have to turn to femtech to fill the gaps left by traditional healthcare services. While the current state of women's healthcare operates as a 'push' factor in the femtech context, the marketing of femtech apps and wearables provides a complimentary 'pull' factor. Much of this marketing centres upon a (highly critiqued and contested)[102] promise to 'empower' women and gender diverse users with knowledge about their own sexual and reproductive health, a promise which may resonate well in light of the frustrating lack of appropriate healthcare.[103] Indeed, a number of femtech apps explicitly capitalise upon this gap, positioning their role as spotlighting existing problems, and contributing towards solving these.[104] For example, Flo (a popular menstrual tracking app) observed in its 2023 'Menstrual and Reproductive

[97] Department for Health and Social Care, *Women's Health Strategy for England* (CP736, Her Majesty's Stationery Office 2022), 7.

[98] All Party Parliamentary Group on Endometriosis 'Inquiry Report; Endometriosis in the UK: Time for Change' (2020) 27.

[99] Department for Health and Social Care (n 97), 2, 6: though note there are ongoing attempts to improve the situation.

[100] Daniela Alaattinoğlu, 'Rethinking Explicit Consent and Intimate Data: The Case of Menstruapps' (2022) 30 *Feminist Legal Studies* 157, 161.

[101] For example, in its 2022 report, the UK Royal College of Obstetricians and Gynaecologists noted that more than half a million women (570,000) were on waiting lists for gynaecological appointments across the UK, and that more than one in 20 patients in England had to wait more than a year for treatment – often for conditions such as endometriosis which have debilitating symptoms. See Renu Khanna, 'Women's health: Why is the health of at least half the global population so often overlooked?' (*World Economic Forum*, 2 Jan 2022). Available at: www.weforum.org/agenda/2023/01/women-health-gap-davos-2023/; Leah Hoctor et al, 'Women's sexual and reproductive health and rights in Europe: Issue Paper' (*Council of Europe Commissioner for Human Rights*, December 2017); Royal College of Obstetricians & Gynaecology, 'Left for too long: understanding the scale and impact of gynaecology waiting lists' (nd). Available at: www.rcog.shorthandstories.com/lefttoolong/index.html; Elvie and Motherly, The Motherload – The Weight of Limited Postpartum Support (2024). Available at: www.elvie.com/assets/main/elvie--the-motherload.pdf.

[102] Michele Estrin Gilman, 'Periods for Profit and the Rise of Menstrual Surveillance' (2021) 41 *Colombia Journal of Gender and Law* 100; Maria Novotny and Les Hutchinson, 'Data Our Bodies Tell: Towards Critical Feminist Action in Fertility and Period Tracking Applications' (2019) 28 *Technical Communication Quarterly* 332; Tereza Hendl and Bianca Jansky, 'Tales of Self-empowerment through Digital Health Technologies: A Closer Look at "Femtech"' (2022) 80 *Review of Social Economy* 29.

[103] NIHR Evidence, 'Women's Health: Why do Women Feel Unheard?' (Health and Social Care Research, 23 November 2023).

[104] See, e.g., Sorina Mihaila, 'Women's pain still not taken seriously, says Clue CEO' (*FemTech World*, 19 Jan 2024). Available at: www.femtechworld.co.uk/news/womens-pain-is-still-not-taken-seriously-says-clue-ceo/.4.

Misinformation' report that women are struggling to access reliable 'information and support around menstrual and reproductive health', concluding that 'Flo purports to actively helping to close the medical research gender gap and producing medically credible content to help inform millions of women.'[105]

While femtech's promise of empowerment for managing sexual and reproductive health is appealing, questions arise about the new ways of controlling women. As observed by Lupton:

> These devices could … be regarded as disciplinary, working to tame the sexual and reproductive body by rendering it amenable to monitoring, tracking, and detailed analysis of the data thus generated …[106]

Women, their bodies, cycles, communications, relationships and activities are constructed as 'monitored subjects'[107] that can be seduced, coerced, disciplined and controlled.[108]

Some femtech products offer an embedded functionality that sends women's period data and other intimate information to partners.[109] Intimate partner surveillance (IPS) often concerns women's sexual and reproductive autonomy issues. IPS that can also be perpetrated through general social media can cause both emotional and physical harm.[110] In the most extreme cases it can lead to violence, including reproductive coercion (which can be perpetrated through femtech) physical assault and even murder.[111] IPS and domestic violence disproportionately affect women. Official reports indicate that, in 2021, '720 women were murdered by an intimate partner, family member or relative in 17 EU Member States'.[112]

Whether femtech data processing complies with the GDPR is at least debatable.[113] Concerns have been raised with regard to, inter alia, data minimisation, transparency and the appropriate legal bases for processing of such sensitive

[105] Flo 'Mind the gaps: Menstrual and reproductive misinformation in the UK in 2023' (2023). Available at: www.flo.health/landings/reproductive-health-report-uk.

[106] Deborah Lupton, 'Quantified Sex: A Critical Analysis of Sexual and Reproductive Self-Tracking Using Apps' (2014) 17 *Culture, Health & Sexuality* 440.

[107] Karen Levy, 'Intimate Surveillance' (2015) 51 *Idaho Law Review* 679, 688.

[108] Rob Kitchin, 'Thinking Critically About and Researching Algorithms' (2017) 20 *Information, Communication & Society* 14, 19.

[109] Sorina Mihaila, 'Period tracking app Flo launches feature for male partners' (*FemTech World*, 20 Oct 2023). Available at: www.femtechworld.co.uk/news/period-tracking-app-flo-launches-feature-for-male-partners/.

[110] Molly Dragiewicz et al, 'Technology Facilitated Coercive Control: Domestic Violence and the Competing Roles of Digital Media Platforms' (2018) 18 *Feminist Media Studies* 609.

[111] R Chatterjee et al, 'The Spyware Used in Intimate Partner Violence' (2018) *IEEE Symposium on Security and Privacy* 441.

[112] There is currently a lack of comprehensive data regarding gender-based violence in the EU. See: European Institute for Gender Equality 'Gender Equality Index. Domain: Violence in the European Union (2023)'. Available at: www.eige.europa.eu/gender-equality-index/2023/domain/violence. More comprehensive data is expected to be published some time in 2024.

[113] See Anastasia Siapka and Elisabetta Biasin, 'Bleeding Data: The Case of Fertility and Menstruation Tracking Apps' (2021) 10 *Internet Policy Review* 4, 5–11.

data, including consent.[114] Indeed, against the current socio-medical landscape, the processing of personal data through femtech apps has been labelled as a 'coercive exchange' – one is required to consent to 'such data collection if one wants to access … services'.[115]

This chapter does not focus on femtech's compliance with the GDPR. Instead, we are interested in investigating the role of the GDPR itself in addressing gendered risks and harms[116] (arising from femtech processing and beyond). What are the potential gendered risks of processing and how could our understanding of risk under the GDPR evolve to encompass gendered risks? Can the GDPR address risks that go beyond individual rights and are embodied, collective and systemic?

Before we attempt to answer these questions, we explain why gender matters within the GDPR.

The GDPR and (the Absence of) Gender: Women's Sexual and Reproductive Rights and Why Gender *Matters* in Data Protection Law

While technology-facilitated surveillance is gendered, the GDPR – and European data protection law in general – is gender blind.[117] Indeed, neither 'gender' nor 'sex' are mentioned anywhere in the GDPR.[118] Article 9 of the GDPR, which deals with the processing of 'special categories' or 'sensitive data' establishes an in-principle prohibition of processing of such data because there is a risk that this might lead to, *among others*, discrimination and includes personal data

> revealing racial or ethnic origin, political opinions, religious or philosophical beliefs, or trade union membership, and the processing of genetic data, biometric data for

[114] Alaattinoğlu (n 100).

[115] Renee Shelby, Jenna Imad Harb and Kathryn Henne 'Whiteness In And Through Data Protection: An Intersectional Approach to Anti-Violence Apps and #MeToo Bots' (2021) 10 *Internet Policy Review* 1, 17.

[116] Broadly speaking, the distinction between risk and harm can be understood as follows: A risk can exist without the outcome actually materialising. A harm, however, is definite in character and generally requires a completed action. Adriana Placani, 'When the Risk of Harm Harms' (2017) 36 *Law and Philosophy* 77, 82.

[117] Malgieri and González Fuster (n 5).

[118] Sex is often used to describe the biological characteristics of a person, whereas gender relates to a person's identity – and is increasingly recognised as being socially and culturally constructed. This approach to understanding the sex/gender distinction is one which has been reflected in both international human rights law and European equality law: European Institute for Gender Equality, 'The EU's Evolving Legal and Policy Approaches to Gender Equality' (*Publications Office of the European Union*, 2022), 11; Damien A Gonzalez-Salzberg, 'The Accepted Transsexual and the Absent Transgender: A Queer Reading of the Regulation of Sex/Gender by the European Court of Human Rights' (2014) 29 *American University International Law Review* 797. However, there is also a prominent body of critical scholarship which aims to unsettle the sex/gender binary: eg, Judith Butler, *Gender Trouble* (Routledge 1990); Catherine Clune-Taylor, 'Is Sex Socially Constructed?' in Sharon Crasnow and Kristen Intemann (eds), *The Routledge Handbook of Feminist Philosophy of Science* (Routledge 2020).

> the purpose of uniquely identifying a natural person, data concerning health or data concerning a natural person's sex life or sexual orientation,

It, however, does not mention 'gender' ('gender identity') or 'sex'.

This appears a significant oversight in light of Article 21(1) of the EU Charter of Fundamental Rights (EUCFR), which provides that 'any discrimination based on any ground such as *sex*, race, colour, ethnic or social origin, genetic features, language, religion or belief, political or any other opinion, membership of a national minority, property, birth, disability, age or sexual orientation shall be prohibited'.[119] Remarkably, 'sex', a protected characteristic of primary EU anti-discrimination law, has not found its way into (or has been (un)consciously excluded from) the provision of the GDPR which aims to address discrimination. The remainder of the text of the GDPR is equally silent on gender (or sex).[120]

The GDPR's gender blindness is not innocuous; it reveals a further significant omission: a lack of acknowledgment of the significance of data protection rights for the safeguarding of women's sexual and reproductive wellbeing and autonomy (which constitutes another gendered problem). As the femtech case study above demonstrates, technology-facilitated gendered surveillance and gendered outcomes are inextricably linked with the sexual and reproductive rights of women and girls (or the lack thereof). According to the UN Working Group on Discrimination Against Women and Girls, 'the full enjoyment of sexual and reproductive health rights is indispensable to the ability of women and girls to exercise all other human rights'[121] and the non-enjoyment of these rights is 'a significant impediment to gender equality, resulting from the persistent failure of States to adequately respect, protect and fulfil those rights'.[122]

As the Council of Europe Commissioner has also observed, without 'effective state action to guarantee sexual and reproductive health and rights … some of the most significant and intimate aspects of our lives as human beings are at risk'.[123] Indeed, there cannot be gender equality without reproductive autonomy.[124] Alongside reproductive rights and autonomy, sexual rights have been recognised not only as 'fundamental human rights', but also as 'an essential component for human development' and 'fundamental to individual health and wellbeing'.[125]

[119] Emphasis added.

[120] 'Sex life' is mentioned in Recital 75 and 'sexual orientation' in Recital 71.

[121] Human Rights Council 'Women's and Girls' Sexual and Reproductive Health Rights in Crisis: Report of the Working Group on Discrimination Against Women and Girls' (A/HRC/47/38, 28 Apr 2021) para 8.

[122] ibid, 1.

[123] Hoctor et al, (n 101) at 5.

[124] See, eg, Carolina Fredrickson, 'Gender Equality Depends on Reproductive Freedom' (*SDG Action*, 2 Mar 2023). Available at: www.sdg-action.org/equality-depends-on-reproductive-rights/; Ranee Thakar, 'Sexual and reproductive health and rights must remain a priority for the UK's agenda for global gender equality' (*RCOG Blog*, 6 March 2023). Available at: www.rcog.org.uk/news/blog-sexual-and-reproductive-health-and-rights-must-remain-a-priority-for-the-uk-s-agenda-for-global-gender-equality/.

[125] Jessie V Ford et al, 'Why Pleasure Matters: Its Global Relevance for Sexual Health, Sexual Rights and Wellbeing' (2019) 31 *International Journal of Sexual Health* 217, 218.

Yet, there remains substantial stigma attached to women's sexuality, sexual pleasure and sexual expression,[126] which has 'negative implications for women's sexual autonomy, agency and freedom' and their wider wellbeing.

Gender inequality – understood as 'systemic disadvantages for women throughout their life cycle'[127] – is tied to women's sexual and reproductive status.[128] Indeed, women experience a number of 'life milestones'[129] such as menstruating, trying to conceive, giving birth and managing the menopause that make them prone to exploitative market practices seeking to capture and capitalise upon data related to these realities.[130] Women are far more likely to make use of femtech given inequalities in access to healthcare, which increases the gendered disparity of this kind of data extraction. Many women and girls regularly face sexual and reproductive crises, such as period poverty, unplanned pregnancy and sexual violence.[131] These crises are linked to 'structural discrimination and fostered by the patriarchal oppression, pervasive gender stereotypes, stigma and taboos that drive gender inequality'.[132] Finally, 'in a context of rising fundamentalisms, backlash against gains in women's equality' once again 'target sexual and reproductive health rights'.[133] Many of the issues that women and girls face in relation to their sexual and reproductive autonomy 'can be ascribed to the instrumentalization and politicization of their bodies'.[134]

Achieving sexual and reproductive justice requires dealing with large, systemic and deeply rooted social ills such as discrimination, poverty, gendered, racial and socio-economic subjugation, and their multiple and complex underlying causes. It would require making the agency and autonomy of women and girls central to all sexual and reproductive health laws and policies.[135]

This chapter undertakes a more modest task: it argues that data protection and privacy have a significant role to play when the sexual and reproductive health

[126] Hoctor et al (n 101) at 26.

[127] Human Rights Council 2021, A/HRC/47/38 (n 121), para 12.

[128] ibid.

[129] Lucy Purdon, 'Unfinished Business: Incorporating a Gender Perspective into Digital Advertising Reform in the UK and EU' (*Mozilla Foundation*, October 2023), 11.

[130] Danielle Keats Citron has noted that women are 75% more likely to use health apps than men: *The Fight for Privacy: Protecting Dignity, Identity, and Love in the Digital Age* (Chatto & Windus 2023) 14–15.

[131] As the UN notes 'an estimated 810 maternal deaths occur each day globally, 15 and 25 million unsafe abortions take place annually, resulting in approximately 47,000 deaths every year, primarily in developing countries and among members of socioeconomically disadvantaged and marginalised populations. Every 16 seconds there is a stillbirth. More than 200 million women who want to avoid pregnancy are not using modern contraception, due to a range of barriers. Millions of women and girls are denied the ability to manage their monthly menstrual cycle safely and with dignity'. Human Rights Council 2021, A/HRC/47/38 (n 122) at para 16.

[132] 'Human Rights Council 2021 (n 121) at para 12.

[133] ibid para 17.

[134] ibid.

[135] ibid.

rights of women and girls are at risk.[136] Indeed, gender *matters* for the enjoyment of the privacy and data protection rights of women.[137] As discussed above, femtech is a form of self-participatory surveillance, where women 'willingly' give information related to their reproductive and sexual activity to apps and wearables (primarily) created by private entities for profit. However, what makes the femtech case study important is that it lies at the intersection of data protection and reproductive rights,[138] and provides useful context on how digital products which process intimate personal data – with consent – might affect women's reproductive rights, autonomy and decision making.

Data protection (and privacy) are 'essential to the free development of individuals personality and identity', serve as 'necessary preconditions for the protection of fundamental values, such as dignity, liberty and equality', and 'facilitate the exercise and enjoyment of other human rights',[139] including bodily integrity and sexual and reproductive autonomy. As digital technologies make it increasingly difficult to distinguish (gendered) 'bodies' from their (gendered) 'data doubles' in the information society,[140] the femtech case study demonstrates that data protection – and the GDPR – is integral to the realisation of sexual and reproductive rights which are 'intrinsic to every woman and girl and tied to their ability to live with dignity and exercise their agency'.[141]

Indeed, the UN Special Rapporteur on the Right to Privacy has emphasised that '[g]ender based breaches of privacy are a systemic form of denial of human rights; discriminatory in nature and frequently perpetuate unequal social, economic, cultural and political structures'.[142] In light of this, he stressed that 'gender should be a key consideration for the development and enforcement of privacy protection frameworks',[143] and has called States to develop frameworks to address and prevent gender based privacy invasions, by actively protecting privacy in policy development, legislative reform and regulatory action.[144]

Regrettably, the GDPR, through its gender-blind approach, fails to recognise that personal data (and data gaps), data subjects[145] and risks of processing – which constitutes the focus of the present chapter – can be *gendered*. Admittedly, sexual

[136] This issue goes beyond 'decisional privacy' as understood in the US context. It concerns data protection as understood in the EU context.

[137] As well as trans and gender diverse individuals. See, eg, Cayce C Hughes, 'Not Out in the Field: Studying Privacy and Disclosure as an Invisible (Trans) Man' in D'Lane R Compton, Tey Meadow and Kristen Schilt (eds), *Other, Please Specify* (University of California Press 2018) 111–25; Toby Beauchamp, *Going Stealth: Transgender Politics and U.S. Surveillance Practices* (Duke University 2019).

[138] See Katie Krumbholz, Alice Militaru and Kyle J Morgan, 'Tracking the Trackers: 'Menstruapp' Privacy Policies Following the Dobbs Decision' (2024) 45 *Journal of Women, Politics & Policy* 167.

[139] Human Rights Council 2019, A/HRC/40/63, (n 73) at para 52.

[140] Kevin D Haggerty and Richard Ericson, 'The Surveillant Assemblage' (2000) 51 *The British Journal of Sociology* 605.

[141] Human Rights Council 2021, A/HRC/47/38 (n 121) para 71.

[142] Human Rights Council 2019, A/HRC/40/63 (n 73) para 104.

[143] ibid.

[144] ibid para 106.

[145] Malgieri and González Fuster (n 5).

and reproductive data could be considered 'data concerning health'[146] and, thus, fall within the special categories of data under Article 9 of the GDPR. However, this is not sufficient; it misses out that such data and more importantly their processing might entail gendered risks associated with sexual and reproductive rights, which are intrinsic to every woman and girl. The lack of any mention of gender seriously weakens any potential link between health data and women's sexual and reproductive rights. These are viewed as 'sensitive data' to the extent that they are regarded as data concerning health, but they lack a recognition of their gendered significance to women and girls.

This reveals a gap in the GDPR: symbolically, the potential gendered impact of processing is not sufficiently important to even be mentioned among the numerous GDPR recitals with the concomitant normative consequences of effacing any relevant legal recognition (for half of the population). The EU legislator's choice to refrain from any mention of gender (or even to the less preferable term 'sex') is 'particularly striking'[147] in light of its significance in relation to personal data processing (although, admittedly, this is not unique to data protection law).[148]

IV. Re-imagining the GDPR: A Gender Responsive Approach

In light of the above analysis, we argue that the GDPR should be(come) gender responsive. This entails a core normative argument calling for a reimagination of the GDPR so that it considers the 'gendered realities' of the society we live in and ensures that 'injustices are not replicated as we race towards digital development'.[149] This proposal continues Tzanou's work on the egalitarian 'reconstruction' of EU data protection law so that this can address substantive justice concerns;[150] in light of the recent Feminist Data Protection research, which calls for an interrogation of data protection so that this pursues intersectional feminist objectives;[151] and Malgieri's and Fuster's important work on the gendered 'vulnerable' data subject.[152]

Our contribution advances these debates by focusing on *gendered risks* under the GDPR. The focus on 'gendered risks' is important for two reasons.

[146] These are defined in GDPR art 4(15) as 'personal data related to the physical or mental health of a natural person, including the provision of health care services, which reveal information about his or her health status'.

[147] Malgieri and González Fuster (n 5).

[148] Gender is seen as 'barely visible in the conceptual armoury of law'. See Joanne Conaghan, *Law and Gender* (OUP 2013) 5.

[149] Sachini Perera, *White Paper on Feminist Internet Research* (Association for Progressive Communications, 2022) 48.

[150] Tzanou (n 4).

[151] Theilen et al (n 4).

[152] Malgieri and González Fuster (n 5).

First, while a risk-based approach is central to the GDPR, the possibility of data processing risks being 'gendered' has not been considered so far by the law, the relevant case law, the data protection authorities,[153] or the academic literature surrounding EU data protection law. More importantly, we consider that the risk-based approach can and should bring gender concerns within the scope of the GDPR in light of the gendered surveillance of women's data and bodies currently undertaken by market actors, states and intimate partners. Indeed, these concerns cannot be fully captured by looking merely at potentially gendered personal data,[154] or by considering the (gendered) data subject as 'vulnerable'.[155] A focus on 'gendered risks' provides a more dynamic and flexible approach, which aligns with the GDPR's focus on risks. It also enables a broader understanding of risks than the one currently adopted by the GDPR, which, beyond *individual* ones, encompasses *collective*, *systemic*, *embodied* and *societal* (*gendered*) risks.

Conceptualising *Gendered* Risks: Definitions and Categories

As discussed, despite its centrality to the GDPR, risk is fraught with conceptual ambiguities. This makes the task of conceptualising *gendered* risks challenging. Based on the dimensions of *event* and *consequences*, the GDPR is concerned with risks to natural persons' rights and freedoms arising from personal data processing. This is useful for our discussion: *gendered* risks could be understood 'as risks to the rights and freedoms of natural persons *related to gender* and arising from personal data processing'.[156] This understanding is broad: it includes risks related to gender that might arise from the processing of *gendered personal data*, risks that might arise from *gendered processing* and, more generally, risks that relate to gender but arise from what could be considered gender neutral processing of personal data. Our focus here is to the potential or the actual adverse effect of personal data processing *relating to gender*; if such a potential adverse effect exists, we submit that this would be considered a *gendered risk*.

This broad understanding of gendered risks includes different types of risk: *individual*, *embodied*, *collective* and *societal gendered risks*.

[153] Though the Data Protection Authorities in both Poland and Spain have drawn a potential connection between *vulnerability* and gender in the data protection context: Malgieri and González Fuster, n.5 at 8. The UK ICO has also recognised the potential for specific data protection concerns to arise in the (gendered) context of menstrual trackers and fertility apps: Information Commissioner's Office (ICO), 'ICO to Review Period and Fertility Tracking Apps as Poll Shows More than Half of Women Are Concerned over Data Security' (*Media Centre*, 7 September 2023) ico.org.uk/about-the-ico/media-centre/news-and-blogs/2023/09/ico-to-review-period-and-fertility-tracking-apps.

[154] It would be difficult to define these and delineate *in abstracto* why they would require enhanced protection as well as clearly distinguish what should be included or excluded from such an exercise.

[155] Malgieri and González Fuster note that 'vulnerability' – and most generally the very notion of 'protection' – is 'a double-edged sword, not necessarily always benefiting the holder of the label': Malgieri and González Fuster (n 5) at 25.

[156] Emphasis added.

Gendered Individual Risks

Our proposed understanding of *gendered risks* captures *individual risks* which constitute the GDPR's focus. Let us take an example from femtech. Assume that a woman uses a fertility and ovulation app to get pregnant and, subsequently, to track her pregnancy. Without the woman's awareness, her data are further shared with third parties, including Facebook and Google, for analytics and marketing purposes.[157] Although such third-party sharing is essential to the business models of several digital technologies, when performed in the femtech context, it predominantly relies on and affects women. As mentioned in III.2, the marketing practices for which this data sharing is employed are gendered, capitalising on reproductive milestones.[158] Such data enable the segmentation of marketing targets into similarly reproduction-related profiles(eg, 'heavy purchaser of pregnancy tests' or 'infertility/IVF').[159]

Based on these data and profiles, marketers make assumptions about women's desires and likely purchases, with the prevalent assumptions being that they desire to conceive or that they will desire baby products nine months after conception.[160] These assumptions feed into advertising practices which, unbeknownst to the femtech users on whose data they rely, might be experienced by women as unnecessary and creepy or even shameful and upsetting, depending on their individual circumstances.[161] For instance, being targeted with Facebook ads about unwanted baby products might be highly distressing for a woman who has just suffered a stillbirth.[162] This sharing of the data with third parties without explicit consent impacts the individual and is, therefore, an individual risk/harm[163] that the GDPR recognises. Additionally, we argue that it is also an example of a *gendered individual risk* because it has an individual adverse effect relating to gender through its inextricable connections to women's reproductive life.

Gendered Embodied Risks

Our understanding of gendered risks further includes *embodied* risks. For example, let us imagine that a woman uses a smart vibrator which is not sufficiently secure and is, therefore, hacked by a third party. Sextech offers women and gender minorities knowledge and control over their sexuality and sexual pleasure,

[157] This is not a hypothetical example. See Zoe Schiffer, 'Period tracking app settles charges it lied to users about privacy' (*The Verge*, 13 Jan 2021). Available at: www.theverge.com/2021/1/13/22229303/flo-period-tracking-app-privacy-health-data-facebook-google.

[158] Purdon (n 129) above.

[159] ibid.

[160] ibid.

[161] ibid.

[162] Gillian Brockwell, 'Dear tech companies, I don't want to see pregnancy ads after my child was stillborn' *The Washington Post* (Washington DC, 12 Dec 2018). Available at: www.washingtonpost.com/lifestyle/2018/12/12/dear-tech-companies-i-dont-want-see-pregnancy-ads-after-my-child-was-stillborn/.

[163] The GDPR does not mention 'harm'. It instead uses 'risk' or 'damage' terminology.

something which has often been denied to them within the patriarchal society. Against this, we submit that the woman in our example has suffered an *embodied gendered* harm. The loss of control over the flow of her intimate data generated through the smart device and accessed by an unwanted third party is an *embodied* harm.[164] As we explain elsewhere,[165] this also gives rise to a further embodied harm understood in the narrow sense: the user's bodily integrity itself is violated since the vibrator is controlled by an unwanted third party (this constitutes a sexual offence type harm).

Embodied risks broadly understood as having an impact on bodily integrity, are not explicitly acknowledged in the GDPR, but we argue that they matter because new technologies and their applications increasingly rode the boundaries between the data and the body. The body is implicated in the use of online spaces and technologies and both this and bodily subjectivity, are 'central to the experience one has in online spaces'.[166]

Digital embodiment offers a response to 'digital dualism', by situating the body 'as central to the lived experience of digital culture'.[167] Popularised by Jurgenson,[168] the concept of 'digital dualism' refers to 'a bias that treats offline/physical life as real and online/digital life as virtual and somehow less real'.[169] Embodiment in this context implies that the harms experienced in the virtual world can have 'real effects, both bodily and psychical' which are 'not tangential, but increasingly central, to how individuals experience and live their everyday lives'.[170] Thus, we can recognise that online, 'noncontact' offences may give rise to embodied harms[171] in the context of autonomy, dignity or bodily integrity. For instance, survivors of image-based sexual abuse experience this harm 'in and through their bodies, altering their sense of bodily integrity, and their corporeal, social and sexual subjectivity'.[172] In the reproductive context, scholars have emphasised the 'experientially profound' nature of pregnancy and birth[173] and highlighted that looking at

[164] ibid.

[165] ibid.

[166] Chandell Gosse, '"Not the Real World": Exploring Experienced of Online Harm, Digital Dualism and Ontological Labour' in Jane Bailey, Asher Flynn and Nicola Henry (eds) *The Emerald International Handbook of Technology-Facilitated Violence and Abuse* (Emerald Publishing Ltd 2021) 49.

[167] ibid, 50.

[168] Nathan Jurgenson, 'Digital dualism versus augmented reality' (*The Society Pages: Cyborgology*, 24 Feb 2011). Available at: www. thesocietypages.org/cyborgology/2011/02/24/digital-dualism-versus-augmented-reality/; Nathan Jurgenson, 'Digital dualism and the fallacy of web objectivity' (*The Society Pages: Cyborgology*, 13 Sept 2011). Available at: https://thesocietypages.org/cyborgology/2011/09/13/digital-dualism-and-the-fallacy-of-web-objectivity/; Gosse (n 166), 48.

[169] Gosse, ibid at 48.

[170] Nicola Henry and Anastasia Powell, 'Embodied Harms, Gender, Shame & Technology Facilitated Sexual Violence' (2015) 21 *Violence Against Women* 758, 766; See also, Jennifer Laffier and A Rehman, 'Deepfakes & Harm to Women' (2023) 3 *Journal of Digital Life & Learning* 1, 3.

[171] Gosse (n 166) at 50; Henry and Powell ibid.

[172] Clare McGlynn et al, '"It's Torture for the Soul": The Harms of Image-Based Sexual Abuse' (2021) 30 *Social & Legal Studies* 541, 550.

[173] Susan Bordo, 'Are Mothers People? Reproductive Rights and the Politics of Subjectivity' in Susan Bordo and L Heywood (eds), *Unbearable Weight: Feminism, Western Culture, and the Body* (University

reproductive issues through the lens of embodiment enables research to examine 'power and how inequality operates on and through bodies'.[174] Combining, therefore, understandings of digital and reproductive embodiment serves to underscore the potential for embodied gendered risks that arises from femtech wearables and apps data processing[175] as the data subjects' lived experience is felt through the body.

Therefore, when thinking about embodied risks in the context of femtech, it is important to consider both embodiment per se, and the gendered aspects of embodiment. Femtech wearables are 'embodied computing technologies'[176] – worn in, on, or around the body, and quantify bodily information through computing. They operate through an 'embodied interaction' with the user,[177] as wireless biosensors placed on the device to collect data flows from within the body. The use of smart (intimate) wearables, thus, implies a 'double embodiment' process whereby the technology is embedded in and works through the user's body,[178] and becomes the means through which the user understands and/or experiences the self. For instance, while placing a smart menstrual cup inside their bodies, users not only do the data work but also use the analytics to understand, track, and manage their menstrual life. The 'double embodiment' thus, produces a 'networked body'[179] – where the intimate self is experienced and embodied through an interconnected assemblage of the biological and the digital. The networked body functions through the data flows between three nodes in the assemblage – the body, the device and the mobile app. These three nodes are interconnected and collectively inform the user's technologically facilitated intimate embodiment.

Overall, we argue that the GDPR should concern itself with *embodied* risks. Emerging technologies, such as wearables, involve contact with the body and, as such, they implicate interests in autonomy and bodily integrity. Crucially, risks to bodily integrity and autonomy are closely linked to human dignity and matter when considering risks under the GDPR.

of California Press 2003) 94 (original emphasis); See also, Iris Young, 'Pregnant Embodiment: Subjectivity and Alienation' (1984) 9 *The Journal of Medicine and Philosophy: A Forum for Bioethics and Philosophy of Medicine* 45.

[174] Katrina Kimport and Krystale Littlejohn, 'What Are We Forgetting? Sexuality, Sex, and Embodiment in Abortion Research' (2021) 58 *The Journal of Sex Research* 863, 868.

[175] This section on embodiment builds from other research on Femtech Wearables and Embodied Harm, conducted as part of the project 'FemTech surveillance: Gendered digital harms and regulatory approaches'. For more information see: www.sheffield.ac.uk/law/research/centres-and-institutes/sciel/projects/femtech-surveillance-gendered-digital-harms-and-regulatory-approaches.

[176] Isabel Pedersen and Andrew Iliadis, *Embodied Computing: Wearables, Implantables, Embeddables, Ingestibles* (MIT Press 2020).

[177] Paul Dourish, *Where the Action Is: The Foundations of Embodied Interaction* (MIT Press 2001).

[178] Federica Buongiorno, 'Embodiment, Disembodiment and Re-embodiment in the Construction of the Digital Self' (2019) 12 *HUMANA.MENTE Journal of Philosophical Studies* 310.

[179] Isabel Pedersen, 'Will the Body Become a Platform? Body Networks, Datafied Bodies, and AI Futures' in Isabel Pedersen and Andrew Iliadis (eds), *Embodied Computing: Wearables, Implantables, Embeddables, Ingestibles* (MIT Press 2020) 21–47.

Gendered Collective and Societal Risks

Although it is unclear whether the GDPR's risk-based approach extends beyond the individual, our proposed understanding of gendered risks encompasses *collective* and *societal* risks. *Collective* or *group* harms occur 'when a group – either aligning with a traditional category or an *ad hoc* group – experiences a harm in their capacity as a member of that group eg, a group of workers, local or indigenous community'.[180] *Societal* harms refer to 'harms affecting larger-scale human groups bounded by persistent interaction, normally sharing the same spatial territory, typically subject to the same political authority and dominant cultural expectations, interests, and norms'.[181] Let us take an example from each category. As part of a workplace wellness programme at a company, employees are given free access to an app which has a period and fertility tracking component and also monitors women's menopausal symptoms.[182] Employees who use the app receive additional benefits and rewards such as reduced health insurance premiums. The employer who has purchased the app for its employees has access to the data generated by the app, supposedly to make appropriate adjustments to the workplace to support employee wellbeing. Over time, it appears that a number of women employees are refused promotions which they would be expected to get or promotions for women are significantly delayed. In fact, the majority of the women who are using the app 'to get pregnant' are not putting themselves forward for a promotion even if they are at the appropriate career stage.

This would be an example of a *gendered collective harm*. It refers to a small grouping of people (here the women employees) of a company and is gendered because it concerns women's sexual and reproductive data and autonomy. While the gendered data use might lead to workplace discrimination and aspects of it would be captured by EU anti-discrimination law,[183] we argue that the GDPR – and data protection law – should care for these problems as well. This is because women employees are disproportionately subjected to a chilling effect of employer surveillance affecting their reproductive autonomy and their consent or the legal

[180] Chris Thomas et al, 'The Case For a Broader Approach to AI Assurance: Addressing "Hidden" Harms in the Development of Artificial Intelligence' (2024) *SRN Electronic Journal* 1, 5; Linnet Taylor, Luciano Floridi and Bart van der Sloot (eds), *Group Privacy: New Challenges of Data Technologies* (Springer International Publishing 2017).

[181] Thomas et al, ibid 5; Luciano Floridi, 'Global Information Ethics: The Importance of Being Environmentally Earnest' (2007) 3 *International Journal of Technology and Human Interaction* 1; Nathalie A Smuha, 'Beyond the Individual: Governing AI's Societal Harm' (2021) 10 *Internet Policy Review* 1.

[182] Drew Harwell, 'Is your pregnancy app sharing your intimate data with your boss?' *The Washington Post* (Washington DC, 10 April 2019). Available at: www.washingtonpost.com/technology/2019/04/10/tracking-your-pregnancy-an-app-may-be-more-public-than-you-think/; Filza Siddiqui 'The Birth of Femtech Lays Fertile Grounds for Pregnancy Discrimination in the Workplace' (2024) 62 *Family Court Review* 413.

[183] Directive 2006/54/EC of the European Parliament and of the Council of 5 July 2006 on the implementation of the principle of equal opportunities and equal treatment of men and women in matters of employment and occupation (recast), OJ L 204, 26.7.2006.

basis used for the processing of such data by their employer is not sufficient to account for the power asymmetries in the context of the employment relationship.

Finally, our understanding of gendered risks includes *gendered societal* risks.[184] As explained, these might also be experienced at an individual level, but their effects might have a systemic and cumulative impact on the lived experiences of women in general. Non-consensual intimate images[185] and deepfakes[186] fall in this category of societal gendered harms and are relevant to the GDPR but let us take another example from the femtech context, which concerns participatory self-surveillance. Imagine that a fertility and ovulation app is funded by anti-abortion campaigners.[187] The app is widely used by women and girls in different countries, including in countries that criminalise abortion and require sharing of such data with law enforcement authorities.

This example – which is not entirely imaginary – raises questions that are difficult to capture within the GDPR's regulatory capacity. First, it involves broader issues around consent.[188] While it could be assumed that women have given valid explicit consent for the processing of their intimate personal data by the app under the GDPR, this consent does not cover femtech's business models and actors involved therein which escape the defined categories found in the GDPR (controller/processor). Would consent under the GDPR to process data by this app cover the fact that the app has been funded by anti-abortion campaigners? How is this fact to be captured when it does not form part of standard privacy policies and terms and conditions but was revealed by the media? Is there any violation of the GDPR at all?

More importantly, we argue that a *societal risk* arises when market surveillance of women's sexual and reproductive autonomy is ultimately used by states to control, police and coerce women's data bodies. We consider this an example of a *gendered societal risk*: the state surveillance and control of women's sexual and reproductive bodies is perpetrated through the 'compelled assistance' of private market companies. The GDPR clearly does not focus on such *gendered societal risks*, but we argue that it *should* be concerning itself with these as a matter of substantive justice.[189]

Overall, as the above examples from the femtech case study demonstrate, gendered risks might produce both *tangible harms* and *intangible harms*. *Tangible harms* refer to physical and material as well as non-material/emotional damage arising from the misuse or abuse of users' personal data, embodied injuries,

[184] See also Bieker (n 41).

[185] Clare McGlynn, Erika Rackley and Ruth Houghton, 'Beyond "Revenge Porn": The Continuum of Image-Based Sexual Abuse' (2017) 25 *Feminist Legal Studies* 25.

[186] Laffier and Rehman (n 170).

[187] Jessica Glenza, 'Revealed: women's fertility app is funded by anti-abortion campaigners' *The Guardian* (London, 30 May 2019). Available at: www.theguardian.com/world/2019/may/30/revealed-womens-fertility-app-is-funded-by-anti-abortion-campaigners.

[188] Alaattinoğlu (n 100).

[189] Tzanou (n 4).

intimate partner surveillance and discrimination and intangible harms relating to the power asymmetries between women and femtech actors, the inhibitive and controlling effects of femtech surveillance and the opacity of femtech's algorithmic predictions. *Intangible harms* can be more indirect,[190] abstract and, therefore, more difficult to determine[191] often lacking an individualistic focus and requiring attention to scale[192] and to both actors involved in femtech surveillance and bodies subject to its incremental everyday techno-management.

In short, this section identified different risks with which the GDPR should be concerned. These are *individual-level* risks (captured by the current focus of the GDPR), but also *embodied, collective* and *societal* risks. These categories are not clear cut but may overlap with each other. It might also be that more than one category of risk is present in a particular case: the risk might be individual, embodied and societal. Crucially, the common characteristic of all these identified types of risk is their *gendered* nature (gender is understood here in an *intersectional* way).[193] While we provided a definition of *gendered risks*, we still need to explain why it is important to identify risks as gendered under the GDPR and, more broadly, in EU data protection law. We now turn to this question.

Why Should the GDPR Recognise Gendered Risks?

There are two main reasons underlying our normative suggestion that the GDPR – and more broadly data protection law – *should* explicitly recognise *gendered* risks. Such a recognition is important for both *symbolic* and *normative* reasons.

Symbolic Significance: Gendered Risks and Epistemic (In)Justice

We argue that in light of the 'likelihood', 'severity' and 'possible consequences'[194] of producing systemic harms to women and girls at both the individual and the societal level as identified above, the lack of an explicit recognition of an adverse impact related to gender of personal data concerning them would constitute at a *symbolic* level an *epistemic injustice.*

[190] Maria Tzanou 'Addressing Big Data and AI Challenges' in M Tzanou (ed), *Health Data Privacy under the GDPR* (Routledge 2021) 106–32.

[191] Orla Lynskey, *The Foundations of EU Data Protection Law* (OUP 2015).

[192] Danielle Keats Citron and DJ Solove, 'Privacy Harms' (2021) 102 *Boston University Law Review* 793.

[193] Kimberle Crenshaw 'Mapping the Margins: Intersectionality, Identity Politics, and Violence Against Women of Colour' (1991) 43 *Stanford Law Review* 1241; Shelby, Imad Harb and Henne (n 115) at 3.

[194] This is the language used by the CJEU in recent cases regarding non-material damages under the GDPR. For instance, in NAP the Court held that 'the risks of a personal data breach caused by the processing concerned, more specifically the likelihood and severity thereof, and the possible consequences for the rights and freedoms of natural persons need to be assessed'. See Case C-340/21 *VB v Natsionalna agentsia za prihodite* EU:C:2023:986.

In her ground-breaking work, Miranda Fricker theorised the intersection of social epistemology with theories of justice. Fricker identified two distinctively epistemic forms of injustice: *testimonial injustice*, which 'occurs when prejudice causes a hearer to give a deflated level of credibility to a speaker's word' and *hermeneutical injustice* which 'occurs when a gap in collective interpretive resources puts someone at an unfair disadvantage when it comes to making sense of their social experiences'.[195] While both forms are relevant here, we focus on hermeneutical injustice which directly links with our discussion of the law (here: the GDPR). Hermeneutical injustice is structural because it arises when a society lacks the interpretive resources to make sense of a speaker's experience, because they or members of their social group have been 'prejudicially marginalized in meaning-making activities'.[196] The example used by Fricker to explain hermeneutical injustice is illuminating in the context of the present discussion. As Fricker explained, prior to the introduction of the concept of sexual harassment into public and institutional discourse, people tended to interpret women's experiences and trauma at unwanted sexual advances as 'hysterical reactions to innocent flirtation'.[197] Sexually harassed women suffered *hermeneutical injustice* because they lacked the interpretive resources to make sense of the injustice they were suffering, due to their prejudicial epistemic marginalisation: women were expected to put up with what was considered 'normal' male behaviour.[198]

While Fricker's hermeneutical injustice theory focuses primarily on the individual level and proposes epistemic virtue as a solution,[199] it is an important analytical framework through which one can consider gender concerns in the GDPR (or the absence thereof). Unlike Fricker, who focuses on the speaker's experiences (eg, those of harassed women), hermeneutical injustice concerns here the *institutional* (the *legislative*) level and, in particular, *how* epistemic injustice may be constructed through legal frameworks and policies. Feminist theory has long discussed 'the way in which relations of power can constrain women's ability to understand their own experiences'.[200] As Nancy Hartsock noted, 'the dominated live in a world structured by others for their purposes – purposes that at the very least are not our own and that are in various degrees inimical to our development and even existence'.[201] Social institutions and practices are structured 'to favour the powerful' and, from an epistemological point of view, 'the powerful have an unfair advantage in structuring collective social understandings'.[202] This entails that

[195] Miranda Fricker, *Epistemic Injustice: Power and the Ethics of Knowing* (OUP 2007) 1.
[196] Fricker (ibid), 158–59; Elizabeth Anderson, 'Epistemic Justice as a Virtue of Social Institutions' (2012) 26 *Social Epistemoly* 163, 166.
[197] ibid.
[198] ibid.
[199] ibid.
[200] Fricker (n 195) at 148.
[201] Nancy Hartsock, *The Feminist Standpoint Revisited and Other Essays* (Westview Press 1998) 241.
[202] Fricker (n 195) at 148.

'in the hermeneutical context of social understanding, … if understandings are structured a certain way, then so are the social facts'.[203]

The explicit recognition of gendered concerns in data protection law is, therefore, significant at a *symbolic* level. This recognition would address the above issue of institutional epistemic injustice and make the GDPR an even more robust fundamental rights' legal instrument which concerns itself with – so far – largely neglected data protection issues. Such a recognition is urgently needed as emerging technologies increase the surveillance capabilities of women's bodies, thereby incurring gendered risks.

This recognition departs from the current GDPR approach and would, therefore, require legislative intervention. In practice, it could be incorporated in one of the GDPR's numerous recitals or included where it provides examples of 'risk' and 'risky processing'. For instance, the GDPR recognises that children require additional protection, particularly in relation to information society services, because they are considered to be 'vulnerable'.[204] It would certainly be important to also acknowledge the data protection risks that girls face daily with regard to menstruation and, more broadly, their sexual and reproductive rights.

It goes without saying that *de lege ferenda*, it would be even more preferable if gender (as well as sexual and reproductive rights) were explicitly recognised in Article 9 of the GDPR which, unlike its recitals, is legally binding. This would better address the issues of epistemic injustice identified above.

Normative Significance: Gendered Risks and the GDPR's Risk-based Approach

An explicit recognition of gender (and gendered risks) within the GDPR is also significant due to its *normative* implications. In particular, the weaknesses of the risk-based approach, identified in Part 2, lend support to the need for a recognition of gendered risks.

First, the ambiguity surrounding the meaning of risk has implications for the implementation of the risk-based approach. As discussed above, GDPR-mandated accountability obligations are scalable, meaning that their scope should be calibrated based on the risks posed to natural persons, specifically the likelihood and severity thereof. Neglecting to identify and manage an entire category of risks (here gendered ones) entails that controllers' accountability obligations are inaccurately calibrated. Such omission, and accordingly such inaccurate scaling, is striking when it comes to gendered risks, which can be both highly likely (since they affect users simply by virtue of their gender) and highly severe (since they can cause bodily, reproductive harms). Therefore, an explicit recognition of gendered

[203] ibid.
[204] See, inter alia, Recitals 38 and 75, as well as GDPR, art 8 (n 2).

risks is necessary for the accurate scaling of controllers' accountability obligations and, more concretely, for the implementation of appropriate technical and organisational measures in service of compliance.

In line with the preceding conceptualisation of gendered risks, as well as the understanding of risk as a scenario describing both an event and its consequences, such a recognition should be broad. It should consider not only gendered processing and the processing of gendered personal data (event) but also the gender-related impacts of such processing (consequences), even when the latter is gender neutral (eg, in cases where compliant data processing may nonetheless lead to technology-facilitated gender-based violence or other violations of bodily integrity). It should, likewise, be broad in terms of the type of risk, including digital as well as embodied, tangible as well as intangible. Beyond the individual-level risks that are currently captured by the GDPR, such a recognition of gendered risks should finally be broad in terms of the risk subjects, encompassing groups/collectives and society at large, as well as individuals.

Second, as the GDPR does not impose a general, independent obligation to protect natural persons' rights and freedoms (but rather one contingent on the compliance of data processing), the relation between rights and risks and the scope of rights to be considered, remain unclear. The explicit inclusion of gendered risks into the GDPR's risk-based approach is therefore needed to expand the scope of rights under consideration and include sexual and reproductive health rights. As demonstrated, reproductive rights are necessary to the enjoyment of other fundamental rights yet often threatened by data-driven technologies, including femtech. Following the WP29's guidance on the scalability of risks versus rights, consideration and respect of such reproductive rights should be upheld even when the data processing itself is of low risk.[205]

Third, given the ambiguities surrounding its exact meaning and scope, the risk-based approach is largely left to the controllers' interpretation, which may or may not include input from data subjects, despite the fact that risk is often subjective and hard to objectively assess. This exclusive reliance on controllers is problematic if we consider that, following general trends in the IT industry, many developers and owners of, for instance, the for-profit femtech products and services are not of the same gender as the users of said products and services.[206] It is therefore less

[205] Article 29 Data Protection Working Party, WP 218 (n 13).

[206] For example, popular femtech apps Flo, Glow and Ovia have male CEOs and (co-)founders at the time of writing: C Tucker, '"Our Goal Is to Showcase What Femtech Can Accomplish and That It Is Worth Investing in": Interview with Flo's (the Period Tracker App) CEO and Co-Founder, Dmitry Gurski' (*EU-Startups*, 22 September 2021). Available at: www.eu-startups.com/2021/09/our-goal-is-to-showcase-what-femtech-can-accomplish-and-that-it-is-worth-investing-in-interview-with-flos-the-period-tracker-app-ceo-and-co-founder-dmitry-gurski/; Glow, 'About Glow: Revolutionizing Women's Health Through Data & AI' (*Glow*, 20 May 2023) Available at: www.glowing.com/about-glow; Forbes, 'Paris Wallace | CEO – Ovia Health' (*Forbes Business Council*). Available at: www.councils.forbes.com/profile/Paris-Wallace-CEO-Ovia-Health/68645c4f-8a41-4631-99d8-8f2afd9ee7be#:~:text=Paris%20Wallace%20is%20CEO%20of,women%20and%20families%20since%202012. On the general trends about female representation in IT with a specific focus on

likely that they will, on their own initiative, identify and anticipate gendered risks, of which they will probably lack first-hand experience. Yet, when these developers and owners act as data controllers, their interpretation of the risk-based approach will, for the most part, be binding. To counter, therefore, controllers' blind spots (in the femtech context and beyond), the possibility of gendered risks should be expressly and authoritatively acknowledged in the law rather than relegated to controllers' self-regulatory initiatives.

A More Moderate Re-thinking of the GDPR: Making Data Protection Law Gender-responsive *de lege lata*

Above we called for legislative intervention that would incorporate gender in the GDPR – for instance, through one of its recitals or its substantive provisions. However, we acknowledge that such a legislative intervention is not forthcoming, at least in the near future. How could we then re-imagine the GDPR – and the data protection ecosystem more broadly – to meet the need for a recognition of gendered risks? In keeping with existing arguments in the literature, we agree that, beyond the realm of gender, the GDPR should broadly complement its atomistic focus on individual data subjects' protection with an equivalent focus on the collective and societal, systemic risks incurred by data-driven technologies.[207] Such legislative changes would be welcome, but probably hard to achieve, so in what follows we propose at least four other (non-legislative) ways to put gendered (especially collective) risks at the forefront of data protection.

First, contrary to their more common individual rendering, data controllers could perform collective DPIAs; we call these, 'Gender-focused DPIAs' or indeed 'Feminist DPIAs'.[208] The development of such sector-, technology- or target group-specific DPIA frameworks would be better suited to account for the more collective sorts of risks and consequences on particular groups. In particular, a (femtech) sector-specific approach to DPIA frameworks would be able to draw on the accumulated sectoral knowledge and address risks arising from relevant data processing activities in a more targeted, detailed manner. This is recommended by the WP29 itself, which suggests that 'a single DPIA could be used to assess multiple processing operations that are similar in terms of the risks presented, provided adequate consideration is given to the specific nature, scope, context and purposes

the EU context, see: European Parliament, 'European Parliament Resolution of 21 January 2021 on Closing the Digital Gender Gap: Women's Participation in the Digital Economy (2019/2168(INI))' (P9_TA(2021)0026, 21 January 2021).

[207] Inge Graef and Bart van der Sloot, 'Collective Data Harms at the Crossroads of Data Protection and Competition Law: Moving Beyond Individual Empowerment' (2022) 33 *European Business Law Review* 153.

[208] Alessandra Calvi, 'Data Protection Impact Assessment under the EU General Data Protection Regulation: A Feminist Reflection' (2024) 53 *Computer Law & Security Review* 1.

of the processing'.[209] More concretely, this applies to cases of (i) data processing within a particular sector; (ii) use of similar technologies for data processing; or (iii) similar data processing activities.[210] Such collective DPIAs would consider not only high-risk processing but also broader risky outcomes (ie, potential violations of rights, including sexual and reproductive rights).

It is crucial that data subjects' engagement is sought by controllers in developing 'Feminist DPIAs'. Given that risks are varied and often subjective, their assessment would benefit from becoming more participative. Facilitated by Article 35(9) of the GDPR, public involvement could help achieve a more comprehensive framing of the relevant risks, factoring in data subjects' knowledge and context, particularly with respect to gendered risks- be they individual, embodied, collective or societal.

Second, considerations of gendered risks could be made prominent in relevant interpretations and guidance. Recital 77 of the GDPR indicatively suggests the provision of guidance by codes of conduct, certifications, EDPB guidelines and data protection officers, all of which could ensure the inclusion of gendered risks. In that regard, the role of data protection authorities is pivotal. DPAs could specifically direct controllers' attention to gendered risks, raise awareness about these and ensure that data subjects have access to redress mechanisms where such risks materialise. A promising example of such efforts is the recently launched review of period and fertility tracking apps by the UK's Information Commissioner's Office (ICO).[211]

Third, without placing the onus of change on data subjects, their 'strength in numbers' could help address the gendered risks of large-scale data-driven technologies (including femtech).[212] Going back to the discussion of group or collective privacy, data subjects, as groups of citizens and/or civil society organisations, could resort to collective means of defence to address correspondingly collective gendered risks. Such collective action, commonly perceived in law as 'the right to procedural class action and/or to the positive protection of a collective interest' could be taken ex post (eg, through strategic litigation) and ex ante (ie, through preventive measures).[213] Indeed, the provisions of Article 80 of the GDPR leave room for not-for-profit bodies, organisations or associations (e.g., digital rights non-profits, consumer associations, trade unions) to start an action on behalf of data subjects (with or without the latter's mandate) albeit under certain conditions and differing national transpositions. Even in the case of (at least seemingly)

[209] Article 29 Data Protection Working Party, WP 248 (n 25).

[210] ibid.

[211] Information Commissioner's Office (n 153).

[212] Jef Ausloos, Jill Toh and Alexandra Giannopoulou, 'The Case for Collective Action against the Harms of Data-Driven Technologies' (*Ada Lovelace Institute*, 23 November 2022). Available at: www.adalovelaceinstitute.org/blog/collective-action-harms/.

[213] ibid.

compliant data processing, data subjects do not necessarily have the (informational or financial) capacity to exercise their rights against resourceful data controllers on an individual basis but may instead require coordination on a collective level.[214] To that end, collectively exercising the right of access has been supported as a means to identify the violation(s) on which subsequent litigation can be based and to help data subjects discern the collective rather than individual risks to which they are exposed.[215]

Fourth, data subjects' engagement could be initiated by local, national and EU policymakers, who would meaningfully include (representatives of) groups that are subject to collective gendered risks across all stages of 'law-making, policy, agenda and strategy setting, litigation, advocacy' as well as 'throughout standardisation processes and broader discussions of technology and digital rights'.[216]

Finally, national and EU courts have an important role to play in recognising gendered risks within data protection law. In particular, the CJEU's widely celebrated pro-data protection/ fundamental rights approach could further develop in this direction to explicitly acknowledge gendered concerns and their link with women's and girls' sexual and reproductive rights.

V. Conclusion

This chapter called for the re-imagination of the GDPR to explicitly recognise gender concerns and argued that its risk-based approach could be a vehicle to achieve this.[217] Indeed, risk is central to the GDPR: it is the object and outcome of data protection regulation, as well as a feature of its regulatory approach. However, the current lack of specification about the conceptualisation and measurement of risk, its complex or even antagonistic relation to rights, and the kinds of knowledge or involvement required for its assessment raise several conceptual and practical challenges.

[214] ibid.

[215] René LP Mahieu and Jef Ausloos, 'Harnessing the Collective Potential of GDPR Access Rights: Towards an Ecology of Transparency' (*Internet Policy Review*, 6 July 2020). Available at: www.policyreview.info/articles/news/harnessing-collective-potential-gdpr-access-rights-towards-ecology-transparency/1487; Ausloos, Toh and Giannopoulou (n 212).

[216] Jef Ausloos, Jill Toh and Alexandra Giannopoulou, 'The Role of Collective Action in Ensuring Data Justice' (*Ada Lovelace Institute*, 1 December 2022). Available at: www.adalovelaceinstitute.org/blog/data-collective-action-justice/.

[217] The need to recognise gendered risks could also support an argument for the re-imagination of other, similarly risk-based, legislative instruments. For instance, the EU AI Act explicitly refers to sex and gender, which lends support to the inclusion of relevant considerations in the GDPR, while also recognising the possibility of intangible and societal harms. Nonetheless, the concept of vulnerability is again left unclear; the AI Act refers to children and migrants as vulnerable individuals but, other than that, it seems to understand vulnerability as a condition caused by age and physical or mental disabilities.

This lack of specification eventually jeopardises data subjects' protection by obscuring the applicability of data subjects' rights and data protection rules more broadly. Focusing on gender, we submitted that while a risk-based approach is central to the GDPR, the possibility of risks or harms of data processing being *gendered* has not, so far, been considered in the law, the case law or the academic literature surrounding EU data protection law. This chapter attempted to fill this regulatory and knowledge gap by conceptualising '*gendered risks*' and by identifying different categories beyond the GDPR's narrow focus on individualistic risks. Despite the conceptual difficulties that the GDPR's risk-based approach poses, we consider that this is the best way to bring gender concerns within its scope, as these cannot be fully and effectively captured by looking merely at potentially gendered personal data, or by considering the (gendered) data subject as 'vulnerable'. In this regard, we argued that a focus on *gendered risks* provides a more dynamic and flexible model, which aligns well with the GDPR's risk-based approach and toolkit on risks mitigation, while probing a reflection on a broader understanding of risks than the one currently envisaged under the GDPR's atomistic focus.

We defined *gendered risks* as risks to the rights and freedoms of natural persons *related to gender* and arising from personal data processing. This conceptualisation of gendered risk focuses on the likelihood of personal data processing resulting in an adverse effect relating to gender; if such a potential adverse effect is likely to materialise this signifies a *gendered risk*. Beyond individual risks, which the GDPR already recognises, we identified and articulated further types of gendered risks that the GDPR -and more broadly EU data protection law- should be concerning itself with. These include *embodied*, *collective* and *societal* gendered risks. To conceptualise these categories of gendered risks, we focused on femtech as a useful case study at the intersection of data protection and reproductive and sexual rights.

We argued that *embodied* risks, broadly understood as having an impact on bodily integrity, should be recognised because new technologies (such as femtech) increasingly blur the boundaries between data and bodies. Furthermore, the GDPR should acknowledge *collective* gendered risks, which occur when a group experiences a harm in their capacity as a member of that group, and *societal* gendered risks, whose effects might have a systemic and cumulative impact on the lived experiences of women and girls in general.

In light of this, we submitted that the GDPR – and more broadly data protection law – *should* explicitly recognise gendered risks. Such a recognition is important for both symbolic and normative reasons. We acknowledged, however, that this re-imagining of the GDPR to make it gender responsive, would require legislative intervention as it departs from the current 'gender-blind' approach. For the sake of completeness of the discussion, we proposed a number of *de lege lata* ways to put gendered risks at the forefront of data protection law, including feminist DPIAs. Further research – which goes beyond the scope of this chapter – is needed into how feminist DPIAs could be (co-)designed and (co-)implemented in practice so that collective interests are properly considered. We intend to undertake this research in the future, but meanwhile aspire to have opened a new way of thinking about the GDPR's risk-based approach, especially on how this can be developed to incorporate substantive (gender) data justice interests.[218]

Acknowledgment

The research for this paper was funded by the Leverhulme Trust Research Project Grant 'FemTech surveillance: Gendered digital harms and regulatory approaches', RPG-2022-015. The drafting of sections 2, 4.2.2 and 4.3 is primarily attributed to Anastasia Siapka; that of sections 3, 3.2, 4, 4.1, 4.2 and 4.2.1 to Maria Tzanou; and that of section 3.1 to Anna Nelson. Sections 1 and 5 were co-drafted. The whole manuscript is shaped by all authors and supported by Anna Nelon's research assistance.

[218] Tzanou (n 4); Linnet Taylor 'What is Data Justice?' (2017) 4 *Big Data & Society* 1; Catherine D'Ignazio and Lauren F Klein *Data Feminism* (MIT Press 2020).

6

Data Transfers, Schrems and the Future of Data Transfers under the GDPR

JAMES KNEALE

I. Introduction

On 10 July 2023, after a long period of negotiations with the US government, the European Commission adopted the EU–US Data Privacy Framework Decision, intended to ensure that organisations in the EU can lawfully transfer the personal data of EU data subjects to the US.[1] The adoption of this decision was intended to be the culmination of a saga of litigation and legislative reform initiated in June 2013 when Max Schrems, then an Austrian postgraduate law student, privacy activist and Facebook user, complained to the Irish Data Protection Commissioner that his personal data were being transferred by Facebook to the US, where they were liable to be accessed by the National Security Agency's ('NSA') bulk surveillance programmes.

Part II of this chapter traces the progress of Mr Schrems' litigation from his initial complaint to the Data Protection Commissioner, by way of the Irish High Court, to the Court of Justice of the European Union ('CJEU') under the then Data Protection Directive. It discusses the important judgments given by the CJEU in *Schrems I*[2] and *Schrems II*[3] where the CJEU invalidated both the Safe Harbour Decision[4] and the Privacy Shield Decision,[5] the predecessors to the EU–US Data Privacy Framework Decision.

[1] Commission Implementing Decision EU 2023/1795 of 10 July 2023 pursuant to Regulation (EU) 2016/679 of the European Parliament and of the Council on the adequate level of protection of personal data under the EU–US Data Privacy Framework [2023] OJ L231/118 ('the EU–US Data Privacy Framework Decision').

[2] Case C–362/14 *Schrems v Data Protection Commissioner* EU:C:2015:650 ('*Schrems I*').

[3] Case C–311/18 *Data Protection Commissioner v Facebook Ireland Ltd* EU:C:2020:559 ('*Schrems II*').

[4] Commission Decision of 26 July 2000 pursuant to Directive 95/46/EC of the European Parliament and of the Council on the adequacy of the protection provided by the safe harbour privacy principles and related frequently asked questions issued by the US Department of Commerce [2000] OJ L215/7 ('the Safe Harbour Decision').

[5] Commission Implementing Decision (EU) 2016/1250 of 12 July 2016 pursuant to Directive 95/46/EC of the European Parliament and of the Council on the adequacy of the protection provided by the EU-U.S. Privacy Shield [2016] OJ L207/1 ('the Privacy Shield Decision').

Part III offers a preliminary assessment of whether the EU–US Data Privacy Framework Decision meets the concerns expressed by the CJEU in *Schrems I* and *Schrems II*. It discusses, in particular, whether the EU–US Data Privacy Framework Decision is likely to withstand an inevitable legal challenge, in the light of the CJEU's findings that Safe Harbour and Privacy Shield did not ensure an essentially equivalent level of protection of data subjects' rights to that guaranteed in the EU legal order. In particular, it addresses whether the new redress mechanisms introduced by the US government to enable EU data subjects to challenge the lawfulness of surveillance by intelligence agencies satisfy the requirement, under Article 47 of the EU Charter of Fundamental Rights ('the Charter'), of effective judicial protection.

II. The *Schrems* Saga: A Game of Cat and Mouse

The Safe Harbour Decision, the Snowden Revelations and Max Schrems' Original Complaint

While transfers of personal data outside of the European Union have become a matter of legal controversy only in recent years, particularly since the Edward Snowden revelations, the EU has had rules requiring a minimum level of protection of its citizens' personal data when being transferred outside of the Union since 1988. Article 25(1) of the Data Protection Directive[6] required that the transfer of personal data to a third country take place only if the third country in question 'ensures an adequate level of protection', with Article 25(6) giving the power to the European Commission to make a finding that a third country 'ensures an adequate level of protection … by reason of its domestic law or of the international commitments it has entered into … for the protection of the private lives and basic freedoms and rights of individuals'.

On foot of this power, on 26 July 2000, the European Commission adopted the Safe Harbour Decision in respect of transfers of personal data to the United States of America. In essence, the Safe Harbour Decision recognised that an adequate level of protection was attained where organisations complied with a set of principles ('the Safe Harbour Principles') issued by the US Department of Commerce and set out in annex to the Decision and implemented in accordance with guidance made by the US Department of Commerce. In an approach that may appear naïve to today's readers, the Safe Harbour Decision operated based on a system of self-certification, where US organisations receiving data from the EU were

[6] Directive 95/46/EC of the European Parliament and of the Council of 24 October 1995 on the protection of individuals with regard to the processing of personal data and on the free movement of such data [1995] OJ L281/31 ('the Data Protection Directive').

permitted to self-certify that they adhered to the Safe Harbour Principles and publicly declare their commitment to comply.

The Safe Harbour Principles essentially required that individuals be notified of the purposes for which their personal data were being collected and used, that individuals be given the choice to opt-out of the onward disclosure or further processing of their data, that reasonable data security and integrity precautions be taken, that individuals have a right of access to and rectification of their data and that recourse be available to individuals where there is non-compliance with the principles. In this regard, the Safe Harbour Principles reflected in broad terms the principles of data protection under the Data Protection Directive.

However, crucially, the Safe Harbour Principles also recognised a wide carve-out for US government action:

> Adherence to these Principles may be limited: (a) to the extent necessary to meet national security, public interest, or law enforcement requirements; (b) by statute, government regulation, or case law that create conflicting obligations or explicit authorizations, provided that, in exercising any such authorization, an organization can demonstrate that its non-compliance with the Principles is limited to the extent necessary to meet the overriding legitimate interests furthered by such authorization …

The ineffectiveness of the Safe Harbour Principles to protect the personal data of EU citizens became abundantly clear in June 2013 with the revelations by Edward Snowden, a US NSA contractor, of the scale of internet and telecommunications interception and surveillance being operated by the NSA. On 6 June 2013, the Guardian newspaper reported that:

> The National Security Agency is currently collecting the telephone records of millions of US customers of Verizon, one of America's largest telecoms providers, under a top-secret court order issued in April.
>
> …
>
> The secret Foreign Intelligence Surveillance Court (Fisa) granted the order to the FBI on April 25, giving the government unlimited authority to obtain the data for a specified three-month period ending on July 19.
>
> Under the terms of the blanket order, the numbers of both parties on a call are handed over, as is location data, call duration, unique identifiers, and the time and duration of all calls. The contents of the conversation itself are not covered.[7]

The same month, on 25 June 2013, the process that would ultimately lead to the striking down of the Safe Harbour Decision (and its successor) commenced with the lodging by Max Schrems, then an Austrian postgraduate law student and Facebook user, of his twenty-third complaint with the Irish Data Protection Commissioner alleging that, in the light of the Snowden revelations, the Safe Harbour Decision was invalid.[8]

[7] See www.theguardian.com/world/2013/jun/06/nsa-phone-records-verizon-court-order.
[8] See www.europe-v-facebook.org/prism/facebook.pdf.

The First High Court Judgment in *Schrems v Data Protection Commissioner*[9]

On 23 July 2013, the Irish Data Protection Commissioner wrote to Mr Schrems to inform him of his view that Facebook, as an Irish-based data controller, had met its data protection obligations in relation to the transfer of personal data to the US, as the US-based entity to which the data were transferred was 'Safe Harbour registered'. Two days later, the Commissioner informed Mr Schrems that he was satisfied that there was no contravention of the Data Protection Act 1988, as amended (which transposed the Data Protection Directive into Irish law) and that the Commissioner had exercised his discretion not to formally investigate the case.[10]

Mr Schrems brought judicial review proceedings in the Irish High Court seeking to quash the decision of the Data Protection Commissioner not to investigate his complaint. In the High Court, Hogan J surveyed the details of the NSA's 'PRISM' surveillance programme which had been revealed by Edward Snowden and noted that, as appeared from press reports in the *Washington Post* and *Guardian* newspapers, the PRISM programme enabled the NSA to collect personal data from internet providers on a mass scale in accordance with orders made by the US Federal Intelligence Surveillance Court ('FISC'). While the activities of the NSA were supervised by the FISC, which is a court enjoying standard constitutional guarantees in respect of tenure and independence, Hogan J noted that its hearings are entirely conducted in secret, with the US security authorities being the only parties who can be heard in respect of applications before it. While orders of the FISC required telecommunications companies to make disclosure of telephone records 'on a vast and undifferentiated scale', the existence or nature of its orders remained secret, making 'an independent assessment of its orders and jurisprudence all but impossible'.[11]

Having regard to these details, Hogan J opined that the operation of the Safe Harbour regime did not appear able to satisfy the requirements of Article 8 of the Charter. In the view of Hogan J, 'the very fact that this oversight is not carried out on European soil and in circumstances where the data subject has no effective possibility of being heard or making submissions and, further, where any such review is not carried out by reference to European Union law are all considerations which would seem to pose considerable legal difficulties'. Given these doubts as to the compatibility of Safe Harbour with the requirements of the Charter, and given that the Safe Harbour Decision, while in force, was binding on the Data Protection Commissioner, the High Court considered it appropriate to refer the following question to the CJEU for preliminary ruling:

[9] *Schrems I* (n 2).

[10] See www.europe-v-facebook.org/DPC_PRISM_all.pdf.

[11] *Schrems I* (n 2) [10]–[15].

> Whether in the course of determining a complaint which has been made to an independent office holder who has been vested by statute with the functions of administering and enforcing data protection legislation that personal data is being transferred to another third country (in this case, the United States of America) the laws and practices of which, it is claimed, do not contain adequate protections for the data subject, that office holder is absolutely bound by the Community finding to the contrary contained in [the Safe Harbour Decision] having regard to Article 7, Article 8 and Article 47 of the Charter …, the provisions of Article 25(6) of Directive 95/46/EC notwithstanding?
>
> Or, alternatively, may and/or must the office holder conduct his or her own investigation of the matter in the light of factual developments in the meantime since that Commission Decision was first published?

The CJEU's Judgment in *Schrems I*[12]

In *Schrems I*, the CJEU broke new ground both in its innovative approach to the procedure which must be available to national supervisory authorities to enforce EU data protection law and in its application of the principles established in its recent judgment in *Digital Rights Ireland*.[13]

The Procedural Innovation

First, the CJEU addressed the dilemma facing a data supervisory authority which (as with the Irish Data Protection Commissioner) considers that it is bound to apply an adequacy decision adopted by the European Commission under Article 25(6) of the Data Protection Directive, but which entertains doubts as to the validity of the decision.

The CJEU found, straightforwardly, that a decision adopted by the European Commission on the basis of Article 25(6) of the Data Protection Directive is addressed to the Member States and 'is binding on all the Member States to which it is addressed and is therefore binding on all their organs'[14] and that, accordingly, until the decision is declared invalid by the CJEU 'the Member States and their organs, which include their independent supervisory authorities, admittedly cannot adopt measures contrary to that decision, such as acts intended to determine with binding effect that the third country covered by it does not ensure an adequate level of protection'.[15] Likewise, a national supervisory authority is not entitled, in the context of examining a complaint made under the Data Protection Directive, to declare a European Commission adequacy decision invalid.[16]

[12] *Schrems I* (n 2).
[13] Joined Cases C-293/12 and C-594/12 *Digital Rights Ireland Ltd v Minister for Communications, Marine and Natural Resources* EU:C:2014:238 ('*Digital Rights Ireland*').
[14] *Schrems I* (n 2) [51].
[15] ibid [52].
[16] ibid [62].

However, contrary to the approach taken by the Irish Data Protection Commissioner in refusing to investigate Mr Schrems' complaint, the CJEU considered that a European Commission adequacy decision cannot prevent a data subject whose personal data may have been transferred to a third country from lodging a complaint with the supervisory authority concerning that processing. The adequacy decision cannot be taken to 'eliminate or reduce the powers expressly accorded to the national supervisory authorities by Article 8(3) of the Charter and Article 28 of the directive' and the supervisory authority 'must be able to examine, with complete independence, whether the transfer of that data complies with the requirements laid down by the directive'.[17]

In order to square this circle, the CJEU innovatively found that where a national supervisory authority considers that a complainant's objections as to the validity of a European Commission decision are well-founded, the authority must be able to engage in legal proceedings to determine the validity of that decision. The CJEU held:

> It is incumbent upon the national legislature to provide for legal remedies enabling the national supervisory authority concerned to put forward the objections which it considers well founded before the national courts in order for them, if they share its doubts as to the validity of the Commission decision, to make a reference for a preliminary ruling for the purpose of examination of the decision's validity.[18]

Validity of the Safe Harbour Decision

The year prior to the *Schrems I* judgment, the CJEU gave its decision in *Digital Rights Ireland* in which it struck down a directive that required providers of electronic communications services to retain communications metadata and permitted competent national authorities to access the retained data for the purpose of the investigation, detection and prosecution of serious crime. In doing so, the CJEU found that the directive in question permitted the retention of the personal data of all persons, in a generalised manner, without differentiation, limitation or exception and regardless of whether there is any evidence of a link between the person concerned and serious crime, and that the directive did not lay down any criteria or substantive or procedural conditions relating to access to the data. Having regard to these considerations, the CJEU found that the directive disproportionately interfered with the right under the Charter to respect for private and life, home and communications and the right to data protection.

In *Schrems I*, the CJEU considered whether the Safe Harbour Decision validly determined that the US 'ensures an adequate level of protection' within the meaning of Article 25(6) of the Data Protection Directive. While the term 'adequate' was not defined in the Data Protection Directive, the CJEU found that it 'must be understood as requiring the third country in fact to ensure, by reason of its

[17] ibid [53]–[58].
[18] ibid [65].

domestic law or its international commitments, a level of protection of fundamental rights and freedoms that is *essentially equivalent* to that guaranteed within the European Union'[19] and that the protections must 'prove, in practice, effective'.[20] The standards established by the CJEU in *Digital Rights Ireland* formed the yardstick against which the CJEU, in *Schrems I*, assessed the adequacy of the protections ensured by the Safe Harbour principles.

Against this backdrop, the CJEU focused its assessment on three features of the Safe Harbour principles. First, the CJEU noted that the Safe Harbour principles are based on a system of self-certification. While it considered that a self-certification system was not in itself impermissible, 'the reliability of such a system … is founded essentially on the establishment of effective detection and supervision mechanisms'. Moreover, the self-certification system applied solely to US organisations receiving personal data from the EU and did not require the US authorities themselves to comply with the Safe Harbour principles.[21] Second, as noted above, the Safe Harbour principles contained a wide carve-out, allowing them to be overridden by 'national security, public interest or law enforcement requirements' or by 'statute, government regulation, or case law that create conflicting obligations or explicit authorisations'.[22] Third, the Safe Harbour Decision did not refer to the existence of effective legal protection against interference with the fundamental rights of data subjects resulting from measures originating from the state.[23]

In light of these features, the CJEU considered whether the protections offered by the Safe Harbour Principles could be considered as *essentially equivalent* to the level of protection of fundamental rights and freedoms in the EU, on the basis of the standards established in *Digital Rights Ireland*. The CJEU found that the protection of the fundamental right to respect for private life 'requires derogations and limitations in relation to the protection of personal data to apply only in so far as is strictly necessary'[24] and held:

> Legislation is not limited to what is strictly necessary where it authorises, on a generalised basis, storage of all the personal data of all the persons whose data has been transferred from the European Union to the United States without any differentiation, limitation or exception being made in the light of the objective pursued and without an objective criterion being laid down by which to determine the limits of the access of the public authorities to the data, and of its subsequent use, for purposes which are specific, strictly restricted and capable of justifying the interference which both access to that data and its use entail
>
> …
>
> In particular, legislation permitting the public authorities to have access on a generalised basis to the content of electronic communications must be regarded as compromising

[19] ibid [73] (emphasis added).
[20] ibid [74].
[21] ibid [80]–[82].
[22] ibid [84]–[87].
[23] ibid [89].
[24] ibid [92].

> the essence of the fundamental right to respect for private life, as guaranteed by Article 7 of the Charter
>
> …
>
> Likewise, legislation not providing for any possibility for an individual to pursue legal remedies in order to have access to personal data relating to him, or to obtain the rectification or erasure of such data, does not respect the essence of the fundamental right to effective judicial protection.[25]

Having regard to these standards, the CJEU found the European Commission had not, in adopting the Safe Harbour Decision, made valid findings or given reasons that the US had in fact ensured a level of protection of fundamental rights that was essentially equivalent to that guaranteed in the EU legal order and, accordingly, it found that the Safe Harbour Decision was invalid.

Back to Ireland

Max Schrems' Reformulated Complaint

As the Safe Harbour Decision had been declared invalid by the CJEU, the matter returned to the Irish courts where, on 20 October 2015, the High Court quashed the Data Protection Commissioner's refusal to investigate Mr Schrems' complaint and remitted the complaint back to the Commissioner for investigation.

In circumstances where the Safe Harbour Decision had been invalidated, Facebook now sought to transfer EU users' personal data to the United States based on so-called 'standard contractual clauses' ('SCCs'). Article 26(2) of the Data Protection Directive provided that Member States may authorise the transfer of personal data to a third country which does not ensure an adequate level of protection within the meaning of Article 25(2) 'where the controller adduces adequate safeguards with respect to the protection of the privacy and fundamental rights and freedoms of individuals and as regards the exercise of corresponding rights; such safeguards may in particular result from appropriate contractual clauses'. Article 26(4) conferred a power on the European Commission to decide that 'certain standard contractual clauses offer sufficient safeguards'. In exercise of this power, the European Commission adopted a number of decisions on standard contractual clauses including, on 5 February 2010, the decision on which Facebook sought to base its continued transfers of personal data to the US after the invalidation of the Safe Harbour Decision ('the SCC Decision').[26]

[25] ibid [93]–[95].

[26] Commission Decision 2010/87/EU of 5 February 2010 on standard contractual clauses for the transfer of personal data to processors established in third countries under Directive 95/46/EC of the European Parliament and of the Council [2010] OJ L39/5.

The SCC decision established several contractual clauses which, if incorporated into a contract between a data controller/exporter in the EU and a data processor/importer in a third country, were deemed as 'offering adequate safeguards with respect to the protection of the privacy and fundamental rights and freedoms of individuals and as regards the exercise of the corresponding rights'. The SCC Decision contained a number of clauses which a data subject could enforce against the data exporter (or in certain circumstances the data importer) as a third-party beneficiary, including the obligation that the data importer will 'promptly notify the data exporter about … any legally binding request for disclosure of the personal data by a law enforcement authority unless otherwise prohibited, such as a prohibition under criminal law to preserve the confidentiality of a law enforcement investigation' (Clause 5(d)). However, importantly, due to the SCCs' contractual nature, data subjects had no ability to sue a state body on foot of the SCCs. Additionally, and crucially, Article 4(1) of the SCC decision permitted national supervisory authorities to:

> exercise their existing powers to prohibit or suspend data flows to third countries in order to protect individuals with regard to the processing of their personal data in cases where … it is established that the law to which the data importer or a sub-processor is subject imposes upon him requirements to derogate from the applicable data protection law which go beyond the restrictions necessary in a democratic society … where those requirements are likely to have a substantial adverse effect on the guarantees provided by the applicable data protection law and the standard contractual clauses.[27]

In the light of Facebook's reliance on the SCC Decision following the invalidation of the Safe Harbour Decision, the Data Protection Commissioner invited Mr Schrems to reformulate his complaint. In his reformulated complaint, Mr Schrems took the view that Facebook could not rely on its contractual agreements to transfer his personal data to the US 'given the situation of factual "mass surveillance" and applicable US law that violate Article 7, 8 and 47 of the [Charter] (as the CJEU has held)', and, having regard to Article 4(1) of the SCC decision, he requested the Data Protection Commissioner to prohibit the transfer of his personal data by Facebook to the US.

The Data Protection Commissioner opened an investigation into Mr Schrems' reformulated complaint and, on 24 May 2016, issued a 'Draft Decision' in respect

[27] By Commission Implementing Decision (EU) 2016/2297 of 16 December 2016 amending Decisions 2001/497/EC and 2010/87/EU on standard contractual clauses for the transfer of personal data to third countries and to processors established in such countries, under Directive 95/46/EC of the European Parliament and of the Council [2016] OJ L344/100, adopted after the Draft Decision but before the hearing of the proceedings leading to the second High Court judgment, replaced Article 4 of the SCC decision with the following text:

> Whenever the competent authorities in Member States exercise their powers pursuant to Article 28(3) of Directive 95/46/EC leading to the suspension or definitive ban of data flows to third countries in order to protect individuals with regard to the processing of their personal data, the Member State concerned shall, without delay, inform the Commission which will forward the information to the other Member States.

of the complaint. In the Draft Decision, the Commissioner formed a view that there were deficiencies in the remedial mechanisms available under US law for EU citizens whose personal data are transferred to the US to enforce their data protection rights and that there was a well-founded objection that there was an absence of an effective remedy in US law compatible with Article 47 of the Charter. The Commissioner considered that the safeguards established by the SCCs did not address this deficiency, in that they did no more than establish a contractual right to a remedy against the data exporter or importer and were not binding on the state. In the light of these deficiencies, the Commissioner formed the view that she could not conclude her investigation without obtaining a ruling from the CJEU on the validity of the SCC Decision by way of the procedural mechanism established by the *Schrems I* judgment. Accordingly, the Commissioner commenced High Court proceedings seeking a declaration as to the validity of the SCC Decision and a reference to the CJEU.

The Intercession of Privacy Shield

On 12 July 2016, after the issuing of the Draft Decision on Mr Schrems' reformulated complaint but before the High Court had the opportunity to give judgment on the Data Protection Commissioner's application, the European Commission adopted the Privacy Shield Decision based on Article 25(6) of the Data Protection Directive, in order to take account of the findings of the CJEU in *Schrems I*. As appears from Recital 13 of the Decision, the European Commission 'carefully analysed U.S. law and practice' including representations and commitments made by US authorities and concluded that 'the United States ensures an adequate level of protection for personal data transferred under the EU-U.S. Privacy Shield from the Union to self-certified organisations in the United States'.

As with the Safe Harbour Decision, the Privacy Shield Decision operated on the basis of a system of self-certification, whereby organisations could self-certify and publicly declare that they adhered to a set of principles ('the Privacy Shield Principles') adopted by the US Department of Commerce in consultation with the European Commission and annexed to the Decision. The Privacy Shield Principles, however, were considerably more detailed than the Safe Harbour principles and, importantly, were accompanied by a number of representations and commitments given by the US authorities. Notably among these, in order to provide a redress mechanism for affected EU data subjects,[28] a 'Privacy Shield Ombudsperson' was established as a person 'independent from the Intelligence Community' reporting directly to the Secretary of State who would receive complaints made by EU data subjects, via national supervisory authorities. However, the Privacy Shield Ombudsperson would operate in relative secrecy and would provide limited remedies:

[28] In response to the findings in *Schrems I* (n 2) [95].

> The Privacy Shield Ombudsperson will provide a response to the submitting EU individual complaint handling body confirming (i) that the complaint has been properly investigated, and (ii) that the U.S. law, statutes, executives orders, presidential directives, and agency policies, providing the limitations and safeguards described in the ODNI letter, have been complied with, or, in the event of non-compliance, such non-compliance has been remedied. The Privacy Shield Ombudsperson will neither confirm nor deny whether the individual has been the target of surveillance nor will the Privacy Shield Ombudsperson confirm the specific remedy that was applied.[29]

Moreover, as with the Safe Harbour Principles, the Privacy Shield Principles could also be limited 'to the extent necessary to meet national security, public interest, or law enforcement requirements' or 'by statute, government regulation, or case law that creates conflicting obligations or explicit authorizations, provided that, in exercising any such authorization, an organization can demonstrate that its non-compliance with the Principles is limited to the extent necessary to meet the overriding legitimate interests furthered by such authorization'.

The Second High Court Judgment in The Data Protection Commissioner v Facebook Ireland Limited[30]

The Data Protection Commissioner's application before the High Court seeking a reference to the CJEU as to the validity of the SCC Decision was ultimately heard over three weeks in February and March 2017, with the court hearing the evidence of five expert witnesses as to the law of the USA; judgment was given on 3 October 2017.

In her judgment, Costello J made a number of findings regarding the system of electronic surveillance in the US. Under section 702 of the Foreign Intelligence Surveillance Act ('FISA'), the Attorney General and Director of National Intelligence may jointly authorise surveillance, conducted within the US, of non-US persons reasonably believed to be located outside the US. Authorisations are approved by the FISC, but the FISC is not informed of the particular non-US person who will be targeted. Moreover, there is no requirement to show 'probable cause'. The FISC is responsible for determining that the procedures being followed are consistent with statute and the Fourth Amendment of the US Constitution (which guarantees protection against unreasonable searches and seizures); however, the rights of non-US persons located outside the US are not protected by the Fourth Amendment. Once surveillance is authorised under section 702, a written directive is sent to electronic communications service providers compelling their assistance, on foot of which the provider will furnish data based on certain 'selectors' such as telephone numbers or e-mail addresses.

[29] The Privacy Shield Decision, Annex III, Annex A, para. 4.e.
[30] *The Data Protection Commissioner v Facebook Ireland Limited* [2017] IEHC 545.

The court heard evidence of two surveillance programmes operated under section 702 of FISA: the 'PRISM' programme and the 'Upstream' programme. Under the PRISM programme, a 'selector', such as an e-mail address, is sent to a US-based electronic communications service provider which must give the communications sent to or from that selector to the US government. All such data is received by the NSA and a select portion thereof is provided to the CIA and the FBI. Under the 'Upstream' programme, data is obtained from service providers that operate the telecommunications network. Telephone calls and internet communications that are 'to' or 'from' (or, prior to April 2017, 'about') a particular selector are obtained. The nature of the communications that are obtained is such that communications between persons who have no connection whatsoever with the target person, and who are not themselves targets, are obtained.

In addition to surveillance programmes under FISA, Executive Order ('EO') 12333 authorises the collection by the NSA of data in transit to, and transiting through, the US, including from deep underwater cables. There is no legal remedy for any actions of the NSA pursuant to this EO.

Having regard to the evidence given as to these surveillance programmes, Costello J concluded that 'there is mass indiscriminate *processing* of data by the United States government agencies, whether this is described as mass or targeted surveillance'.[31]

Costello J then went on to consider the data protection and privacy protections that were available to EU data subjects, including the various Constitutional and statutory protections and remedies available. Costello J concluded that, while a number of judicial remedies are available to EU citizens under various statutes, restrictive rules on *locus standi* mean that EU citizens are faced with 'a substantial obstacle to maintaining any of the causes of action'.[32] Moreover, Costello J noted, with regard to judicial oversight, that:

> … there is no judicial approval of individual selectors to query the data collected under s. 215 or tasked for collection under s. 702. The FISC operates *ex parte* and in secret. Its orders and opinions are classified, unless they are declassified. Increasingly, more material has been declassified. There is no judicial oversight of the collection of foreign intelligence outside the US, including pursuant to transit authority, under EO 12333.[33]

Having regard to these findings, Costello J concluded that the argument, made by the Data Protection Commissioner, that the laws and practices of the US do not respect the essence of the right to an effective remedy before an independent tribunal as guaranteed by the Charter, was well founded and that there were well-founded concerns that the limitations on the exercise of the right to an effective remedy are not proportionate or strictly necessary.[34] With regard to

[31] ibid [190].
[32] ibid [222].
[33] ibid [239].
[34] ibid [298].

the Ombudsperson mechanism established under Privacy Shield, Costello J also found that there was a well-founded argument that the Ombudsperson does not respect the essence of the fundamental right to an effective remedy, where the Ombudsperson is not a judge and is not independent of the executive, her decisions are not subject to judicial review, and there is no remedy by way of damages, injunctive or declaratory relief available to data subjects.[35]

In circumstances where Costello J found that the Data Protection Commissioner had well-founded concerns regarding the adequacy of the protection afforded to EU data subjects under the Privacy Shield Decision and the SCC Decision, she referred a number of questions as to the validity of these decisions to the CJEU.

The CJEU's Judgment in *Schrems II*[36]

The Order for Reference was made on 4 May 2018. Shortly afterwards, the General Data Protection Regulation ('GDPR') came into effect. Because of this, while the questions referred to the CJEU by the High Court were phrased in terms of the Data Protection Directive, in circumstances where Mr Schrems' complaint before the (now) Data Protection Commission was still pending, the CJEU made its decision by reference to the provisions of the GDPR.

Like the Data Protection Directive, Article 45 of the GDPR permits the transfer of personal data to a third country 'where the Commission has decided that the third country … in question ensures an adequate level of protection'. Article 45(2) of the GDPR enumerates a number of elements which the Commission must take into account in assessing the adequacy of the level of protection, including:

> rule of law, respect for human rights and fundamental freedoms, *relevant legislation, both general and sectoral, including concerning public security, defence, national security and criminal law and the access of public authorities to personal data, as well as the implementation of such legislation*, data protection rules, professional rules and security measures, including rules for the onward transfer of personal data to another third country or international organisation which are complied with in that country or international organisation, case-law, as well as *effective and enforceable data subject rights and effective administrative and judicial redress* for the data subjects whose personal data are being transferred.[37]

Article 45(3) confers on the Commission a power, after assessing the adequacy of the level of protection, to decide that a third country ensures an adequate level of protection.

In the absence of an adequacy decision under Article 45, Article 46 of the GDPR permits the transfer of personal data to a third country 'only if the controller or

[35] ibid [310].
[36] *Schrems II* (n 3).
[37] (Emphasis added).

processor has provided appropriate safeguards, and on condition that enforceable data subject rights and effective legal remedies for data subjects are available'. To this end, Article 46(2) provides that appropriate safeguards may be provided for by 'standard data protection clauses adopted by the Commission'. Article 46(5) provides that decisions on standard contractual clauses made by the European Commission under the Data Protection Directive are to remain in force until amended, replaced or repealed by a decision adopted by the Commission under Article 46(2) of the GDPR.

'Appropriate Safeguards' and the SCC Decision

The CJEU considered the level of protection that is required to be provided by the 'appropriate safeguards' which a controller is entitled to rely on under Article 46 of the GDPR. While Article 46 does not specify the nature of such requirements, the CJEU noted that Article 46 is contained within Chapter V of the GDPR, the purpose of which is to 'ensure the continuity of that high level of protection [guaranteed by the GDPR] where personal data is transferred to a third country'. Within Chapter V, Article 45 permits the transfer of personal data to third countries which ensure an 'adequate level of protection', which term was interpreted in the *Schrems I* judgment as requiring 'a level of protection of fundamental rights and freedoms that is essentially equivalent to that guaranteed in the European Union'.

To the same effect, the CJEU took the view that the 'appropriate guarantees' referred to in Article 46 must also 'be capable of ensuring that data subjects whose personal data are transferred to a third country pursuant to standard data protection clauses are afforded, as in the context of a transfer based on an adequacy decision, a level of protection essentially equivalent to that which is guaranteed within the European Union'.[38] This assessment must take into consideration *both* the contractual clauses *and* the relevant aspects of the legal system in the third country governing access to personal data by public authorities, including those aspects enumerated in Article 45(2).[39]

Where (in the absence of a valid adequacy decision adopted by the European Commission under Article 45) the SCCs cannot be complied with or cannot ensure the requisite 'essentially equivalent' standard of protection of fundamental rights, the CJEU found that the controller or processor or, in default of action being taken by the controller or processor, the national supervisory authorities, must suspend or prohibit the transfer of personal data to the third country in question.[40]

However, contrary to the concerns held by the Data Protection Commissioner in the Draft Decision, the CJEU found that the inability of the SCCs in a particular

[38] *Schrems II* (n 3) [92]–[96].
[39] ibid [104]–[105].
[40] ibid [121].

case to ensure the requisite level of protection of fundamental rights did not call into question the validity of the SCC decision. In this regard, the CJEU found that, unlike in the case of an adequacy decision (as in *Schrems I*), the validity of the SCC Decision does not depend on the European Commission having assessed and made a finding as to the adequacy of the level of protection ensured in a third country.[41] Rather, the CJEU recognised that there are situations where the SCCs will 'not constitute a sufficient means of ensuring, in practice, the effective protection of personal data', such as where the law of the third country allows for the interference with the fundamental right to privacy and data protection by the public authorities.[42] Given that the SCCs, by their contractual nature, are not capable of binding the public authorities of a third country, a controller or processor may be required on a case-by-case basis to supplement the protections offered by the SCCs with additional safeguards.[43]

However, where it is not possible for the controller or processor to implement adequate safeguards, such as where the law in the third country requires the recipient of personal data to carry out certain actions which are contrary to the level of protection of privacy and personal data guaranteed in the EU, the CJEU confirmed that the controller or processor (or, failing that, the national supervisory authority) must step in to suspend or prohibit the transfer of personal data.[44] So long as the possibility for a supervisory authority to step in and suspend or prohibit the transfer exists as an escape valve in the SCC Decision, the CJEU found that the validity of the SCC Decision is not undermined by the fact that the SCCs may not, in themselves, be capable of ensuring an essentially equivalent level of protection to that guaranteed in the EU legal order.[45]

Validity of the Privacy Shield Decision

While the SCC Decision escaped the CJEU's scrutiny unscathed, the Privacy Shield Decision suffered a different fate.

In line with its judgment in *Schrems I*, the CJEU confirmed that a supervisory authority is not permitted to suspend or prohibit transfers of personal data to a third country in respect of which an adequacy decision has been made by the European Commission, unless and until that decision is declared invalid by the CJEU. However, it reaffirmed its finding in the *Schrems I* judgment that this does not impact on the right of an affected individual to make a complaint to a supervisory authority regarding the transfer of their personal data (and, thereafter, the obligation on a supervisory authority to bring court proceedings seeking a

[41] ibid [129]–[130].
[42] ibid [126].
[43] ibid [133]–[134].
[44] ibid [135].
[45] ibid [136]–[137].

preliminary reference to the CJEU in an appropriate case, in accordance with the procedural mechanism established in *Schrems I*).[46] Given this, the CJEU considered the validity of the Privacy Shield Decision.

The CJEU went on to note that, by virtue of the derogation under the Privacy Shield Principles which enables the principles to be limited where necessary for national security, public interest, or law enforcement requirements or by measures taken by state authorities, the Privacy Shield Decision 'enables interference, based on national security and public interest requirements or on domestic legislation of the United States, with the fundamental rights of the persons whose personal data is or could be transferred'.[47]

In the light of this derogation, the CJEU considered that the surveillance schemes operated by the US authorities (as detailed in the judgment of Costello J) did not contain sufficient guarantees for non-US persons potentially targeted and did not grant EU data subjects actionable rights before the US courts, enforceable against the public authorities. Moreover, the CJEU considered that the surveillance programmes did not sufficiently delimit the scope of the bulk collection of personal data and could not be regarded as limited to what was strictly necessary. As such, the CJEU found that 'it is impossible to conclude, as the Commission did in the Privacy Shield Decision, that United States law ensures a level of protection essentially equivalent to that guaranteed by Article 47 of the Charter'.[48]

Finally, the CJEU considered whether the Privacy Shield Ombudsperson mechanism established by the US authorities was sufficient to remedy the defects identified. In this regard, the CJEU took as the starting point of its analysis that 'data subjects must have the possibility of bringing legal action before an independent and impartial court in order to have access to their personal data, or to obtain the rectification or erasure of such data'.[49] The CJEU noted that the Privacy Shield Ombudsperson is 'appointed by the Secretary of State and is an integral part of the US State Department', and that there is nothing in the Privacy Shield Decision 'to indicate that the dismissal or revocation of the appointment of the Ombudsperson is accompanied by any particular guarantees, which is such as to undermine the Ombudsman's independence from the executive' or to indicate that the Ombudsperson 'has the power to adopt decisions that are binding on those intelligence services'.[50] In the light of these characteristics, the CJEU found that the Privacy Shield Ombudsperson did not provide guarantees essentially equivalent to those required by Article 47 of the Charter. Accordingly, it found the Privacy Shield Decision to be incompatible with Article 45(1) of the GDPR and invalid.

[46] ibid [156]–[158].
[47] ibid [165].
[48] ibid [178]–[192].
[49] ibid [194.].
[50] ibid [195]–[196].

III. The EU–US Data Privacy Framework – Adequacy at Last?

On 10 July 2023, for the third time, the European Commission adopted a decision finding that the US ensures an adequate level of protection for personal data transferred from the EU to the US.

Following the judgment in *Schrems II*, the European Commission entered into lengthy negotiations with the US government with a view to resolving the concerns expressed by the CJEU. The result of these negotiations was that the US Government adopted two measures, an Executive Order, EO 14086, and an accompanying regulation issued by the US Attorney General ('the AG Regulation'). In the light of the concerns expressed in the judgment of Costello J and the *Schrems II* judgment, these measures are important in two major respects: first, new limitations and safeguards are imposed on the collection of and access to data obtained via section 702 of FISA and EO 12333, and second, a new redress mechanism is introduced for data subjects to enforce their rights.

Limitations and Safeguards

Recitals 124 to 141 of the EU–US Data Privacy Framework Decision explain that on 7 October 2022, EO 14086 on Enhancing Safeguards for United States Signals Intelligence was issued by the President. This EO introduces binding 'limitations and safeguards' which must be applied by intelligence agencies when engaging in surveillance activities under section 702 of FISA and EO 12333 and requires intelligence agencies to update their policies and procedures to bring them in line with the EO. In particular, the EO requires that data can be collected in pursuit of specifically enumerated 'legitimate objectives' only, and the pursuit of certain other objectives is explicitly prohibited. These legitimate objectives must be further substantiated, for operational purposes, into concrete intelligence priorities developed by the Director of National Intelligence and approved by the President. Once an intelligence priority has been established, a number of procedural requirements are imposed. First, signals intelligence may only be collected following a determination that the collection is necessary to advance a specific intelligence priority, having considered the availability, feasibility and appropriateness of other less intrusive sources and methods. Second, the collection of signals intelligence must be as tailored as feasible and not disproportionately impact privacy and civil liberties. While targeted collection must be prioritised, where bulk collection is carried out under EO 12333, 'methods and technical measures' must be applied to limit the collection to what is necessary, and the collection of non-pertinent information must be minimised. Information collected in bulk may only be used for specifically enumerated objectives and may only take place where necessary to advance a validated intelligence priority.

Redress

More crucially, Recitals 175 to 195 detail a redress mechanism established under EO 14086, which represents a substantial improvement on the Privacy Shield Ombudsperson mechanism in several respects.

EO 14086 and the AG Regulation enable an individual in the EU to submit a complaint, via their national supervisory authority, to a redress mechanism. An initial investigation of the complaint is carried out by the Civil Liberties Protection Officer of the Director of National Intelligence ('the CLPO'). The CLPO is independent in the conduct of their investigation, with intelligence agencies being prohibited from impeding or improperly influencing their review and can only be dismissed by the Director of National Intelligence for cause.

The CLPO will determine whether a violation of the law has occurred and will decide on appropriate remediation, such as terminating the unlawful acquisition of data, deleting unlawfully collected data, and restricting access, and its decisions are binding on the intelligence agencies. The CLPO must maintain documentation of its review and produce a classified decision explaining the basis for its factual findings. On completion of its review, it will inform the complainant (via the national supervisory authority) that either the review did not identify any violations or that the CLPO issued a determination requiring appropriate remediation. In this respect, (with the exception of the binding nature of its decisions) the operation of the CLPO is broadly similar to the Privacy Shield Ombudsperson mechanism.

Either the complainant or the intelligence community may seek a review of the CLPO's decision before a newly established 'Data Protection Review Court' ('DPRC'). The DPRC is an independent tribunal consisting of six judges who hold renewable four-year terms, appointed in accordance with the same criteria as federal judicial candidates, and who must be practising lawyers with appropriate experience in privacy and national security law. At least half of the appointed judges must have prior judicial experience. Judges are subject to impartiality guarantees. They may not have any other official duties or employment within the US Government, are protected from interference or improper influence by the executive, and may be dismissed only for cause (misconduct, malfeasance, breach of security, neglect of duty or incapacity).

Each panel of the DPRC is assisted by a 'Special Advocate' who ensures that the complainant's interests are represented and that the panel is informed of all issues of law and fact, and the Special Advocate may seek information from the complainant through written questions. The DPRC may either (a) decide that there is no evidence indicating that signals intelligence activities occurred involving the complainant's personal data, (b) decide that the CLPO's determinations were legally correct and supported by substantial evidence, or (c) if it disagrees with the CLOP's determination, issue its own determination. Where it determines that a violation of applicable rules has occurred, it will decide on appropriate remediation measures, and its decision is binding and final. While the DPRC adopts a written decision, the complainant is merely notified that the DPRC has completed its review and that 'the review wither did not identify any covered violations or the DPRC issued a determination requiring appropriate remediation'.

Notwithstanding these reforms, it remains that case that under the EU–US Data Privacy Framework Principles, the adherence to the principles may be limited 'to the extent necessary to comply with a court order or meet public interest, law enforcement, or national security requirements, including where statute or government regulation create conflicting obligations [or] by statute, court order, or government regulation that creates explicit authorizations'.[51]

Schrems III?

While the enhanced EU–US Data Privacy Framework Decision represents a substantial improvement on the Safe Harbour and Privacy Shield decisions, it is not clear that all of the concerns expressed by the CJEU in *Schrems I* and *Schrems II* have been addressed.

As discussed above, of crucial importance to the CJEU in *Schrems II* in invalidating the Privacy Shield Decision was the absence of an effective redress mechanism for EU data subjects. The CJEU examined whether the Privacy Shield Ombudsperson mechanism was capable of satisfying the requirement of effective judicial protection under Article 47 of the Charter, starting from the premise that 'data subjects must have the possibility of bringing legal action before an independent and impartial court in order to have access to their personal data, or to obtain rectification or erasure of such data'.[52]

The CJEU ultimately found that the Privacy Shield Ombudsperson did not offer essentially equivalent guarantees of effective judicial protection to those guaranteed under Article 47 of the Charter on the basis that (a) the Ombudsperson reported directly to the Secretary of State and was an integral part of the US State Department, (b) there was nothing in the Privacy Shield Decision to indicate that the dismissal or revocation of appointment of the Ombudsperson is accompanied by any particular guarantees, and (c) there was nothing in the Privacy Shield Decision to indicate that the Ombudsperson had the power to adopt decisions that were binding on the intelligence services.

The redress mechanism introduced under the EU–US Data Privacy Framework addresses these concerns, to an extent, insofar as the European Commission has identified measures which, in its view, ensure the independence and impartiality of the CLPO and the DPRC and insofar as the decisions of the CLPO and DPRC have binding effect. However, while the CJEU focused on these three deficiencies in the Ombudsperson mechanism in *Schrems II*, the requirements discussed by the

[51] EU–US Data Privacy Framework Decision, Annex 1, para 5.
[52] *Schrems II* (n 3) [194].

CJEU do not represent the entirety of the requirements flowing from Article 47 of the Charter as interpreted in the case law of the CJEU.

The CJEU's case law on the requirements of Article 47 of the Charter is well developed. Aside from the requirements of independence and impartiality of a decision-maker, it is well established that the principle of effective judicial protection comprises 'the rights of the defence, the principle of equality of arms, the right of access to a tribunal and the right to be advised, defended and represented'.[53] As part of these rights, the CJEU has found that a party to proceedings has, amongst other things, a right to effectively participate and be heard in the proceedings and a right to be given reasons for a decision.

The right to participate and be heard in proceedings recognised by the CJEU extends far beyond the right to initiate a complaint. Rather, a party to proceedings is required to have a right to 'a process of inspecting and commenting on the evidence and observations submitted to the court' and to 'be apprised of, and … be able to debate and be heard on, the matters of fact and of law which will determine the outcome of the proceedings'.[54] Where a decision significantly affects a person's interests, that person 'must be placed in a position in which they can effectively make known their views as regards the information on which the authorities intend to base their decision'.[55] In addition to being apprised of the evidence and submissions of the other party to proceedings, the right to be heard 'also implies a right for the parties to be apprised of pleas in law raised by the court of its own motion, on which it intends to base its decision, and to discuss them'.[56] The right of a party to be heard must be under conditions that do not place him at a 'substantial disadvantage vis-à-vis his opponent'.[57]

As a corollary of the right to be heard, Article 46 of the Charter imposes an obligation on the decision-maker to 'pay due attention to the observations submitted by the person concerned, examining carefully and impartially all the relevant aspects of the individual case and giving a detailed statement of reasons for their decision'.[58] The decision-maker must give reasons for a decision adverse to a party which are 'sufficiently specific and concrete to allow the person concerned to understand the reasons for the refusal of his request'.[59] This obligation applies not only to a court, but also to a decision-maker whose decisions are subject to judicial review, so as to allow an affected party decide whether to exercise a right to review.[60]

[53] Case C–199/11 *Europese Gemeenschap v Otis NV* EU:C:2012:684, [48].

[54] Case C–413/18 P *H v Council of the European Union* EU:C:2019:1044, [103]–[104].

[55] Case C–189/18 *Glencore Agriculture Hungary Kft v Nemzeti Adó- és Vámhivatal Fellebbviteli Igazgatósága* EU:C:2019:861, [39].

[56] Case C–472/11 *Banif Plus Bank Zrt v Csaba Csipai* EU:C:2013:88, [30].

[57] Case C–199/11 *Europese Gemeenschap v Otis NV* EU:C:2012:684, [71].

[58] Case C–230/18 *PI v Landespolizeidirektion Tirol* EU:C:2019:383, [79].

[59] ibid [79].

[60] Case T–15/11 *Sina Bank v Council of the European Union* EU:T:2012:661, [64].

The CJEU has, admittedly, recognised that Article 47 rights are not absolute and may be restricted 'provided that the restrictions in fact correspond to objectives of public interest pursued by the measure in question and do not constitute, in the light of the objectives pursued, a disproportionate and intolerable interference which impairs the very substance of the rights thus guaranteed'.[61] However, even where certain information cannot be disclosed to the person concerned for reasons of state security, the procedure applied must nevertheless accommodate 'the need to ensure sufficient compliance with the person's procedural rights, such as the right to be heard and the adversarial principle'.

Moreover, the existence and validity of the reasons invoked with regard to state security must, themselves, be subject to judicial review by an independent court. In any event, the person concerned must be informed of the 'essence of the grounds which constitute the basis of the decision'.[62] In practical terms, the CJEU has held that the balancing of a person's Article 47 rights against the exigencies of national security, in the light of the requirement that remedies be 'effective' cannot 'place that person in a situation where neither he or she nor his or her representative would be able to gain effective knowledge, where applicable in the context of a specific procedure designed to protect national security, of the substance of the decisive elements contained in that file'.[63]

It is highly doubtful that the participatory rights guaranteed to data subjects under the EU-US Data Privacy Framework by way of the Special Advocate, and the standard of decision which is required to be rendered by the CLPO and DPRC, are compatible with these requirements. As noted above, while EO 14086 and the AG Regulation permit an EU data subject to submit a complaint to the redress mechanism, the complainant does not actively participate in either the review by the CLPO or, on appeal, the proceedings of the DPRC. In particular, the DPRC's proceedings are secret and the complainant's 'interests' are represented by a 'Special Advocate' who may (but is not required to) seek information from a complainant by way of written questions. No evidence is provided to the complainant, nor is the complainant informed of the evidence or submissions given by any other party. While the CLPO and the DPRC are obliged to make a decision, this decision is classified, and the outcome notified to the complainant is limited to confirmation that either no violations of applicable law were identified or appropriate remediation was ordered. It is difficult to see how, based on the information set out in the EU–US Data Privacy Framework Decision, the essence of a complainant's Article 47 rights is protected by the redress mechanism established by the US authorities.

[61] Case C–189/18 *Glencore Agriculture Hungary Kft. v Nemzeti Adó- és* EU:C:2019:861, [43].
[62] Case C–300/11 *ZZ v Secretary of State for the Home Department* EU:C:2013:363.
[63] Case C–159/21 *GM v Országos Idegenrendézeti Főigazgatóság* EU:C:2022:708, [53].

IV. Conclusion

In adopting the EU–US Data Privacy Framework Decision, the European Commission sought to bring to an end the 10-year saga begun by Max Schrems' 2013 complaint to the Irish Data Protection Commissioner. It is clear that the decision represents a significant improvement on the situation prevailing at the time of the Snowden revelations when, as the CJEU stated in *Schrems I*, the Safe Harbour Decision did not

> … contain any finding regarding the existence, in the United States, of rules adopted by the State intended to limit any interference with the fundamental rights of the persons whose data is transferred from the European Union to the United States, interference which the State entities of that country would be authorised to engage in when they pursue legitimate objectives, such as national security. … Nor [did it] refer to the existence of effective legal protection against interference of that kind.[64]

However, despite these improvements, there remain significant doubts whether the redress mechanism introduced under the EU–US Data Privacy Framework offers an essentially equivalent level of judicial protection to that protected under Article 47 of the Charter. It remains to be seen whether the CJEU will require, for the purpose of its adequacy assessment, a tribunal of a third country (in particular, one acting in the domain of national security) to comply with the full panoply of requirements that apply to Member State courts under Article 47 of the Charter. It is nevertheless clear, however, that the characteristics of the redress system under the EU–US Data Privacy Framework are fertile ground for a *Schrems III*-style challenge.

[64] *Schrems I* (n 2) [89]–[90].

7

Silent Reforms of the GDPR in the EU Digital Market Legal Revolution

MICHAËL VAN DEN POEL AND GIANCLAUDIO MALGIERI

I. Introduction

Six years on from the applicability of the GDPR and almost eight since its adoption, the GDPR has not been amended. The contentious negotiations leading up to its adoption have made multiple actors weary of discussions on the substance of the GDPR, with commissioner Reynders comparing the reopening of the GDPR to that of Pandora's box.[1] Resistance against amending the GDPR can equally be found in the Commission proposal on additional procedural rules relating to the enforcement of the GDPR.[2] While several of the provisions in the proposed regulation bring significant changes to the framework envisioned by the GDPR, the Commission is adamant in proclaiming that the proposal merely complements it.[3]

[1] Jorge Liboreiro, 'Brussels Pitches GDPR Reform but without Opening "Pandora's Box"' *euronews* (5 July 2023). Available at: www.euronews.com/my-europe/2023/07/04/brussels-pitches-gdpr-reform-but-without-opening-pandoras-box, last accessed 28 November 2023. See also the speech of the EDPS at the conference on 'The Future of Data Protection', stating that 'the EDPS is not proposing to reopen the discussions on the substance of the GDPR'. Wojciech Wiewiórowski, 'EDPS Speech' (Future of Data Protection: Effective Enforcement in the Digital World conference, Brussels, 17 June 2022). Available at: https://edps.europa.eu/system/files/2022-06/2022-06-17-edps-conference-speech_en.pdf, last accessed 28 November 2023.

[2] Commission, 'Proposal for a Regulation of the European Parliament and of the Council Laying down Additional Procedural Rules Relating to the Enforcement of Regulation (EU) 2016/679 (General Data Protection Regulation) COM(2023) 348 Final'.

[3] An example of how the proposal would change the GDPR can be found in art 18 of the proposal, which would disable the possibility for concerned supervisory authorities to comment on the scope of the investigation when putting forward relevant and reasoned objections, contrary to the view of the EDPB. EDPB, 'Guidelines 09/2020 on Relevant and Reasoned Objection under Regulation 2016/679, Version 2.0'. Available at: https://edpb.europa.eu/system/files/2021-03/edpb_guidelines_202009_rro_final_en.pdf nr, 26–29.

The main concern in reopening is however not related to procedural provisions but focuses instead on the substantive provisions.[4] At first sight, the lack of amendments might reflect a status quo on the substantive provisions of the GDPR, which has seen interpretation by the Court of Justice, national courts and DPAs alike, but no changes to the text itself. An in-depth look at the broader EU Digital Strategy reveals that the GDPR has nonetheless been subject to several amendments, albeit silent and in the form of provisions in several adjacent regulations. This chapter focuses on three such silent reforms, found in the AI Act and the Digital Services Act.

II. Debiasing AI with Sensitive Data as a Substantial Public Interest: How Article 10(5) of the AI Act Builds on Article 9(2) of the GDPR

A first example of possible reform of the GDPR through other digital regulation can be found in how the AI Act introduces an exception for the use of sensitive personal data to monitor, detect and correct bias in AI.[5] This section will explore how this exception builds on the GDPR, by taking an innovative approach on sensitive data processing. It will first discuss literature on the intersection of data protection law, computer science and anti-discrimination to build the case for using sensitive data in debiasing AI. Next, it will discuss how sensitive data is protected in the GDPR. The next two parts will discuss both how the AI Act will implement the substantial public interest exception to allow sensitive data to be processed for debiasing AI, and how this exception builds on and relates to the GDPR. It will conclude with a discussion on how this is innovative, and how this will change data protection law.

The Need to Use Sensitive Data to Counter Bias and (Indirect) Discrimination in AI

Recent advances in the field of AI have been attributed to a combination of big data and machine learning.[6] The application of deep learning on large sets of training data has many advantages over older expert systems, which encoded existing human knowledge and required more human effort to build and maintain.[7]

[4] Wiewiórowski (n 1).

[5] AI Act, art 10(5).

[6] Stuart J Russell and Peter Norvig, *Artificial Intelligence: A Modern Approach* (4th edition, global edition, Pearson 2022) 35–45; Giovanni Sartor and Francesca Lagioia, *The Impact of the General Data Protection Regulation on Artificial Intelligence.* (Publications Office 2020) 9. Available at: https://data.europa.eu/doi/10.2861/293, last accessed 29 November 2023.

[7] Russell and Norvig (n 6) at 40–42.

Effective deep learning requires appropriate training data. This data should not only be available in large quantities,[8] but should also be of high quality. Where a model is trained on incorrect data, the eventual predictions it outputs will reflect these incorrections.[9] The need for large quantities of qualitative data has resulted in increased data collection, and has been described as AI 'data hunger'.[10] Efforts to increase the accuracy of models by increasing the number of characteristics, allowing to better approximate the person analysed by the AI system,[11] in turn further reinforce data collection and use in training.[12]

Parallel to the increased data collection to train more performant AI systems, researchers and developers of AI systems have focused on measuring, preventing and correcting for bias.[13] Preventing bias is of importance for AI to comply with non-discrimination law. When AI systems are biased on characteristics which are protected by non-discrimination law,[14] their predictions can result in indirect discrimination.

This form of discrimination is defined in several EU directives as occurring 'where an apparently neutral provision, criterion or practice would put persons of a racial or ethnic origin at a particular disadvantage compared with other persons, unless that provision, criterion or practice is objectively justified by a legitimate aim and the means of achieving that aim are appropriate and necessary'.[15] Noteworthy is that this form of discrimination can occur even when the person or algorithm that takes the discriminatory decision has no knowledge of the protected characteristics.[16]

Two main approaches have been explored in efforts to counter discrimination. These approaches can equally be applied to indirect discrimination by algorithms. A first approach attempts to stop disparate treatment through ignoring protected characteristics. Seemingly simple, this approach has several shortcomings. Redlining and masking, whereby human or algorithmic decision-makers use proxies that correlate with protected characteristics, allow

[8] Sartor and Lagioia (n 6) at 15–18.

[9] Philipp Hacker, 'A Legal Framework for AI Training Data – From First Principles to the Artificial Intelligence Act' (2021) 13 *Law, Innovation and Technology* 257, 260–61.

[10] Sartor and Lagioia (n 6) at 15–18.

[11] On the issues of proxies of human action, see Mireille Hildebrandt, 'The Issue of Proxies and Choice Architectures. Why EU Law Matters for Recommender Systems' (2022) 5 *Frontiers in Artificial Intelligence*. Available at: www.frontiersin.org/articles/10.3389/frai.2022.789076 accessed 4 October 2023.

[12] Sartor and Lagioia (n 6) at 15–16.

[13] For an overview, see Sandra Wachter, Brent Mittelstadt and Chris *Russell*, 'Why Fairness Cannot Be Automated: Bridging the Gap between EU Non-Discrimination Law and AI' (2021) 41 *Computer Law & Security Review* 494–620.

[14] Listed under the Charter of Fundamental Rights of the European Union [2012] OJ C326/391 ('CFR' or 'Charter'), art 21(1).

[15] Council Directive 2000/43/EC of 29 June 2000 implementing the principle of equal treatment between persons irrespective of racial or ethnic origin [2000] OJ L180/22, art 2(2)(b).

[16] Indrė Žliobaitė and Bart Custers, 'Using Sensitive Personal Data May Be Necessary for Avoiding Discrimination in Data-Driven Decision Models' (2016) 24 *Artificial Intelligence and Law* 183, 185.

for indirect discrimination to persist.[17] A second approach takes into account the context of discrimination, allowing an analysis of the outcomes and their relation with protected characteristics.[18] Applying this latter approach to algorithmic processing and machine learning results in a use of protected characteristics of individuals to analyse the impact on the predictions.[19] When this impact can be mitigated, indirect discrimination can be prevented.

Sensitive Data Protection under the GDPR

The use of protected characteristics relating to individuals brings us to the field of data protection law. In the EU, the GDPR restricts the use of what it calls special categories of personal data, further referred to as sensitive data.[20] The compliance of the second approach to counter discrimination with EU data protection rules will thus be dependent on either the non-applicability of the GDPR or the compliance with its rules on processing sensitive data. This part will first discuss these rules, before covering the possibilities to avoid their applicability, and finally how to comply with the current legal framework where they are applicable.

Sensitive Data Processing Ban and Exceptions in GDPR, Article 9

The current framework for the use of sensitive data under the GDPR consists of a general processing ban in Article 9(1) of the GDPR, followed by ten exceptions provided by Article 9(2), certain of which can further be implemented in EU or member state law.

The GDPR contains a list of special categories of personal data in Article 9(1), the use of which it restricts through a general ban on processing. The list of prohibited categories is quite extensive, including racial or ethnic origin, political opinions, health data and data on sexuality.[21] Processing these types of data is allowed only where one of the ten exceptions contained under Article 9(2) apply. These cover a wide range of use-cases, including explicit consent,[22] vital interests

[17] Sandra G Mayson, 'Bias in, Bias Out' (2018) 128 *Yale Law Journal* 2218, 2263–70; TGK Calders and I Zliobaite, 'Why Unbiased Computational Processes Can Lead to Discriminative Decision Procedures (Chapter 3)' in BHM Custers and others (eds), *Discrimination and Privacy in the Information Society: Effects of Data Mining and Profiling Large Databases* (Springer 2013) 185.

[18] Mayson gives the example of the following quote by US Supreme Court Justice Sotomayer: '[t]he way to stop discrimination on the basis of race is to speak openly and candidly on the subject of race, and to apply the Constitution with eyes open to the unfortunate effects of centuries of racial discrimination'. Mayson (n 17) at 2263–64.

[19] See Žliobaitė and Custers (n 16) at 185 arguing that the use of protected characteristics is 'necessary in the modeling process, in order to be able to remove discrimination'.

[20] GDPR, art 9.

[21] ibid. art 9(1).

[22] ibid. art 9(2)(a). The threshold for explicit consent is higher than consent as a legal basis in GDPR, art 6(1)(a). Ludmila Georgieva and Christopher Kuner, 'Article 9. Processing of Special Categories of

of a data subject who is unable to give consent,[23] and a substantial public interest.[24] The full list in Article 9(2) is to be interpreted restrictively and is exhaustive,[25] but does leave room for EU and member state law to further develop several of the exceptions.[26]

Personal data which falls outside of the scope of Article 9(1) of the GDPR, including characteristics which might be protected by non-discrimination law, such as gender, age, social class, and mental disability will still need to be processed in line with the GDPR, but are not reliant on fulfilling one of the exceptions in Article 9(2).[27]

Avoiding the Applicability of the GDPR Through Anonymisation

A first option in dealing with the restrictions posed by Article 9 of the GDPR is by preventing the applicability of data protection law altogether. The material scope of the GDPR is limited to personal data, which is defined as any information relating to an 'identified or identifiable natural person'.[28] It does not apply to anonymous data, which is referred to in Recital 26 of the GDPR as 'personal data rendered anonymous in such a manner that the data subject is not or no longer identifiable'.

To distinguish between personal and non-personal data, recital 26 GDPR notes that 'account should be taken of all the means reasonably likely to be used'. In practice, this criterion has been subject to legal uncertainty and academic debate. The strict guidelines by the then-WP 29[29] were followed by a critical reception from academia, with the argument mostly focussing on the possibility of re-identification.[30]

As recent advances in computer science have increased risk for re-identification,[31] authors argue that a zero-risk approach is not fit for purpose, and a risk-based

Personal Data' in Christopher Kuner and others, *The EU General Data Protection Regulation (GDPR): A Commentary* (Oxford University Press 2020) 377.

[23] GDPR, art 9(2)(c).

[24] ibid. art 9(2)(g).

[25] Georgieva and Kuner (n 22) 375.

[26] GDPR, art 9(2)(b) and (g)–(j).

[27] Marvin van Bekkum and Frederik Zuiderveen Borgesius, 'Using Sensitive Data to Prevent Discrimination by Artificial Intelligence: Does the GDPR Need a New Exception?' (2023) 48 *Computer Law & Security Review* 105770, 5.

[28] GDPR, arts 2(1) and 4(1).

[29] Article 29 Data Protection Working Party, 'Opinion 05/2014 on Anonymisation Techniques'. Available at: https://ec.europa.eu/justice/article-29/documentation/opinion-recommendation/files/2014/wp216_en.pdf, last accessed 31 January 2024.

[30] Michèle Finck and Frank Pallas, 'They Who Must Not Be Identified – Distinguishing Personal from Non-Personal Data under the GDPR' (2020) 10 *International Data Privacy Law* 11; Sophie Stalla-Bourdillon and Alison Knight, 'Anonymous Data v. Personal Data-False Debate: An EU Perspective on Anonymization, Pseudonymization and Personal Data' (2016) 34 *Wisconsin International Law Journal* 284.

[31] Paul Ohm, 'Broken Promises of Privacy: Responding to the Surprising Failure of Anonymization' (2009) 57 *UCLA Law Review* 1701, 1716–31. A significant number of these advances are the result of using AI to re-identify. Sartor and Lagioia (n 5) at 35–38; Michael Veale, Reuben Binns and

approach should be implemented.[32] Some even argue that the concept of personal data should be abandoned altogether.[33] Whilst anonymised data might be an option for developers of AI wishing to detect, prevent and correct for bias in AI, this might not always be practical, in particular because the implementation of anonymisation processes can still face legal uncertainty.

Compliance with Article 9 GDPR

Without legal certainty on anonymisation, the GDPR will have to be considered as applicable by developers of AI.[34] The applicability of the GDPR activates a full suite of obligations and principles with which AI developers will have to comply, but these are not further discussed here. Zooming in on Article 9 of the GDPR, developers will have to find an exception which is most able to suit their approach.

Specific exceptions relating to employment and social security,[35] vital interest when the data subject is unable to consent,[36] non-profit organisations,[37] data made manifestly public,[38] legal claims[39] and health data,[40] have a narrow and well-described field of application and will not be further discussed.[41] This leaves three possible exceptions: explicit consent; substantial public interest and archiving; and research or statistics, which will be further discussed.

A first possibility would be to obtain explicit consent from the data subjects before using their sensitive data.[42] This exception builds upon consent as a legal basis,[43] but by emphasising that this consent should be 'explicit', sets a higher standard. Georgieva and Kuner note that for the exception, 'consent cannot be implied, and requires a high degree of precision and definiteness in the declaration of consent, as well as a precise description of the purposes of processing'.[44] Several obstacles stand in the way of an effective implementation of this exception to reduce bias in AI.

Lilian Edwards, 'Algorithms That Remember: Model Inversion Attacks and Data Protection Law' (2018) 376 *Philosophical Transactions of the Royal Society A: Mathematical, Physical and Engineering Sciences* 20180083.

[32] Finck and Pallas (n 30); Stalla-Bourdillon and Knight (n 29). Similarly, specifically for AI training data, Hacker (n 9) at 265–68.

[33] Nadezhda Purtova, 'The Law of Everything. Broad Concept of Personal Data and Future of EU Data Protection Law' (2018) 10 *Law, Innovation and Technology* 40.

[34] This is the case even when data is pseudonymised, see GDPR, recital 26.

[35] GDPR, art 9(2)(b).

[36] ibid. art 9(2)(c).

[37] ibid. art 9(2)(d).

[38] ibid. art 9(2)(e).

[39] ibid. art 9(2)(f).

[40] ibid. art 9(2)(h) for providing health care and art 9(2)(i) for the public interest in the area of public health.

[41] For an explanation on these exceptions, we refer to Georgieva and Kuner (n 22) at 377–81.

[42] GDPR, art 9(2)(a).

[43] ibid. arts 4(11), 6(1)(a) and 7.

[44] Georgieva and Kuner (n 22) 377.

First, Member States, as well as the EU itself, can prohibit the use of this exception, which can introduce legal uncertainty through different regimes.[45] Second, the use of explicit consent is not allowed where there is a power imbalance between the controller and data subject.[46] This limits the use of this exception in sectors such as employment where the employer is unable to use consent to collect sensitive data.[47] Finally, the use of consent might enable some collection of sensitive data, but not on the large scale necessitated for machine learning. Techniques described above to counter bias in AI involve using statistics and further machine learning, which in turn requires large amounts of relevant data. Acquiring consent to acquire a sufficiently large dataset would not only involve prohibitive costs but might also come at the cost of the representativeness of the resulting dataset.[48]

A second possibility would be to use the exception intended for archiving, research and statistics.[49] The latter two are, in principle, compatible with AI. As Sartor and Lagioia note, analysing datasets with AI can be considered as processing for statistical purposes.[50] Similarly, AI can be used in research.[51] Where sensitive data is inherently needed, such as in medical research, this exception can be used subject to implementation by Member States or the EU. This is less certain for machine learning which does not necessarily require the processing of sensitive data.

A restrictive interpretation, in combination with the proportionality requirement of the exception in Article 9(2)(j) of the GDPR,[52] would, in our view, require not only the strict necessity to process sensitive data, but also a clear link between this processing and the goal of statistical processing or research. Legislators and developers would need to cross a high bar to implement and use this exception for debiasing AI. They would first need to establish that they are using machine learning for statistical or research purposes, after which they will have to prove the strict necessity of debiasing using sensitive data for the statistical or research purposes that machine learning is aiming to accomplish.

This leads to the final exception, allowing the processing of sensitive data for substantial public interests.[53] According to Georgieva and Kuner, this exception should be interpreted as having a higher threshold than Article 6(1)(e) of the

[45] GDPR, art 9(2)(a).

[46] ibid. recital 43.

[47] EDPB, 'Guidelines 05/2020 on Consent under Regulation 2016/679'. Available at: https://edpb.europa.eu/our-work-tools/our-documents/guidelines/guidelines-052020-consent-under-regulation-2016679_en, last accessed 16 February 2024 7–9; van Bekkum and Zuiderveen Borgesius (n 27) 6–7.

[48] Hacker (n 9) at 291–92; Sartor and Lagioia (n 6) at 49; van Bekkum and Zuiderveen Borgesius (n 27) at 7; Žliobaitė and Custers (n 16) at 198.

[49] GDPR, art 9(2)(j).

[50] Sartor and Lagioia (n 6) at 70–72.

[51] Hacker (n 9) 294. See, e.g., Mahsa Shabani and Pascal Borry, 'Rules for Processing Genetic Data for Research Purposes in View of the New EU General Data Protection Regulation' (2018) 26 *European Journal of Human Genetics* 149; Rossana Ducato, 'Data Protection, Scientific Research, and the Role of Information' (2020) 37 *Computer Law & Security Review* 105412.

[52] Georgieva and Kuner (n 22) at 380–81.

[53] GDPR, art 9(2)(g).

GDPR, which provides for a legal basis for processing in the 'public interest'.[54] Examples given in the recitals include humanitarian emergencies or the processing of voter data for electoral purposes.[55] The operationalisation of this exception is subject to the existence of an appropriate EU or Member State law, which will need to fulfil the three cumulative criteria.[56] The first two criteria, proportionality and respecting the essence of the right to data protection,[57] are similar to the general conditions for restrictions on fundamental rights in the Charter.[58] Additionally, the GDPR requires that such a law should contain 'suitable and specific measures to safeguard the fundamental rights and the interests of the data subject'.[59]

It is this need for careful consideration and drafting by the legislator which is irreconcilable with the approach suggested by Hacker, who proposes Article 20 'Equality before the law' and Article 21 'Non-discrimination' CFR as a basis to process sensitive data under Article 9(2)(g) of the GDPR.[60] Neither provision considers proportionality vis-à-vis the right to data protection nor do they contain any specific safeguards. Whilst equality and non-discrimination could be used as arguments in secondary EU law or by Member States,[61] a mere reference by AI developers to the Charter will not suffice. An implementation of this exception would thus be needed to allow sensitive data processing in order to debias AI.

The current absence of such implementation results in legal uncertainty for developers, who cannot rely on a dedicated exception. As was more broadly the *ratio legis* for the AI Act,[62] this legal vacuum leaves open room for national governments to adopt diverging rules, such as an exception on research already adopted in Germany.[63] To avoid this divergence for AI, the Commission included a harmonised exception in the AI Act proposal, which was eventually adopted in the final text.

How the AI Act would Allow Sensitive Data Processing for Debiasing AI

The exception introduced by the AI Act, to use sensitive data to debias AI, is limited to high-risk AI systems, and is situated within a broader article on data and

[54] Georgieva and Kuner (n 22) 379.

[55] GDPR, Recitals 46 and 56. See ibid.

[56] Contained in GDPR, art 9(2)(g).

[57] Studied extensively in Gloria González Fuster, 'Study on the Essence of the Fundamental Rights to Privacy and to Protection of Personal Data'. Available at: https://edps.europa.eu/system/files/2023-11/study_en.pdf, last accessed 18 December 2023.

[58] CFR, art 52(1).

[59] GDPR, art 9(2)(g).

[60] Hacker (n 9) 294.

[61] Hacker rightly mentions approaches taken by both the German and UK regulator, with van Bekkum and Zuiderveen Borgesius also referencing the UK approach. ibid; van Bekkum and Zuiderveen Borgesius (n 27) at 8.

[62] Commission, 'Proposal for a Regulation of the European Parliament and of the Council laying down harmonised rules on Artificial Intelligence (Artificial Intelligence Act) and Amending Certain Union Legislative Acts COM(2021) 206 Final' 6 (hereafter: Commission Proposal).

[63] Hacker (n 9) at 294.

data governance. This section will first contextualise the exception, by discussing how it fits in with the data governance requirements and how the AI Act defines high-risk AI. A second subsection will discuss the exception itself.

Data Governance for High-risk AI

Article 10 of the AI Act is situated within Chapter III, titled 'High-Risk AI Systems'. As such, its applicability is limited to these systems.[64] High-risk AI systems are classified as such either due to their nature as safety components or standalone products regulated by EU legislation in Annex I,[65] or due to their inclusion in Annex III.[66] The AI Act further provides for limited exceptions,[67] to be further clarified by the Commission,[68] which also has the ability to amend both these exceptions and the categories in Annex III.[69] Notable examples include machinery and medical devices,[70] as well as the sectors of critical infrastructure and justice.[71]

The obligations on data quality and data governance are applicable to all testing data used for high-risk AI systems.[72] Where these systems additionally use data to train, the obligations expand to training and validation datasets.[73] These datasets are required to comply with 'data governance and management practices appropriate for the intended purpose of the high-risk AI system'.[74] These practices include data collection and preparation,[75] but also an 'examination in view of possible biases that are likely to affect the health and safety of persons, have a negative impact on fundamental rights or lead to discrimination prohibited under Union law'.[76] Where these biases are detected, 'appropriate measures to detect, prevent and mitigate possible biases' should be undertaken.[77] In addition, data should be 'relevant, sufficiently representative, and to the best extent possible, free of errors and complete' and should take into account the setting in which the AI system is intended to be used.[78] Finally, Article 10(5) of the AI Act contains the exception for sensitive data processing.

The AI Act's Exception for Sensitive Data Processing

The exception allowing for the use of sensitive data in Article 10(5) of the AI Act is subject to two general conditions and several safeguards. It explicitly aims

[64] AI Act, art 10(1).
[65] ibid. art 6(1).
[66] ibid. art 6(2).
[67] ibid. art 6(3).
[68] ibid. art 6(5).
[69] ibid. arts 6(6) and 7.
[70] ibid. Annex I, Section A, paras 1 and 11.
[71] ibid. Annex III, paras 2 and 8.
[72] ibid. art 10(1) and (6).
[73] ibid. art 10(1).
[74] ibid. art 10(2).
[75] ibid. art 10(2)(b) and (c).
[76] ibid. art 10(2)(f).
[77] ibid. art 10(2)(g).
[78] ibid. art 10(3) and (4).

to implement the substantial public interest exception in Article 9(2)(g) of the GDPR, with Recital 70 of the AI Act noting that 'providers should [...] be able to process also special categories of personal data, as a matter of substantial public interest within the meaning of Article 9(2)(g) of [the GDPR]'.

A first condition, stemming from both the substantial public interest exception in the GDPR and the limitations on fundamental rights in the CFR, is the strict necessity requirement.[79] The purposes of 'bias detection and correction' have been reduced from the Commission proposal, which additionally included bias monitoring,[80] and are further limited by a reference to Article 10(2)(f) and (g) of the AI Act. Whilst the latter provision reiterates the purposes of detection, prevention and mitigation of biases, Article 10(2)(f) limits the concept of biases in the context of data quality requirements to those 'likely to affect the health and safety of persons, negatively impact fundamental rights or lead to discrimination prohibited under Union law'. This limitation was not present in the original Commission proposal but was added based on the European Parliament mandate.[81] The AI Act further introduces a consequence of the strict necessity requirement, requiring that no effective alternatives can be used for sensitive data. This includes both anonymous and synthetic data.[82]

The second condition, already discussed above, is the limitation to high-risk AI systems. Possible uses of sensitive data to avoid bias in non-high-risk AI systems will not be able to rely on the exception in the AI Act, retaining their current uncertainty. This has been criticised by Hacker, who notes that providers of these systems should be able to use the exception for voluntary balancing.[83]

Next to these conditions, the AI Act contains several safeguards. These are required by Article 9(2)(g) of the GDPR, which requires that the EU or Member State laws implementing substantial public interest exceptions should 'provide for suitable and specific measures to safeguard the fundamental rights and the interests of the data subject'. The initial Commission Proposal was quite limited in this department, providing only general references to security, pseudonymisation and encryption.[84] This led to criticism from the EDPS and EDPB who remarked in their Joint Opinion that '[the] provision requires additional safeguards, also giving examples'.[85]

[79] GDPR, art 9(2)(g) and CFR, art 52(1).

[80] Commission Proposal, art 10(5).

[81] European Parliament, 'Amendments Adopted by the European Parliament on 14 June 2023 on the Proposal for a Regulation of the European Parliament and of the Council on Laying down Harmonised Rules on Artificial Intelligence (Artificial Intelligence Act) and Amending Certain Union Legislative Acts' 156, Amendment 285. Available at: www.europarl.europa.eu/doceo/document/TA-9-2023-0236_EN.pdf, last accessed 21 January 2024.

[82] AI Act, art 10(5)(a).

[83] Hacker (n 9) at 298.

[84] Commission Proposal, art 10(5).

[85] EDPB and EDPS, 'Joint Opinion 5/2021 on the Proposal for a Regulation of the European Parliament and of the Council Laying Down Harmonised Rules on Artificial Intelligence (Artificial Intelligence Act)' 20–21. Available at: https://edps.europa.eu/node/7140_en, last accessed 1 November 2023.

The European Parliament mandate included such additional safeguards, and served as the basis of the final text.[86] First, the AI Act requires that there are 'technical limitations on the re-use of the personal data and state of the art security and privacy-preserving measures, including pseudonymisation'.[87] The security aspects are further specified, with examples such as controls and documentation on access, including confidentiality obligations.[88] The sensitive data collected for debiasing can also not be transferred to other parties,[89] and needs to be deleted after their use, or at the end of the retention period.[90] Finally, the use of sensitive data and their strict necessity for debiasing should be motivated and kept in the records of processing activities.[91]

How the Exception in the AI Act Builds on the GDPR

Combining both the analysis of the sensitive data framework in the GDPR and the novel exception in the AI Act allows for a reflection on how these two regulations intersect on this topic. This section will first consider whether the novel exception complies with the requirements of the substantial public interest exception in the GDPR, before considering how the approach of the AI Act is novel. Finally, it will expand to a consideration of the broader topic of European versus national approaches.

How Article 10(5) AI Act complies with Article 9(2)(g) GDPR

To comply with the substantial public interest exception in Article 9(2)(g) of the GDPR, the exception in Article 10(5) of the AI Act must adhere to the four conditions discussed above.

First, the exception is based on an EU or Member State law. The choice of instrument as an EU law, and not of the Member States, will be further discussed below. Second, the AI Act adequately considers proportionality. The exception is limited to situations where they are strictly necessary, specifying that this is not the case where alternatives, such as anonymous or synthetic data, offer an alternative.[92] The most noticeable restriction is the limitation to high-risk AI systems.[93] Whilst potentially affecting the use and efficacy of the exception,[94]

[86] European Parliament (n 81) Amendment 290 at 158–59.
[87] AI Act, art 10(5)(b).
[88] ibid. art 10(5)(c).
[89] ibid. art 10(5)(d).
[90] ibid. art 10(5)(e).
[91] ibid. art 10(5)(f).
[92] ibid. art 10(5)(a).
[93] ibid. art 10(5).
[94] Hacker (n 9) 298.

these limitations ensure that sensitive data is only used where no plausible alternatives exist, and where the legislator considers the risk of biased AI higher than that of using sensitive data. Third, the exception presumably meets the criterium of respect for the essence of the right to data protection. Whilst evaluating this criterion is not straightforward as it is not well-defined,[95] the limited scope and safeguards in the exception makes compliance with this criterion likely.

Finally, the safeguards contained in Article 10(5)(b)–(f) of the AI Act are both expansive and precise and, as such, seem reasonable in view of the risk. In light of this analysis, it seems likely that the exception provided in the AI Act complies with the relevant criteria in the GDPR.

How the AI Act Tries to Reconcile AI with the Protection of Sensitive Data

By allowing sensitive data to be processed to address bias and discrimination in AI, the AI Act takes a spin on the academic debate on inferential discrimination. The pragmatic answer to this debate, is implemented through the substantial public interest exception in the GDPR.

The debate on discrimination through the use of data has focused on the novel risks of big data analytics and machine learning, which have given rise to a new category of risks due to the inference of data.[96] Critics have put into question the distinction between sensitive and non-sensitive data in light of big data and AI,[97] against the backdrop of an ever-increasing concept of what can be considered sensitive data.[98] Instead of debating the concept of sensitive data or amending it, the AI Act chose a different, risk-based approach.

Recognising that bias and unintentional[99] discrimination can occur, it gives developers the tools to address inferential bias using newly collected, instead of inferred, sensitive data. Whilst this might lead to tension with principles of data minimisation and the concept of sensitive data, it should be considered a pragmatic approach to the problem of discrimination that the concept of sensitive data similarly, although indirectly, aims to address.

Besides the novel answer to this debate, the implementation in the AI Act also features an innovative use of the substantial public interest exception. Whilst

[95] González Fuster (n 57).

[96] Brent Daniel Mittelstadt et al, 'The Ethics of Algorithms: Mapping the Debate' (2016) 3 *Big Data & Society* 1, 8–9.

[97] Tal Zarsky, 'Incompatible: The GDPR in the Age of Big Data' (2017) 47 *Seton Hall Law Review* 1013. Available at: https://scholarship.shu.edu/shlr/vol47/iss4/2, last accessed 28 December 2023; Daniel Solove, 'Data Is What Data Does: Regulating Based on Harm and Risk Instead of Sensitive Data' (2024) 118 *Northwestern University Law Review* 1081.

[98] Case C-184/20 *OT v Vyriausioji tarnybinės etikos komisija* [2022] EU:C:2022:601, paras 117–28.

[99] For a discussion of how AI and big data analytics give rise to unintentional discrimination, instead of the intentional discrimination laying at the basis of the additional protection of sensitive data, see Zarsky (n 97) at 1014; Antoinette Rouvroy, '"Of Data and Men". Fundamental Rights and Freedoms in a World of Big Data' 16–17.

examples of implementations in Member States often concern uses of sensitive data to the direct benefit of the data subjects,[100] the AI Act would take a more collective approach. Indeed, processing the sensitive characteristics in training might not help the data subject directly, or even ever, but will contribute to the broader goal of creating fairer AI.

The Limited Role of Member States in Implementing Sensitive Data Processing

Finally, it should be remarked that while Member States have, in theory, had the possibility since 2016 to introduce the changes foreseen in the AI Act, in the end it is the EU which will implement them. Whilst subsidiarity was a significant concern during the negotiation of the GDPR, the discussion was less present preceding the adoption of the AI Act.[101] The most prominent cause of limited attention for subsidiarity concerns is the global nature of AI development, with tools such as ChatGPT becoming globally prominent in mere months, resulting in a global race towards AI governance.[102]

A secondary cause can be identified in the limited use Member States have made of the possibilities to further implement the GDPR. As van Bekkum and Zuiderveen Borgesius note, no national legislation has aimed to fill the gap the AI Act will address, despite the possibility thereto provided by the substantial public exception in the GDPR.[103] Even where use has been made of this and similar possibilities for exceptions by Member States, this has been criticised, including by the European Parliament, as 'detrimental to the achievement of full data protection harmonisation and to the elimination of diverging market conditions'.[104] The combination of both causes has thus resulted in the adoption of this exception by the EU, and not by Member States.

Conclusion: How Article 10(5) of the AI Act Changes Data Protection Law

In summary, this part has discussed how the AI Act would introduce an exception allowing the processing of sensitive data for debiasing AI. In doing so, the AI Act implements an exception provided by the GDPR for substantial public interests.

[100] See, e.g., Dutch legislation permitting the use of sensitive data for positive discrimination. Uitvoeringswet Algemene Verordening Gegevensbescherming, art 25.

[101] See the limited attention given to subsidiarity in Commission Proposal 6.

[102] Nathalie A Smuha, 'From a "Race to AI" to a "Race to AI Regulation": Regulatory Competition for Artificial Intelligence' (2021) 13 *Law, Innovation and Technology* 57.

[103] van Bekkum and Zuiderveen Borgesius (n 27) at 8.

[104] European Parliament, Resolution of 25 March 2021 on the Commission evaluation report on the implementation of the General Data Protection Regulation two years after its application (2020/2717(RSP)) 2021, para 23.

The AI Act is novel in taking a risk-based and pragmatic approach to sensitive data, balancing both the risk of processing sensitive data and the potential discrimination risk from inferences and machine learning.

III. How Article 14 of the AI Act Supplements the Automated Decision-making Ban in Article 22 of the GDPR

The EU's Decade-long Path of Subjecting Automated Decision-making to Human Oversight

A second silent reform can be formed in Article 14 of the AI Act, which aims to oblige human oversight measures for high-risk AI systems. Both Article 22 of the GDPR and Article 14 of the AI Act can be seen as part of the EU's decade-long attempt to regulate against the overreliance on computers in decision-making. A first attempt, which Bygrave traces back to the Commission's attempt 'to uphold human dignity in the face of machine determinism, in particular by enabling humans […] to maintain the lead role in "constituting" themselves', was included as Article 15 of the Data Protection Directive ('DPD').[105] Closely resembling the current wording of Article 22 of the GDPR, Article 15 of the DPD saw divergent implementations by Member States, varying from an individual right to object to automated decision-making to a prohibition of these decisions.[106] Contributing to a lack of clarity, it saw only limited application in enforcement actions and no rulings by the Court of Justice.[107]

The GDPR expanded on Article 15 of the DPD by broadening the scope to automated decisions, abandoning the prior restriction to just profiling.[108] Being a regulation, it also introduced a single wording throughout the EU. Despite this, ambiguity remained as to whether Article 22(1) of the GDPR should be interpreted as a right for individuals to object to automated decision-making, or as a prohibition.[109] This ambiguity was only recently settled by the Court of Justice

[105] Lee A Bygrave, 'Article 22. Automated Individual Decision-Making, Including Profiling' in Christopher Kuner and others (eds), *The EU General Data Protection Regulation (GDPR): A Commentary* (Oxford University Press 2020) 526. Directive 95/46/EC of the European Parliament and of the Council of 24 October 1995 on the protection of individuals with regard to the processing of personal data and on the free movement of such data [1995] OJ L281/31 ('DPD').

[106] ibid. 529.

[107] ibid. 526–29.

[108] ibid. 530.

[109] Most authors sided with the WP29 and later EDPB, arguing that GDPR, art 22(1) should be seen as a principle, with exceptions provided in art 22(2), with a notable dissent from Luca Tosoni, see 'The Right to Object to Automated Individual Decisions: Resolving the Ambiguity of Article 22(1) of the General Data Protection Regulation' (2021) 11 *International Data Privacy Law* 145.

which, concurring with Advocate General Pikamäe's opinion,[110] ruled that Article 22(1) 'lays down a prohibition in principle, the infringement of which does not need to be invoked individually by such a person'.[111] The judgment by the Court of Justice coincides with a more general uptick in Article 22 cases, signifying an increased interest in countering algorithmic decisions.[112]

This leads to the status quo before the AI Act becomes applicable, consisting of three different scenarios.[113] First is a scenario where the resulting decision does not cross the material threshold of Article 22(1) of the GDPR. This is crossed only when a decision produces legal effects, or where it 'similarly significantly affects' a data subject.[114] This concept should be broadly interpreted to include (albeit only serious) economic and social impacts.[115] Second, Article 22(1) of the GDPR can be complied with through the implementation of a human in the loop.[116] This human intervention should be extensive enough to be considered 'meaningful'.[117] Where a decision falls within the scope of Article 22(1) of the GDPR, yet no meaningful human intervention is present, the exceptions in Article 22(2) and the safeguards in Article 22(3) apply. These provisions allow automated decision-making where necessary for a contract,[118] authorised by EU or Member State law[119] or based on explicit consent.[120] Where contract and explicit consent are used to use automated decision-making, data subjects remain able to claim an *ex post* human intervention to challenge the decision.[121]

How the AI Act Fills the Human Oversight Gaps in the GDPR

Despite the increasing use of Article 22 of the GDPR in enforcement, it still has several limitations decreasing its effectiveness in tackling unwanted algorithmic

[110] Based on the context of GDPR, art 22(1) provided in recital 71 and art 22(2). Case C-634/21 *SCHUFA* [2023] EU:C:2023:957, Opinion of AG Pikamäe, para 31.

[111] Case C-634/21 *SCHUFA* ECLI:EU:C:2023:220, para 52.

[112] Notable enforcement action can be seen in the Italian *Garante* cases against Foodinho and Deliveroo. Both food delivery platforms were fined for infringements of GDPR, art 22. Guillermo Lazcoz and Paul De Hert, 'Humans in the GDPR and AIA Governance of Automated and Algorithmic Systems. Essential Pre-Requisites against Abdicating Responsibilities' (2023) 50 *Computer Law & Security Review* 105833, 4.

[113] Schematically set out in ibid. 9–12.

[114] GDPR, art 22(1).

[115] Case C-634/21 *SCHUFA* (n 110), Opinion of AG Pikamäe, paras 34, 38 and 46.

[116] The prohibition on automated decision-making in GDPR, art 22(1) (and its predecessor in the DPD) has thus been described as a right to a human in the loop, see Meg Leta Jones, 'The Right to a Human in the Loop: Political Constructions of Computer Automation and Personhood' (2017) 47 *Social Studies of Science* 216, 223–24; Lazcoz and De Hert (n 112) at 9.

[117] Lazcoz and De Hert (n 112) 11–13.

[118] GDPR, art 22(2)(a).

[119] ibid. art 22(2)(b).

[120] ibid. art 22(2)(c).

[121] ibid. art 22(3).

decisions. The main limitation results from the scope of the GDPR. As data protection rules only start to apply as soon as personal data is processed,[122] only the final user inputting personal data to an AI system will have to comply with Article 22. Whilst developers of these systems might consider future human intervention to ensure compliance with the requirements for human intervention in the GDPR,[123] they are under no obligation to do so.[124] The AI Act addresses this gap, recognising the importance of human involvement throughout the development stage.[125] This lifecycle approach is reflected in Recital 73 of the AI Act: 'High-risk AI systems should be *designed and developed* in such a way that natural persons can oversee their functioning, ensure that they are used as intended and that their impacts are addressed *over the system's lifecycle* [Own emphasis]', which also stipulates that 'appropriate human oversight measures should be identified by the provider of the system before its placing on the market or putting into service'.

These legislative goals are implemented throughout several provisions of the AI Act. The bulk of the obligations on human oversight are limited to high-risk AI and are contained in Article 14 of the AI Act. This provision obliges deployers to take steps to enable human oversight by deployers through one of two possible measures. In the first and preferred scenario, AI providers identify and build oversight measures into their systems, before placing it on the market or putting it into service.[126]

Only where this is not feasible can the provider limit itself to identifying the measures, which should nonetheless be 'appropriate to be implemented by the deployer'.[127] In both cases, the AI Act provides several conditions for these measures. They should enable effective oversight through 'appropriate human-machine interface tools',[128] should aim to 'prevent or minimise the risks to health, safety or fundamental rights'[129] and should be 'commensurate to the risks, level of autonomy and context of use' of the AI system.[130]

Finally, Article 14(4) of the AI Act specifies the different aspects that human oversight should entail. These five aspects should be provided in an 'appropriate and proportionate' manner to the human responsible for oversight. First, those overseeing AI should be able to understand both relevant capabilities and limitations

[122] ibid. art 22(1).

[123] In GDPR, art 22(1) and (3) respectively. In the former case, ex ante human intervention can be used to avoid decisions *solely* based on automated decision-making, whilst in the latter case ex post human intervention is required as a safeguard for permitted automated decision-making under the contractual necessity and explicit consent exceptions in art 22(2). See Lazcoz and De Hert (n 112) 9–10.

[124] ibid. 6.

[125] ibid.

[126] AI Act, art 14(3)(a).

[127] ibid. art 14(3)(b).

[128] ibid. art 14(1).

[129] ibid. art 14(2).

[130] ibid. art 14(3).

of the system, which should allow them to duly monitor operations and detect unexpected behaviour.[131] Second, human overseers should be aware of automation bias, a phenomenon widely described in literature which leads humans to overvalue computer-issued recommendations.[132] Third, humans should be able to interpret the output.[133] Fourth, they should be able to decide to ignore, override or not use the AI system.[134] Fifth, human overseers should be able to stop the AI system in a safe state.[135]

Besides these obligations on developers, Article 26 of the AI Act adds some obligations for deployers, defined as entities 'using an AI system under its authority'.[136] These should only assign human oversight duties to humans who have adequate competences, training, authority, and support, but remain free to organise their human oversight resources and activities as they see fit.[137] Human oversight also plays a role in Fundamental Rights Impact Assessments ('FRIAs'),[138] where the assessment should include 'a description of the implementation of human oversight measures'.[139] Finally, the more generic provision in Article 4 of the AI Act, requiring AI literacy for staff involved in the operation and use of AI within organisations, also applies to human oversight.

First, the AI Act greatly expands human oversight obligations for high-risk AI. Whilst the DPD and later the GDPR took important steps to protect humans from arbitrary automated decisions, their limitations became clear in recent years, leading to uncertainty which was only partly remedied by guidance from regulators and by the Court of Justice. The AI Act will provide a far more detailed set of rules for human oversight, which should be read in combination with the existing provision in Article 22 of the GDPR.

This expands the duty to take human oversight into account from controllers and processors to developers of AI systems, which should simplify compliance with the automated decision-making ban in the GDPR as it eases implementation of meaningful human intervention. As regards to what constitutes *meaningful* human intervention, the conditions contained in Article 14(4) of the AI Act should provide additional guidance. Whilst Article 14 only applies to high-risk AI systems, even for other AI systems Article 4 of the AI Act and its conditions on AI literacy will apply, setting a minimum standard for human overseers to have a 'sufficient level of AI literacy'.

[131] ibid. art 14(4)(a), which adds on the more general requirement of art 4.

[132] ibid. art 14(4)(b). See, e.g., Danielle Keats Citron, 'Technological Due Process' (2008) 85 *Washington University Law Review* 1249, 1271–72.

[133] ibid. art 14(4)(c).

[134] ibid. art 14(4)(d).

[135] ibid. art 14(4)(e).

[136] ibid. art 3(4).

[137] ibid. art 26(2) and (3).

[138] Further discussed below.

[139] AI Act, art 26(1)(e).

IV. Changing Approaches to the Impact Assessment Model

The introduction of the Digital Services Act (DSA) and the AI Act (AIA) has served as a testament to the evolving nature of these frameworks, particularly in enhancing the concept of risk and impact assessments originally laid out by Article 35 of the GDPR.[140] This evolution underscores a critical transition towards more nuanced, comprehensive and inclusive approaches in assessing and mitigating the privacy and fundamental rights implications of data processing activities.

The Data Protection Impact Assessment (DPIA), as mandated by Article 35 of the GDPR, was a proactive step designed for organizations to identify, evaluate, and mitigate privacy risks in data processing activities, particularly those that could result in high risks to individuals' rights and freedoms. However, this initiative encountered several challenges.[141] The GDPR offered limited guidance on how to measure risks to fundamental rights, leading to ambiguity around what constituted a 'high risk'. There was no requirement for an external audit of the DPIA, raising concerns about the potential for biased self-assessments that might prioritise organisational interests over the protection of the rights of data subjects. Additionally, the GDPR did not mandate the public disclosure of DPIA results, curtailing the opportunity for external scrutiny and accountability. The absence of a mandate for the involvement of impacted stakeholders in the DPIA process has further limited the opportunity for a diverse and comprehensive risk assessment.

Recognising these limitations, the Digital Services Act (DSA) through its Article 34, and the AI Act (AIA) through Article 27, have introduced measures to address and surpass the shortcomings of Article 35 of the GDPR. The DSA explicitly identifies the fundamental rights at stake, grounding the assessments in a rights-based framework and introducing audit requirements to ensure assessments' reliability and objectivity. Furthermore, it promotes transparency regarding the outcomes of these assessments, enhancing public scrutiny and accountability. Although not as pronounced as in the AIA, the DSA acknowledges the importance of stakeholder participation, signalling a shift towards more inclusive assessment processes.[142]

[140] Kosta, Eleni, 'Article 35 Data protection impact assessment', in Christopher Kuner, and others (eds), *The EU General Data Protection Regulation (GDPR): A Commentary* (New York, 2020; online edn, Oxford Academic). Available at: https://doi.org/10.1093/oso/9780198826491.003.0072, last accessed 19 April 2024.

[141] Atoosa Kasirzadeh and Damian Clifford. (2021) 'Fairness and Data Protection Impact Assessments'. In Proceedings of the 2021 AAAI/ACM Conference on AI, Ethics, and Society (AIES '21). Association for Computing Machinery, New York, NY, USA, 146–53. Available at: https://doi.org/10.1145/3461702.3462528.

[142] Alessandro Mantelero, 'Fundamental rights impact assessments in the DSA', Verfassungsblog, 2022. Available at: https://verfassungsblog.de/dsa-impact-assessment/; ECNL and Access Now, Towards Meaningful Fundamental Rights Impact Assessment under the DSA, 2023. Available at: https://ecnl.org/publications/human-rights-impact-assessments-are-key-effective-dsa-enforcement.

Article 27 of the AI Act takes this progression a step further with the introduction of the Fundamental Rights Impact Assessment model.[143] This model not only mandates the public disclosure of assessment results, fostering transparency and building public trust, but it also emphasises the critical role of stakeholder participation in the assessment process. This approach advocates for a democratic and inclusive method to identify and mitigate risks, valuing the insights and perspectives of those directly impacted by technological developments.

This evolving legislative framework, marked by the DSA and AIA, reflects a significant advancement in the EU's approach to digital governance. By addressing the identified gaps in the GDPR's DPIA process, these legislations not only complement but also significantly enrich the protective mechanisms envisioned by the GDPR. This development illustrates a profound understanding of the complex interplay between technology, privacy, and fundamental rights, indicating a forward-thinking commitment to safeguarding individual freedoms in the digital age.

V. Conclusion: Fil Rouge

As this chapter's exploration draws to a close, we are left to ponder the intricate tapestry of legislative measures that have collectively redefined the landscape of data protection and AI regulation within the EU. Beginning with the GDPR's unwavering presence as a cornerstone of data protection law and culminating in the nuanced advancements proposed by the AI and Digital Services Acts, this journey has unveiled a series of silent, yet profound, reforms.

The introduction highlighted the hesitancy to amend the GDPR, an apprehension born from the contentious negotiations of its inception. Yet, despite this reluctance, the need for continuous adaptation in the face of technological advancement has driven the emergence of complementary legislative frameworks. These frameworks do not merely append to the GDPR; they expand, refine, and sometimes boldly reinterpret its foundational concepts.

The intersection of AI and sensitive data presents a particularly compelling narrative. Through the respective lenses of Article 10(5) of the AI Act and Article 9(2) of the GDPR, we have observed a deliberate, careful balancing act. The AI Act's provisions for the use of sensitive data in debiasing AI respond to the GDPR's protective stance, crafting exceptions that strive for a symbiotic relationship between innovation and privacy.

The discourse around automated decision-making and human oversight, while rooted in Article 22 of the GDPR, has gained additional layers of complexity

[143] Heidi Waem, Jeanne Dauzier and Muhammed Demircan, Fundamental Rights Impact Assessments under the EU AI Act: Who, what and how?, DLA Piper, 2024. Available at: www.technologyslegaledge.com/2024/03/fundamental-rights-impact-assessments-under-the-eu-ai-act-who-what-and-how/.

through Article 14 of the AI Act. This evolution signifies a deepening commitment to human-centric AI, bridging gaps that were once only tentatively addressed.

Our focused analysis on impact assessments has shed light on the shifting paradigm from the GDPR's DPIA to the more robust and rights-aware provisions found in Article 34 of the DSA and Article 27 of the AIA. These advancements reflect a keen understanding of the intricate dance between risk, technology, and fundamental rights – a dance that demands ever more vigilant choreography as the digital age marches forward.

The 'fil rouge', the underlying thread that weaves through this chapter, is clear. It is one of progression and cautious optimism. The GDPR, while steadfast in its principles, has not been static. It has been silently reformed through the adjacent legislative initiatives of the EU, reflecting a dynamic approach to the intersection of technology, fundamental rights and the law. This silent reform has not been without its critics, yet it is undeniable that the EU's legal order is incrementally adapting to the challenges posed by the digital revolution. As we reflect on these developments, we recognise that the narrative is far from complete. The legal, social and ethical questions posed by AI and data protection remain open-ended, inviting continued scholarly debate and legislative scrutiny. Nonetheless, this chapter serves as a testament to the EU's proactive stance and its determination to foster a digital environment where rights, innovation and societal values coexist harmoniously.

In conclusion, the GDPR may not have been amended explicitly, but through the ongoing legislative discourse and the introduction of the DSA and AIA, it has been shaped into a framework fit for the challenges and opportunities of our time. As the digital horizon continues to expand, one can only anticipate the next chapters of reform and adaptation that will inevitably be written in response to the ever-evolving digital saga.

8

Data Protection's Intersections: Reconciling Data Protection Requirements with Regulated Data Use Beyond the GDPR

KATHERINE NOLAN

I. Introduction

Lawful data processing is not merely a question of compliance with the General Data Protection Regulation ('GDPR').[1] Rather, data processing is often subjected to overlapping regulatory requirements, deriving from multiple legislative instruments. While the GDPR is thus the starting point to assess legality of data processing, it is often far from being the only consideration. For this reason, understanding the relationship between the GDPR and other legislation which impacts data processing is a crucial component of data protection law. This chapter will engage with some of the key ways in which the GDPR intersects with other legislation in this area.

A number of scholars have engaged with the relationship between the GDPR and other instruments. Each of these tended to be with respect to particular legal instruments, for example the relationship with the ePrivacy Directive,[2] the Digital Markets Act,[3] the Data Governance Act[4] and the Data Act.[5] More broadly,

[1] Regulation (EU) 2016/679 of the European Parliament and of the Council of 27 April 2016 on the protection of natural persons with regard to the processing of personal data and on the free movement of such data, and repealing Directive 95/46/EC (General Data Protection Regulation) [2006] OJ L 119.

[2] Andrew Cormack, 'The Draft ePrivacy Regulation: No More Lex Specialis for Cookie Processing?' (2017) 14 *SCRIPT-ed* 345; Christiana Etteldorf, 'European Union – EDPB on the Interplay between the ePrivacy Directive and the GDPR' (2019) 5 *European Data Protection Law Review* 224.

[3] Konstantina Bania, 'Fitting the Digital Markets Act in the Existing Legal Framework: The Myth of the "Without Prejudice" Clause' (2023) 19 *European Competition Journal* 116; Damien Geradin, Konstantina Bania and Theano Karanikioti, 'The Interplay between the Digital Markets Act and the General Data Protection Regulation' [2022] *SSRN Electronic Journal*. Available at: www.ssrn.com/abstract=4203907, accessed 16 October 2023; Oskar Nilsson, 'Digital Competition Law and Data

other scholars have considered enforcement overlaps between data protection and other areas of law, particularly competition and consumer law.[6] However, a holistic account of the GDPR's relationship with other laws which require data processing has yet to be made during these first five years of the Regulation's existence, and this chapter offers such a contribution.

Multiple factors are making data protection's overlaps and intersections ever more relevant and complex, both in theory and in practice. Data protection's material and personal scope have been interpreted expansively, resulting in a law which captures most actors and most types of data.[7] Further, data processing is central to many commercial activities and is also often required to comply with certain legislative or regulatory obligations. Moreover, the EU digital strategy has resulted in an avalanche of new legislation in the digital governance space, much of which engages with concepts of data, personal data and data-intensive commercial

Privacy in the EU – The Overlap and Interplay between GDPR, Article 102 TFEU, and DMA' (Lund University 2023).

[4] Lusine Vardanyan and Hovsep Kocharyan, 'The GDPR and the DGA Proposal: Are They in a Controversial Relationship?' (2022) 9 *European Studies* 91.

[5] Bárbara Lazarotto and Gianclaudio Malgieri, 'The Data Act: A (Slippery) Third Way beyond Personal/Non-Personal Data Dualism?' (*European Law Blog*, 4 May 2023). Available at: europeanlawblog.eu/2023/05/04/the-data-act-a-slippery-third-way-beyond-personal-non-personal-data-dualism, last accessed 26 October 2023.

[6] For example, Christopher Kuner and others, 'When Two Worlds Collide: The Interface between Competition Law and Data Protection' (2014) 4 *International Data Privacy Law* 247; Orla Lynskey, *The Foundations of EU Data Protection Law* (Oxford, Oxford University Press, 2015); Maurice E Stucke and Alan P Grunes, *Big Data and Competition Policy* (New York, Oxford University Press, 2016); Francisco Costa-Cabral and Orla Lynskey, 'Family Ties: The Intersection between Data Protection and Competition in EU Law' (2017) 54 *Common Market Law Review* 11; Natali Helberger, Frederik J Zuiderveen Borgesius and Augustin Reyna, 'The Perfect Match? A Closer Look at the Relationship between EU Consumer Law and Data Protection Law' (2017) 54 *Common Market Law Review* 1427; Damian Clifford and Jef Ausloos, 'Data Protection and the Role of Fairness' (2018) 37 *Yearbook of European Law* 130; Damien Clifford, 'Data Protection and Consumer Protection: The Empowerment of the Citizen Consumer' in Gloria González Fuster, Rosamund E Van Brakel and Paul De Hert (eds), *Research Handbook on Privacy and Data Protection Law: Values, Norms and Global Politics* (Cheltenham, Edward Elgar Publishing, 2022); Orla Lynskey, 'Grappling with "Data Power": Normative Nudges from Data Protection and Privacy' (2019) 20 *Theoretical Inquiries in Law* 189.

[7] See discussions in: Natalie Purtova, 'The Law of Everything. Broad Concept of Personal Data and Future of EU Data Protection Law' (2018) 10 *Law, Innovation and Technology* 40; Benjamin Wong, 'Delimiting the Concept of Personal Data after the GDPR' (2019) 39 *Legal Studies* 517; Rene Mahieu, Joris van Hoboken and Hadi Asghari, 'Responsibility for Data Protection in a Networked World – On the Question of the Controller, "Effective and Complete Protection" and Its Application to Data Access Rights in Europe' (2019) 10 *Journal of Intellectual Property, Information Technology and Electronic Commerce Law* 39; Lee A Bygrave and Luca Tosoni, 'Article 4(1). Personal Data' in Christopher Kuner and others (eds), *The EU General Data Protection Regulation (GDPR): A Commentary* (Oxford, Oxford University Press, 2020); Lilian Edwards and others, 'Data Subjects as Data Controllers: A Fashion(Able) Concept?' *Internet Policy Review*. Available at: www.policyreview.info/articles/news/data-subjects-data-controllers-fashionable-concept/1400, last accessed 21 October 2019; Michèle Finck, 'Cobwebs of Control: The Two Imaginations of the Data Controller in EU Law' (2021) 11 *International Data Privacy Law* 333; Jiahong Chen and others, 'Who is Responsible for Data Processing in Smart Homes? Reconsidering Joint Controllership and the Household Exemption' (2020) 10 *International Data Privacy Law* 279; Katherine Nolan, 'The Multi-Faceted Role of the Individual in EU Data Protection Law' in Hideyuki Matsumi and others (eds), *Data Protection and Privacy, Volume 15: In Transitional Times* (Oxford, Hart Publishing, 2023).

activities. As Bania writes, none of these laws 'apply in a vacuum', but rather interact with other applicable rules at EU and national level.[8]

As a result, the GDPR's relationship with other legal regimes will be central to understanding the GDPR and EU data protection law more broadly in the coming years. This chapter contributes to such an understanding by explaining how data protection intersects holistically with other areas of law, particularly those which create data processing obligations. This contribution is important on two levels. First, we are able to better understand data protection law, its reach and power across the broader legal landscape. Second, grasping the points of intersection helps us to identify where regulatory overlaps and gaps may appear, which will be vital to the continued viability of the GDPR, and the future shape of EU digital governance more broadly.

By way of methodological note, this chapter takes a doctrinal approach to the GDPR's relationship with other legislation involving data processing. It operates from an EU law perspective, as manifested in EU legislation and case law of the Court of Justice of the European Union ('CJEU'). Intersections at a national level from a domestic legal perspective in respective Member States are clearly also significant, but beyond the scope of this chapter.

Therefore, to respond to the question of what the GDPR's relationship is to other legislation which requires data processing, this chapter considers three key intersections between the GDPR and other such legislation. First, the formal relationship between the GDPR and other legislation which mandates data processing is considered, and the function of Articles 6 and 23 of the GDPR is explained. Second, I consider the intersection between such legislation and the rights to respect for private life and to protection of personal data (hereinafter, 'the right to privacy' and 'the right to data protection'),[9] and observe that that these rights subject relevant legislation to a second tier of legal scrutiny. Finally, some of the new digital governance legislation emerging from the EU is considered, and some thoughts are offered on the challenges of reconciling such new legislation with the GDPR.

II. The Formal Relationship between the GDPR and Other Mandating Legislation

The first intersection to be considered is that between the GDPR and other legislation which mandates data processing (I will refer to such legislation as 'mandating legislation'). Under the GDPR, mandating legislation can provide the lawful justification for processing data, for both public and private data controllers. We see

[8] Bania (n 3) at 117.

[9] Charter, arts 7 and 8. Article 8 of the European Convention on Human Rights ('ECHR') is also relevant, although it was more frequently cited before the Charter's adoption.

this arising in two senses: first, mandating legislation can provide a lawful basis for processing data, and second, mandating legislation can support a derogation from the requirements of the GDPR.

We recall that controllers can only process data under the GDPR if they comply with the data protection principles under Article 5 of the GDPR and if they have a lawful basis for processing data under Article 6 of the GDPR. The first data protection principle requires that data only be processed 'lawfully'. This principle interacts with Article 6 of the GDPR, which prescribes the possible legal bases for processing. There are six possible legal bases for processing data. Significantly, two of the legal bases for processing allow for data processing are grounded by mandating legislation.

Mandating legislation can support data processing under Articles 6(1)(c) and (e) of the GDPR. Under Article 6(1)(c), processing may be lawful where it is 'necessary for compliance with a legal obligation to which the controller is subject'. Such a legal obligation must be specified in a legal act, such as EU or Member State legislation.[10] Under Article 6(1)(e), processing may be lawful where it is 'necessary for the performance of a task carried out in the public interest or in the exercise of official authority vested in the controller'. Again, such processing should have a basis in either EU or Member State law.[11]

Thus, the simplest intersection between the GDPR and mandating legislation is found in these provisions of Article 6, which recognise the legitimacy of such legislation as a lawful basis to process data. The processing will still need to comply with the other requirements of the GDPR in order to be regarded as lawfully processed, but nevertheless, the mandating legislation can provide the justification necessary under Article 6. However, depending on the nature of the mandating legislative obligation, this is not always so straightforward. For example, the mandating legislation will not always accord with the requirements or logic of the GDPR. As Brewczyńska and Kosta have written in the context of obligations associated with anti-money laundering legislation, 'lack of precise legislative provisions ordering data sharing' contribute to challenges of identifying an appropriate legal basis to process data.[12] If the legislation does not specifically prescribe data processing, or the relevant actor is not foreseen by the mandating legislation, the controller may have to assert another basis for processing (e.g. legitimate interest under Article 6(1)(e) of the GDPR) but they are left in a position of legal uncertainty.

[10] Or some other binding legal acts deriving from public law. See GDPR, Recital 45 and the discussion in Waltraut Kotschy, 'Article 6. Lawfulness of Processing' in Christopher Kuner and others (eds), *The EU General Data Protection Regulation (GDPR): A Commentary* (Oxford, Oxford University Press, 2020) 332–33.

[11] ibid.

[12] Magdalena Brewczyńska and Eleni Kosta, 'From the Fight against Money Laundering and Financing of Terrorism towards the Fight for Fundamental Rights: The Role of Data Protection' in Hideyuki Matsumi and others (eds), *Data Protection and Privacy, Volume 15: In Transitional Times* (Oxford, Hart Publishing, 2023).

Mandating legislation can also render data processing lawful by providing the basis for a derogation to the GDPR's requirements under Article 23 of the GDPR. Article 23 allows for derogations from certain obligations and rights under the GDPR by way of EU or Member State law, in pursuit of certain specified goals including, *inter alia*, national security, objectives of public interest, crime detection or prevention, the protection of judicial proceedings. Such mandating legislation must contain specific provisions including the purposes of processing, scope of restrictions, and safeguards.[13]

Moreover, even where the mandating legislation provides a clear basis for the processing data, things are still not simple. The overlap between the GDPR and other mandating legislation is not so neat as one of mutual recognition. Rather, there is a second tier of scrutiny, as such mandating legislation must also comply with the rights to respect for private life and to the protection of personal data, as will be explained in the next section.

III. The Rights to Privacy, Data Protection and Other Legal Instruments

While data processing might be nominally legitimised based on a piece of EU or Member State legislation, that mandating legislation must still be compliant with fundamental rights. The rights to privacy and data protection are particularly relevant. This chapter does not purport to address the academic debate as to the uncertain relationship between these rights, and the nature of the right to data protection.[14] Rather, as the CJEU tends to deal with the rights collectively, so shall I, by noting the way in which these rights have served to import data protection standards and norms into other areas of law. I observe that the rights to privacy and data protection have two important functions, first as a source of interpretation of mandating legislation, and second as a source of review or challenge of such mandating legislation. This can create tensions with other rights and interests, and I highlight particular challenges with regards to balancing the rights to data protection and privacy against interests in public access to information.

[13] Charter, art 23(2).

[14] See, e.g., Gloria González Fuster and Raphael Gellert, 'The Fundamental Right of Data Protection in the European Union: In Search of an Uncharted Right' (2012) 26 *International Review of Law, Computers & Technology* 73; Raphael Gellert and Serge Gutwirth, 'The Legal Construction of Privacy and Data Protection' (2013) 29 *Computer Law & Security Review* 522; Juliane Kokott and Christoph Sobotta, 'The Distinction between Privacy and Data Protection in the Jurisprudence of the CJEU and the ECtHR' (2013) 3 *International Data Privacy Law* 222; Orla Lynskey, 'Deconstructing Data Protection: The "Added-Value" of a Right to Data Protection in the EU Legal Order' (2014) 63 *International and Comparative Law Quarterly* 569; A Forde, 'The Conceptual Relationship between Privacy and Data Protection' (2016) 1 *Cambridge Law Review* 135; Maja Brkan, 'The Essence of the Fundamental Rights to Privacy and Data Protection: Finding the Way Through the Maze of the CJEU's Constitutional Reasoning' (2019) 20 *German Law Journal* 864.

The rights to privacy and data protection have been adopted by the CJEU to important interpretative effect. First, we have seen in a number of cases that where there is a balancing exercise to be conducted within the context of other legal regimes, that the rights to privacy and data protection must be weighed in that balance where those rights are impacted. This has been significant in a number of copyright cases, particularly concerning the disclosure of information in relation to copyright infringement. For example, in *Promusicae*, the CJEU clarified that both the eCommerce Directive[15] and ePrivacy Directive[16] must be transposed with 'an interpretation of the directives which allows a fair balance to be struck between the various fundamental rights protected by the Community legal order'.[17] Given the involvement of the rights to data protection and privacy, the CJEU advised that the internet services provider did not have an obligation to communicate the data regarding alleged file sharing on their network.[18] Similar interpretative effect was seen in *LSG-Gesellschaft*, where the relevant copyright directives had to be interpreted as to allow a fair balance to be struck between various rights, including the rights to data protection and privacy.[19] This requirement to interpret copyright and associated legislation in light of data protection and privacy has continued through a range of subsequent cases.[20] Moreover, the interpretative effect of the rights of data protection and privacy has also been seen in cases relating to EU legislation on customs,[21] money laundering[22] and passenger name record data.[23]

Beyond interpretative effect, the rights to data protection and privacy have also been important sources of review of mandating legislation. There are broadly three mechanisms by which these rights come to operate as a source of review: (a) through the review of legislation which nominally justifies data processing under Article 6 of the GDPR, (b) through the assessment of legislation which falls within the derogations to the GDPR's obligations under Article 23 of the GDPR, and (c) as an independent source of challenge to the legislation through the assertion of rights under the Charter or ECHR.

In the previous section, I noted that there is a formal connection between mandating legislation and the GDPR through Article 6, which allows data

[15] Directive 2000/31/EC of the European Parliament and of the Council of 8 June 2000 on certain legal aspects of information society services, in particular electronic commerce, in the Internal Market [2000] OJ L 178.

[16] Directive 2002/58/EC of the European Parliament and of the Council of 12 July 2002 concerning the processing of personal data and the protection of privacy in the electronic communications sector [2002] OJ L 201.

[17] Case C-275/06 *Promusicae v Telefónica de España* [2008] ECR I-00271, para 68.

[18] ibid para 70.

[19] Case C-557/07 *LSG-Gesellschaft zur Wahrnehmung von Leistungsschutzrechten* [2009] ECR I-01227, para 28.

[20] See, e.g., Case C-70/10 *Scarlet Extended* [2011] I-11959; Case C-360/10 *SABAM* EU:C:2012:85; Case -461/10 *Bonnier Audio and Others* EU:C:2012:219.

[21] Case C-496/17 *Deutsche Post* EU:C:2019:26.

[22] Case C-235/14 *Safe Interenvios* EU:C:2016:154.

[23] Opinion 1/15 *Passenger Name Record Agreement* EU:C:2016:656; Case C-817/19 *Ligue des droits humains* EU:C:2022:491.

processing which is necessary for compliance with a legal obligation or task in the public interest or under official authority. The mandating legislation which requires such processing will only be sufficient to legitimise that data processing if it conforms to a rights test,[24] as has been made clear in a number of CJEU cases. In *Manni*, legislation requiring the listing of personal data on the companies register was said to satisfy several legal bases under the Data Protection Directive,[25] but nevertheless the CJEU went on to analyse that legislation in light of affected fundamental rights, ultimately determining that there was no disproportionate interference with the fundamental rights of persons concerned.[26] A similar observation was made in *Puškár*, concerning personal data collected for the collection of tax and combating tax fraud.[27] The CJEU found that such legislation must comply with the principle of proportionality, considering in particular the right to privacy and the limiting derogations to that right to what is strictly necessary.[28] In *OT v Vyriausioji tarnybinės etikos komisija* the CJEU considered national legislation which provided for an online register of declaration of private interests for certain recipients of public funds.[29] The CJEU analysed that legislation in light of interferences with the rights to data protection and privacy, ultimately determining that aspects of the legislation did not reflect the appropriate balances in particular given the serious interferences with the relevant rights.

Notably, there is inconsistency across the CJEU judgments as to the precise legal rationale by which the rights test becomes relevant. For example, in the *Puškár* judgment, the CJEU frames the review of the mandating legislation as complying with the conditions of lawfulness under the Data Protection Directive, and thus derives the proportionality test from the Directive, interpreted in light of the Charter.[30] By contrast, in *OT*, the CJEU finds that processing on the basis of public interest/compliance with legal obligation, read together with the requirement in Article 6(3) that such mandating legislation shall meet an objective of public interest and be proportionate, constitutes an expression of Article 52(1) of the Charter and therefore should be interpreted in light of that provision.[31] This raises questions as to precise relationship between data protection legislation and the Charter rights which goes beyond the scope of this chapter but, in any case, what emerges is a consistent application of rights standards to national mandating legislation. Accordingly, mandating legislation which nominally legitimises data processing under Article 6 will nevertheless also need to conform to a rights analysis if it is to fully render such data processing lawful.

[24] See GDPR, art 6(3).
[25] *Manni*, para 42.
[26] ibid para 56.
[27] Case C-73/16 *Puškár* EU:C:2017:725.
[28] ibid para 112.
[29] Case C-184/20 *OT v Vyriausioji tarnybinės etikos komisija* EU:C:2022:601.
[30] *Puškár* (n 28) paras 111–12.
[31] *OT v Vyriausioji tarnybinės etikos komisija* (n 30) para 69.

A rights analysis of mandating legislation is also engaged by Article 23 of the GDPR. Any legislation which derogates from the protections of the GDPR under that Article must 'respect[t] the essence of the fundamental rights and freedoms', and satisfy necessity and proportionality tests.[32] The CJEU has only considered Article 23 a few times, but in each case it clearly subjected the relevant mandating legislation to a fundamental rights analysis. In *Österreichischer Rundfunk*, considering the equivalent predecessor provision under the Data Protection Directive, before the Charter was adopted in the Lisbon Treaty, the Court considered that such legislation must be analysed in accordance with Article 8 of the ECHR.[33] The relevant Austrian legislation, which provided for the disclosure of data relating to employees for certain public bodies could be compatible with Article 8, but only if the nature of the data to be disclosed was proportionate.[34]

In *Norra Stockholm Bygg*, the CJEU considered certain Swedish civil procedure rules which allowed the judiciary to make disclosure orders and had to assess whether these rules provided a legal basis for the processing of data.[35] The CJEU read Article 23 of the GDPR together with Article 6(4) in order assess the legality of the processing of the data by the judiciary. The reasoning of the CJEU is somewhat peculiar in parts,[36] but again illustrates that the CJEU requires the mandating legislation to comply with a fundamental rights analysis. The Court referred the civil procedure code back to the referring court to consider whether the power to order the data disclosure satisfies one of the relevant objectives under Article 23 and whether the code is 'necessary and proportionate to the said objectives'.[37] In *La Quadrature du Net* the CJEU clearly articulated the safeguarding role of Article 23, and that derogating mandating legislation cannot be allowed to escape rights scrutiny.[38] The CJEU clearly states that 'Article 23(1) and (2) … cannot be interpreted as being capable of conferring on Member States the power to undermine respect for private life, disregarding Article 7 of the Charter, or any of the other guarantees enshrined therein' and that 'the power conferred on Member States by Article 23(1) of Regulation 2016/679 may be exercised only in accordance with the requirement of proportionality, according to which derogations and limitations in relation to the protection of personal data

[32] GDPR, art 23(1). See also GDPR, Recital 73, which provides in part: 'Those restrictions should be in accordance with the requirements set out in the Charter and in the European Convention for the Protection of Human Rights and Fundamental Freedoms.'

[33] Joined Cases C-465/00, C-138/01 and C-139/01 *Österreichischer Rundfunk* [2003] ECR I-5014, para 72.

[34] ibid, para 90. See also Case C-473/12 *IPI* EU:C:2013:715 which followed a similar approach in relation to derogations from the Data Protection Directive.

[35] Case C-268/21 *Norra Stockholm Bygg* EU:C:2023:145.

[36] See the discussion in Katherine Nolan, 'Data Protection Meets Civil Procedure – the ECJ Decision in Norra Stockholm Bygg' (*European Law Blog*, 24 March 2023). Available at: europeanlawblog.eu/2023/03/24/data-protection-meets-civil-procedure-the-ecj-decision-in-norra-stockholm-bygg/, last accessed 10 November 2023.

[37] Case C-268/21 *Norra Stockholm Bygg* EU:C:2023:145, para 39.

[38] Case C-511/18 *La Quadrature du Net* EU:C:2020:791.

must apply only in so far as is strictly necessary'.[39] Again we see that any legislation which falls within Article 23 must also satisfy a rights analysis in order to render the derogation from the obligations of the GDPR lawful.

Further, the rights to privacy and data protection can also serve as independent sources of review of or challenge to mandating legislation. These rights have been asserted by claimants in a variety of actions, and to powerful effect.[40] These rights have been successfully deployed to invalidate of a number of legislative measures, including the Data Retention Directive,[41] aspects of common agricultural policy law,[42] two adequacy decisions which legalised data transfers,[43] national surveillance measures,[44] an article of the Fifth Money Laundering Directive,[45] and national implementation measures of the PNR Directive.[46] The rights have also been asserted unsuccessfully to challenge the use of biometrics in travel documentation.[47]

We can therefore see that the rights to privacy and data protection can act as vectors bringing data protection concerns into any area of law which engages personal data processing. Given that mandating legislation inevitably acts in pursuit of some other interest, these cases often come down to questions of balancing rights and interests.[48] Such balancing can be challenging, difficulties which are reinforced by the umbrella nature of the right to privacy,[49] and data protection's uncertain nature.[50] One particular tension which has emerged in the case law of the CJEU is the conflict between public access to data/information and data protection. This question has arisen in a few contexts, and the balance between these interests is far from easy to determine.

In the context of the so-called "right to be forgotten", the CJEU have introduced a series of factors to be weighed in order to balance the public's interest in access

[39] ibid, para 210.

[40] See Nolan (n 7) at 102–04.

[41] Joined Cases C-293/12 and 594/12 *Digital Rights Ireland and Seitlinger and Others* EU:C:2014:238.

[42] Case C-92/09 *Volker und Markus Schecke and Eifert* [2010] I-11063.

[43] Case C-352/14 *Schrems* EU:C:2015:650; Case C-311/18 *Facebook Ireland & Schrems* EU:C:2020:559.

[44] Joined Cases C-203/15 and C-698/15 *Tele2 Sverige* EU:C:2016:970; Case C-623/17 *Privacy International* EU:C:2020:790; Case C-511/18 *La Quadrature du Net and Others* EU:C:2020:791; Case C-140/20 *Commissioner of an Garda Síochána and Others* EU:C:2022:258.

[45] Joined Cases C-37/20 and C-601/20 *Luxembourg Business Registers* EU:C:2022:912.

[46] Case C-817/19 *Ligue des droits humains* EU:C:2022:491.

[47] Case C-291/12 *Schwartz* EU:C:2013:670; Joined Cases C-446/12 to C0449/12 *Willems and Others* EU:C:2015:238.

[48] See C Docksey, 'Four Fundamental Rights: Finding the Balance' (2016) 6 *International Data Privacy Law* 195.

[49] There is an extensive literature on the nature of privacy, see e.g., Daniel J Solove, 'Conceptualizing Privacy' (2002) 90 *California Law Review* 1087; Bart J Koops and others, 'A Typology of Privacy' (2017) 38 *University of Pennsylvania Journal of International Law* 483; Oskar J Gstrein and Anne Beaulieu, 'How to Protect Privacy in a Datafied Society? A Presentation of Multiple Legal and Conceptual Approaches' (2022) 35 *Philosophy & Technology* 3.

[50] See, e.g., Fuster and Gellert (n 14); Gellert and Gutwirth (n 14); Kokott and Sobotta (n 14); Lynskey, 'Deconstructing Data Protection,' (n 14); Forde (n 14).

to information and a data subject's right to be forgotten.[51] The CJEU's treatment of the right to be forgotten, including repeated assertions that the right to data protection should generally override the public's interest in accessing that data via search listings,[52] have been controversial.[53] At the same time, the nature of information de-listing in the specific right to be forgotten cases is relatively limited, and thus it is with the greater issue of principle we might be more concerned.

This broader tension between public access to information and data protection has also manifested in recent cases relating to anti-corruption and anti-money laundering legislation. The anti-money laundering regime comes into tension with data protection, as 'the realisation of the [customer due diligence] measures requires from the obliged entities wide collection and processing of personal data of the customers'.[54] Public access to certain regulated information has been asserted by Transparency International as an important safeguard against corruption, amongst other purposes.[55] Nevertheless in two recent cases of the CJEU, the Court determined that legislation providing for such public access disproportionately interfered with the rights to data protection in privacy. In *OT v Vyriausioji tarnybinės etikos komisija*, Lithuanian law requiring the declaration of private interests by certain public servants was considered by the CJEU.[56] The Court accepted that combatting corruption was an objective of general interest recognised by the EU,[57] but that the law went further than was strictly necessary, in particular insofar as information regarding spouses, cohabitees or partners was to be disclosed, which was said to represent a particularly serious infringement.[58]

Similarly, in *Luxembourg Business Registers*, the publication of registers of beneficial ownership was asserted to be necessary to combat money laundering and terrorist financing, but the CJEU rejected such an argument, finding that the interferences with the rights to privacy and data protection went beyond what was strictly necessary.[59] The general public's access to the information under the Fifth Anti-Money Laundering Directive was said to amount to a considerably more serious interference with the fundamental rights guaranteed in Articles 7 and 8 of the Charter, without that increased interference being capable of being offset

[51] See Case C-131/12 *Google Spain and Google* EU:2014:317; Case C-136/17 *GC and Others* EU:C:2019:773; Case C-460/20 *TU, RE v Google* EU:C:2022:962.

[52] *Google Spain and Google* ibid, para 81; *GC and Others* ibid, para 66; *TU, RE v Google* ibid, para 62.

[53] See, e,g, Muge Fazlioglu, 'Forget Me Not: The Clash of the Right to Be Forgotten and Freedom of Expression on the Internet' (2013) 3 *International Data Privacy Law* 149; Susanna Lindroos-Hovinheimo, 'Legal Subjectivity and the "Right to Be Forgotten": A Rancièrean Analysis of Google' (2016) 27 *Law and Critique* 289; Mark R Leiser, '"Private Jurisprudence" and the Right to Be Forgotten Balancing Test' (2020) 39 *Computer Law & Security Review* 105458.

[54] Brewczyńska and Kosta (n 12) at 163.

[55] Á Földes, 'Personal Data Protection Has a Sole Purpose, and Shielding Corporate …' (*Transparency.org*, 5 September 2023). Available at: www.transparency.org/en/blog/personal-data-protection-has-sole-purpose-cjeu-ruling-beneficial-ownership-transparency accessed 13 November 2023.

[56] *OT v Vyriausioji tarnybinės etikos komisija* (n 30).

[57] ibid para 80.

[58] ibid paras 87–116.

[59] Joined Cases C-37/20 and C-601/20 *Luxembourg Business Registers* EU:2022:912, para 75–77.

by any benefits which might result from the latter regime as compared against the former regime, in terms of combating money laundering and terrorist financing.'[60]

One challenge is that the framing of these issues before the CJEU tends to be shaped as one of an individual's interest in data protection or privacy versus a public or generalised interest. Absent from these cases is any type of societal or systematic analysis of whether there is a public interest in data protection,[61] and or the societal purpose of data protection rights and legislation, and the limits of such reach. The right to data protection has been a powerful instrument to challenge mandating legislation, resulting in cases resolved in terms of individual rights claims. However, to date, a cohesive sense of the nature of the balance between access to information and data protection has not emerged, an issue which is undoubtedly going to recur as more legislation has been introduced in the sphere, and more and more rights, interests and objectives are to be balanced.

IV. Intersecting Legislation – An Increasing Thicket

Recent years in EU digital governance have been characterised by multiple new legislative proposals, many of which have come to fruition and some of which are still in development. Much of this new legislation is founded on ideas of economic exploitation of data, and as we shall see, there is a considerable potential for overlap between the GDPR and these new laws. Unpicking the relationships between the new laws is far from simple. By contrast to earlier data laws, explicit provisions to clarify the relationships between the laws are absent. Predominantly, new laws are said to apply 'without prejudice' to the GDPR but create significant potential for material and functional overlaps. Some scholars have pointed to the use of the *lex specialis* doctrine for resolving conflicts, but the potential for conflicting normative positions makes this challenging.

In 2018, the current generation of data protection legislation were adopted in quick succession: the GDPR, the Law Enforcement Directive,[62] the EU Institutions Data Protection Regulation[63] and the Non-Personal Data Regulation.[64] For the

[60] ibid, para 85.

[61] See also Katherine Nolan, 'The Individual in EU Data Protection Law' (Doctor of Philosophy, London School of Economics and Political Science 2023).

[62] Directive (EU) 2016/680 of the European Parliament and of the Council of 27 April 2016 on the protection of natural persons with regard to the processing of personal data by competent authorities for the purposes of the prevention, investigation, detection or prosecution of criminal offences or the execution of criminal penalties, and on the free movement of such data, and repealing Council Framework Decision 2008/977/JHA [2016] OJ L 119.

[63] Regulation (EU) 2018/1725 of the European Parliament and of the Council of 23 October 2018 on the protection of natural persons with regard to the processing of personal data by the Union institutions, bodies, offices and agencies and on the free movement of such data, and repealing Regulation (EC) No 45/2001 and Decision No 1247/2002/EC [2018] OJ L 295.

[64] Regulation (EU) 2018/1807 of the European Parliament and of the Council of 14 November 2018 on a framework for the free flow of non-personal data in the European Union [2018] OJ L 303.

most part, there is a logical or conceptual distinction between these pieces of legislation such that the relationships between these regimes, at least in terms of scope, is relatively clear. The Law Enforcement Directive applies to processing of personal data by certain designated authorities,[65] and the GDPR excludes such processing from its scope.[66] The EU Institutions Data Protection Regulation applies to personal data processing by the EU institutions and bodies,[67] which is excluded from the Law Enforcement Directive[68] and GDPR[69] in turn. The Non-Personal Data Regulation applies to data other than personal data, and Article 2(2) provides for a division of responsibility between the GDPR and the Non-Personal Data Regulation.[70] Thus, while there can certainly be issues of interpretative and enforcement consistency between the two regimes, at least at a formal level, there is a clear demarcation of applicable regimes.

By contrast, the latest generation of EU digital governance laws do not have the same consistency. Rather, the relationships between the GDPR and these new data laws are complex. I shall primarily consider the intersections between the GDPR and newly adopted laws, but I note also the potential for conflict in relation to certain proposed new laws.

The dominant approach in recent data and digital governance laws is for such laws to be said to apply 'without prejudice' to the GDPR. This is the case with the Digital Markets Act,[71] the Digital Services Act,[72] NIS2 Directive[73] and the Data Governance Act.[74] The same 'without prejudice' language is also found in the new Data Act[75] and the proposed European Health Data Space Regulation.[76] The Digital

[65] Directive (EU) 2016/680, art 2(1).

[66] GDPR, art 2(2)(d).

[67] Regulation (EU) 2018/1725 (n 65) art 2(1).

[68] ibid art 2(3)(b).

[69] GDPR, art 2(3).

[70] Regulation (EU) 2018/1807, art 2(2) provides: 'In the case of a data set composed of both personal and non-personal data, this Regulation applies to the non-personal data part of the data set. Where personal and non-personal data in a data set are inextricably linked, this Regulation shall not prejudice the application of Regulation (EU) 2016/679.'

[71] Regulation (EU) 2022/1925, Recital 12 of the European Parliament and of the Council of 14 September 2022 on contestable and fair markets in the digital sector and amending Directives (EU) 2019/1937 and (EU) 2020/1828 (Digital Markets Act) [2022] OJ L 265.

[72] Recital 10, Regulation (EU) 2022/2065 of the European Parliament and of the Council of 19 October 2022 on a Single Market For Digital Services and amending Directive 2000/31/EC (Digital Services Act) [2022] OJ L 277.

[73] Directive (EU) 2022/255 of the European Parliament and of the Council of 14 December 2022 on measures for a high common level of cybersecurity across the Union, amending Regulation (EU) No 910/2014 and Directive (EU) 2018/1972, and repealing Directive (EU) 2016/1148 (NIS 2 Directive) [2022] OJ L 333, art 2(12), Recital 14.

[74] Regulation (EU) 2022/868 of the European Parliament and of the Council of 30 May 2022 on European data governance and amending Regulation (EU) 2018/1724 (Data Governance Act) [2022] OJ L 152, art 1(3), Recital 4.

[75] Regulation (EU) 2023/2854 of the European Parliament and of the Council of 13 December 2023 on harmonised rules on fair access to and use of data and amending Regulation (EU) 2017/2394 and Directive (EU) 2020/1828 (Data Act) [2023] OJ L (22 December 2023), art 1(5).

[76] Commission, 'Proposal for a Regulation of the European Parliament and of the Council on the European Health Data Space' COM (2022) 197 final, art 1(4).

Services Act further provides that '[t]he protection of individuals with regard to the processing of personal data is governed solely by the rules of Union law on that subject, in particular Regulation (EU) 2016/679 and Directive 2002/58/EC'.[77] The Platform to Business Regulation does not have a general without prejudice clause, but the provisions providing for access to data by business users of online intermediation services to certain personal data associated with those services are said to apply 'without prejudice' to the GDPR.[78] The relationship between the proposed AI Act and the GDPR is still in flux through the legislative negotiations, but in the initial Commission proposal, the Commission wrote in the explanatory memorandum that the intent was for the proposed Act to be 'without prejudice and complemen[t]' the GDPR.[79] Notably, the proposed ePrivacy Regulation does not take such an approach, but continues in the pattern of the ePrivacy Directive to 'particularise and complement the general rules on the protection of personal data laid down in [the GDPR] as regards electronic communications data that qualify as personal data'.[80]

Despite these assertions of application 'without prejudice' to the GDPR, there are multiple areas of overlap between these pieces of legislation and the GDPR.

First, some of these new pieces of legislation create new obligations which are closely related to obligations found in the GDPR. The Digital Markets Act creates a new obligation relating to data portability, which is said to 'complemen[t] the right to data portability' under the GDPR.[81] Nevertheless, the scope of this right to data portability differs, and regulated actors who are caught by both regimes will notionally have to figure out how to operationalise two 'complementary' rights. Geradin et al highlight that 'there are significant differences in every single aspect of the respective provisions, ranging from the normative goals they pursue, the scope of data covered, the legal basis on which the users' right to data portability rests and the (transactional and technical) conditions under which data portability should take place'.[82] The Digital Services Acts prohibits certain prohibitions on profiling, including profiling based on sensitive personal data[83] and on ad profiling to children.[84] In this sense, additional obligations are imposed on top of GDPR requirements, which create specialised data protection rules applicable to certain

[77] Digital Services Act, Recital 10.

[78] Regulation (EU) 2019/1150 of the European Parliament and of the Council of 20 June 2019 on promoting fairness and transparency for business users of online intermediation services [2019] OJ L 186.

[79] Commission, 'Proposal for a Regulation of the European Parliament and of the Council Laying Down Harmonised Rules On Artificial Intelligence (Artificial Intelligence Act) and Amending Certain Union Legislative Acts' COM (2021) 206 final.

[80] Commission, 'Proposal for a Regulation of the European Parliament and of the Council concerning the respect for private life and the protection of personal data in electronic communications and repealing Directive 2002/58/EC (Regulation on Privacy and Electronic Communications)' COM (2017) 010 final.

[81] Digital Markets Act, art 6, Recital 9.

[82] Geradin, Bania and Karanikioti, (n 3) at 4.

[83] Digital Services Act, art 26(3).

[84] ibid art 28.

types of actors. Similarly, the Digital Services Act purports to ban so-called 'dark patterns' but then seeks to carve out and distinguish such practices from those already addressed by the GDPR. The Act provides that the relevant prohibition 'shall not apply to practices covered by Directive 2005/29/EC or [the GDPR]'.[85]

More complicated overlaps exist where new legislation borrows or piggy-backs on concepts within the GDPR. Thus, both the Data Governance Act and Digital Markets Act interact with the GDPR's notion of consent. The Data Governance Act provides that consent for data altruism must be in compliance with consent within the meaning of the GDPR,[86] which is relatively straightforward. However, the Data Markets Act also prohibits certain uses of personal data, including in relation to online advertising, unless consent within the meaning of the GDPR has been provided, and then further provides that this is without prejudice with the ability of the gatekeeper to rely on certain other legal bases for processing.[87] While the consent is to be within the meaning the GDPR, the recitals to the Digital Markets Act contain fairly extensive guidance as to the nature of the consent to be obtained.[88] Even more murkily, the concept of 'data' as distinct from 'personal' or 'non-personal' data has also been adopted in the Data Governance and Data Acts. Both speak of obligations in relation to 'data' and 'data users'. As Lazarotto and Maglieri point out, this creates a risk of ambiguity with regards to overlaps between the GDPR and these new obligations.[89]

Another type of overlap which manifests between these new laws and the GDPR relates to the legitimating of processing. The need to process data to comply with certain obligations under new legislation means that, in certain cases, we can consider these new laws as mandating legislation, necessarily bringing Articles 6 and 23 of the GDPR and the rights to privacy and data protection, into the picture. The Data Governance provides the clearest indication of its status, explicitly not legitimating further processing of personal data, providing that that 'this Regulation should not be read as creating a new legal basis for the processing of personal data for any of the regulated activities, or as amending the information requirements laid down in Regulation'.[90] The proposed EHDS Regulation contains a complex but comprehensive recital setting out certain circumstances in which the Regulation provides a legal basis for the processing of health data, and when a primary basis under Article 6 of the GDPR is required.[91] In other cases there is uncertainty, as the legislation does not seem to formally recognise that mandating legislation can be a legal basis under Article 6 of the GDPR. For example, the Data Act explicitly

[85] ibid art 25(2). See also Recital 67, which provides: 'Those rules on dark patterns should be interpreted as covering prohibited practices falling within the scope of this Regulation to the extent that those practices are not already covered under Directive 2005/29/EC or Regulation (EU) 2016/679.'

[86] Data Governance Act, art 25.

[87] Digital Markets Act, art 5(2).

[88] ibid, Recital 37.

[89] Lazarotto and Malgieri (n 5).

[90] Data Governance Act, Recital 4.

[91] EDHS Regulation, Recital 37.

'does not constitute a legal basis for collection or generation of personal data' by the holder but, where the data holder has an obligation under the Act to make data available to data subjects or at the subject's request, it refers back to the requirement to satisfy Article 6 of the GDPR.[92] It seems implicit in the language not to consider the Data Act itself as mandating legislation under Article 6, but it is at least ambiguous.[93] The NIS2 Directive is similarly unclear, providing that relevant actors 'shall process personal data to the extent necessary for the purposes of this Directive and in accordance with Regulation (EU) 2016/679, in particular such processing shall rely on Article 6 thereof'.[94] Other pieces of legislation are silent as to legal basis, but seem to at least potentially require the processing of personal data in order to comply with obligations or monitor ongoing compliance.

Thus, this assertion that new laws are to be 'without prejudice' to existing protections and rights under the GDPR can be seen as a convenient fiction. The legislation purports not to undermine existing data protection law, but these uncertainties and overlaps will necessarily have an effect on the GDPR's operation. It appears that the Data Governance Act is the only of these new instruments which contains an explicit conflicts of laws provision in favour of data protection.[95] In other instances, regulated actors will have to figure out how to implement overlapping requirements, and regulators will have to coordinate with each other across functionally related areas. The European Data Protection Board and the Court will almost certainly be called upon to clarify the relations between these laws,[96] and in that uncertainty is created both a compliance cost and a space for regulated entities to avoid regulation by pursuing defensive litigation. It is unfortunate that there is less consistency of approach and that this complicated reconciliation of

[92] Data Act, Recital 7.

[93] ibid. This provides in part: 'This Regulation does not constitute a legal basis for the collection or generation of personal data by the data holder. This Regulation imposes an obligation on data holders to make personal data available to users or third parties of a user's choice upon that user's request. Such access should be provided to personal data that are processed by the data holder on the basis of any of the legal bases referred to in Article 6 of Regulation (EU) 2016/679. Where the user is not the data subject, this Regulation does not create a legal basis for providing access to personal data or for making personal data available to a third party and should not be understood as conferring any new right on the data holder to use personal data generated by the use of a connected product or related service. In those cases, it could be in the interest of the user to facilitate meeting the requirements of Article 6 of Regulation (EU) 2016/679. As this Regulation should not adversely affect the data protection rights of data subjects, the data holder can comply with requests in those cases, inter alia, by anonymising personal data or, where the readily available data contains personal data of several data subjects, transmitting only personal data relating to the user.'

[94] NIS2 Directive, art 2(14).

[95] Data Governance Act, art 1(3), Recital 4 requiring that '[i]n the event of a conflict between this Regulation and Union law on the protection of personal data or national law adopted in accordance with such Union law, the relevant Union or national law on the protection of personal data should prevail'.

[96] Just as the EDPS did with regards the ePrivacy Directive, but only after a number of cases before the CJEU. See European Data Protection Board, 'Opinion 5/2019 on the interplay between the ePrivacy Directive and the GDPR, in particular regarding the competence, tasks and powers of data protection authorities' 12 March 2019. Available at: https://edpb.europa.eu/our-work-tools/our-documents/opinion-board-art-64/opinion-52019-interplay-between-eprivacy_en; see also Etteldorf (n 2).

obligations will fall to be worked out by regulated actors and in the courts, instead of being proactively addressed by the legislators, who could have anticipated these overlaps.

Some have pointed to the *lex specialis* rule as having a role to play in demarcating the respective roles of overlapping laws in the digital governance space. The doctrine comes from a Latin principle: *Lex specialis derogate legi generali*, meaning 'special law repeals general laws', or the principle that priority be given to specialist laws over general laws.[97] Thus, notionally, if there is a conflict between two laws, the principle can guide the determination of the applicable law, by determining which law is more specific, and applying that law. The GDPR has been characterised as a *lex generalis* in terms of data protection law.[98] The main discussion of the *lex specialis* rule in the data protection context to date has largely been in relation to the ePrivacy Directive.[99] The ePrivacy Directive is generally thought to be *lex specialis* only with regard to the storing and accessing cookies, not subsequent processing.[100] Thus, the ePrivacy Directive does not displace the entirety of the GDPR, but rather is relevant only to one potential conflict: the legitimation of the storing and accessing of cookies and similar technologies on user devices.

As Conway identifies, applying the *lex specialis* rule is not always easy and it can be subject to multiple conceptions.[101] Even simply applying the rule as a straightforward conflict rule requires characterisation of the underlying laws, to determine which is the general and which is the specific.[102] Such characterisation is not always self-evident. If the conflict is not straightforward, the rule can be further deployed as an interpretative technique, to assess the underlying intention of the legislator as part of judicial reasoning.[103] It becomes more challenging when we consider different types of conflicts which can arise between overlapping laws, and the characterisation issue that Conway identifies manifests. First, we might consider where we have two laws which set out regimes for the protection of personal data. In such a conflict, we can see how the GDPR might represent a more generalist version than a sector-specific articulation of the level of desirable protection. Yet, even in the case of the relationship between the GDPR and ePrivacy Directive, this has not been without uncertainties. Second, more challenging conflicts can arise where the conflict represents a difference of norms more than simply a technical legal overlap. This has been raised by others. As Gerardin

[97] Aaron X Fellmeth and M Horwitz, 'Lex Specialis Derogat Legi Generali', *Guide to Latin in International Law* (New York, Oxford University Press, 2011). Available at: www.oxfordreference.com/display/10.1093/acref/9780195369380.001.0001/acref-9780195369380-e-1303, last accessed 18 November 2023.

[98] Magdalena Kędzior, 'GDPR and beyond – a Year of Changes in the Data Protection Landscape of the European Union' (2019) 19 *ERA Forum* 505.

[99] Cormack (n 2); Kędzior (n 98).

[100] Cormack, ibid at 349.

[101] Gerard Conway, 'Conflicts of Competence Norms in EU Law and the Legal Reasoning of the ECJ' (2010) 11 *German Law Journal* 966.

[102] ibid 986.

[103] ibid.

et al highlight, clashes of normative goals pursued between legislation can arise.[104] They highlight that the Digital Markets Act may be regarded as *lex specialis* as a sector-specific instrument in some cases, but given different normative goals pursued, this raises a potential concern as to whether the application of the Digital Markets Act can be truly 'without prejudice' to the GDPR.[105] Similarly, Vardanyan and Kocharyan characterise the Data Governance Act as 'an attempt by the EU to become an active player in promoting the monetization of personal data'.[106] They warn of a 'risk of collision' in terms of the GDPR and Data Governance Act, particularly with regards to individual control over personal data.[107]

The desirable balance between competing normative goals (such as the economic exploitation of data versus data protection) is contested. Thus, in reconciling conflicting laws, in many cases, a balancing of normative goals will be engaged. The lesson from the case law of the CJEU in relation to the reconciliation of mandating legislation and the GDPR is that affected fundamental rights cannot be divorced from such a balance. Therefore, the character of data protection and privacy as fundamental rights under the Charter, and the GDPR's role in giving expression to those rights,[108] should inform any balancing of normative conflicts between the GDPR and the new suite of EU digital governance laws. However, this is an exercise more comfortably conducted proactively by legislators or reactively by the judiciary, rather than regulated entities who have a different set of incentives driving their behaviour.

At best, we can see that regulated persons will have lots of overlapping regimes to be navigated. This raises questions as to the business and compliance costs created. At worst, conflicting requirements will have to be resolved both legally and operationally. While the *lex specialis* doctrine is notionally available to resolve some of those conflicts, it is challenging to apply, particularly in the context of conflicts of laws which embody competing normative frameworks. In both instances, conflicts and overlaps will also have to be resolved by those called upon to enforce these laws. One of the persistent criticisms of the GDPR has been in relation to enforcement,[109] and this challenge may be confounded given these new digital governance laws will be supervised by a variety of new regulators and oversight bodies. We can look forward to activities by national supervisory authorities under the Data Governance Act,[110] proposed AI Act,[111] the Data Act,[112] and

[104] Geradin, Bania and Karanikioti (n 3) at 2.

[105] ibid 4.

[106] Vardanyan and Kocharyan (n 4) at 92.

[107] Ibid 106.

[108] Elise Muir, 'Of Ages In – and Edges Of –EU Law' (2011) 48 *Common Market Law Review* 39; Elise Muir, 'The Fundamental Rights Implications of EU Legislation: Some Constitutional Challenges' (2014) 51 *Common Market Law Review* 219.

[109] See Giulia Gentile and Orla Lynskey, 'Deficient by Design? The Transnational Enforcement of the GDPR' (2022) 71 *International and Comparative Law Quarterly* 799; Filippo Lancieri, 'Narrowing Data Protection's Enforcement Gap' (2022) 74 *Maine Law Review* 59.

[110] Data Governance Act, art 23.

[111] Proposed AI Act, art 59.

[112] Data Act, art 37.

guidance and coordination via a new European Health Data Space Board[113] and a European Data Innovation Board.[114] In a space where coordination amongst GDPR regulators has already been sufficiently trying as to warrant proposals of legislative reform,[115] the need to manage intersecting roles and responsibilities will doubtless be difficult.

V. Conclusion

What emerges from this consideration of the intersection between the GDPR and other legislation is a complex picture.

Mandating legislation can, in principle, legitimise processing under the GDPR, either in providing a legal basis for processing under Article 6 or providing a derogation from GDPR obligations under Article 23. In either case, there can be problems in terms of fit between such legislation and the requirements of the GDPR, which can create uncertainty as to the legality of the data processing. Moreover, such legislation must also comply with the rights to privacy and data protection. This is seen through the interpretation of mandating legislation in light of Charter rights, and the willingness of the CJEU to review mandating legislation for compliance with such rights. This inevitably engages questions of competing normative purposes and balancing of rights and other interests. Such a balancing exercise is not easily predicted. As the cases concerning the balance between the public interest in access to information versus privacy/data protection illustrate, a cohesive sense of desirable societal or systematic levels of data protection has not yet emerged.

These intersections are only bound to raise more problems in light of the proliferation of EU digital governance legislation in recent years. Considerable potential for overlap is evident in the suite of legislation emerging from the EU, and yet the legislation does not adequately reconcile such overlaps. Rather, predominantly such legislation provides that it is to apply 'without prejudice' to the GDPR, even though clear overlaps in terms of scope, obligations and use of concepts are evident. This inevitably will create at least operational challenges for entities which operate across these suites of legislation – both the regulated and the regulators. While the *lex specialis* doctrine has potentially some function to play in resolving conflicts between overlapping laws, the doctrine is not particularly useful where those conflicting laws represent competing contested normative positions. In such cases, the rights to privacy and data protection should have an important role in ensuring conflicts do not have the effect of undermining rights protections, nor that new legislation founded on economic conceptions of data usage can supplant the GDPR.

[113] See Proposed EHDS Regulation, Chapter VI.

[114] See Proposed Data Act, art 42; Data Governance Act, art 29.

[115] Commission, 'Proposal for a Regulation of the European Parliament and of the Council laying down additional procedural rules relating to the enforcement of Regulation (EU) 2016/679' COM (2023) 388 final.

9

Article 82 GDPR and Non-Material Damages: Torn between Social and Economic Functions?

RÓISÍN Á COSTELLO

I. Introduction

The digital spaces in and through which we conduct so much of our social interactions and economic activity today have generated fundamental challenges for data protection law. In the first half decade of the existence of the GDPR, the form and function of the Union's data protection infrastructure, the centralisations (and diffusions) of power it enables, and how it is used by commercial, state and individual actors has generated a growing body of jurisprudence.

A central issue which recurs in several of the contributions to this volume is the Union's somewhat conflicted view of the GDPR's character. The Regulation is premised on the protection of individual autonomy[1] and specifically frames the Regulation in Recital 4 in the following terms

> The processing of personal data should be designed to serve mankind. The right to the protection of personal data is not an absolute right; it must be considered in relation to its function in society and be balanced against other fundamental rights, in accordance with the principle of proportionality. This Regulation respects all fundamental rights and observes the freedoms and principles recognised in the Charter as enshrined in the Treaties, in particular the respect for private and family life, home and communications, the protection of personal data, freedom of thought, conscience and religion, freedom of expression and information, freedom to conduct a business, the right to an effective remedy and to a fair trial, and cultural, religious and linguistic diversity.

[1] See the notice and consent architecture established in arts 6, 7 and 9 of Regulation (EU) 2016/679 of the European Parliament and of the Council of 27 April 2016 on the protection of natural persons with regard to the processing of personal data and on the free movement of such data, and repealing Directive 95/46/EC (General Data Protection Regulation) (Text with EEA relevance) *OJ L 119, 4.5.2016, pp 1–88, as well as the disclosure obligations imposed, in particular, by* arts 12–14. See also, Recitals 7 and 32 which particularly emphasise this.

The Regulation is thus explicitly concerned with normative framing and with the substantive vindication of fundamental rights – both in terms of protecting those rights directly implicated by its text (data protection, privacy) as well as those fundamental rights, freedoms and principles which might be indirectly implicated where data protection is invoked (freedom of expression being, perhaps, the most obvious though others are also explicitly mentioned). Interestingly, several of those rights which are explicitly referred to – rights such as linguistic diversity and cultural identity would appear to mirror the broad contours of some of the rights recognised as part of Article 8 of the ECHR in as much as they are concerned with identity, personality development and the constitution of self within society and as between individuals and social groups.[2]

Despite this emphasis on autonomy and fundamental rights in its framing, the Regulation is also, fundamentally, characterised by its market-facing concerns. As a result and following in a consistent pattern from Recital 4 onwards there are multiple references throughout the text to the Regulation's function as a measure which will facilitate and enable the better regulation and functioning of the European market.

These two streams of concern could, of course, continue in parallel uninterrupted and untroubled by each other. The Regulation does not clearly choose to proceed in this way. Recital 2, for example, marries the social objectives of the Regulation with its function in advancing the market, noting that the GDPR is intended 'to contribute to the accomplishment of an area of freedom, security and justice and of an economic union, to economic and social progress, to the strengthening and the convergence of the economies within the internal market', but that it is also intended to contribute to the well-being of natural persons.

In framing the manner in which these social, rights-based and market aspects of the Regulation's functions and objectives are served, the GDPR is notable for emphasising that its work to foster greater 'trust' is required in order to 'allow the digital economy to develop across the internal market'.[3] Further on, the Recitals to the Regulation note the need for harmonised measures across the Union in order to minimise obstacles 'to the pursuit of economic activities at the level of the Union' and 'distort competition'[4] and note the GDPR is necessary to provide 'legal certainty and transparency for economic operators'.[5]

The Regulation's combination of social objectives (advancing and securing the protection of fundamental rights) and market objectives (improving the seamlessness and efficiency of the single market) is the most recent manifestation of the

[2] On the right to have a personal name recognised under Article 8 ECHR including in a particular language, see, e.g., *Aktas & Ors v Turkey*, App nos 18684/07 and 21101/07 (ECHR, 25 June 2019). On the right to culture or the protection and freedom to enjoy culture see, e.g., *Ahunbay & Ors v Turkey*, App no 6080/06 (ECHR, 29 January 2019).

[3] Regulation (EU) 2016/679 (n 1) Recital 7.

[4] ibid. Recital 9.

[5] ibid. Recital 13.

Union's broader attempt to identify and define an internally coherent constitutional identity which can encompass both the Union's traditionally market-oriented constitutional order and its progressive development of a rights-based order.[6] The GDPR is, at once, a central aspect of the Union's fundamental rights architecture – as well as being perhaps one of the most influential aspects of it[7] – while also functioning as an economically orientated regulatory mechanism which enables a more competitive digital single market.

Recital 5 of the GDPR refers to '[t]he economic and social integration resulting from the functioning of the internal market' and the increase in cross-border flows of personal data which has resulted from this. The Regulation thus acknowledges both in the factors which drove its creation, and its orienting objectives that both economic and social spheres of activity are engaged. Yet the GDPR lacks a clear perspective on whether its social and economic objectives are to be advanced equally and (perhaps more fundamentally) how this can be achieved. Indeed, the overall picture which emerges from the first years of the GDPR is of a law which is acknowledged as exercising significant normative influence but whose interpretation often remains firmly rooted in economic and market-based analysis, as several of the other contributions to this volume have examined.

This chapter seeks to contextualise this uneasy relationship between the GDPR's normative power, and its market-enabling objectives by adopting a political economy analysis which challenges the division between 'market' and 'social' concerns. Political economy approaches are particularly appropriate in the case of EU law for two reasons. The first, is that the constitutional core of the Union by its nature blurs the boundaries between public and private law as part of a constitutional identity which was traditionally premised on furthering exclusively market objectives, but which rapidly adopted 'public law' constitutional features – first as part of the fundamental rights jurisprudence which emerged through the general principles and then as an explicit aspect of the Treaties and Charter. The second, related, reason is that the Union itself is fundamentally ordoliberal in its regulatory approach and as part of that approach it seeks to achieve positive social outcomes through market interventions, thus exposing for consideration the manner in which the social and market aspects of the Union's constitutional identity can interact and operate.

Using the political economy model articulated by Karl Polanyi, this chapter analyses the GDPR's integration of its commitments to, on the one hand, the promotion and protection of fundamental rights and, on the other hand, the

[6] See Dorota Leczykiewicz, 'The Charter of Fundamental Rights and the EU's Shallow Constitutionalism', in Maria Cahill and Richard Ekins NW Barber (eds), *The Rise and Fall of the European Constitution* (Hart, 2019).

[7] Anu Bradford, *The Brussels Effect: How the European Union Rules the World* (Oxford University Press, 2020). See also, Róisín Á Costello, 'The Brussels Effect: Regulatory Standard-Setting and Constitutional Conflicts in Post-Brexit Privacy Law' in Celeste et al (eds) *Data Protection and Digital Sovereignty Post-Brexit* (Hart, 2023), 165.

promotion of market efficiency and competition. The chapter asks to what extent, and how successfully, these ends have been vindicated in the Regulation's enforcement and, in so doing, focuses (in particular) on the CJEU'S recent decisions on non-material damages under Article 82 of the GDPR and how both the market enabling and fundamental rights protecting functions of the Regulation have been employed in that jurisprudence.

Parts II and III examine the relationship between social and economic values in the European legal order and, more specifically, in the European Union's data protection law. Part IV then proceeds to consider the CJEU's developing jurisprudence on Article 82 and to analyse how the Court has sought to marry the social and market aspects of the Regulation in their decisions on this article.

II. Social and Market Values in EU Law

Proposals for a European community as a functional remedy for Europe's cyclical periods of conflict and despotism had long been mooted, first by William Penn[8] and subsequently by Bellers[9] and Rousseau, the latter building on the work of Abbé St Pierre.[10] Yet none of these thinkers drew a necessary or desirable connection between their imagined European alliances and the protection of individual rights and when the first European community emerged following the Second World War it was fashioned in an explicitly (and exclusively) economic mould.

The European Coal and Steel Community (ECSC) resulted from two opposing forces. The first was a desire, following the Second World War, to ensure German military capacities were limited (accomplished indirectly through impositions of controls coal and steel). The second, more fundamental and somewhat more abstract desire, was to create a community of European states defined and unified, largely, by their opposition to the emerging political environment of Eastern Europe. While the ECSC accomplished its ends through collective buy-in to the institutional structure of the Community[11] and associated market regulations, an explicitly social or substantive element to accompany the economic co-ordination was absent.

[8] William Penn, 'An essay toward the present and future peace of Europe' (1693) Section IV, 406. Available at: www.fredsakademiet.dk/library/penn.pdf, last accessed 1 February 2024 in which the author envisions the creation of a European parliament.

[9] John Bellers, *Some Reasons for a European State* (1710) in which the author argues for a model based on Swiss cantonal system.

[10] Jean-Jacques Rousseau, 'Extrait Du Projet De Paix Perpétuelle De Monsieur Abbé Saint Pierre', in Jean-Jacques Rousseau (ed), *Ouvres Complètes Iii – Du Contrat Social – Écrits Politiques* (La Plaéaide, Éditions Gallimard, 1964), 563.

[11] See generally, Craig de Paul and Grainne De Burca, *Eu Law: Text, Cases, and Materials* (6th edn, Oxford University Press, 2015), 3. For a detailed examination of the ECSC see John Gillingham, *Coal, Steel, and Rebirth of Europe: The Germans and French from Ruhr Conflict to Economic Community* (Cambridge University Press, 2005).

The particular source of this reluctance, however, was specific – borne of British reluctance to support more comprehensive political integration. Some years later, a more general reluctance on the part of other States to engage in deeper political integration also led to the failure of the European Defence Community (EDC) and the European Political Community (EPC). Though the question of fundamental rights was considered by both the *Comité d'Études sur une Constitution Européene* and the Ad Hoc Assembly between 1951 and 1952[12] as part of the process of developing the EPC and EDC the rights inclusive constitutional texts produced by both groups were abandoned in favour of texts whose emphasis in achieving integration was on economic rather than social standards.[13]

As a result of the failure to progress towards a more broadly integrated constitutional identity – to be realised through the EDC and EPC – the European community remained an entity defined by institutional and economic motivations and constraints into the early 1960s until the Community's judicial institutions took a decisive role in advancing a more substantive vision of the Union's constitutional identity.

More fundamentally, the failure of both the EDC and EPC led proponents who favoured greater European integration to favour explicitly market-led models. In this respect, the Dutch proposal for a more developed understanding of the common market, which had been included within the EPC, re-emerged in discussions over the creation of a European Economic Community (EEC) in Messina in 1955. The resulting report, published in 1956, which contained the proposed scheme (later adopted in the Rome Treaty[14]) for the EEC and Euratom retained much of the ESCS's institutional character. The constitutional identity it advanced continued to be distinctly economic prioritising the creation of the common market which removed barriers to trade as well as seeking to promote a more efficient market. The broader aims of the Community, to increase the standard of living, improve stability and promote closer relationship between Member States hinted, for the first time, at a social as well as market aspect to the Community's identity – an aspect which would emerge more fully in subsequent revisions to the Treaties.[15]

Indeed, it was ultimately the activism of the European Courts that drove the concrete emergence of fundamental rights as a feature of Community law and part of the European integration agenda.[16] The undiluted economic character of the

[12] Johan Van Haersolte and Jan-Kees Wiebenga, 'The Role of the European Parliament in the Fundamental Rights Architecture of the European Union', in Ben Vermeulen Marjolein Van Roosmalen, Frien Van Hoof and Marten Oosting (eds), *Fundamental Rights and Principles* (Intersentia, 2013), 153, 155–57.

[13] Allan Rosas and Lorna Armati, *EU Constitutional Law: An Introduction* (3rd edn, Hart, 2018).

[14] European Union, Treaty Establishing the European Community (Consolidated Version), Rome Treaty, 25 March 1957.

[15] Stephen Weatherill, *Law and Values in the European Union* (Oxford University Press, 2016), 4–5.

[16] Though the Court initially resisted the attempt to 'smuggle in' fundamental rights through judicial decisions. See Case C-1/58 *Stork v High Authority* EU:C:1959:4; Joined Cases 36, 37, 38 and 40/59

Community's integration agenda did not prevent the CJEU from subsequently finding, in *Stauder*,[17] that the 'general principles' of Community law included the protection of fundamental rights.[18] While the decision can be read as a delayed recognition of the need to accommodate social as well as market concerns within the European project, the motivations of the Court in recognising fundamental rights as a general principle of European law has been queried.

The decision in *Stauder* followed a period of intense discussion within the EU's institutions on the status of European law. The shift occasioned by the decision in that case has been attributed to the Court's expectation that, following the enumeration of the principles of primacy and direct effect in *Costa*[19] and *Van Gend En Loos*,[20] the Community would encounter opposition if it sought to require states to accept those principles in circumstances where the Community's own legal order did not itself respect fundamental rights, and instead subordinated them to market concerns.[21]

This motivation finds support in the Courts' dicta in *Siragusa*[22] and *Hernandez*[23] to the effect that the reason for requiring fundamental rights review of Member State action within the scope of EU law is the same as the original reason for requiring fundamental rights review of EU action in *Handelsgesellschaft* – to ensure the supremacy of EU law.[24]

As a result, while it is tempting to classify *Stauder* as representative of a sea-change it is more likely that a practical concern with promoting further economic integration was the motivation behind the decision.[25] The delay following *Stauder*,

Geitling v High Authority EU:C:1960:36; Case 40/64 *Scarlata and Others v Commission of the EEC* EU:C:1965:36. See, generally, Alec Stone Sweet, *The Judicial Construction of Europe* (Oxford University Press, 2004), 9. Gerard Conway, *The Limits of Legal Reasoning and the European Court of Justice* (Cambridge University Press, 2012), 21–49, 53; Ulrich Haltern, 'Integration through Law', in Tanja Diez and Thomas Risse Antje Wiener (eds), *European Integration Theory* (Oxford University Press, 2004), 183; Jason Coppel and Aidan O'Neill, 'The European Court of Justice: Taking Rights Seriously' (1992) 29 *Common Market Law Review* 669; Anna Bredimas, *Methods of Interpretation and Community Law* (North Holland Publishing Company, 1978); Hjalte Rasmussen, *On Law and Policy in the European Court of Justice: A Comparative Study in Judicial Policymaking* (Martinus Nijhoff Publichers, 1986), 167; JHH Weiler, 'The Reformation of European Constitutionalism' (1997) 35(1) *Journal of Common Market Studies* 104.

[17] Case C-26/69 *Stauder v City of Ulm* at [7].

[18] The significance of the general principles to the current scheme of fundamental rights within the European Union is examined in the proceeding section, see Chapters 5 at p 157 and 6 at p 197.

[19] Case C-6/64 *Costa v ENEL* EU:C:1964:66.

[20] ibid.

[21] De Burca (n 11) at 383; Jan Weiler, *The Constitution of Europe: 'Do the Clothes Have an Emperor' and Other Essays on European Integration* (Cambridge University Press, 1999). 107–8; Allan Rosas, 'The European Court of Justice and Fundamental Right: Yet Another Case of Judicial Activism?', in C Baudenbacher and H Bull (eds), *European Integration through Interaction of Legal Regimes* (Oslo Universitetsforlaget, 2007), 33, 36–39.

[22] Case C-206/13 *Siragusa* EU:C:2014:126. See also, Case C-40/11 *Ilida* EU:C:2016:691; Case C-87/12 *Ymeraga* EU:C:2013:291.

[23] Case C-198/13 *Julian Hernandez* EU:C:2014:2055.

[24] Case C-7/14 *Handelsgesellschaf* EU:C:2015:205.

[25] Manfred A Dauses, 'The Protection of Fundamental Rights in the Community Legal Order' (1985) 10 *European Law Review* 398.

of the emergence of any institutional recognition of fundamental rights within the Union further supports this position – indeed it was not until the 1990s that fundamental rights received institutional recognition in European law.[26] It was not until the Charter of Fundamental Rights achieved binding status in 2009 that the Union's commitment to fundamental rights was articulated as an enumerated list of protections. However, even following the introduction of the Charter, the Union's fundamental rights competence remains restricted.

The Rome Treaty was succeeded, in 1986, by the Single European Act which was generally recognised as a substantial revision of the Community's constitutional structure in both institutional and substantive terms. The most significant of these was the adoption of Article 100a of the EEC (now TFEU art 114) which conferred a broad legislative power on the Union to enact secondary law with a view to 'progressively establishing the internal market' defined as 'an area without internal frontiers in which the free movement of goods, persons, services and capital is ensured'.[27]

Though the Act was seen as advancing an integration agenda which extended beyond purely economic issues – including areas of social policy and cohesion within the Union's competences, it was notable for its continued failure to include fundamental rights within the Union's constitutional documents – despite the CJEU's recognition of fundamental rights as part of the general principles of Community law.[28] Weiler and others thus characterised the SEA as focused primarily on offering new, legislative, mechanisms to 'kick start' the fulfilment of the Community's economic objectives.[29] While Weiler argued the new competences in respect of social policy constituted a recognition that the Community's market objectives were connected to social forces,[30] the SEA was nevertheless understood as being characterised predominantly by its single market aims and economic character with the newly introduced social objectives considered secondary.

The Maastricht Treaty further strengthened the Union's legislative powers (subsequently augmented once more by the Treaty of Amsterdam)[31] though the Treaty on the European Union (TEU) continued to lack a substantial, social element.[32] Article B of the TEU continued to platform an ordoliberal view through

[26] The Convention had previously been described by the Court in *Loizidou v Turkey* (Preliminary Objections) Application No 15318/99 (ECHR, 28 July 1996) as 'a constitutional instrument of European public order' and had been treated by the CJEU as a 'special source of inspiration' for fundamental rights. See, JWF Allison, *The English Historical Constitution*, (Cambridge University Press, 2007), 54.

[27] See Treaty Establishing the European Community (Consolidated Version), Rome Treaty, art 8a.

[28] See White Paper on the Completion of the Internal Market COM(85) 310.

[29] JHH Weiler, 'The Transformation of Europe' (1991) 100 *Yale Law Journal*, 2403, 2454; De Burca (n 11) at 10.

[30] Weiler (n 29).

[31] Treaty of Amsterdam amending the Treaty on European Union, the Treaties establishing the European Communities and certain related acts (2007), OJ C 340; European Union, Treaty on European Union (Consolidated Version), Treaty of Maastricht , 7 February 1992, *Official Journal of the European Communities* C 325/5 (2002).

[32] Deirdre Curtin, 'The Constitutional Structure of the Union: A Europe of Bits and Pieces' (1993) 30 *Common Market Law Review* 17–69.; Alkuin Kölliker, 'Bringing Together or Driving Apart the Union? Towards a Theory of Differentiated Integration' (2001) 24(4) *West European Politics* 125–51.

the promotion of economic and social progress by market mechanisms, and although rights were referred to in the same article, this was framed by reference to national law. While Article F of the document did refer to the Union's commitment to respecting fundamental rights under the ECHR but it did not clarify the relationship of fundamental rights as recognised by the CJEU with this commitment or with the constitutional documents of the Community itself. The most substantive development which heralded an explicit augmentation of the Union's constitutional character to include social characteristics as well as economic ones came at this juncture.

The introduction of the Charter as a document with binding force within the EU constitutional order in 2009 and its application to the Union, and those activities within the scope of EU law, was intended to add an additional layer of socially orientated constitutional values to this market-orientated core through the incorporation of systemic commitments to social aims which would operate in addition to pre-existing market-based objectives.[33] A complementary reorientation of the Treaties following the Treaty of Lisbon, highlighted the Union's foundation on the values of human rights and human dignity[34] and emphasised the promotion and preservation of the European values.[35]

This re-orientation of the Union's constitutional core seems transformational, prioritising the integration of these aspects as a fundamental aspect of the Union's constitutional identity and thus ensuring, in theory, that such social, constitutional values and principles were integrated in quotidian practice and policy. Moreover, the move seemed also to recognise that the EU exercises both power and responsibility in a State-like manner,[36] which requires a concomitant augmentation of any constitutional identity premised on the narrow recognition of economic integration.[37]

While the TEU set out the shared constitutional basis of the Union and her Member States,[38] as well as the structural restraints on the scope of EU law as imposed by its values[39] and objectives[40] and the principles of EU law,[41] its most significant aspects from the perspective of integrating fundamental rights as part of the Union's constitutional identity come in Article 6 which outlines the sources of human rights norms applicable in the Union's legal order (including the obligation of accession to the ECHR).

[33] Leczykiewicz, (n 6) at 124, 143.
[34] TEU, art 1.
[35] ibid. arts 6 and 7.
[36] Weatherill (n 115) at 405.
[37] On the shortcomings of this approach see Leczykiewicz (n 6).
[38] See Title I of European Union, *Treaty on European Union (Consolidated Version), Treaty of Maastricht*, 7 February 1992, *Official Journal of the European Communities* C 325/5; 24 December 2002.
[39] ibid. arts 1 and 2.
[40] ibid. art 3.
[41] ibid. arts 4 and 5.

Article 6 establishes the Charter as part of the primary law of the Union and provides that it has the same legal value as the Treaties and, as such, has binding force. The Charter is thus not subordinate to the Treaties and should, in theory, ensure that fundamental rights (as the social component of the Union's constitutional identity) act as the standard of review for EU secondary laws and are integrated within them, afforded equal weight in balancing exercises involving the economic or market concerns provided in the Treaties.

What emerges from an analysis of the EU's constitutional history is a system characterised by an ongoing struggle to integrate the two strands of market/economic and social constitutionalism within the overarching constitutional identity of the Union, and to fully realise the interdependence and inter-relation of those two aspects in a coherent and sustained manner.

Polanyi's Theory of Political Economy and the European Union

Tracing a similar pattern to those identified by Marx[42] and Foucault,[43] Polanyi identified the gradual emergence of the legal mechanisms of enclosure, appropriation of natural resources, and marketisation or labour as having reconceptualised the basic factors of social life as commodities resulting in conceptual shifts which disassociated those areas which could still be considered 'social' from the market while simultaneously generating a popular perception that a vast array of social goods and objectives were, in fact, economic and fundamentally related to and the subject of the market.[44]

Polanyi's central critique of this process focuses on the loss of, or departure from, the concept of 'embeddedness' which, he argues, has traditionally characterised market-based societies.[45] Polanyi uses the term embeddedness to express the idea that the economy is not an autonomous and distinct force, as it has been understood in neoliberal and ordoliberal theory, but is and should be understood as an aspect of the social life of communities. In Polanyi's account, the market is an aspect of society which has traditionally been interwoven and subordinated to the values of politics, religion and social relations. It is, fundamentally, a theory that contends for the integration of social and market objectives.

[42] Karl Marx, *Capital: A Critique of Political Economy (1887)* (New York: International Publishers, 1967).

[43] James Boyle, 'Foucault in Cyberspace: Surveillance, Sovereignty and Hardwired Censors' (1997) 66 *University of Cincinnati Law Review* 177; Michel Foucault, *Discipline and Punish*, trans. Alan Sheridan (London: Penguin, 1991).

[44] Karl Polanyi, *The Great Transformation: The Political and Economic Origins of Our Time* (2nd edn, Beacon Press, 2001), 171 *et seq.*

[45] ibid. xxiii.

In contrast to this, Polanyi argues that modern economic thought has been, and is, premised on an understanding of the economy as an interlocking system of markets that automatically adjusts supply and demand through price mechanisms, independent of and unrelated to social factors. In this modern model, social values and objectives are achieved through market functions – which is to the say that the market is the dominant force to which social values are subordinated, or from which they are removed. This understanding, he argues, fails to reflect the reality of societies throughout history in which the economy has existed as a socially embedded mechanism and not an independent one whose operation was held in tension to social objectives.[46]

Specifically, Polanyi argues that this disembedded view of market and social has emerged only with the radical works of Malthus and Ricardo[47] and should be understood in that context, as a radical departure from the accepted and established pattern as it had existed to that point and which gained popular endorsement during the economic liberalism of the 1830s.[48] The result, Polanyi argues, is a popular misconception that this radical view represents a conservative and enduring fidelity to a long-established status quo. On the contrary, however, the reality is that the economy has become the dominant organising force of society, within which social relations must seek to accommodate themselves – which is far from being representative of the place, embedded in social relations, which it occupied for much of history.

As part of this re-orientation, the system for social ordering has been required to accommodate private economic activity rather than the reverse and economic and social areas of concern are viewed as incidentally complementary but largely distinct. Polanyi's primary concern is to challenge to ascendancy of this view and to argue for a reversion to the original pattern of embedded market societies. His more abstract concern, however, is with the impact of this modern pattern on the capacities of individuals to realise that they themselves are social citizens and on the freedom of those viewed as units of consumption and production.[49]

The 'social' aspect of the Union's ordering, within Polanyi's articulation, can be understood as referring to those measures which determine the normative infrastructure of individual goods underpinning the Union's legal system whose constitutional character is, as outlined above, predominantly market based, and provides a constitutional footing to the normative goods which comprise its

[46] ibid. 257.

[47] ibid.

[48] ibid. 145 et seq.

[49] ibid. 171 and 257. Cohen has applied Polanyi's analysis in an account that seeks to understand struggles over the conditions of information flow and the design of information architectures as part of which law is enlisted to help produce the economic and sociotechnical shifts that have accompanied the emergence of the informational economy and which have, in turn, shaped how the law has developed. See Julie E Cohen, *Between Truth and Power: The Legal Constructions of Informational Capitalism* (Oxford University Press, 2019). On the two strands of Polanyi which Cohen addresses, see Fred Block, (2008) 'Polanyi's Double Movement and the Reconstruction of Critical Theory', *Revue Interventions Économiques*, 38.

'social' aspect only in so far as they impact, or facilitate, the market aspect of the Union's identity. This is perhaps most notable by reference to the text of the treaties themselves where social values are notable for their rarity – the exceptions being the constitutionalised principles of non-discrimination in Article 19, and data protection in Article 16 of the TFEU. While these principles, and fundamental rights more generally, form part of the Union's constitutional infrastructure they are notably framed in terms of their contribution to, and facilitation of, a more efficient and competitive Union market.

This is a feature of the ordoliberal ideology which characterises the approach to legal interventions and constitutional identity, within the Union.[50] The Union's vision of ordoliberalism envisions a strong role for the State in ensuring the market functions at close to pure efficiency but emphasises that political power rather than restricting itself, or refraining from regulation of the market, should prefer, and regulate to ensure, the presence of market based rules to enhance competition and market efficiency while ensuring certain basic welfare protections.[51]

From the Treaty of Rome (which has been described, with slight exaggeration, as 'a triumph for German ordoliberalism')[52] onwards, the European Community's constitutional character has been markedly ordoliberal.[53] Indeed, the EU explicitly grounds its legitimacy on its constitutional commitment to this market focus[54] and has legitimised its own expansion, and competences by reference to the a-political value of market health. In doing so, the Union's proliferation of new legal and policy standards, while not unchallenged, is rendered palatable to national sovereignty concerns.[55] However, the market emphasis which characterises ordoliberalism, necessarily involves the decoupling of the market and social aspects of Union law and policy.[56] This is particularly evident in the development of the Union's digital policy agenda from the latter half of the 1990s.

[50] See Jotte Mulder (2019) 15(2) 'Re-Conceptualising a Social Market Economy for the EU Internal Market', *Utrecht Law Review* 16–39.

[51] It is notable that Alexander Rüstow, who first articulated neoliberalism in 1938, is himself regarded as an ordoliberal in contemporary analysis. See Taylor C Boas and Jordan Gans-Morse, 'Neoliberalism: From New Liberal Philosophy to Anti-Liberal Slogan' (2009) 44(2) *Studies in Comparative International Development* 137.

[52] Bernard Moss, 'The European Community as Monetarist Construction: A Critique of Moravcsik', (2000) 8(1) *Journal of European Area Studies* 247, 260.

[53] Christian Joerges, 'What Is Left of the European Economic Constitution? A Melancholic Eulogy', (2005) 30 *European Law Review* 461.

[54] Edward N Megay, 'Anti-Pluralist Liberalism: The German Neoliberals' (1970) 85(3) *Political Science Quarterly* 422.

[55] David Gerber, 'Ordoliberalism: A New Intellectual Framework for Competition Law' in David Gerber (ed), *Law and Competition in Twentieth-Century Europe* (Oxford University Press, 2001), Chapter 7.

[56] Traditionally this was accommodated through the bifurcation of the economically orientated constitutional documents of the Union, which looked to the market, and nationally embedded social law and policy which operated to protect fundamental rights, apart from the Union's legal schema though the boundaries of this bifurcation have blurred over time. See Manfred E Sreit and Wener Mussler, 'The Economic Constitution of the European Community: From Rome to Maastricht' (1994)

III. Social and Market Values in EU Data Protection Law

European interventions to regulate the digital sphere through a digital policy have been predominantly market based since their inception. Thus the 1997 European Initiative in Electronic Commerce sought to encourage the growth of e-commerce and create a coherent regulatory framework building on existing Single Market legislation but did not consider social aspects of the digital market. Indeed, by seeking to articulate the digital space as a market created a context in which national regulation for the achievement of social objectives in digital contexts was significantly curtailed as conflicting with EU law by imposing barriers to trade.[57]

The 1997 Initiative was followed by the Lisbon Declaration and the e-Europe Initiative,[58] the Union's Digital Agenda for Europe[59] and the 2015 Digital Single Market Strategy[60] which each in turn emphasised market rather than social justifications for, and aims in, the development of digital policy focusing on consumer engagement, market efficiency and economic growth.

Parallel attempts to ensure a similar development of socially oriented policy governing the digital market from which the GDPR would, eventually, emerge were equally concerned with markets and, in particular, maximising the Union's capacity to compete with the United States. Thus, the 1973 Communication on Community policy in the area of data processing suggested it was necessary to devise a systematic system of support for European capacities in data processing which would enable European actors to compete internationally. As part of these efforts the Commission proposed in a 1973 measure that there was a need to adopt 'common measures for the protection of the citizen'.[61]

The 1973 communication is significant for its suggestion that harmonised measures for protecting consumers were necessary to enable the development of a competitive digital market but also its contextualisation of these measures as being, by default, economically orientated – targeted at achieving greater market

5 *Constitutional and Political Economy* 319; Wolf Sauter, 'The Economic Constitution of the European Union' (1998) 4 *Columbia Journal of European Law* 27; Stefano Giubboni, *Social Rights and Market Freedom in the European Constitution* (Cambridge University Press, 2006), 15–29.

[57] European Commission, 'A European Initiative in Electronic Commerce, Communication to the European Parliament, the Council, the Economic and Social Committee and the Committee of the Regions', in Com(97)157 (Brussels, 1997).

[58] Communication from the European Commission, 'E-Europe: An Information Society for All Com(1999)687', (1999), repeated in the conclusion of the Stockholm European Council in March 2001.

[59] Communication from The Commission, 'A Digital Agenda for Europe Com(2010)245', (Brussels, 2010).

[60] Communication from The Commission, 'A Digital Single Market Strategy for Europe Com(2015)192', (Brussels, 2015).

[61] Commission for European Communities, 'Community policy on data processing' (Communication of the Commission to the Council) SEC(73) 4300 final, 13.

participation and competition.[62] As the OECD and Council of Europe began to consider the same issues of consumer protection in digital spaces, the European Parliament ordered a report in 1974 on the rights of individuals in the field of data processing and subsequently adopted a resolution based on its contents calling for the adoption of a Directive on individual freedom and data processing.[63] However, no response was forthcoming and there followed a considerable period during which the Union's institutions undertook examinations and studies as well as passing further resolutions without advancing concrete legal or policy developments.[64]

Indeed, it was only with the adoption of a package of proposals related to data protection that the proposal for a data protection Directive began to take shape.[65] However, beginning with the 1995 Directive on Data Protection,[66] followed by the Directive on Data Retention[67] and the e-Privacy Directive,[68] the Union's secondary laws developed with the expressed aim of harmonising national laws which sought to protect the 'fundamental rights of individuals, and in particular the right to privacy'.[69] The 1995 Directive, in particular, while it was adopted as a measure necessary for the functioning of the internal market under Article 100a of the ECT, couched its language in terms of the protection of individuals.[70]

This orientation, deriving the Directive's legitimacy from a market- rather than rights-based basis, has caused some to label to Directive as a tool which was used to neutralise national rights in favour of economic efficiency.[71] However, Fuster argues that the Directive and the other measures adopted should be seen instead as part of a wider trend in Community law which viewed fundamental rights as the legitimate means of derogation from internal market freedoms.[72]

Such language augured well from a rights perspective, indicating that the market-orientated approach which had contextualised the development of such laws was to be tempered by fundamental rights concerns. However, while the Directive aimed to protect individuals it also prohibited restrictions on the free flow of personal data,[73] prioritising market functionality over restrictions on

[62] For a discussion of the issue see Gloria Gonzalez Fuster, *The Emergence of Personal Data Protection as a Fundamental Right of the EU*, Pompeu Casanovas and Giovanni Sartor (eds) (Law, Governance and Technology Series, 16 (Springer, 2014), 113–14.

[63] Resolution of the European Parliament on the protection of the rights of the individual in the face of developing technical progress in the field of automatic data processing [1975] OJ C60/48.

[64] See again, Fuster (n 62) at 117–24.

[65] Commission of the European Communities COM(90) 314 final [1990] OJ C277/1.

[66] Directive 95/41/EC.

[67] Directive 2006/24/EC.

[68] Directive 2002/58/EC.

[69] COM(90) 314 final, 5.

[70] Directive 95/46/EC, art 1.

[71] Jean-Baptiste Thomas-Sertillanges and Elisabeth Quillatre, 'Libre Circulation Des Données Á Une Caractére Personnel Au Sein Du Marché Intérieur Et De L'espace De Liberté Sécurité Justice: Vers Une Diversification Des Instruments De Régulation', (2011) 400(3) *Petites Affiches* 9.

[72] Fuster (n 62) at 135.

[73] ibid. art 1(2).

market activity. The result was an uncomfortable marriage of competing social and market-orientated aims. This is not to say that the Directive did not advance fundamental rights. Decisions like *Google Spain*,[74] clearly indicate a capacity for significant and, at times controversial, rights-led expansion based on the Directive's text. However, it is probably more accurate to characterise the Directive as a law concerned, primarily, with marked-oriented goods as part of a traditionally ordoliberal model.

The practical reality was thus that the trend identified by Fuster remains very much alive – with measures like the Data Protection Directive best understood as part of a wider trend in Community law as part of which fundamental rights are viewed as the legitimate means of derogating from internal market freedoms.[75]

This perspective, while not clearly rejecting ordoliberal perspectives on market regulation, certainly approaches a position more aligned with a Polanyian reintegration of the social and market aspects of regulatory design. The subsequent legislative package, consisting of the GDPR and the (still proposed) e-Privacy Regulation, is notable for its retrenchment of this trend with the aim of achieving a more balanced dual emphasis on fundamental rights *and* market functions. The CJEU's decisions interpreting the GDPR have reinforced this trend – demonstrating an incrementally more active engagement with the social functions of data protection since the Regulation's entry into force. In particular, the Court's jurisprudence on non-material damages under Article 82 GDPR displays an increasing tendency to view breaches of the GDPR as resulting in social harms even where there is no, substantive, economic harm occasioned by the breach.

IV. The Damages Jurisprudence of the CJEU

Since its entry into force the GDPR has demonstrated a potential to be used as a means of expanding the scope of data protection law, as other contributions to this volume have ably examined. The CJEU's judgment in Case C-184/20 *OT v Vyriausioji tarnybinės etikos komisija*[76] is perhaps the most dramatic illustration of this capacity, though the CJEU's active engagement with the issue of cross-border transfers of personal data to the United States[77] (and arguably the Court's data retention decisions[78]) also illustrates the very real concern which the Court has for not only the practical but also the normative impacts for EU citizens where data protection law breaks down. The Regulation has, in this respect, firmly established

[74] Case C-131/12 *Google Spain SL v AEPD, Costeja* EU:C:2014:317.

[75] Fuster (n 62) at 135.

[76] Case C-184/20 *OT v Vyriausioji tarnybinės etikos komisija* ECLI:EU:C:2022:601.

[77] For a summary see Róisín Á Costello, 'Schrems II: Everything is Illuminated?' (2020) 5(2) *European Papers* 1045.

[78] See Joined Cases C-293/12 and C-594/12 *Digital Rights Ireland* EU:C:2014:238; Case C-203/15 *Tele2 Sverige* EU:C:2016:970; Case C-511/18 *La Quadrature du Net and Others* EU:C:2020:791; Case C-140/20 *GD v Commissioner of An Garda Síochána* EU:C:2022:258.

itself as being concerned just as much with the social functions of data protection law in modern society, as the market-enabling role that the GDPR, and the Directive before it, have played within the single market.

I focus, in this portion of the chapter, on how this trend has been drawn out in the CJEU's Article 82 jurisprudence for two reasons. The first, is that the decisions concerning Article 82 which have thus far come before the court have frequently involved claims for damages which are nominal and are sought not for the monetary value of the award but as a recognition of the breach of the applicant's rights. They are, in effect, a form of normative damages which seek to require a data controller to acknowledge the social harm occasioned by their act or omission.

In this respect, the cases expose how far data protection law has travelled from its own expressed roots of being a market enabling branch of EU law – intended to facilitate a more competitive European market and expose how much data protection law has come to be regarded as an integrated and active part of the Union's fundamental rights architecture.

This, in turn, leads to the second reason the CJEU's Article 82 decisions are important. In coming to this view of data protection, the Court has implicitly endorsed aa political-economy analysis in which it is accepted that social and market aims are not distinct but rather must be viewed as part of an integrated whole. Whether this will yield more seismic results in future remains to be seen but it certainly offers a compelling glimpse into how a rights-oriented view of market regulation might develop within the Union in the twenty-first century.

Article 82 of the GDPR and Non-material Damages

Article 82 of the GDPR provides, inter alia, that

1. Any person who has suffered material or non-material damage as a result of an infringement of this Regulation shall have the right to receive compensation from the controller or processor for the damage suffered.
2. Any controller involved in processing shall be liable for the damage caused by processing which infringes this Regulation. A processor shall be liable for the damage caused by processing only where it has not complied with obligations of this Regulation specifically directed to processors or where it has acted outside or contrary to lawful instructions of the controller.
3. A controller or processor shall be exempt from liability under paragraph 2 if it proves that it is not in any way responsible for the event giving rise to the damage.

Much of the current approach to the issue is led by the CJEU's approach in Case C-300/21 *UI v Osterreichische Post*.[79] In that case, the Austrian postal service

[79] Case C-300/21 *UI v Osterreichische Post AG* EU:C:2023:370.

had collected information on the political affinities of the population and sold that data to various organisations to use in targeted advertising.[80] The plaintiff had not consented to this collection and processing of his data and claimed to have suffered upset, a loss of confidence and a feeling of exposure as a result[81] and sought compensation for non-material damage amounting to some €1,000 in damages.[82]

The Austrian Supreme Court referred three questions to the CJEU for a preliminary ruling namely,

1. Does the award of compensation under Article 82 of [the GDPR] also require, in addition to infringement of provisions of the GDPR, that an applicant must have suffered harm, or is the infringement of provisions of the GDPR in itself sufficient for the award of compensation?
2. Does the assessment of the compensation depend on further EU-law requirements in addition to the principles of effectiveness and equivalence?
3. Is it compatible with EU law to take the view that the award of compensation for non-material damage presupposes the existence of a consequence [or effect] of the infringement of at least some weight that goes beyond the upset caused by that infringement?'

Interestingly, the respondent in the proceedings objected to the first question referred to the CJEU was inadmissible on the basis that it was hypothetical.[83] The CJEU rejected this objection in a relatively summary fashion noting that the question went to the application of a rule to compensation provided under the Regulation and the determination of damage where rights were infringed.[84] This, in itself, was an interesting approach from the CJEU and clearly signalled that it viewed breach of the Regulation, and damage distinct from the breach.[85] In this respect the early signs of a more expansive approach to damage under the Regulation were, perhaps, evident in the judgment's opening paragraphs.

In its decision the CJEU noted, at the outset, that where there is no reference to national or Member State law, the presumption must be that a measure is fully harmonising and that, as the GDPR makes no reference to national law in Article 82, that provision is fully harmonising and must be interpreted in a uniform manner by Member States.[86] In this respect the Court's judgment began (much as had the Opinion of the Advocate General[87]) with a considered engagement with the Regulation's aim of improving market efficiency and promoting harmonisation

[80] ibid. [11].
[81] ibid. [12].
[82] ibid. [13].
[83] ibid. [21].
[84] ibid. [24]–[27].
[85] ibid. [24].
[86] ibid. [29]–[30].
[87] ibid.

of regulatory standards as part of the 'strengthening and the convergence of the economies within the internal market' as Recital 2 of the GDPR notes.

However, the Court then transitioned from explicating the regulatory and market justifications of the Regulation to a contextual interpretative approach to Article 82. Noting that the wording of the article focused on the fact that 'damage' must have been 'suffered' with a causal link between the infringement alleged and the damage[88] the Court noted that it could not be said that a breach of the GDPR, prima facie, afforded a right to compensation absent these 'cumulative' criteria.[89] The Court dwelt in particular on the broader landscape of the Regulation in making this finding, noting that Recitals 75, 85 and 146 all indicated that compensable damage must be actualised rather than potential.[90] Moreover, the Court noted that the existence of alternative remedies, under Articles 77 and 78 as well as 83 and 84 lent further weight to a contextual interpretation which would limit non-material damages to a discrete range of actualised harms.[91]

On this basis, the Court found that an infringement alone could not attract compensation under Article 82 absent a harm which had been proven to have been suffered by the plaintiff. In this respect, the approach of the Court in particularly interesting. There is, at first blush, a clear emphasis on reading the Regulation holistically, bearing in mind not only its market-harmonising function but also its aim of protecting the well-being of citizens and vindicating their rights.

Yet there is also a pragmatic tone which hints at an arguably ordoliberal perspective in this portion of the judgment. While the Court found discrete non-material harms can be compensated where proven, the broader underlying point is that there is no right to a remedy in the form of compensation for breach of rights under the Regulation at a broad level. This, of course, would run counter to the manner in which constitutional and fundamental rights are vindicated in many systems and could perhaps be considered contrary to the spirit (if not always the function) of *Francovich* damages in EU law more generally.

The Court's emphasis on harmonisation was reinforced in its consideration of the third question referred by the Austrian court. In considering that question, the Court noted that making compensation for non-material damage subject to a certain threshold of seriousness would risk undermining the coherence of the rules established by the GDPR, because such a threshold would be liable to fluctuate according to the assessment of the courts seised.[92] This would seem to be the ideal point at which to retrench the objectives of the Regulation in promoting market integration, efficiency and standardisation. However, the Court did not adopt this approach and, instead, noted that the objective of ensuring that varying thresholds for recovery did not subsist was not only the objectives of the

[88] ibid. [32].
[89] ibid. [32]–[33], [36].
[90] ibid. [37], [46]–[47].
[91] ibid. [39]–[40].
[92] ibid. [49], [51].

Regulation generally but specifically the need to vindicate 'a consistent and high level of protection of natural persons' with regard to their data protection rights.[93]

Nevertheless, the Court noted that a person who alleged an infringement of the GDPR and claimed to have suffered negative consequences on foot of that infringement could not be relieved of the need to demonstrate that those consequences constituted non-material damage within the meaning of Article 82 of that regulation.[94]

The Court did not address whether 'loss of control' or 'hurt feelings' could be sufficient to constitute non-material damage such that claims based on loss of trust, or loss of autonomy as a result of a loss of control over data might be vindicated under the Regulation, thus widening its scope[95] though that issue did come to be considered in the reference in Case C-456/22, *VX and AT v Gemeinde Ummendorf*.[96] In that case, a municipal council had, without the consent of the applicants in the main proceedings, published the agenda of a meeting of the municipal council online. The names of the applicants were referred to on several occasions in that publication, and also referenced a judgment delivered by the Administrative Court which included their surnames and forenames as well as their addresses. The applicants took the view that the publication was intentional and asked the municipality to compensate them for the non-material damage which they claimed to have suffered, as a result of the publication. In response, the municipality claimed that, compensation for 'non-material damage', within the meaning of Article 82(1) of the GDPR, requires proof of a noticeable disadvantage and an objectively comprehensible impairment of personal interests.

The referring court considered that the mere loss of control over the personal data of the applicants was not sufficient to constitute non-material damage within the meaning of Article 82(1) of the GDPR, in particular where the data subjects had lost control over their data only for a short period of time and where that had occurred without causing a noticeable disadvantage or an objectively comprehensible impairment to the personal interests of the applicants.

The Court rejected this view referring to its decisions in C-300/21 *UI v Osterreichische Post* as well as the further decision of Case C-340/21 *VB v Natsionalna agentsia za prihodite*,[97] (discussed below) and found that Article 82(1)

[93] ibid. [48].

[94] ibid. [50]. The Court also noted that, in the absence of EU rules, it is for the national legal order of each Member State to establish procedural rules to give effect to this view, [53]–[54].

[95] However, the decision of the UK's Supreme Court in *Lloyd v Google* [2021] UKSC 50 would seem to offer some support to an argument that such injuries may not be compensable. Subsequent decisions have confirmed that there is a *de minimis* threshold implicit in English law which claimants must satisfy to seek damages for actual loss or distress. See *Rolfe v Veale* [2021] EWHC (QB) and *Johnson v East light* [2021] EWHC 3069 (QB). Similar developments in the case law of Ireland have not yet rendered as definitive a position from a Superior Court. See *Kaminski v Ballymaguire Foods* [2023] IECC 5 and contrast that decision with *Cuniam v Parcel Connect* [2023] IECC 1. More recently, in an Irish context, see *Keane v CSO* [2024] IEHC 20 and *Dillon v Irish Life Assurance plc* [2024] IEHC 203.

[96] Case C-456/22, *VX and AT v Gemeinde Ummendorf* EU:C:2023:988.

[97] Case C-340/21 *VB v Natsionalna agentsia za prihodite* EU:C:2023:986, [78]; Case C-300/21 *UI v Osterreichische Post* (n 79).

of the GDPR must be interpreted as precluding national legislation or a national practice which sets a '*de minimis* threshold' in order to establish non-material damage caused by an infringement of that regulation.[98]

As the CJEU alluded to in *VX*, this concern with mere normative harms and their remediation under Article 82 was considered, albeit to a limited extent, by the Court in Case C-340/21 *VB*.[99] In that case, the national revenue service of Bulgaria had been subject to a hacking attack and the personal data of some 6 million data subjects had subsequently been published online. The referring court asked, inter alia, whether an award of compensation for non-material damage could be made to a person whose personal data, held by a public agency, was published on the internet following a hacking attack where no further harm resulted, or where the data subject experienced only 'fear' that such misuse may occur in future, and whether the intervention of a third party could relieve the controller of liability for any breach.

In respect of the argument premised on 'fear' the Court found that this was capable of grounding a claim for non-material damages where it was extant, albeit that it might be premised on an event which had not yet occurred.[100] In coming to that conclusion, the Court reiterated its finding from *UI v Osterreichische Post* in respect of the cumulative factors required to ground a claim for non-material damages under Article 82,[101] but noted that there was nothing within the text of the Regulation which required that non-material damage be 'linked to a misuse of his or her personal data by third parties that has already occurred, at the date of his or her claim for compensation, or, secondly, is linked to that person's fear that such use may occur in the future'.[102] In this respect, the Court reiterated its position that a contextual reading and one undertaken by reference, inter alia, to Recital 146 of the GDPR would favour the adoption of a broad reading of the term 'damage'[103] as would the first sentence of Recital 85 of the GDPR which suggested that mere loss of control over data was intended to be included as a type of damage, as was an apprehension of misuse of data even where such misuse had not yet occurred.[104]

As such, the Court concluded that a reading of Article 82 which excluded the award of non-material damages would be inconsistent with the context of the Regulation as well as the broader objectives of the law, while sounding a final note of caution that even 'fear' while it was compensable would need to be proved,[105] and well-founded.[106] This, final, addendum that any fear in order to be

[98] Case C-456/22 *VX and AT v Gemeinde Ummendorf* [16], [23].
[99] ibid.
[100] ibid. [79]–[80]; [86].
[101] ibid. [76]–[78].
[102] ibid. [79].
[103] ibid. [81].
[104] ibid. [82]–[83].
[105] ibid. [83]–[84].
[106] ibid. [85].

compensable must be well-founded is somewhat jarring. The CJEU noted in *UI v Osterreichische Post* that it was not desirable that national courts seised with cases in which plaintiffs' sought non-material damages would apply varying thresholds for recovery, yet the establishment of a 'well-founded fear' would appear to invite the courts of Member States to do just that.

These matters, however, are of somewhat less concern in the context of the present piece. Rather, what is particularly interesting, in *VB* as in *Osterreichische Post*, is the Court's broad emphasis on what might be considered the *most* 'social' harms – experiences of apprehension and fear, threatened misuse and loss of control. In the facts of *VB* and the Court's decision there is an implicit, but no less trenchant, concern for the lived reality of what data protection breaches mean for citizens of the Union, and how those experiences impact their own wellbeing. Indeed, the market objectives of the GDPR fade into the background of the decision in *VB*, even in respect of the broader set of questions referred by the Bulgarian court.

A similar approach is evident in the Opinion of Advocate General Collins in the as-yet-pending decision in Case C-182/22 *JU*.[107] In that case, there had been a theft of special category data belonging to the claimants by an unknown party from the data controller's trading platform. The referring court asked whether this theft could give rise to a right to compensation for non-material damage and, upon satisfying the criteria established in *Osterreichische Post* in circumstances where no further damage was suffered, whether a claim of identity fraud might be mounted on that basis.

In his opinion the Advocate General considered that the theft gave right to a claim where the *Osterreichische Post* criteria were satisfied. However, the Advocate General noted that,

> 30. Recitals 75 and 85 of the GDPR distinguish between the example of 'loss of control' or being prevented from 'exercising control' over personal data and the example of 'identity theft or fraud'. As a consequence, the theft of personal data alone does not constitute identity theft even if that theft may lead to future (mis)use of that data. Identity theft requires an additional action or step with detrimental effects for the data subject that go beyond the theft of personal data. A person who steals a data subject's personal data must (mis)use or take concrete steps to (mis)use them for unlawful purposes without that person's consent. Such action typically involves fraud or some other form of deceit and is generally carried out for financial or other gain or in order to harm the data subject or his or her entourage.
>
> 31. It follows from the foregoing that while the theft of personal data does not constitute identity theft or fraud, that theft may give rise to non-material damage and a right to compensation pursuant to Article 82 of the GDPR.

[107] Case C-182/22 *JU v Scalable Capital GmbH*. No ECLI or any other provision has been assigned by court as yet.

The Advocate General also specifically noted that, as such, the GDPR does not provide for a system of strict liability and that punitive damages are not available under the Regulation, although he did note that compensation for breach of the Regulation must be 'full and effective'.

This is perhaps the most interesting issue which remains to be resolved under Article 82 and one which the referring court in Joined Cases C-182/22 and C-189/22 *SO*[108] has also asked the CJEU to address in the context of determining whether damages under the Regulation serve a general or specific dissuasive function or are intended to be purely compensatory.

The answer which the Court gives to this, and further pending matters is likely to shed further light on the specific relationship which the Court understands to exist between the Regulation's market and social functions. The matter of punitive damages will be particularly interesting in this context in as much as such damages are specifically envisaged in many legal systems as serving to recognise the breach of a particularly fundamental or significant normative threshold, including one which may be difficult to establish. In this respect, the answer to whether punitive damages can be awarded may expose more clearly how the CJEU conceptualises the balance between the GDPR's social and market functions.

V. Conclusion

A series of further preliminary references variously pending before the court at the time of writing, or in which judgment was delivered after this volume had been typeset, are asking the court to consider, variously; whether accidental disclosure impacts a non-material damage claim,[109] whether failure to use data obtained through a breach impacts on an award of non-material damage,[110] whether compensable non-material damage can include an impairment of the legal position of party, whether damages under Article 82 are to be set by reference to the fines provided in Article 83,[111] and whether in calculating compensation under the Regulation, account can be taken of parallel breaches of national laws governing data protection (but which are not delegated or implementing acts adopted in accordance with that regulation or Member State laws which specify provisions of that regulation).[112]

[108] Joined Cases C-182/22 and C-189/22 *JU and SO* EU:C:2023:820.

[109] Case C-741/21 *GP v Juris GmbH* EU:C:2024:288.

[110] Case C-687/21 *BL v Saturn Electro-Handelsgesellschaft GmbH Hagen* EU:C:2024:72.

[111] Case C-741/21 *GP v Juris GmbH*. No ECLI or any other provision as none has been assigned by court as yet.

[112] Case C-590/22, *AT, BT v PS GbR, VG, MB, DH, WB, GS*. No ECLI or any other provision as none has been assigned by court as yet.

Such is the range of these questions, and their nuanced relationship both to each other and to the character and scope of data protection law as a whole, that it is evident that Article 82 will provide some of the conceptually richest decisions of the GDPR's first decade. This capacity to add to the jurisprudence in a still-developing area will make these decisions compelling reading. What they can tell us about the CJEU (and the Union's) evolving relationship to ordoliberal regulatory approaches – and the integration (or perhaps reintegration) of the social and market aspects of the Union's constitutional identity will be still more intriguing.

Conclusion

RÓISÍN Á COSTELLO AND MARK LEISER

What emerges from the contributions to this volume is a timely portrait of the complexity and nuance of the field of data protection in EU law – as well as an insight into the attendant challenges for national law and national supervisory authorities, which the GDPR has occasioned during its first, early, years in force. What comes through, perhaps still more clearly, in the contributions is how rapidly this complexity has developed and, as a result, how dense data protection, as a practice area and a field of academic study, can be for the uninitiated.

Data protection is not just a theoretical concept, as the contributors to this volume have ably illustrated. It is an area rich with both practical and normative questions – the answers to which have, and will continue to have, the potential to touch EU citizens in their daily lives, to support equality and reduce discrimination, to enhance and safeguard intimacy and personal relationships, to protect reputation and to advance individual autonomy and control. Few areas of study can aspire to such lofty and such grounded ends, underscoring the importance and relevance of our discussion.

As we move towards the final years of the GDPR's first decade in force, it is evident that the rapid development that characterised its early years is primed to continue. Perhaps most significantly, the first amendment of the GDPR's text, contained in the Commission proposal on additional procedural rules relating to the enforcement of the GDPR, is a significant change that may well be passed shortly, further shaping the evolving landscape of data protection in the EU. In closing, we provide an overview and analysis of this crucial development and how transnational enforcement of the GDPR remains a site of controversy and change even now, some six years after the Regulation entered into force.[1]

I. Report on the First Two Years of the GDPR

The proposed amendments to the Regulation follow from and are, to some extent, based on a report produced by the European Commission in 2020 (the 2020 Report),

[1] Commission, 'Proposal for a Regulation of the European Parliament and of the Council Laying down Additional Procedural Rules Relating to the Enforcement of Regulation (EU) 2016/679 (General Data Protection Regulation)' COM(2023) 348 final.

a document that continues to exert significant influence in the ongoing discussions on the need for reform of the GDPR, and the form which any such reforms should take. The 2020 Report placed particular emphasis on the need for further progress to strengthen the harmonisation of the handling of cross-border cases under the GDPR and to make that process more efficient in light of diverging national procedures and interpretations of the Regulation.[2]

The Report made findings regarding several areas in which the Commission had identified a need for further engagement to improve the functioning of the GDPR. Those areas included, inter alia, those identified below but it is notable that, as with many of the long-standing criticisms of the EU's data protection regime both prior to and following the GDPR's enactment – there is a preponderant focus on transnational enforcement in the recommendations.

Co-operation and Consistency Mechanisms

The 2020 Report noted the progress of the EDPB in advancing cooperation and consistency alongside national supervisory authorities, including through the development and provision of Guidelines which stakeholders had generally welcomed despite apparent inconsistencies between national and EDPB Guidelines. Noting the utility of these tools, the 2020 Report emphasised the need for ongoing engagement through Guidelines as well as additional practical advice, including the use of concrete examples.[3]

The Report also noted a need for data protection authorities to be equipped with the necessary human, technical and financial resources to carry out their tasks effectively. This resource-hunger was perhaps among the most controversial issues while pre-dated the entry into force of the GDPR, as documented by Ruohonen and others[4] and the 2020 Report confirmed that concerns remain about the consistency of the investigation and engagement by national supervisory authorities, as well as highlighting a parallel concern about the allocation of resources among the supervisory authorities of Member States.[5]

In particular, the 2020 Report noted that while a majority of supervisory authorities benefitted from an increase in staff and budget between 2016 and 2019 – the supervisory authorities of Ireland and Luxembourg, as lead supervisory authorities in many important cross-border cases, required still more

[2] Communication from the Commission to the European Parliament and the Council, 'Data protection as a pillar of citizens' empowerment and the EU's approach to the digital transition – two years of application of the General Data Protection Regulation' (COM/2020/264 final).

[3] ibid 5–6.

[4] Jukka Ruohonen and Kalle Hjerppe, 'The GDPR Enforcement Fines at a Glance' (2022) 106 *Information Systems* 101876.

[5] See, Orla Lynskey, 'The "Europeanisation" of Data Protection Law' (2017) *Cambridge Yearbook of European Legal Studies* 252.

extensive resources than the populations of those Member States would otherwise suggest.[6]

Fragmentation and Divergence between Various National Regimes

Linked to the 2020 Report's concern in respect of co-operation, the Report equally expressed the view that because the GDPR requires Member States to legislate in some areas but also allows them to provide supplementary protection in others, there is a resulting margin of Member State activity where divergences in procedure and approach may emerge.

The Report noted that a degree of fragmentation does prevail among the Member States of the EU, citing, in particular, the divergent approaches to ages of consent for children in respect of information society services, which it noted creates uncertainty regarding the application of children's data protection rights within the Single Market.[7] Another example cited in the Report was the divergence between Member States regarding reconciling and balancing the rights of freedom of expression and data protection.[8]

The Report noted that while specific national regimes adhere to a principle of precedence for freedom of expression, others prioritise the protection of personal data and exempt the application of data protection rules only in limited contexts and still others adhere to statutory or case-by-case assessments as regards derogations from specific provisions of the GDPR.[9]

Empowering Individuals to Control their Data

In respect of empowering individuals, the Commission specifically cited the right to data portability which, it noted, 'has a clear potential, still not fully used', to centre individuals within the data ecosystem by enabling them to switch between

[6] Communication from the Commission to the European Parliament (n 2) at 6.

[7] See, on children's consent, Clare Feikert-Ahalt et al., 'Children's Online Privacy and Data Protection in Selected European Countries: European Union, Denmark, France, Germany, Greece, Portugal, Romania, Spain, Sweden, United Kingdom' (Law Library of Congress Global Legal Research Directorate, 2021).

[8] Communication from the Commission to the European Parliament (n 2) at 7. This debate also pre-dates the entry into force of the GDPR but remains unresolved by the Regulation. See, for some examples, David Erdos, 'European Union Data Protection Law and Media Expression: Fundamentally Off Balance' (2016) 65(1) *International and Comparative Law Quarterly* 139; Magdalena Jozwiak, 'Balancing the Rights to Data Protection and Freedom of Expression and Information by the Court of Justice of the European Union' (2016) 23(3) *Maastricht Journal of European and Comparative Law* 404; David Erdos, 'European Regulatory Interpretation of the Interface between Data Protection and Journalistic Freedom: An Incomplete and Imperfect Balancing Act?' (2016) 3 *Public Law* 631.

[9] Communication from the Commission to the European Parliament (n 2) at 8.

different service providers, combine different services, and to choose services most compatible with their data protection preferences. The Commission noted that the result would be improved competition and support for innovation and that, as such, maximising data portability should remain a priority to advance these ends and avoid 'lock-in' effects.[10]

Challenges for Small and Medium-Sized Enterprises

As some of the contributions to this volume have touched on, the Report argued that the GDPR, alongside the provisions of the Free Flow of Non-Personal Data Regulation, is a crucial aspect of ensuring a level playing field. However, it also noted that stakeholders had reported challenges for SMEs in ensuring compliance.[11] In recognition of this, the Commission noted it was working on standard contractual clauses that SMEs could use, linked to its work on using similar clauses in the context of international data transfers.[12]

The Application of the GDPR to New Technologies

As several of the chapters have also examined, one of the central challenges for the GDPR is how to engage with and apply its provisions to new technologies given its technology-neutral terms and the need to understand how existing principles might be extended to new operations or technologies.[13]

II. The Proposed Amendment to the GDPR

Before the entry into force of the GDPR, there was a notable (and problematic) absence of coordination between supervisory authorities for transnational enforcement efforts. Under the Data Protection Directive, several authorities might claim that they were each competent to investigate a particular matter, with each authority applying its own rules and standards for cooperation with other national authorities and a consequent potential for a regulatory race to the bottom, and for forum shopping by both data controllers, and complainants.[14]

[10] On the problems of interoperability and lock-ins, see Heiki Schweitzer and Robert Welker, 'A Legal Framework for Access to Data – A Competition Policy Perspective' in German Federal Ministry for Justice and Consumer Protection and the Max Planck Institute for Innovation and Competition (eds) *Data Access, Consumer Interests and Public Welfare* (2021), 103–54.

[11] Communication from the Commission to the European Parliament (n 2) at 9.

[12] ibid 10.

[13] ibid.

[14] See Lynskey, 'The "Europeanisation" of Data Protection Law' (n 5) at 252.

The current rules in respect of cross-border cases retain a legacy of this beginning. Those rules, at present, require supervisory authorities first to engage in dialogue with each other and, if needed, to refer the matter to the EDPB for a binding decision under Article 65 of the GDPR where no consensus can be reached as between the authorities involved. The procedure has been criticised by some as inefficient, leading to inconsistent enforcement due to the emergence of 'hawks and doves' among national supervisory authorities.[15] Others, notably Gentile and Lynskey, have gone further, arguing that under-enforcement of the GDPR in transnational contexts is, in fact, a result of the deficient design of the Regulation itself, including its provisions governing transnational enforcement. As such, Gentile and Lynskey contend that the shortcomings of the Regulation are not merely a result of the regulatory appetites of those tasked with enforcing its terms but are built into the Regulation itself.[16]

In light of this reality, the GDPR sought, on its entry into force and through the now proposed amendments, to secure a legally harmonised and practically effective approach to the transnational enforcement of its provisions, which prioritised coordination between the national supervisory authorities.

In this respect, the GDPR sought to (and pending its amendment still does) coordinate the use, and the form and substance, of the mechanisms provided in the Regulation to effect its objectives. However, rules of procedure facilitating much of this activity were considered to be a matter for provision in and through national law.[17] It is these national procedures which, in the early years of the GDPR, were identified by the 2020 Report as a source of fragmentation – allowing for different time limits, procedural rights and thresholds for admissibility in respect of complaints, among other effects, and thus stymying the transnational enforcement of the Regulation.

In a Resolution after the 2020 Report, the European Parliament, cognisant of this identified divergence and the need for greater co-ordination and efficacy in enforcement, urged the Commission to assess, in particular, whether national administrative procedures hindered the effectiveness of Article 60 of the GDPR.[18] In addition, the Parliament called on the European Data Protection

[15] Thomas Streinz, 'The Evolution of European Data Law' in Paul Craig and Gráinne de Búrca (eds) *The Evolution of EU Law* (3rd edn, Oxford University Press, 2021) 902, 914.

[16] See, Giulia Gentile and Orla Lynskey, 'Deficient by Design? The Transnational Enforcement of the GDPR' (2022) 71 *International and Comparative Law Quarterly* 799, 800. For examples of the criticisms made in respect of the use of Article 65 mechanisms in context see, Lisette Mustert, 'The First Article 65 Decision – Correct and Consistent Application of the GDPR Ensured?' (2021) 7 *European Data Protection Law Review* 94; Lisette Mustert, 'The EDPB's Second Article 65 Decision – Is the Board Stepping up Its Game?' (2021) 7 *European Data Protection Law Review* 416.

[17] These are sometimes referred to as 'composite administrative procedures' see, Filipe Brito Bastos, 'An Administrative Crack in the EU's Rule of Law: Composite Decision-making and Nonjusticiable National Law' (2020) *European Constitutionalism* 63, 66.

[18] European Parliament resolution of 25 March 2021 on the Commission evaluation report on the implementation of the General Data Protection Regulation two years after its application (2020/2717(RSP)).

Board to establish a basic architecture which would provide a standard administrative procedure for handling complaints in cross-border cases under Article 60. In 2020, the Board launched a reflection on improving cooperation between national supervisory authorities in cross-border cases. That culminated in the adoption by the Board of its 2022 'Statement on Enforcement Co-operation'.[19]

The 2022 Statement committed the EDPB to identifying a list of procedural matters that could be harmonised more fully and to prioritising cooperation with and support of DPAs to identify cross-border cases of strategic importance. The statement also committed the Board to making greater use of opinions – as permitted under Article 64(2) – and engaging in internal training to encourage and support the increased use of that mechanism and consistency in its use, as well as, finally, agreeing (as between the EDPB and national authorities) to annual enforcement priorities.

In October 2022, the Board transmitted this list of procedural matters to the Commission, which were then reformulated as a proposal for a reform of the GDPR drawing on the 2020 Report, the Board's list, and conclusions from the Commission's monitoring of the enforcement of the Regulation since its entry into force, alongside input from the GDPR Multi-stakeholder Expert Group, the GDPR Member States Expert Group, and comments received in response to a Call for Evidence launched in February 2023.[20]

The proposed changes aim to tackle divergences in the form and procedure of valid complaints under the GDPR, including through harmonising procedural rights of parties under investigation, imposing consistent deadlines (including for cooperation and dispute resolution procedures)[21] and harmonising other procedural rights. Crucially, however, they propose these changes in relation only to cross-border cases.[22]

Submission and Handling of Cross-border Complaints

Chapter II of the proposed amending Regulation outlines new rules on the submission and handling of cross-border complaints and prescribes the information required for such complaints under Article 77 of the GDPR. The proposed amendments include, inter alia, Article 3, which requires complainants to use the Form provided in the Annex to the amending Regulation to make their complaint and, having done so and provided the information required, obliges supervisory authorities to provide the complainant with an acknowledgement of their

[19] European Data Protection Board, 'Statement on Enforcement Co-operation' (2022).

[20] Proposal for a Regulation of the European Parliament and of the Council laying down additional procedural rules relating to the enforcement of Regulation (EU) 2016/679 COM/2023/348 final, 6–8.

[21] ibid 3.

[22] ibid 3–4.

complaint. Articles 11–13, contained in Section 2 of Chapter III of the proposed amendment, impose a further set of requirements in respect of the rejection of complaints, including the sharing of draft decisions rejecting a complaint (in whole or in part), and allowing the complainant to comment before the issuing of a final rejection.

In considering whether to investigate a complaint received and complying with the requirements of Article 3, Article 4 provides three factors that supervisory authorities must consider. These include the 'relevant circumstances' and an apparently non-exhaustive list of three matters, including the gravity of the alleged infringement, the extent to which the infringement is systemic or repetitive, and the expediency of delivering a timely and effective remedy.

The proposed Article 5 formalises the amicable settlement mechanism and imposes a one-month objection period. Finally, in Chapter II, Article 6 provides the proposed amendments and detailed rules for translating documents during cross-border cooperation.

Co-operation between Supervisory Authorities

Chapter III of the proposed amendment concerns cooperation between supervisory authorities in cross-border cases under Article 60 of the GDPR. Article 8 of the Chapter provides that national supervisory authorities shall 'regularly update' other supervisory authorities concerned and provide them with all 'relevant information once available'. The materials falling within the definition of 'relevant information' under Article 8(2) include information about the alleged infringement, the investigative powers to be used and the key issues identified for investigation, the reasons the authority intends to reject the complaint (if relevant), and the authority's preliminary findings.

These are significant requirements and retrench the interdependence of national supervisory authorities by supplementing the cooperation mechanisms provided in the GDPR with procedural provisions by which those mechanisms should be effected, though they also maintain the superiority of the 'one-stop-shop' system.

Thus, under Article 9, once the lead supervisory authority has formed a preliminary view on the investigation, it is required to send a 'summary of critical issues' identifying the main findings of fact and the lead authority's views on the case to the other supervisory authorities concerned. The articulated purpose of this measure is to allow the concerned authorities to engage in a meaningful way with the investigation at an early stage and to identify and resolve disagreements regarding the assessment of the issues and the scope of the investigation at an early stage, thus reducing the likelihood of later dispute, and appeal. However, there is no formal mechanism to force the hand of the lead authority if it is perceived by other authorities to be in default in terms of commencing, accepting or progressing an investigation.

If a disagreement does arise between the lead and concerned authorities, Article 7 now obliges the concerned authority to engage with the lead supervisory authority under Articles 61 (mutual assistance) or 62 (joint operations) of the GDPR and, in the absence of agreement following the use of these mechanisms, to then move under Article 10 to request an urgent binding decision of the EDPB. The proposed amendments thus effectively introduce a hierarchy of cooperative mechanisms through which national authorities must move, but without substantively altering the balancing of power between lead and concerned supervisory authorities.

Procedural Rights for Parties

Further procedural provisions are included in Chapter III of the proposed amendment, which contains, in Section 3, a series of Articles which aim to harmonise the rights of parties under investigation to be heard. Thus, Article 14 provides that the lead supervisory authority shall submit its preliminary findings (including proposed corrective measures) to concerned supervisory authorities and the party being investigated, but also requires that the investigating authority present any party under investigation with the allegations raised in an exhaustive and sufficiently clear way to enable the party to understand the conduct being investigated. The investigated party will then be entitled to respond to any preliminary findings, setting out any objections raised in their defence. This is complemented by the provisions of Article 15 which impose obligations on supervisory authorities to whom a complaint is made to communicate preliminary findings to the complainant.

Where no objections are received, Article 16 provides for the adoption of a final decision, subject to the right of the parties under investigation under Article 17 to be heard regarding any revisions to the draft decision following.

Article 18 proposes to codify the submission of relevant and reasoned objections under Article 4(24) – in terms of permissible content and the basis for such objections, as well as concerning the permissible form and structure of objections. Interestingly, the basis on which this codification is proposed would appear to narrow the possible objections that might be classified as 'relevant and reasoned' compared with extant guidance from the EDPB. However, this matter's precise scope is also before the General Court in the pending decision in Joined Cases T-70/23, T-84/23 and T-111/23, case C-97/23 P and case T-682/22.

In addition, while provisions for being heard in respect of draft decisions are not absent from the GDPR's existing text, the focus of existing provisions in Article 60 and Recital 127, for instance, is very much on the views of other supervisory authorities, with procedural rights determined through national legislation. The proposals in Chapter III thus represents a significant step towards further harmonisation.

Access to Administrative File

Articles 19 and 20 of the proposed amendment provide detailed rules regarding access to the administrative file related to the investigation of any infringement and the treatment of confidential information contained within that file – including business secrets or other confidential information collected or obtained by the supervisory authority.

While Article 21 outlines the balancing to be undertaken where business secrets or confidential information are at issue, the provisions of Chapter IV do not consider how confidentiality is determined or by whom. Confidentiality is defined in divergent (and often incomplete) ways between the Member States of the Union.[23] In addition, it is not clear to what extent legal privilege, though it might be considered a form of confidentiality on some basis, is distinct from the concerns raised in Chapter IV.

The Article 65 Dispute Resolution Procedure

Chapter V provides procedural rules to govern the dispute resolution procedure in Article 65 of the GDPR. In particular, the proposed Article 22 specifies the information to be provided by the lead supervisory authority to the EDPB when submitting a matter to dispute resolution, imposes deadlines and provides a list of the documents required to be submitted to the EDPB.[24]

Article 24 obliges the Board to provide for the hearing of the parties under investigation or, in the case of rejection of a complaint, the complainant, as well as furnishing the relevant parties with a statement of reasons explaining the decision it intends to adopt.[25] These provisions seek to facilitate the swift and efficient conclusion of the dispute resolution procedure by clarifying the roles of all actors and providing deadlines for certain procedural steps.

Articles 25 and 26, as proposed, now lay down detailed arrangements for the submission of matters to dispute resolution under Articles 65(1)(b) and (c) of the GDPR, mainly related to the documents which must be provided to the Board by the supervisory authority referring the matter to it for resolution, as well as further documents which the Chair of the Board may request.

[23] See, Róisín Á Costello, *Privacy Law in Ireland* (Bloomsbury, 2023), [9.2.2].

[24] In addition, Article 23 of the proposed amendment provides that any referral to the Board made under Article 25 must be registered within one week of receipt of the documents outlined.

[25] It is at the discretion of the Board, under the current text, as to whether to accompany any statement of reasons with the retained relevant and reasoned objections on which it intends to base its decision.

Urgency Procedure

Chapter VI lays down detailed procedural rules for the urgency procedure currently provided for in Article 66 of the GDPR providing, in Article 27, for timelines within which requests under Article 66 can be made as well as the information which must be provided at the time of making the request, and (in proposed Article 28) the timelines for the Board's decision and the matters which that decision must contain.

The Amended GDPR – Revolution or Missed Opportunity

Perhaps the most notable aspect of the proposed amendments to the GDPR is what they do not do. They do not, for example, grapple with the substantive ambiguities that many of the chapters to this volume examine, nor do (or can) they address the insufficient and uneven funding of supervisory authorities that is at the root of much of the delay and procedural divergence that the amendments seek to remedy.

Indeed, Mildebrath[26] has observed, as merely one example, that the proposals have failed to address the imbalances between concerned supervisory authorities and the lead supervisory authority, which, at present, means concerned authorities 'have to make do with uncertain and cumbersome procedures to overcome LSA inactivity'.[27] A change to introduce a formal request mechanism for concerned supervisory authorities through which they might request the commencement or pursuit of an investigation was suggested by the German Data Protection Authorities during the GDPR trilogues but is not reflected in the now proposed text.

Analysing the proposals, Mildebrath has ventured that,

> [O]verall, the proposal may fail to reach its efficiency objective because it primarily builds on the GDPR's cooperation and consistency mechanism and risks inheriting or exacerbating crucial flaws instead of remedying them. It would likely strengthen the role of the lead supervisory authorities (LSAs), some of which are heavily criticised for stifling vigorous enforcement and shielding controversial industry data practices. Conversely, it would limit the powers the current guidelines ascribe to the supervisory authorities concerned (CSAs) and the European Data Protection Board (EDPB) to undertake corrective action against the possibly flawed approaches of LSAs. Furthermore, it seems doubtful whether the additional procedural steps would accelerate enforcement, considering that they build on ambiguous concepts and lack (hard) disciplinary measures such as deadlines.[28]

[26] Hendrik Mildebrath, 'An Analysis of the newly proposed rules to strengthen GDPR enforcement in cross-border cases' (European Parliamentary Research Service, 2014).

[27] Ibid, 3 citing Advocate General Bobek in Case C-645/19 *Facebook Ireland* EU:C:2021:5.

[28] ibid [2].

It is somewhat trite to say that more significant and dynamic changes might have been made to the GDPR. However, the suggested changes appear to introduce more procedural detail but little substantive reform – smoothing some rough edges without addressing outstanding queries regarding the substance of the Regulation itself.

III. The Enforcement Battle Continues

What is clear, on the basis of the proposed amendments outlined above, is that the Regulation continues, six years following its entry into force, to struggle with enforcement. This has been cast into still-higher relief by the Opinion of Advocate General Pikamäe in Case C-768/21 *TR v Land Hessen*.[29]

Under the Data Protection Directive, national supervisory authorities did not enjoy a power to impose financial penalties. This lacuna was viewed as undercutting the efficacy of the Directive and its enforcement. Following the entry into force of the GDPR, this position changed significantly with powers granted to national supervisory authorities to impose administrative fines pursuant to Article 83 of the GDPR in addition to, or in place of, another corrective measure under the Regulation.

In respect of the efficacy of those powers once granted, Article 83(4) and (5) provided for two schema of financial penalty. The first, under Article 83(4) of the GDPR permitted a maximum fine of the greater of €10 million or 2% of the data controller's total worldwide annual turnover in the previous financial year for violations of Articles 8, 11, 25–30, 41(4), 42 or 43. In addition Article 83(5) of the GDPR permitted the imposition of a maximum fine of the greater of €20 million or 4% of the data controller's total worldwide annual turnover in the previous financial year for violations of core provisions of the GDPR including, inter alia, Articles 5, 9 and 12–22.

The fines imposed pursuant to either regime are required to be effective, proportionate and dissuasive relative to the facts of each individual case, and in accordance with Article 83(1) of the GDPR. Subject to this proviso the regime established by the GDPR would appear to provide (and indeed require) a broad range of genuinely dissuasive penalties that incentivise compliance with the Regulation's provisions. However, concerns continue to be expressed, in particular by advocacy organisations, that supervisory authorities are insufficiently proactive in imposing fines.

The issue has come before the CJEU recently in the Opinion of Advocate General Pikamäe in Case C-768/21 *TR v Land Hessen*.[30] In *TR*, a savings bank notified the relevant national supervisory authority (the HDBI) of a personal

[29] Case C-768/21 *TR v Land Hessen* EU:C: 2024:291.
[30] ibid.

data breach as part of which there had been unlawful access by one of the bank's employees to the personal data of TR, a customer. TR subsequently learned of the breach and made a complaint to the relevant supervisory authority alleging the bank had breached his rights under the GDPR by failing to report to him that a breach had occurred, and alleging the internal safeguards and systems within the bank were unsatisfactory to redress the potential for a recurrence of similar breaches, or to act as a corrective measure.[31]

The HDBI investigated the complaint and confirmed there had been a breach of the GDPR,[32] but did not consider that there were grounds for taking corrective action against the bank, in circumstances where the bank had already taken disciplinary measures against the employee concerned and had indicated it would review and alter its internal systems and procedures.[33] TR challenged that refusal to take corrective action[34] and asserted that the HDBI should have fined the bank on the basis that where a breach of the GDPR is established, the HDBI did not have discretion not to act.[35]

Advocate General Priit Pikamäe found that in cases where a breach of the Regulation has been found to be present there is an obligation for the supervisory authority to take action 'in the interests of the principle of legality'[36] and 'in all cases, whatever the severity of the breach' by reference to the measures contained in Article 58(2) of the GDPR. This will generally mean identifying the most appropriate corrective measure to address the infringement. The Advocate General appeared to base this finding on four interlinked reasons.

First, it would be incompatible with the mandate of the supervisory authority to be able to ignore an infringement, where one was identified.[37] Second, the corrective powers afforded to supervisory authorities under Article 58(1) of the GDPR would be of little value if an authority were forced to confine itself to an investigation only.[38] Third, enforcement forms a central component of the idea of control under Article 16(2) TFEU and Article 8(3) CFREU.[39] Finally, the supervisory authority acts in the interests of the data subject when engaging in an investigation and the wording of Articles 57(1)(f) and 77(2) of the GDPR impose obligations in this respect not only in relation to the progress of the investigation but also to its outcome.[40]

Having outlined this position, the Advocate General proceeded to find that the question of whether a supervisory authority must intervene is to be

[31] ibid [13].
[32] ibid [15].
[33] ibid [14].
[34] ibid [16].
[35] ibid [17].
[36] ibid [40].
[37] ibid.
[38] ibid [41].
[39] ibid.
[40] ibid.

distinguished from the question of what form that intervention must take. In this respect, he noted that the wording of Article 58(2) of the GDPR itself implied the existence of a choice on the part of the supervisory authority as to the powers used.

In addition, he noted that the language of Recital 129 (which states that measures should be 'appropriate, necessary and proportionate' in the particular circumstances of the case) indicates that the power conferred is one which is accompanied by a discretion concerning the form and manner in which it is to be used in order to bring the 'situation back into compliance with EU law'.[41]

Since the discretion afforded to supervisory authorities under Article 58 of the GDPR is subject to the requirement that the measure identified be 'necessary', the Advocate did not exclude the possibility of situations in which the problem which led to the breach had been resolved or had ceased – thus rendering a particular intervention unnecessary.[42] In such cases, the Advocate General found that there was no obligation to impose administrative fines.[43] However, he did also acknowledge that in cases where there is a serious risk of infringement of fundamental rights, an authority might, equally, be obliged to adopt a specific measure.[44]

The Advocate General acknowledged that 'autonomous' measures taken by a controller itself may remedy the issue in dispute. In such cases, he noted that the discretion afforded to the supervisory authorities under Article 58(2) of the GDPR could permit them to decline to take further action. However, he considered that this would need to be subject to 'some legal requirements'[45] which he posited might take the form of

- a 'rigorous examination' of the situation in light of Recital 129 of the GDPR;
- a requirement for the supervisory authority to give its express consent to such a measure; and
- an agreement with the data controller that it would carry out the 'autonomous measure' and that the supervisory authority would have a right to intervene if its instructions in respect of this compliance are not complied with.[46]

These criteria, nowhere in evidence in the text of the Regulation, offer a clear example of activism on the part of the Court. What the decision in *TR* ultimately illustrates is that the issue of enforcement is still very much alive – not only at the level of large-scale fines for large cross-border undertakings but also for individual data subjects, and that the proposed amendments to the GDPR represent only

[41] ibid [43]–[45].

[42] ibid [47]–[48], [50].

[43] ibid [64]–[73].

[44] ibid [58]–[62] and referring to his Opinion in *SCHUFA* as well as the CJEU's previous decision in Case C-311/18.

[45] ibid [51]–[53].

[46] ibid [53].

one source of the often sudden change in the area of data protection with which academics and practitioners alike must contend.

IV. Conclusion

The next five years will be a period of perhaps still more significant, and more rapid, change for data protection law in the European Union. The proposed amendment to the GDPR considered here will be subject to scrutiny by the European Parliament and Council of Ministers, both of which must agree on the text and formally adopt it before it can become law and, subsequently, enter into force. If it does enter into force, perhaps the most serious accomplishment of the amendment will be to demonstrate that change is possible and that the GDPR can be amended to improve the efficacy of data protection law and, perhaps in the future, clarify the ambiguities that have been identified in its text during its first years in force.

INDEX